D1559267

The Heimwehr and Austrian Politics

The
Heimwehr
and Austrian Politics
1918–1936

C. EARL EDMONDSON

THE
UNIVERSITY OF GEORGIA PRESS
ATHENS

Library of Congress Cataloging in Publication Data

Edmondson, Clifton Earl, 1937–
    The Heimwehr and Austrian Politics, 1918–
1936.
    Bibliography.
    Includes index.
    1. Heimatschutz—History.   2. Austria—Poli-
tics and government—1918–1938.   I. Title.
DB97.E32   943.6'05   77-21924
            ISBN 0–8203–0437–9

Contents

Preface

Like all who undertake research in historical topics, I have incurred a number of debts, the most notable of which I would like to acknowledge here. I am grateful to the government of Austria and to the officials of the Austrian State Archives, especially Dr. Renate Grün, Professor H. L. Mikoletzky, and Dr. Walter Goldinger, for permission to use documents originating after 1925. I am also grateful to the provincial governments of Styria and Upper Austria for allowing me to examine at least some of the documents contained in their archives. The late Professor Ludwig Jedlicka graciously granted me access to much helpful material in the Austrian Institute for Contemporary History at the University of Vienna. Herr Wagner assisted me very graciously while I was using the valuable diplomatic reports in the Political Archives of the German Foreign Office (Bonn). Dr. Eduard Hochenbichler, an assistant to the chief of Austria's Federal Police and director of the police archives, was especially cordial. The staff in the United States National Archives, notably Mr. John Taylor in the military records division, expertly expedited my work there. I also wish to acknowledge the patient assistance of the staffs of the National, University, Parliamentary, and Municipal Libraries in Vienna; of the German Federal Archives in Koblenz; of the Public Record Office in London; and of the libraries of Duke University, the University of North Carolina at Chapel Hill, and Davidson College.

Particular gratitude goes to Professor Andrew Whiteside, who first suggested this topic to me (although he might not recognize the offspring), and to Professors Joel Colton, Ludwig Jedlicka, R. John Rath, Klemens von Klemperer, and the late John Snell, all of whom gave me valuable assistance, encouragement, and guidance. Several younger colleagues have also provided good advice and needed spurs: Professors Bruce F. Pauley, John J. Haag, Reinhart Kondert, and Gabor Vermes.

Other individuals to whom I owe a debt of gratitude are Professor Anton Porhansl, the executive secretary of the Austrian Fulbright Commission, and other members of his staff; Dr. Friedrich Rennhofer of the

Austrian National Library, who shared with me a document from Vienna's Diocesan Archive; Drs. Christa Fessl, Josef Hofmann, Anton Staudinger, and Franz Schweiger, who shared their findings with me; Dr. Gertrude and Dr. Ernst Schmitz, who permitted me to use their father's papers in the State Archives; and several Viennese friends who invited me into their homes and showed me the environs of their lovely city. Finally, without the cooperation and the graciousness of those persons who allowed me to interview them this project would have been neither as meaningful nor as enjoyable (although naturally there are some differences of interpretation).

Chapter two of this book appeared in substantially the same form in the *Austrian History Yearbook* (8 [1972]: 105–147). I am grateful for permission to use that material here.

Grants from the university research council of the University of North Carolina at Chapel Hill, from the Piedmont University Center (Winston-Salem, N.C.), and from the committee on faculty research at Davidson College helped underwrite the later stages of the project.

The completion of the work owes more to the assistance and patient encouragement of my wife, Patricia, than I can express here.

Abbreviations

ABP	Archiv der Bundespolizeidirektion (Vienna)
Abt.	Abteilung
Alp. HtW	*Alpenländische Heimatwehr* (Innsbruck)
AS	Austrian Schillings
AVA	Allgemeines Verwaltungsarchiv (Vienna)
A-Z	*Arbeiter-Zeitung*
Bgld.	Burgenland
BKA	Bundeskanzleramt
BR	Bundesrat
Car.	Carinthia
CSP	Christian Social Party (Christlichsoziale Partei)
DBA	Deutsches Bundesarchiv (Koblenz)
DBFP	*Documents on British Foreign Policy*
DGFP	*Documents on German Foreign Policy*
FF	Fatherland Front (Vaterländische Front)
FHB	Freiheitsbund (Freedom League)
FKV	Frontkämpfervereinigung (Front Veterans' Association)
F.O.	Foreign Office (British)
FRUS	*Foreign Relations of the United States*
Gesch.	Geschichte or geschichtliche
HB	Heimatblock (parliamentary group)
HD	Heimatdienst
HS	Heimatschutz
HSV	Heimatschutzvervand
HS-Ztg	*Heimatschutz-Zeitung* (Klagenfurt)
HtW	Heimatwehr (Tyrolean)
HW	Heimwehr
L.A.	Lower Austria
MID	Military Intelligence Division
MRP	Ministerratsprotokol
NEF	National Estates Front (Nationalständische Front)
NFP	*Neue Freie Presse* (Vienna)
N-ö HW	*Niederösterreichische Heimwehr* (Vienna)

NPA	Neues politische Archiv (Vienna)
NR	Nationalrat
NSDAP	Nationalsozialistische Deutsche Arbeiterpartei (Nazis)
NYT	*New York Times*
Oe, Oesterr.	Oesterreich
OeIZ	Oesterreichisches Institut für Zeitgeschichte, archive of (Vienna)
Oesterr. VW	*Oesterreichischer Volkswirt* (Vienna)
OSS	Ostmärkische Sturmscharen (East Mark Storm Troops)
PADAA	Politisches Archiv des Deutschen Aussenamtes (Bonn)
PRO	Public Record Office (London)
RGFO	*Records of the German Foreign Office*, Microcopy T–120
RM	Reichsminister
RP	*Reichspost* (Vienna)
SB	[Republikanischer] Schutzbund (Republican Defense League)
Sbg.	Salzburg
SD Jahrbuch	*Jahrbuch der österreichischen Arbeiterbewegung*
SDP	Social Democratic Party (Sozialdemokratische Partei)
SSV	Selbstschutzverband (Self-Defense League)
StSek	Staatssekretär
U.A.	Upper Austria
Ungedr.	Ungedruckte (unpublished)
USNA	United States National Archives (Washington)
Vbg.	Vorarlberg

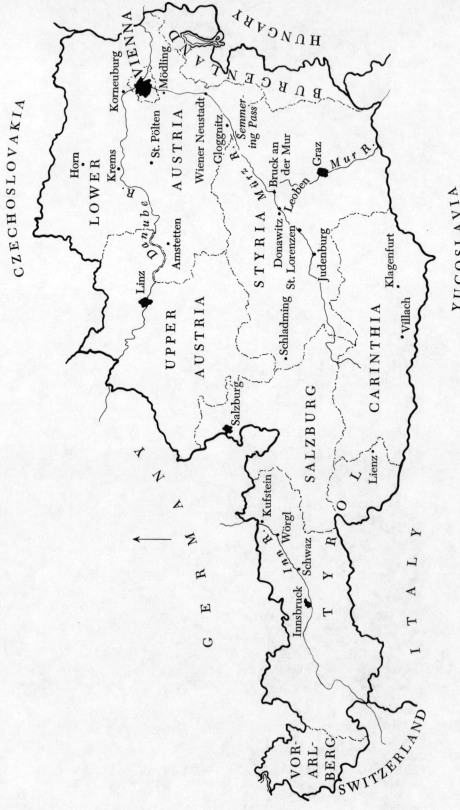

The Heimwehr and Austrian Politics

Introduction

The democracy ushered in by the collapse of empires in central Europe after World War I was at once militarized and polarized by the conditions attending its birth. In central and eastern Europe the war had toppled rickety old political institutions and shattered the framework of traditional social and national relationships. This was a time of unsettling geopolitical changes, each creating a milieu in which extremist approaches to politics could flourish. The brutality of the long war itself, the bitterness of national rivalries, and the intense emotions aroused by the social revolution underway in Russia and threatening elsewhere, all contributed to a widespread willingness to use force in political affairs. Thus, despite efforts to establish democratic and pluralistic constitutions in central Europe, partisans of the new and old social orders fought for control of the body politic, with the result that throughout the interwar years life was marred by violence and by paramilitary activity. Ultimately, the Right swept the Left from the field, and by the early 1930s fascist or semifascist regimes based largely on arbitrary police power governed most states in central Europe.

Ernst Nolte, who has led the way in trying to interpret fascism from a philosophical standpoint, calls the years from 1918 to 1945 a "fascist era," one that must be understood largely through the mentality and actions of fascists and their sympathizers throughout Europe.[1] Nolte's singular emphasis on fascism might be too restrictive, but there is no question that, broadly interpreted, it forms an integral part of the European story between the two world wars. For many years students of fascism and of paramilitary activity on the Right concentrated on Italy and Germany, but fascist movements elsewhere are no longer neglected subjects. In the last few years there have appeared several works, mostly general treatments or edited collections of articles, on fascist ideology and movements in other countries and on the conditions fostering fascism.[2]

Because of the significant role it played as the voice of domestic reaction and as a tool of foreign governments, the Austrian Heimwehr qualifies as one of the most important right-wing movements outside

Germany and Italy. The Heimwehr belongs in both the paramilitary and, with some qualifications, in the fascist categories. Although it failed in its efforts to build and maintain a mass following and in its bids to secure a monopoly on political power, it did contribute to two major developments, both interrelated. Aided by counterrevolutionary regimes in Italy and Hungary, as well as by Austrian backers, the Heimwehr served as the bludgeon that weakened and eventually destroyed both Austria's socialist party and the country's democratic institutions. In turn, leading elements of the Heimwehr worked successfully to align Austria with Italy and Hungary in international affairs during the early 1930s.

Study of the Heimwehr has generally been subsumed under treatments either of Seipel's political legacy or of Dollfuss's and Schuschnigg's authoritarian regime.[3] Otherwise it has received mainly summary or peripheral treatment,[4] although Lajos Kerekes has treated at length its connections with Italy and Hungary in certain periods of its history.[5] The present work attempts to provide an overall picture of the Heimwehr's origins and development, its goals and ideology, and its role in Austrian politics from its inception in 1918 and 1919 to its dissolution in 1936 by the dictatorial government that it had helped create.

Clearly the child of an unstable and contingent age, the Heimwehr cannot be divorced from its milieu. The small Austrian republic created after World War I, which stood at the strategic crossroads of central Europe, presented a classic example of the sociopolitical conflicts that ravaged Europe after the war. Austria was a country but partially modernized, in which peasants and small townsmen comprised over half the population. Ideas of liberalism had never deeply penetrated these groups generally taught by Church and school to defer to authority. Now they faced the anguish of defeat, the fear of revolution, the flux of social and economic upheaval. A stable new order could hardly be perceived, much less accepted. Many people saw no alternative to the secular collectivism threatened by the socialists but some kind of authoritarian countercollectivism pledged to defend property, nation, and traditional values. The appeals of demagogues intensified existing forces of fear and hatred among nationalities and social classes and pitted group against group in bitter conflict. Like its host of siblings in Austria and elsewhere, the Heimwehr thrived on this conflict, especially after its leaders set about to use it as a means of undoing the revolutionary settlement and of gaining power for themselves. All along they threatened the use of force to achieve some absolute end—if only the political destruction of their opponents.

The Heimwehr was paramilitary in that it was composed of unofficial and/or semiofficial groups of men who were armed and trained for the purposes of influencing political affairs, of keeping politics in a state of cold war, and potentially of waging civil war.[6] Such political armies flourished on both the Left and the Right in those states whose official armed forces were required by treaty to be extremely small, or in states whose people were for some reason terribly unhappy with postwar conditions. In some cases these political armies were controlled by the leadership of established parties (this was generally true more of the Left than of the Right); but in Austria the rightist paramilitary groups were formed either to wrest power for their leadership or to bring pressure to bear on the political parties. At the same time they formed the nucleus of a fascist party.

According to its own brash boasts—openly after 1930 and, in fact, before then—the Heimwehr would have to be considered a fascist movement. Even so, the degree to which it qualifies as fascist depends on the characteristics one ascribes to fascism. Unfortunately, scholars have yet to arrive at a commonly accepted definition either of fascist ideology or of its characteristics; and they still debate its place in European history. Many scholars emphasize the negative aspects of fascism. In the philosophic sense discussed by Nolte, it resisted "transcendence," that is, the hopeful and eager acceptance of a reforming society. As if they were all one and the same, fascism opposed Marxism of all hues, any kind of aggressive working-class movement, and liberal, pluralistic democracy with its emphases on the individual and on government by law and discussion. Many fascists would add big industry and finance-capitalism to the list. Accordingly, fascism can be seen as essentially counterrevolutionary, even reactionary. In this sense fascism was the way many Europeans who were comfortably accustomed to a stable and stratified society and to authoritarian rule responded to what they perceived to be a mortal threat to their hallowed ways of life, a threat they thought caused by the ill-conceived peace treaties, by the example of social revolution in Russia, by the exhaustion of society's "natural" leaders, and by the rise of party machines led by self-serving "bosses." They were against it all. What they wanted was the stability, the order, the social harmony that they remembered from the *Kaiserzeit*. As Organski and Weiss suggest, the principal functions of fascist movements were to depoliticize the newly emerging masses, the proletarians and egalitarians, and to enlist the intermediate masses, who could claim some prior status, for the counterrevolutionary and authoritarian cause.[7]

Probably most supporters of fascism were at first attracted by its counterrevolutionary promise. Undoubtedly, however, most of them also believed the values it preached to be positive. Fascist leaders, some more sincerely than others, extolled the common welfare, loyalty to and superiority of the nation, military strength, traditional property rights, social stability, and authoritarian government. Another concept adopted by some fascist movements was that called corporative government, that is, rule by the elite of the major functional groups in the economy, but this appeal was largely a cover for totalitarian aspirations. These values may have seemed positive to their proponents, but for the most part they represented traditional central European conservative values. To that extent John Weiss is justified in discerning a "fascist tradition."

But there is another side to fascism. Scholars also realize that the exigencies of the postwar situation made revolutionaries out of counter-revolutionaries. The times were too out of joint, and the process of social change, often misunderstood, was too inexorable for it to be otherwise. In general, men from the professional middle and even lower classes assumed leadership of popular conservative movements. While most of them valued various aspects of the antirevolutionary tradition, including rule by an elite, they had to cope with popular sovereignty at a time when traditional social and political relationships were dissolv-ing. The very fact of the emergence of the masses into political partici-pation meant that the old order could not be restored. Astutely combin-ing nostalgia for the old and eagerness for the new, successful fascist leaders created mass movements that could justify their claims to power.

In a "revolutionary" and "democratic" age, conservative leaders had to borrow from their enemies. Many fascists, especially the most radical ones, talked more about the future than about the past. Instead of claiming to be just defenders of the old order or spokesmen for class-oriented special interest groups, many popular right-wing leaders criti-cized what they called the cowardice, the staidness, and the selfishness of the bourgeoisie, from whom, in fact, they drew most of their support. Influenced by and appealing to the irrationalist and primitivist currents that were strong at the time, they called for new and dynamic methods to revitalize society. They prided themselves on leading all-encompass-ing "movements of renewal" or even of "revolution," and they intended to create a new "people's" world, one that would satisfy man's elemental longing both for action and mastery and also for order and security. Most insisted on the rectitude—indeed the infallibility—of their own views. Like religious revivalists, fascist leaders demanded unwavering commitment to the crusade. Good was pitted against evil, and one force alone would emerge totally triumphant. Society must be cleansed of its impurities and reordered, and the nation must be infused with a new sense of community, self-sacrifice, discipline, and purposeful productivity.

To master mass man and to subvert the meaning of popular sovereignty, fascist leaders employed the leadership principle and paramilitary organization. It was argued that only hierarchical and authoritarian leadership, much like that of a vast army on the march, could effect the swift decisions and rapid action that the times required. Leadership was best vested in one man, who was deemed to have almost mystic powers to discern both the best interests of the nation and the best means of realizing them. In many movements emphasis was placed on the personal loyalty that members owed to the leader, whose word was law. Thus, the followers were responsible to the leader, not the leader to the people. This identification of leader with movement and of movement with nation led naturally to the effort to acquire a monopoly on political power and, where fascist movements were most successful, to a totalitarian claim to control all aspects of life that far surpassed the practice of traditional authoritarianism. Thus, fascist leaders were forced into ambiguous positions vis-à-vis exiled monarchs and royal pretenders. If these "new men" were going to save the nation by leading their movements to power, they were not likely to defer to relics—temporal or spiritual—who claimed to have inherited sovereign authority.

As will be seen, the Heimwehr shared in varying degrees many of these fascist characteristics.[8] Perhaps it can best be seen as part of the antirevolutionary triad described by Arno J. Mayer.[9] In general the Heimwehr was the expression and vehicle of counterrevolution. While there were many conservatives in its leadership, its most effective leaders came from the middle class (Steidle, Pfrimer) or from the middle officers' caste (Pabst, Fey) rather than from the old elites. Starhemberg might be considered an exception, but his formative experiences linked him with the déclassés. These leaders took advantage of what Mayer calls a double-edged crisis situation to seek not so much to preserve traditional relationships—despite their rhetoric, which was "drawn from the reactionary *cum* conservative dialogue"—but rather to build a popular following of disparate elements to win for new men "the physical control of the state apparatus." They pessimistically rejected their world and its modernizing direction and hoped for a militaristic order that would preserve or enhance their status and some accustomed values. Thus, while they bemoaned successive crises and exaggerated

the threat of revolution, they tried to mobilize the unsettled intermediate, or "crisis," strata with the promise of renewal (not just return)
and offered themselves as a new political elite. Throughout, they both
assailed and seemed to threaten the old conservative elites, whom they
would like to push aside or outmaneuver, but at the same time they depended on and cooperated with this "upper cartel of anxiety." They
demanded law and order even while they were disturbing it; they
stirred social discord while decrying it. And they achieved a measure of
success by their use of paramilitary organization, discipline, and drill
and of aggressive and provocative violence, by which they tried to
demonstrate the élan and indispensability of their movement.

At first Heimwehr leaders preached almost exclusively the anti-
Marxist line: they had to stem the tide of revolution, to defend the good
old ways. Accordingly, most Heimwehr followers probably saw their
task as defensive. But it was not long before ambitious leaders began
thinking in terms of seizing power for themselves instead of saving it for
the moderately conservative parties in the parliamentary system. These
ambitions were aroused well before the Heimwehr had a sizeable following and depended primarily on military preparations for a coup
d'état. Nevertheless, the leaders sought to make the Heimwehr into a
Volksbewegung, portrayed as a mass "movement of renewal" that
would destroy Austria's socialist movement and sweep away the de-
spised parliamentary system. Not surprisingly, they were more eager for
the practice of power than for the fulfillment of doctrine. Although they
never had a clear idea of the society they hoped to rule, they leaned
toward and for a while championed the concept of the corporative
state, although true to form this appeal was largely a smoke screen for
their own desires for arbitrary power, which grew more pronounced as
the parliamentary regime crumbled.

Less convincingly than in Italy and Germany, Heimwehr leaders
attempted to appear dynamic, elemental, and martial. The use of uniforms, outdoor rallies, parades, and military maneuvers became the
hallmark of the Heimwehr, just as they did of other fascist movements.
Its core of dedicated followers must have been moved by emotions that
led to similar activity elsewhere: fear and suspicion of western, liberal,
socialist, and other "un-German" forms of government; pride of race
and/or nationality; attraction of martial pageantry (however provincial
and pallid); and promise of place in a new regime. In addition, there
were the more universal desires for camaraderie and a few schillings.

There were, however, several major factors that stunted the Heimwehr's full growth, and in general its aspirations remained more fascist

than its achievements. While conditions in interwar Austria clearly fostered paramilitary activity, they also militated against the success of a native fascist movement. In brief, postwar Austria was too new, too small, too dependent, too Catholic. Probably the most serious limitation to fascism in Austria was the fact that it could not make full use of the nationalistic appeal. Austrian nationalism did not yet exist, and the Heimwehr ultimately lost its most fervent nationalist adherents to groups dedicated solely to bringing about union with Germany. Furthermore, Austria as a state and the Heimwehr as a movement were both excessively dependent on outside support and hence subject to outside influence. The Heimwehr's taking power would neither restore past glories nor hold out much prospect for future ones. Austria's Catholic tradition, too, hampered Heimwehr attempts to gain a monopoly on political power. As long as the Heimwehr could be seen as the militant guard supporting the conservative party dominated by loyal Catholics, the Church gave it its blessings. But when the Heimwehr began making totalitarian claims, the Church successfully sought to keep it only a junior partner in Austria's authoritarianism.

Other disadvantages limited the chances for lasting Heimwehr success. The movement suffered all along from inadequate leadership. While various aspirants made the effort to establish themselves in undisputed control, there was no leader with both the charisma and the ruthlessness of a Mussolini or a Hitler, so that most of the time there was a largely independent leader in each province, a few of whom actually served at the pleasure of the intermediate leadership. Personal and ideological rivalries were a permanent feature of the Heimwehr scene. This weakness helps account for the failure of the Heimwehr to draw and hold the spontaneous mass following needed to win by political processes. Thus, circumstances forced it to remain most of the time a feudallike army of retainers organized along hierarchical lines within each province, where leaders were often concerned more with weapons than with ballots. Under these circumstances the Heimwehr claimed throughout the 1920s to be nonpolitical or supraparty; that is, it did not seek votes but sought instead to support all nonsocialist political parties, for which its members were free to vote. In reality, Heimwehr leaders bitterly condemned the passiveness of the bourgeoisie and tried to badger the political parties into doing their bidding.

With the help of domestic and foreign funding and also of the overall trend of developments in Europe during the depression, the Heimwehr accomplished its chief negative goal—the destruction of the Social Democratic Party and Austria's parliamentary system. But because of the obstacles already described, the Heimwehr failed to win total control of the little country.

In summary it can be suggested that the Heimwehr, since it failed to seize power by a coup d'état, demonstrated *konkurrenz* fascism both in ideology and leadership characteristics. That is, beyond a basic "fascist minimum" found in all right-wing movements, the Heimwehr followed the lead of and competed with the example of its larger neighbors. In this sense the history of the Heimwehr simply reflected the conditions of central Europe in the interwar period. The Heimwehr was not merely a group of mean men. True, the "military desperadoes" of whom Wolfgang Sauer writes,[10] could be found at all levels of the movement, and these ruffians occasionally had their day (although in the long run the Nazis attracted those men who were most virulently anti-Semitic and/or most disposed to use terrorism and violence). Most Heimwehr leaders were limited to a depressing degree, but few of them were perverse or vicious. Their activities and their fleeting triumphs simply serve to demonstrate the fact that, given the anxieties of postwar Europe, the appearance of groups seeking extreme solutions to poorly perceived problems was all but unavoidable.

However, regardless of the extent to which the Heimwehr was or was not fascist, it proved to be a significant force in Austrian political affairs. This was clearly so after the political crisis that occurred in July 1927, but potentially so in the years before that. The following chapters describe its role in the political life of the first Austrian republic.

1

The Austrian Setting

For convenience one can delineate three major periods between Austria's emergence after World War I and its absorption into Nazi Germany in 1938. The basic division is that between the parliamentary democracy that lasted into 1933 and the authoritarian regime established in 1933 and 1934. However, the political effects of the bloodshed in Vienna on 15 July, 1927, and of the nationwide strikes that followed, were so enormous that that crisis must be seen as a turning point in the history of the First Republic. That event opened the way to a sustained counterrevolutionary thrust and the rapid growth of the Heimwehr, which played its most crucial role in Austrian politics between 1927 and 1934. Still, the Heimwehr also played distinctive roles in the early period of cautious consensus that dissolved into political cold war, as well as for a while in the later period of dictatorial rule.

The defeat in war and the collapse of the monarchy inaugurated an era of instability and despair for many Austrians. Those people happily accustomed to the authoritarian rule of Franz Josef, and for the most part also to traditional Catholic teaching, were now caught up in calamitous changes, frightening uncertainty, and momentous challenges; at the same time many people in the working classes placed their hopes in social revolution. To the extent that a new state with a democratic system of government emerged and that the propertyless classes acquired more political power and social security than they had previously had, there was a revolution in Austria after the war. But many socialists were frustrated because it was not more thorough, while nonsocialists—the landed aristocracy, the industrialists, the petite bourgeoisie, and the Catholic hierarchy—thought it much too sweeping. Thus, throughout the period people of all ages and pursuits were beset by bitter disillusionment, sullen resentment, and anxious intolerance heightened by many fears and lightened by very few hopes.

Such conditions precipitated paramilitary activities on both the Right and the Left, the one side seeking to prevent social revolution, the other hoping to make one, or rather to prevent counterrevolution. For several years the victorious western powers kept a lid on the contest between the two opposing sides. The Allies were inconsistent, however, in their attitudes toward the contestants. On one hand they feared the rearmament of their former enemies, and on the other hand they feared even more bolshevism and movements akin to it. Thus, they tolerated armed groups on both ends of the spectrum to balance each other and then tried to foster a regime of the Center which would, they hoped, become like themselves.

Given the extent of postwar confusion, the "revolution" was effected with remarkably little violence. Sensibly, the last Habsburg emperor, Charles, provided legality both to the dismemberment of the empire and also to the transition from a government responsible to him to one responsible to the German-speaking delegates elected to parliament in 1911. On 12 November 1918, while huge crowds of workers demonstrated outside the parliament building in Vienna, this Provisional Assembly voted to establish a representative democracy that they hoped would become part of the new German republic, a union prevented by France and Italy. The Assembly then continued to govern until a national constituent assembly was elected in February 1919. Both before and after these elections the two major parties, the Social Democrats and the Christian Socials, cooperated in keeping the revolution one in which discussion instead of violence would prevail. The socialist leaders, basically moderate men who had thirty years of legal party and union activity behind them, knew that both the opposition of the peasants in the particularist provinces and Austria's dependence on the victorious Allies for food made it impossible to carry out a thoroughgoing social revolution. Conservative spokesmen, not at all happy with what was happening, sensed that there was no peaceable and practicable alternative to the creation of a democratic republic in which the industrial workers would gain substantial social securities and political influence. It was a revolution of the possible—one might almost say inevitable—in which anarchy and extreme social conflict were avoided.

The new country's economic limitations form one of its most striking characteristics. What became Austria had been, together with Bohemia, the old empire's industrial area, while the lands to the east and south had been its food basket. After the war Austria's industry was deprived of much of its market, its banks of many of their connections, and its industrial population of much of its food supply. Furthermore, most of the civil and military servants of the House of Habsburg became wards of this state, not of the other successor states. Nearly a third of its population of 6.5 million was crowded into Vienna, and most of the rest were located in the three large provinces in the eastern part of the country. Though these three—Lower Austria, Upper Austria, and Styria—were roughly balanced between agriculture and industry, only about a third of the country's total population was engaged in agriculture, and their productivity of food was limited by the mountainous terrain in the western and central parts of the country. Thus, as long as economic nationalism in central Europe kept tariff barriers high, Austria was faced with the constant problem of selling enough abroad to be able to feed its people. Barred by the victorious Allies from union with Germany, Austria had to depend on loans from the western nations, a dependency that heightened political tensions within the country.

Once German Austria had to face the future simply as Austria, its democratically elected coalition of socialists and moderate conservatives proceeded to establish a federal parliamentary republic, with the new constitution going into effect in October 1920. The "revolution by consensus" had produced a classic compromise. The Christian Socials managed to secure a greater measure of decentralization than the Social Democrats theoretically preferred, thereby preserving their power base in the historic provinces. On the other hand the socialists eventually won recognition of Vienna as a separate province in which they thought their power base would be secure. The federal legislature was bicameral: the upper house, with only a suspensive veto, represented the provincial governments according to size and political complexion; and the sovereign lower house was elected by universal suffrage according to a proportional-list plan. The cabinet was appointed by and responsible to the Nationalrat, the lower house; and the indirectly elected president was but a figurehead, at least until the constitutional revision of 1929. In political life parties became all-important, since party affiliation was a requisite for campaigning and since voting was for party rather than personality. People who were accustomed to having their interests represented by professional and economic chambers could not readily accept this primacy of politics and politicians.

The basic lines of political division within the country proved to be remarkably stable. Classic by now is Adam Wandruszka's admirable essay on Austria's three major political traditions—Christian conservatism, democratic socialism, and German nationalism—which he traces from their emergence in the 1880s through the restoration of the republic after 1945.[1] The most cohesive of the three Lager was the Social Democratic party (SDP), which consistently polled from 36 to 42 percent of the votes in national parliamentary elections. Their chief rivals were the Christian Social party (CSP) and its provincial affiliates; these had slightly greater polling strength but were much less homogeneous. The smallest camp, the nationalists, was divided into two parties, the Pan-German People's party and the Agrarian League (Landbund). Together they attracted from 15 to 20 percent of the popular vote in national elections, until the rise of the National Socialists after 1932. While each camp encompassed a wide spectrum of political opinion, each also tended to see its own vision of society as exclusively right, a tendency more marked in the larger two camps than in the pre-Nazi nationalist circles, which included much of what remained of Austria's anticlerical liberal outlook. But until the Nazis radicalized and collectivized the nationalist camp, it was able to cooperate, even if uncomfortably, with the Christian Socials against the Social Democrats.

Broadly speaking, then, the Austrian polity was divided into two main groups—the Social Democrats and their opponents. In a tragic irony of the time, both sides shared the delusion that the socialists would be able to transform social and economic relationships if they could only obtain a bare majority in parliament. Acting on the fears engendered by the assumption, some antisocialists proved willing to use any means available to forestall such a shift in the voting returns—from making the ballot less significant to using bullets. By the same token the socialists, self-proclaimed revolutionaries, concentrated their efforts on gaining a parliamentary majority. But they failed to recognize the limitations of their own political hopes and theories. Led by Otto Bauer, a brilliant analyst and orator who tried to combine theory and practice in good Marxian tradition, the Social Democrats promised their followers a victory they could not achieve and then at times sought both to hold the doubters in their ranks and also to overawe their opponents with demonstrative displays of self-confidence that made them appear more immoderate than they really were.

The socialists counted on two achievements to make possible a nation-wide victory at the polls. The first was their success in maintaining the unity of the working-class party at a time when most workers' movements in Europe were divided into moderate "parliamentary" parties and extreme "revolutionary" parties participating in the Communist International. As already noted, however, the Austro-Marxists achieved their unity by dressing essentially moderate policies in the garb of orthodox Marxist rhetoric which made them sound much more radical than they actually were. Anyone who carefully followed the intraparty debates in conventions and the press knew that their theorists were men of peaceful persuasion. But even intelligent opponents generally heard only the demagogic appeals or threats. By the tactics that seemed necessary to keep their followers united, including at times the obstruction of parliamentary business, the socialist leaders frightened much of their all-too-credulous opposition into uncompromising enmity.

The second source of strength for the Social Democrats was their political power in the eastern part of the country. They controlled Vienna and several other industrial cities from the collapse of the monarchy until the civil war of February 1934, and had strong representation in the governments of several provinces, especially Styria and Lower and Upper Austria. The municipalities in which they had the dominant voice, including Vienna, accounted for slightly over half the population of Austria. Thus, even though at the federal level the party stood in opposition from 1920 until its dissolution in 1934, it did have its bases of power and it did demonstrate its capacity for sensible and responsible participation in government. Nevertheless, where they could, socialists clearly governed for the benefit of the working-class majority. Hence, the fact that many socialists in government proved to be men of ability and of moderation did little to lessen hostility to their policies.

Red Vienna became a symbol of Austria's political polarization. There municipal socialism—an extension of that initiated by the Christian Social Mayor Karl Lueger at the turn of the century—was concentrated in the fields of housing, health, and secular education. The national rent ceiling insisted on by the city's ruling party was also popular with poorer nonsocialists. But socialist achievements in Vienna and a few of the larger cities of the provinces, widely admired outside Austria, were supported by heavy taxation on wealth and luxuries and even hampered small-scale independent entrepreneurs. Those whose interests were adversely affected, as well as those whose earlier aristocratic, military, or bureaucratic status simply could not be maintained in the postwar world, sulked bitterly and waited for a chance to turn back the clock. By the same token Church authorities resented the anticlericalism of the socialists and of the Vienna school system, and preached throughout the country against the atheists. Thus, among the peasantry and the provincial middle classes, as well as among the Viennese rentiers and small independents, there developed a deep antipathy toward the socialist capital, a feeling reinforced by "states rights" politicians who were in any event suspicious of centralizing tendencies emanating from the capital, except when they might be used to weaken social democracy.

Another aspect of Austrian social democracy disliked by its opponents was its network of affiliated associations. These ranged from "free" labor unions, which enrolled nearly 80 percent of the country's union members, and the well-organized paramilitary Republican Defense League (Schutzbund) to adult education programs and a multiplicity of athletic and leisure-time clubs. Without social democracy the workers would have been splintered and neglected, hence more susceptible to revolutionary appeals. As it was, social democracy amounted to a state within a state which tended to cut the working classes off from the rest of the population and to exert political pressure on waverers and on nonsocialist workers. Antisocialists, ignoring the positive contributions of these associations to the lives of the industrial workers and blind to the stability which they imparted to the life of the nation, trembled when a half million citizens in Vienna and other industrial centers could be mobilized for demonstrations—however orderly—on the workers' festival days. Such comprehensive organization and massive demonstrations represented physical and spiritual terror in the eyes of many antisocialists and could be countered ultimately only by similar means.

The most heterogeneous of Austria's three political *Lager* was that of the Christian conservatives. It tenuously held together most ex-aristocrats, industrialists, and financiers; all those still strongly influenced by the Catholic Church, especially the peasants (if not their youngest sons); and those who were first and foremost antisocialist particularists, that is, much of the small town professional and business population. The various economic and cultural associations through which these people acted usually exercised more influence over the politicians than did political theory, and they generally supported the Christian Social party. The socialist threat encouraged more cohesiveness within the Christian-conservative camp than might have been expected of such a heterogeneous grouping. Party discipline nearly always held fast in parliament, and most of the time after 1922 the CSP named the federal chancellor and thus had the major voice in government.

Naturally a party composed of such disparate elements had within it several schools of social and political thought. These ranged from the federalists' pragmatic acceptance of representative democracy to the centralists' desire for an authoritarian, if paternalistic, regime that would restore the traditional social and spiritual norms. Many of the new entrepreneurs and profiteers, who had considerable influence in the CSP, favored a classic liberal and antiunion policy, but the middle classes that had been hard hit by the revolution were attracted by schemes for "Romantic" corporatism that would protect their status and

property. The Christian Socials willing to accept the republic on practical grounds were usually leaders in the provinces, where (except in
Styria) they learned to live with the socialists. It was partly to mollify
them as well as to counter the centralizing thrust of the socialists that
the republic was given a federal constitution. As time passed, however,
the CSP's "Vienna school" of nondemocratic corporative centralizers
came increasingly to the fore. Faced with socialist power in Vienna and
in the largest labor unions, and backed by industrial allies, they were
most eager to find some alternative to parliamentary democracy and
socialist theory.

The bridge between the federalists and the centralists was Ignaz
Seipel. A priest, Seipel became a chief architect of the republican consensus, the CSP's leading politician, and chancellor of Austria for five
years (1922–1924, 1926–1929). While his accommodation with the
democratic forces of the revolutionary era may have been sincere and
flexible, his first concern was for the molding of a Christian society as
he perceived it should be and not for any particular form of government. Over the years his attitude toward the socialists hardened and his
search for "true" democracy became increasingly associated with
Romantic corporatism and counterrevolution.[2] His personal crusade, in
whose service he enlisted the Heimwehr, failed, but changing circumstances enabled his successors to unite superficially the CSP and the
Heimwehr as the major pillars of an authoritarian and ostensibly Christian regime.

The smallest of the three major political groups was itself subdivided.
Aligned in the Pan-German People's party were large numbers of the
middle and upper echelons of the bureaucracy and part of the provincial professional and small independent groups. The Agrarian League
was strongest among anticlerical and well-to-do farmers chiefly in
Styria and Carinthia. The significance of the nationalist camp lay in the
fact that it held the balance of power in the federal parliament. The
Pan-Germans cooperated with the Christian Socials most of the time
from 1922 to 1932; and the Agrarian League was in the cabinet, with a
brief interruption, from 1927 to 1933. Such "bourgeois blocks" were at
best tenuous arrangements, and the rise of National Socialism early in
the 1930s made it impossible to maintain them.

During the interwar years these *Lager* differed over several major
issues. The most significant among them were *Anschluss;* foreign sources
of economic aid and the political price exacted for it; social legislation,
especially in Vienna; the composition and political orientation of the

federal army; and the role of the various paramilitary formations. After the crisis of mid-1927 the very nature of the constitution and of the nation's political system became matters of great moment.

As a state without a national tradition of its own, Austria was unique in postwar Europe. It became "the state that nobody wanted,"[3] a country thought incapable of supporting itself (as it probably was until basic economic and psychological adjustments were made). Most Austrians longed vaguely for their former great-power status, if not in the old empire then as part of greater Germany. But *Anschluss* was forbidden by the Treaty of Saint-Germain and by pledges made to foreign creditors in 1922 and again in 1932, and not all Austrians wanted to become an appendage of Germany. Naturally, union with Germany was the cardinal principle of the nationalist camp. The Social Democrats, who wished to join forces with Germany's socialists, also condemned Seipel for renouncing *Anschluss* in return for foreign loans and, until Hitler's accession, demanded the national self-determination promised by the Allies. The Christian Socials were divided over this issue. Many of the leaders, while paying lip service to the idea of *Anschluss* to please their nationalist allies, were skeptical of what union with Germany would do to their way of life. Much of the Catholic population would have been apprehensive at union with a predominantly Protestant country, and many industrialists did not wish to compete with German manufacturers. Before the depression, enthusiastic German nationalists formed but a minority of Austria's population. The Heimwehr, drawing its support from both the Christian-conservative and the nationalist camps, was also divided over the issue, but its eventual legacy, especially after the National Socialists had become competitors, was that of support for Austrian independence.

Important to the question of the paramilitary formations was the whole matter of military policy. In contrast to the situation in Germany, where the command structure and social caste of the army survived intact, the multinational Habsburg military institutions dissolved in the breakup of the monarchy. In what emerged as Austria, a new army had to be established. Again in contrast to what happened in Germany, the Austrian socialists, in control of the war ministry until late in 1920, saw to it that the officers and especially the men of this new army, called at first the Volkswehr, were sympathetic to the republic. At the same time the socialists prevented the new people's army from becoming a "red" army at a time when bolshevism seemed to be flaming on all sides and threatening within, a signal service only too little appreciated by their political opponents. With the aid of the peace treaty, the Austrian socialists managed to create an army that would be neither a seedbed for radical and violent revolution nor a tool of reaction that would fire upon the workers.

The terms of the treaty limited the size of the army to thirty thousand men and prescribed long-term recruitment instead of short-term conscription. In fact, because of Austria's economic straits, for a decade and a half the new army seldom exceeded twenty-two thousand men. With their soldiers' councils and their guarantee of political rights to the soldiers, the socialists hoped to keep the army republican in outlook and to prevent a return to the full measure of traditional military discipline as insurance against the possibility that the officers might regain their self-confidence and the backing of a bourgeois regime. In truth, for many years the federal army, the Bundesheer, as it was renamed in 1920, was not much of an army. Although it fought valiantly in 1919 and 1920 to save Slovenian Carinthia and the Burgenland for German-Austria, it was no match for the army of any of its neighbors except perhaps for that of Hungary.

After they assumed control of the federal government, the Christian Socials began gradually to transform the army's political coloration, a job that for over a decade was in the hands of Minister Carl Vaugoin. His "depoliticalization" was really a "repoliticalization" designed to make the army into a decisive weight in the internal political balance, not into a nonpartisan national defense force. This process was well along by 1927 but was accelerated after the Viennese workers' "revolt" of that year. When the political system was changed in 1933 and 1934, the army proved its value to the conservatives in the brief civil wars in February and July of 1934. Thereafter successful efforts were made to enlarge the army, to prevent its infiltration by too many pro-Nazis, and to use it as a counterweight to the "totalitarian" demands of the Heimwehr, much as was the case in the army–SA rivalry in Nazi Germany.

Clearly, then, the new Austrian army stood in the "shadow of the parties" and their political armies.[4] The paramilitary formations together had far more men under arms—even if they were generally poorly trained and often undependable—than did the army and the federal police forces combined. Each side could argue that the weakness or the partisanship of the army necessitated the maintenance of the paramilitary self-defense formations, as they were always called. But only the SDP openly claimed and controlled its party guard, the republican Schutzbund. The various antisocialist armed groups, foremost among them the Heimwehren, were not so closely tied to or restrained by the bourgeois parties. Indeed, they claimed to be supraparty, that is, to be above and independent of "petty partisan politics." They were, however, often seen by conservative provincial governments as auxiliary police forces, and in the 1920s they were welcomed by the army ministry as reserve troops. Throughout the existence of the First Republic the martial groups from the Right and the Left kept it in a state of permanent civil war. Such was one result of the militarized democratization of Europe during the First World War, and of the popular notion—fostered by the leaders on both sides—that one side or the other must ultimately gain complete control of the country.

Although this study focuses primarily on the Heimwehr in Austria—its organizational development and its role in domestic politics—an effort has been made to take note of its foreign connections. More than was the case with most European countries at the time, Austrian domestic history reflected the international situation. Of course, significant aspects of Austria's development did depend on domestic factors, especially its essentially authoritarian tradition and its people's unwillingness or inability to accept the postwar geopolitical and constitutional settlements as final. In large measure, however, external forces, far more than the actions of any domestic groups, determined the fate of the country. The prohibition of *Anschluss* and the vacillation of France and Britain were factors beyond Austrian control. Danubian cooperation, which Austria needed so badly to counter her economic prostration, could not be effected because of the determination of Czechoslovakia, Yugoslavia, and Romania to remain aloof from the former ruling groups of the old empire (i.e., Austria and Hungary). Austria's domestic history reflected the international situation in other ways as well. For example, because of the soviet regimes proclaimed in Hungary and Bavaria in 1919, many Austrian rightists remained convinced that all socialists wanted to follow the example of the Russian bolsheviks. To a great extent, then, Austria's antisocialists, including the Heimwehr, simply reflected the sentiments prevailing in Europe, especially in the central and eastern areas, between the two world wars. Political polarization and the readiness to use violence were key features of that tragic era.

2

Aims and Activities before July 1927

Paramilitary groups in Austria sprang into existence as a natural consequence of the crumbling of the imperial regime and of the fearful chaos of the immediate postwar period. The collapse of the empire and its army left the people of the German provinces of old Austria filled with uncertainty and fear, compounded by the economic deprivations following in the wake of the lost war. Thousands of soldiers, many of them non-German, threatened property and food supplies along the main routes as they streamed homeward in disarray from the battlefronts, while rumors of rampaging Italian prisoners also added to the fears of the Austrian populace.[1] In these circumstances it was only natural that people began to organize themselves for self-defense. The formation of such self-defense groups, virtually spontaneous and ill coordinated, occurred under a variety of auspices, including private and political groups, localities, and provincial governments, which helped provide arms to the citizens, in some cases without regard to their social status.[2] Nevertheless, Austria's demography was such that these armed groups generally took on a class complexion, especially in the industrial cities, so that once the common danger from the marauding soldiery was past, class consciousness led everywhere to a clearer distinction between workers' groups on one hand and bourgeois-peasant groups on the other, with each side taking a different view of the social and political changes taking place in Austria.

In Vienna the Social Democrats used their de facto control of the war ministry to create the volunteer Volkswehr, or people's militia, which was to become the nucleus of the republic's new army. Manned chiefly by unemployed industrial workers, it was disciplined by party cadres, who kept the most radical elements under control, at least in the vicinity of the capital. The Volkswehr was not only an official force but also in effect an adjunct of the Social Democratic party, which controlled the war ministry under Dr. Julius Deutsch until October 1920. There were also groups called Arbeiterwehren (Workers' Guards) or Ordnerwehren (Order Guards) which, depending on conditions in the various cities and the strength of the local workers' and soldiers' councils,

served to keep order, to protect socialist meetings, to deter armed reaction, and in some cases to requisition foodstuff from the countryside.
Furthermore, there were numerous occasions on which radical workers
used the permissiveness of the times to intimidate their social antagonists when they tried to express themselves politically. And countless
imperial army officers felt themselves degraded and humiliated by the
brusque, if not hostile, treatment they received upon their return to
Vienna.[3]

In the face of all this energetic activity by the workers, nonsocialists
of all hues began to think in terms of an armed counterpoise, a concern
heightened by the fact that social and religious reactionaries tried to
blame postwar ills on the international-minded and secular socialists.
As a consequence, groups formed primarily to protect the German *Volk*
from the flood of fleeing soldiery began to turn their attention to the
threat of social revolution. Reinforced by returning veterans, peasants
and townsmen continued to join formations designated variously as
citizens', peasants', rural, or simply home guards. Until the Treaty of
Saint-Germain, which severely limited the number of men Austria could
legally keep under arms, went into effect in 1920, provincial and local
officials in areas governed by nonsocialists recognized these groups as
auxiliary police forces.

Events in the spring of 1919 stimulated the creation of such groups.
The establishment of short-lived communist regimes in neighboring
Bavaria and Hungary long served as a bogy for the marshaling of antisocialist sentiment. There were also communist-led disturbances in several
Austrian cities in mid-April, although at that time some local bourgeois
units cooperated with moderate workers' guards in maintaining order.[4]
What really compelled Austrians of all persuasions to take up arms,
however, was the invasion of Carinthia by irregular bands of Yugoslavs.
The successful defense of the province eventually provided a Heimwehr
legend, but, because this early Carinthian Heimatschutz not only cooperated with the Volkswehr but also included many workers in its
ranks,[5] nearly a year passed before a clearly partisan, bourgeois organization was firmly established in Carinthia.

One might have expected that Austria's varied armed guards would
have slowly disappeared once the serious threats of disorder were over.
This was particularly the case in the mountain provinces, which were
governed by nonsocialist majorities wielding extensive local powers
under the new federal constitution of 1920. In fact, in many of these
regions the local defense formations soon assumed positions similar to
that traditionally enjoyed by veterans' associations, volunteer fire de-

partments, gymnastic and rifle clubs, and the like.[6] They were respectable and in ways influential, but they did not threaten to take power into their own hands or to disfranchise their political opponents. However, two factors saved the nonsocialist self-defense groups for the counterrevolutionary cause. In the first place, extreme rightists took heart from the fact that the Left's postwar victory was incomplete, and they determined to undo the partially achieved social revolution. In the second place, Austria's counterrevolutionaries received encouragement and support from like-minded agitators in Bavaria and Hungary who were not content with their triumphs at home.

From Bavaria came money, large quantities of smuggled weapons, and leaders already skilled in paramilitary organization. In this regard two names stand out, Dr. Georg Escherich and Rudolf Kanzler. Escherich was a forester and Kanzler a surveyor who got swept up in the counterrevolutionary movement and made big names for themselves in paramilitary activities. Through an umbrella organization, called Orgesch, Escherich, a fervent nationalist, was trying to unify all rightist paramilitary groups in Germany, many of which were known as Citizens' Guards (Einwohnerwehren). Kanzler, who received a government subsidy early in 1919 to create armed groups in southeastern Bavaria,[7] collaborated closely with Escherich and was commissioned to promote paramilitary activity in Austria in behalf of Orgesch. Both men had close ties with the Bavarian government, and Kanzler, perhaps more particularist than nationalist, soon developed significant contacts with the Hungarian government.

From Budapest came both intense pressure on the Austrian rightists to replace parliamentary government with a conservative dictatorship and also large sums of money. These were distributed through a secret umbrella union of antirepublican groups in Austria called the Association for Order and Law, in which the future chancellor, Ignaz Seipel, played a noticeable role. The Hungarian government also talked about providing a successful putschist regime with fifteen hundred carloads of flour and with five to six carloads of potatoes and corn to meet Austria's persistent food shortage.[8]

Accordingly, throughout 1920 and 1921 Austria's rightist paramilitary groups found themselves caught up in a variety of nefarious intrigues launched from within and without the country. All schemes had in common the aim of establishing an antisocialist, authoritarian regime in Austria. But beyond that the various foreign sponsors had differing goals. In return for their aid the Hungarians wanted guarantees that they could retain the Burgenland, the largely German-speaking West

Hungary of prewar days. Some dreamers hoped to create a Catholic German-Magyar kingdom under either the Habsburgs or the Wittelsbachs (the champions of the two houses did not always cooperate); and others, especially German-nationalists, hoped to enlarge the Reich by dividing Austria between Bavaria and Hungary.

The Austrian counterrevolutionaries, badly divided between pro-German nationalists and Habsburg legitimists and hence doubtful of success, never attempted a coup. Having less-grandiose aspirations than their foreign backers, they lost much of their sense of urgency after the position of the nonsocialist parties was strengthened in parliamentary elections in October 1920. Nevertheless, further encouragement from abroad, as well as agitation for a putsch in some Austrian circles, continued even after the Social Democrats withdrew from the coalition later in the year. Indeed, this formative period, which saw the activities of Austria's paramilitary Right closely connected with those throughout central Europe, lasted through 1923. By the end of that year the moderate Right had clearly regained a predominant share of political power both in Germany and in Austria. Together with the restoration of a semblance of economic stability, this development served to lessen the urgency of the appeal from the paramilitary Right and to form a natural divide in its story before July 1927. The earlier phase provided the basis for much of the Heimwehr's later aims and activities, and thus warrants a closer look.

The Tyrol, a province long known for jealousy of its prerogatives, was from the outset one of the chief centers of Heimwehr activity. In November 1918 Dr. Richard Steidle, a politically active lawyer with no record of military service, organized a volunteer city militia in Innsbruck similar to those established in other towns along main highways. At the time of the soviet regime in Munich in the spring of 1919 the provincial government appointed Steidle chairman of a Tyrolean defense committee charged with setting up new local groups and with arranging for close collaboration between them. Despite efforts by the Social Democrats to sever the close ties between the provincial government and the conservative paramilitary groups late in 1919, Steidle eagerly continued his promotional efforts, which he oriented around the Tyrol's traditional rifle clubs. In March 1920 he established contact with Kanzler, the Bavarian paramilitary organizer who had already helped establish a vigorous Heimwehr in Salzburg. Under Kanzler's guidance, Steidle's Ordnungsblock called for the creation of a province-wide antibolshevist association, and on May 12 a Tyrolean self-defense league, the Heimatwehr, was formally established with the ambitious

Steidle as its chief and the province's lieutenant governor as his deputy. The leaders drafted a resolution justifying the new association on the ground that public security forces were too weak to guarantee the maintenance of order. By the end of 1920 the Heimatwehr may have had as many as twenty thousand members.[9]

Styria, stretching from the Alpine heart of the country southeastward to the borders of its Slavic and Magyar neighbors, eventually rivaled the Tyrol as a center of Heimwehr activities. After facing the flood of returning warriors in 1918, Styria then experienced the fear of the communist revolution in Hungary and of invasion from the south, where the Drava region was transferred to Yugoslavia. Numerous self-defense groups sprang up, some affiliated with political parties, others claiming independence, all eventually competing for membership and support. Intense rivalry, if not hostility, between the Christian Social party and the Agrarian League, which spoke for the nationalistic and anticlerical landowners in the southern part of Austria, prevented the creation of a unified paramilitary organization. Nevertheless, top government officials, most notably Governor Anton Rintelen and Lieutenant Governor Jakob Ahrer, both Christian Socials with nationalist leanings, were instrumental in securing support for the larger self-defense groups. They also aided Kanzler in his efforts to bring the various factions together. Following civil disturbances in Graz in June 1920, Kanzler succeeded in persuading the three major antisocialist parties to cooperate in supporting a provincewide paramilitary union in Styria. However, this collaboration actually restricted the activities of the Heimwehr leaders, especially after the party patrons agreed early in February 1921 that the armed formations should undertake no action unless the order were signed by representatives of at least two of the parties. Some of the paramilitary groups, principally the one under Dr. Walter Pfrimer, who eventually became the leading Heimwehr figure in the province, refused to accept this directive and soon withdrew from the tenuous paramilitary union organized by the three political parties.[10]

During 1920 the bourgeois and peasant participants in Carinthia's struggle against Yugoslavian incursions of the previous year were transformed into the antisocialist Heimatschutz. Larger—with perhaps forty thousand members—and more uniform in outlook—thoroughly nationalistic—than similar forces in Styria, the Carinthian Heimatschutz was always active and provided an appearance that occasionally made Austria's Heimwehr movement look more formidable than it really was, especially in the years before 1927. Because of German support for the anti-Yugoslavian propaganda in 1919, the Carinthian rightists maintained close ties with Bavarian organizations through 1923. However, despite its size and uniformity, the Carinthian Heimatschutz never achieved a leading role in the Heimwehr movement. This was partly because the province's proletarian population was not as important as in Styria and partly because the Heimatschutz leadership lacked the driving ambition of its Tyrolean counterpart.

The area around Vienna was another significant center of paramilitary activities during the early 1920s. In Vienna, the citadel of socialist power, the middle classes were more intimidated and, at the same time, more heterogeneous than elsewhere. While various rightist political groups were formed for mutual commiseration, bourgeois paramilitary formations did not appear in the capital during the first postwar year. But during the winter of 1919/1920 some militant antisocialists, mostly ex-officers embittered by their degradation and unpopularity at the end of the war, began to regain their nerve when their worst fears of revolution were not borne out.

In February 1920 retired officers of the imperial army created a committee to guide the Front Veterans' Association (Frontkämpfervereinigung [FKV]) of officers and enlisted men. They adopted a variation of the slogan that became common to rightist antirepublican groups: "The general good must come before petty party politics." Colonel Hermann von Hiltl, a fanatical German nationalist and anti-Semite, who already led a kind of free corps of officers personally loyal to him, emerged as the leading figure of the association. The first public assembly took place on March 8, and promoters claimed that fifteen hundred persons were present. Spokesmen for the new group railed against the "eastern elements" (i.e. Jews) who, manipulating misery and hunger, forced "against the wall" those patriots who should be directing affairs in Austria.

At first rigorously military in composition, the FKV soon dominated all antisocialist paramilitary activity in Vienna and the surrounding areas of Lower Austria. Branches were established throughout the country, and by the end of 1920 the FKV claimed fifty thousand members. But, except in the core areas around Vienna, the members tended to consider themselves fraternal societies and to participate in other paramilitary organizations. Close collaboration developed between the FKV and provincial Heimwehr groups, although there was some friction because of the FKV's vehement anti-Semitism.[11]

Other antisocialist elements in the region of the capital turned to the Bavarians for assistance, even though Kanzler was not eager to get involved in Vienna until his work in the provinces was further along.

He found almost insurmountable the hostility between Habsburg loyalists and extreme German nationalists, some of whom regarded clericals as a greater danger than bolshevists. Nonetheless, in spite of Kanzler's misgivings, the leaders of several gymnastic, veteran, and student associations worked out a fragile agreement to collaborate with him. To satisfy the nationalists, it was agreed that there would be no discussion of the dynastic question until the *Anschluss* problem had been clarified. Prominent representatives of both the Pan-German party and the Christian Social party, including Seipel, took part in the negotiations. This enterprise also received financial support from the Hungarian government.[12]

All this activity on the local and provincial levels set the stage for Kanzler's effort to create an all-Austrian union of paramilitary organizations in the summer of 1920. At a meeting with Escherich and Kanzler in Munich on July 25, paramilitary leaders from all parts of Austria agreed to work together in a union to be known as the Organization Kanzler (Orka). Promising the Austrians all the assistance they could provide, the Bavarians asserted that their goal was the unification of all Germans and claimed that they did not intend to interfere in internal Austrian politics.[13]

Nevertheless, Kanzler's position in the Austrian paramilitary union was never as strong as his zealous organizing activities would seem to indicate. It was not long before several Austrian leaders, including Steidle, began to question Kanzler's intimate collaboration with Hungarian conspirators, who were urging an armed putsch against Austria's coalition government (there were several meetings to discuss a putsch in August and September 1920[14]). They suspected that Kanzler was interested more in gaining Hungarian support for separating Bavaria from the German Republic than in uniting all Germans (in some circles there was even talk of dividing Austria between Bavaria and Hungary). As a result of these concerns, Kanzler had to struggle to retain the confidence of the Austrians and to keep them united. Through the fall and winter the provincial military chieftains met once a month, but Kanzler failed to establish a generally accepted leadership, and this initial effort to unify Austria's paramilitary associations lasted little more than a year.

In 1920 and early 1921 the inter-Allied military control commission, fully aware that weapons were being smuggled into Austria from Germany and stolen from government armories, tried to get the Austrian government to disband and disarm the paramilitary formations. Their efforts were prompted by rumors of putsch schemes beginning early in

1920.[15] While the commission never seemed to fear that the union under Kanzler would ever be more than a nominal organization, its members regarded the arming of civilians as a breach of the peace treaty and became convinced that on the provincial level the Heimwehren were no longer spontaneous self-defense groups, and a self-justifying report by Steidle to the commission only belied the claim that they were.[16] Following the first provincial "shooting match" staged by the Tyrolean Heimatwehr in November 1920, the Allied military officials in Austria revived their efforts to force a dissolution of the paramilitary associations and to have depots of weapons, if not individually held arms, confiscated, efforts that they intensified again in the wake of new rumors of right-wing conspiracies against the republican government in the spring and summer of 1921. However, the Allied capitals still considered the bolshevist threat in central Europe so serious that they did not press the matter on the Austrian government as assiduously as some of the commissioners thought they should.[17]

To soothe the Allies, Austrian officials asserted their intention to honor the peace treaty, and they also argued that any illegal paramilitary organizations that might exist would automatically disappear when conditions returned to normal.[18] Under pressure, the federal government did gingerly invite the provincial officials to withhold legal approval from any private associations of a military character, which none of them professed to be anyway. A year later the federal government prevailed upon the provincial governments to publish explicit prohibitions on the use of military weapons and training and to get the associations to agree to comply with them.[19] But at all levels of administration, Austrian officials thwarted Allied demands with dilatory tactics and half-hearted measures. Provincial governors often simply refused to act on directives they received from Vienna; and the Tyrolean government would not prosecute men caught smuggling arms from Germany on the grounds that they were patriots obeying instructions and that the man who was "morally" responsible, Steidle, enjoyed immunity from prosecution by virtue of his membership in the provincial diet. Furthermore, nonsocialist officials at all levels could point to the fact that workers' guards also had arms, which they occasionally displayed in public.[20]

The meddling of Allied officials thus had no apparent effect on Heimwehr activities, and its provincial leaders continued to meet frequently well into 1921. In January they discussed the possibility that Austria might not hold together and deliberated on how they should respond to various contingencies. Joined by Kanzler and Rintelen, the conferees concluded that everywhere except in the area around Vienna the Heimwehren were strong enough to keep internal order (that is, to quell a communist or socialist uprising) but not to repel a foreign invasion. They agreed that it would be permissible for the Carinthian Heimat-schutz to risk asking for Italian aid if the Yugoslavs renewed their attacks and concurred that in the event of a putsch from the Left or of a breakdown in central authority the provinces should declare themselves independent and singly seek union with Germany.[21]

As already indicated, well into 1921 Austria's rightists continued to think about establishing an authoritarian government, even though the functioning cabinet, which was composed of bureaucrats instead of politicians, leaned toward the bourgeois parties. With that end in view, on February 26 Seipel and the former imperial foreign minister, Nationalrat member Ottokar Czernin, addressed to the Hungarian government a request for aid in outfitting a strong antisocialist force in Austria. (About the same time Czernin allegedly told a British officer that a putsch organized with Hungarian help was "not unlikely.")[22] Perhaps in connection with putsch plans, on March 5 Lieutenant-Governor Ahrer persuaded the Styrian Manufacturers' Association, prominent bankers, and some of the great landowners to contribute 5 million crowns to the Heimwehren.[23] It was also during these months that the Tyrolean Heimatwehr alone allegedly received fourteen thousand marks a month from some source in Bavaria.[24]

For several reasons, however, these early efforts at union failed and the conspiracies crumbled. Most important among them were the ideological and personal rivalries. Some Austrian rightists were Catholic-conservative in outlook and hoped to restore something like the the old monarchy. Others, völkisch-nationalist and often anticlerical in outlook, wanted to be part of an authoritarian greater Germany. Moreover, the would-be putschists were pragmatic enough to have an understandable fear of failure or of adverse repercussions at a time when Austria was desperately dependent on the Allies for foodstuffs. To this was added the disenchantment and confusion following ex-King Charles's unsuccessful attempt to regain his throne in Hungary in the spring of 1921, a failure which dampened the hopes of Austria's legitimists. Another blow came when the dispute between Austria and Hungary over the Burgenland led Hungarian conservatives to curtail greatly their support for rightist groups in Austria. At the same time Kanzler's tenuous union of Austrian Heimwehren began to break up, with the result that there was another sharp reduction of foreign subsidies toward the end of 1921. It was to be some years before such close ties and such putsch plans were revived.

The events surrounding the collapse of the paramilitary union under Kanzler, which had never really gained a firm footing, revived to the full the rivalries among the Austrian leaders and their foreign connections. King Charles's fruitless putsch attempt revived suspicion among nationalists in the Heimwehr that Kanzler was involved in schemes that might lead to the dismemberment of Germany. Kanzler denied the charges and claimed that personal rivals in Bavaria unjustly fomented mistrust of him, but the dissolution of the German Einwohnerwehren in June 1921 greatly weakened his base of operations. By mid-August he felt compelled to send a letter of resignation as leader of Orka, the Austrian union of rightist paramilitary organizations, to each of the provincial Heimwehren as requested by the pro-*Anschluss* head of the Carinthian Heimatschutz.[25]

Kanzler's withdrawal, however, by no means ended German involvement in Heimwehr affairs. His successor as leader of Orka, which continued to exist in name for several months, was Dr. Otto Pittinger. As head of the Bund Bayern und das Reich, Pittinger exerted considerable influence in Austrian circles into the summer of 1923, long after the collapse of paramilitary union in Austria. But he had rivals. General Erich Ludendorff, who made a highly publicized visit to Carinthia in February 1923, wanted to organize a *völkisch*-oriented paramilitary force under his leadership that would help revive Germany's drive to the east. His representative in Austria, Colonel Max Bauer, set up headquarters in Vienna and attempted to become the central figure in a new Heimwehr union. Thus, until the fruitless Hitler-Ludendorff putsch in Munich in November 1923 temporarily ended the favorable climate for rightist paramilitary activities in Bavaria, Germans of Christian-conservative, often anti-Prussian, sentiments competed with Germans who were *völkisch*-nationalist in outlook for leadership over the Austrian Heimwehren, where all had their adherents. But none succeeded as well as Kanzler had, and the continued involvement of competing Germans in Heimwehr affairs hindered new efforts by Austrian leaders to reunite the separate paramilitary organizations.[26]

The next significant step in that direction occurred after Seipel became chancellor in May 1922. The financial crisis of that year and the persistent uncertainty about the country's economic viability provided continuing impetus for paramilitary activities, and Seipel hoped to mold the various Heimwehr groups into a reliable military support for the republic's first clearly partisan nonsocialist government. He urged the industrialists, who were already supporting the principal Heimwehr groups in the five western provinces, to channel their contributions through the federal government, which would insist that the recipients form a united Heimwehr front that would back his regime. Seipel especially wanted the Heimwehr groups in Lower Austria, Vienna, and Styria, where the ideological and personal differences among the competing paramilitary leaders were the most pronounced, to agree on a common program and leadership. The creation of such a Heimwehr front proved to be a difficult task, however, for many groups throughout the country, still unwilling to think in "Austrian" terms, insisted on retaining their primary ties with Bavarian organizations.

For a brief period the chancellor did succeed in bringing into being a united Heimwehr under Austrian leadership. Seeking to extend their influence beyond the Tyrol, Steidle and his able chief-of-staff, the German émigré Waldemar Pabst, gave their support to Seipel's plan for the establishment of a paramilitary union to be directed by representatives of the three nonsocialist parties. In a cautiously phrased memorandum addressed to Seipel in June 1922, Pabst offered to help create a military organization that would plan for various emergencies and would provide the government with reliable armed support. Pabst demanded no political concessions or government posts for Heimwehr men. Welcoming these assurances of support, Seipel named a four-man committee of party representatives with Steidle, one of the two delegates from the Christian Social party, as chairman. Responding to Seipel's request, on July 10 Steidle submitted a budget proposal calling for 50 million crowns for the monthly operation of his committee and also for the maintenance of military units and technological assistance units for each of the provinces. In anticipation of central control of the Heimwehren, various conservative groups, especially the Central Association of Manufacturers, promised to provide Steidle's committee with the requested funds, of which 30 million crowns were to be used in Vienna and Lower Austria.[27] In September the total subsidy was trebled because of rampant inflation, and then 80 million crowns went to Vienna and Lower Austria. With assurances of such generous financial support at least through February 1923, the competing groups in these two provinces reached accords that permitted the creation of a new, albeit tenuous, all-Austrian Heimwehr union.

But this handsomely subsidized paramilitary union barely survived its birth. The continuing rivalry for leadership was a serious handicap from the outset. German-nationalist groups, especially in Styria and Carinthia, complained bitterly that they received less than their fair share of the money. Equally important, many of the constituent organizations proved unwilling to support Seipel's renunciation of *Anschluss* in return

for a large international loan under the auspices of the League of Nations. Moreover, various Heimwehr leaders accused the chancellor of agreeing to treat the socialists gently in exchange for their permitting his Geneva loan treaty, which they publicly opposed, to receive parliamentary approval (they abstained). All these dissatisfactions led to a serious challenge to Steidle's leadership, which seemed based on collaboration with Seipel. As a result Steidle felt compelled to demand from Seipel dramatic evidence of the Heimwehr's influence in affairs of state.

A peremptory ultimatum that Steidle sent the chancellor on 16 January 1923 ended the promising cooperation between the government and the Heimwehr front. In his undiplomatic letter, Steidle clearly revealed not only his impatience with the supporting role prescribed by Seipel but also his grandiose ambitions for the Heimwehr. Demanding direct access to the chancellor's office, he informed Seipel that he intended to make the Heimwehr the determinative factor in Austrian politics and to see all parliamentary and party-political practices become superfluous. Seipel responded to Steidle's imperious demands by cutting off the subsidies. As much as he felt that he needed paramilitary support, the chancellor preferred to see the Heimwehr front split into its constituent provincial groups rather than give its leaders the upper hand in governmental affairs. At the end of January Steidle resigned from the front's executive committee. The ensuing struggle between the pro-Ludendorff and pro-Pittinger factions for the dominant voice in the Austrian Heimwehr completely disrupted the front. Brief as it was, however, this first Austrian-led Heimwehr union forms the chief connecting link with the history of the Heimwehr of the middle and late 1920s, especially in that it introduced Steidle and Pabst to the national stage.

Steidle eventually became one of the country's most prominent Heimwehr leaders. As a south Tyrolean (he was born near Meran in 1881), he was inclined toward German nationalism, but politically he remained closely associated with the Tyrolean Peasants' League, an affiliate of the Christian Social party, for which he held various positions on both the provincial and federal levels from 1918 to 1934. Although recognized as one of the more intelligent Heimwehr leaders, Steidle never transcended his provincial outlook and often allowed his passions to overpower his intelligence. His greatest assets were his perseverance and his talent as a public speaker. A slightly stooped man, with a short, pointed beard and the appearance of a mild-mannered burgher, Steidle on the rostrum released a flood of bombastic demagogy. In speeches that a

German consular official once called "irresponsibly sanguinary,"[28] he vehemently denounced the bourgeoisie for their "undemocratic" compromises with the self-proclaimed "ninety percent bolsheviks" and threatened his adversaries with political annihilation. He won numerous admirers, among them the young Prince Ernst Rüdiger Starhemberg, who while briefly a student at the University of Innsbruck fell under the spell of Steidle's "sharp and rhetorically brilliant speeches."[29]

If Steidle spoke for the Heimwehr during its early years, his chief-of-staff, Captain Waldemar Pabst, gave it organizational substance. A former member of the German general staff and a political refugee from Prussia, Pabst was a tireless worker and a born intriguer. In postwar Berlin he earned dubious renown as the man who ordered the murder of Karl Liebknecht and Rosa Luxemburg in January 1919. He then became one of the instigators of the Kapp putsch in March 1920 and fled the country in the wake of its failure. After a brief stay in Hungary he moved to the Tyrol where, through the good offices of its hospitable government, he received the right of domicile—a kind of tentative citizenship—in the village of Mieming. Promoting himself to "Herr Major,"[30] Pabst quickly sensed the reactionary potential in the Heimatwehr and joined forces with Steidle, thus forming a team who worked together for ten years.

More than anyone else, Pabst kept alive the ambitious project of initiating nationwide Heimwehr activities during the years before 1927. Although he did not officially become Steidle's chief-of-staff until 1 May 1922, he made his presence felt at once. As early as January 1921 he was ordering Prince Starhemberg to steal cannon from a government depot. He knew how to get money and weapons; he had important contacts abroad; and he was adept at planning demonstrations that kept the Heimwehr in the public eye. Moreover, from the beginning of his activities in Austria he sought to infiltrate the state's official armed forces—army, police, gendarmerie—with men susceptible to his influence, which was sometimes established by his keeping careful tabs on their personal indiscretions. "Waldemar der Grosse," as the adventurer was called, also knew how to look out for himself and in a way to serve his native country as well. For twelve thousand marks per annum Pabst served German Foreign Minister Stresemann as intelligence agent for Austrian and South Tyrolean affairs and as intermediary with the Tyrolean government. If Pabst was guided by any principle at all, it was a steadfast anti-Marxism that led him to oppose any form of political socialism and, by extension, of republican democracy in Austria and Germany.[31]

After the failure of Seipel's effort to unify the Heimwehren, nearly six years passed before another union with any effectiveness was established. Meanwhile, Steidle and Pabst by no means gave up their ambitions. Although Steidle and Seipel eventually achieved a measure of reconciliation, the Tyroleans seemed determined to seek their own sources of support for making the Heimwehr an independent political force. Accordingly, they hesitated to work with their counterparts in Vienna and Lower Austria, whose weak and splintered organizations remained largely dependent on the mediation of Seipel and/or Police President Schober for whatever financial assistance they received. Nearer home Steidle and Pabst lost no time in acquiring the predominant influence in the League of the Alpine Provinces (Bund der Alpenländer) founded by the Heimwehren of Vorarlberg, the Tyrol, Salzburg, Carinthia and Upper Austria in February 1923. At first this confederation was nominally affiliated with Pittinger's German-based association, but to end that attachment Steidle argued that Pittinger was losing influence in Bavaria and that the Austrians should remain aloof from the dangers confronting Germany because of the Ruhr crisis and mounting inflation. By late April Steidle got himself elected federal leader (Bundesführer) of this Alpine league, in which, however, each constituent organization still retained considerable autonomy. Evidently the provincial governments and manufacturers' associations provided adequate financial assistance to the Heimwehren in these western provinces.

All this Heimwehr activity heightened the alarm felt by the Social Democrats, who sensed that both foreign and domestic developments already boded ill for their future. Much of Europe surrounding Austria showed signs of the ascendancy of reactionary forces. After Mussolini's triumph in October 1922, Italy joined Horthy's Hungary as an inimical neighbor, and conservative Munich was much closer to Vienna than was socialist Berlin. At home the Social Democrats knew that in Chancellor Seipel they had an astute, powerful, and hostile adversary, even though they may not have known that, along with the promise of a loan, he also brought back from Geneva in the fall of 1922 unofficial assurances that the Allies would not oppose the development of non-socialist paramilitary formations.[32] The inability of the Heimwehren to stay united seemed of little consequence to the socialists. They were keenly aware that the private organizations were increasing their armaments (largely by theft); they were distressed by the frequent Sunday parades and demonstrations in towns and villages throughout Styria, Carinthia, and the Tyrol, where peasants were warned that the Reds

intended to burn their farms; and they were greatly alarmed by the
tense armed confrontation between striking workers in Judenburg,
Styria, and several thousand Heimwehr men under Pfrimer in November 1922.[33] Moreover, Julius Deutsch's Christian Social successor at the
army ministry, Carl Vaugoin, was beginning to give the Bundesheer a
more conservative complexion. Together the army and the Heimwehr
might one day constitute a serious threat to the very existence of the
Social Democratic party, not to mention its political dominance in
Vienna.

The Social Democrats responded to these developments with both
propaganda and concrete countermeasures. To bring public attention
to the situation, Julius Deutsch published two pamphlets in which he
warned about the "fascist danger" and asked, "Who is arming for civil
war?" With a keen eye for history, he laid the foundation for claiming
his party's innocence in this arms race by proposing the disarmament of
all unofficial civic guards.[34] (Not surprisingly, his opponents never
tested the sincerity of the proposal.) Meanwhile, either not expecting or
not wanting an agreement, socialist leaders completed plans early in
1923 for transforming their own different party guards into a nationwide organization of armed workers, the Republican Defense League
(Schutzbund), both to provide a military counterforce to the Heimwehr
and to protect and control socialist demonstrations. In most respects
this step represented but a streamlining of the earlier formations, which,
while formally decentralized, had apparently recognized Deutsch as
national leader and had been closely coordinated with the Volkswehr
through the soldiers' councils. The avowed aims of the new "private
association" approved by the federal government were not very different from those of the provincial Heimwehr organizations (for the record
they never mentioned their armed character). However, in contrast to
their opponents, the Schutzbund was responsible to the central leadership of the Social Democratic party, not to local chieftains often almost
as hostile to the bourgeois parties as to the Marxists.[35]

Although the formation of the Schutzbund may have been a defensive reaction by the socialists, it gave Heimwehr leaders more apparent
justification for asserting that they had to protect the country from a
Red army. They also used other incentives in 1923, such as the excitement aroused by the French occupation of the Ruhr Valley and by
parliamentary elections in Austria, to enlarge their organizations. They
attempted to keep the membership devoted and alert by means of
parades and flag dedications, shooting matches, and military maneuvers.
In September 1923 fifteen thousand people assembled for a flag dedica-

tion and rally in a meadow near Klagenfurt. The crowd included a thousand Styrians led by Pfrimer and a small Tyrolean contingent under Steidle, who gave one of the principal speeches. Another important factor in keeping the Heimwehr alive was the regular occurrence of clashes of various sorts with socialists. Usually the incidents were minor affairs—fist fights that grew out of tavern arguments or that were provoked by hecklers at political rallies, and violence connected with strikes. But in 1923 two socialists were killed in political brawls that the Social Democrats blamed on the Nazis and the FKV.

However, just when it seemed that the lines were being drawn for a major battle between the private armies, only a long period of minor skirmishing ensued. By late 1923 a new, albeit grim kind of "normalcy" began to settle over the country. Financial help from abroad; the elections of October 1923, which reconfirmed the moderate Right's control of the government; and the easing of the Ruhr and inflation crises in Germany—all helped bring about a measure of stability to the political life of the frail republic. During these years the paramilitary associations played a less obvious role than at any other time between 1919 and 1936. Their potential for violence and for exerting political influence remained, but by and large neither the socialist nor the antisocialist armies were much in the public eye, and the populace had little reason to fear civil war before the early part of 1927.

To call the years from 1924 to 1926 stable is not to say that Austria was then economically or politically sound. Seipel's financial reconstruction (*Sanierung*) brought him considerable prestige and seemed to strengthen his party, but it came at the cost of painful austerity. The rigorous economies required by the foreign lenders led to the dismissal of thousands of civil servants and a reduction in military personnel to slightly more than twenty thousand by 1926, thus enhancing the relative power of the private political armies. Moreover, the end of inflation required a readjustment in the industrial sector that led to the liquidation of many new undertakings and at first to a crisis of declining production and growing unemployment. After the stabilization of the currency was achieved and the budget balanced, however, industry was able to attract some capital, and, largely through rationalization, production rose gradually but steadily from 1925 to early 1929. But this increase in production had an inverse effect on employment, and after late 1924 the number of jobless never fell below one hundred thousand.[36]

On the political front hardly anyone was prepared to accept prevailing conditions as permanent ones. Nevertheless, during these years the battle for power was generally contained within the regular political institutions. After the parliamentary elections of late 1923, in which support for the CSP climbed from 42 to 45 percent and that for the SDP from 36 to almost 40 percent, each side hoped that the long-range trend would give it permanent ascendancy. Three hundred thousand additional votes would give the Social Democrats a parliamentary majority. The Christian Socials, who in combination with the Pan-Germans easily controlled the Nationalrat (92 of 165 seats), hoped, on the other hand, to see nonsocialists acquire the two-thirds majority in parliament required to enact constitutional changes affecting such matters as the municipal housing programs begun by the socialists, the national rent ceiling, civil marriage laws, secular education, and much of the other postwar social legislation. Seipel, who was disappointed because his party's gains had not been greater, remained chancellor until October 1924, when his cabinet, which favored increased powers for the central government, gave way to one more representative of the provincial elements in the Christian Social party. For almost two years Dr. Rudolf Ramek, a parliamentary deputy from Salzburg, headed a cabinet which, despite some legislative achievements, is best remembered for the banking scandals that compromised a number of provincial Christian Social luminaries, including Finance Minister Ahrer, the former lieutenant governor of Styria, who left the country early in 1926. By that time the Ramek government was mired in the general despondency over what appeared to be a permanent economic malaise. In October 1926 Seipel once again took the top cabinet post, supposedly with the comment, "Things aren't so bad in Austria that I must assume the chancellorship, but neither are they good enough that I can afford not to do so."[37] From that point, with each major party talking increasingly in terms of its solutions to the country's problems, the acrimony of domestic politics grew sharper.

Little is known about the activities of the Heimwehr during these years of relative stability. The disruption of ties between the Bavarian rightists and Austria's paramilitary organizations ended one source of information. The official history of the movement, first published in 1934, devotes a few pages to the Heimwehr's "heroic origins" in each province and then jumps to its "positive" response to the socialist "threat" after July 1927. Moreover, between 1923 and 1926 German diplomats virtually stopped sending reports on the Heimwehr, and there was almost no mention of it in the Nationalrat in this period.

In many ways, however, this silence is deceptive. Although the Heimwehr organizations in Vienna, where there were several rival factions, and in Upper and Lower Austria had to struggle to stay alive, those

groups in the western and southern regions that were already well
established by 1923 did more than merely hold their ground. There
Heimwehr leaders and many of their financial backers had "positive"
aspirations for the Heimwehr long before the rank and file were aware
of them. They looked upon it as an instrument for preventing further
changes and possibly for undoing much of the social reform of the revolution. The example of Mussolini's dictatorial ambitions appealed to
many Heimwehr leaders, as did his fascism and other vague notions of
corporatism. Without realizing how completely the prewar world was
gone, they wanted to restore an order in which the social hierarchy
would be dominated by a combination of wealthy men and military
commanders and in which the interests of the petite bourgeoisie
(Kleinbürgertum) and of the independent peasantry would somehow be
protected. Once rescued from the influence of socialist deceivers, the
workers, they believed, would be happy to support such a regime and
to bear the weight of the social pyramid.

The Tyrol remained the center of Heimwehr activities and ambitions.
As indicated by Steidle's letter to Seipel in January 1923, the Tyrolean
leaders were already thinking about exercising supreme power in Austria. From their base in the Tyrol Steidle and Pabst maintained contacts
with their associates in the loose Alpine Heimwehr confederation that
they headed and also with those in the east. They also worked to create
an all-Austrian Heimwehr army with which they could some day seize
power and make Austria the kernel of a "healthy German state," as
Pabst later put it. Their immediate objectives were to win youth to the
Heimwehr, to promote a militant mentality (Wehrgedanke), to contest
control of the streets of industrial cities, thus to form a defense against
"Red terrorism" and free the German worker from communism, enabling everyone to seek his individual welfare.[38] Like Heimwehr leaders
elsewhere, Steidle and Pabst cultivated close ties with the provincial
army command and made plans to collaborate with the army in the
event of war or revolution.[39] They also conducted military maneuvers
and allowed their men to compete with socialists in breaking up each
other's meetings. Pabst maintained his ties in Germany and Hungary,
through which he developed contacts in Italy that were later to become
significant. In October 1924 the Tyrolean Heimatwehr began publishing
the Tiroler Heimatwehr-Blätter, of which twenty-two issues had appeared by the end of 1925; with the second volume, beginning in January 1926, the name was changed to Alpenländische Heimatwehr, and
publication became somewhat more regular. The sheet was stridently
antisocialist.

During the middle years of the twenties the paramilitary leaders in Styria devoted most of their efforts to reuniting the nationalistic, anti-party Heimatschutz with the smaller, Christian-conservative Heimwehr. In 1925 the district units of both organizations agreed to form a united military command under the direction of the leader of the Front Veterans' Association in Graz, although politically they remained separate through 1926. Meanwhile, the more military-minded leaders of the Heimwehr sought to escape the influence of the political parties. Governor Rintelen, never a loyal Christian Social and ever conspiratorial, supported efforts to create a large paramilitary organization that would be less "party" and more "Rintelen-oriented," as indeed the Heimatschutz, led by Walter Pfrimer after December 1925, already was. During 1925 Rintelen tried without success to get financial assistance from Mussolini to equip a private army capable of marching on Vienna "at the first favorable opportunity," where presumably he would set up a military dictatorship that would prepare the way for a fascist regime.[40]

Although the provincial Heimwehr of Upper Austria was a member of Steidle's Alpine confederation, it proved difficult to keep it well organized. A major obstacle was the reluctance of Governor Johann Hauser, a democratically-inclined priest, to support it. Princess Fanny Starhemberg, a devout Catholic and friend of Seipel's, an active member of the Bundesrat, and the mother of the future Heimwehr leader, tried to mediate between representatives of the self-defense league and the nonsocialist parties at her villa at Bad Ischl in July 1925. Heimwehr chroniclers praised her effort as a milestone in the development of the Upper Austrian Heimwehr. But according to Peter Revertera, whose estate at Helfenberg was an early base of Heimwehr operations, the meeting resulted only in a truce with the parties, not an alliance. Revertera recalled that organizational efforts had to be repeated time and again during the mid-1920s.[41]

Despite all the particularism and the rivalries prevalent in the Heimwehr movement, Pabst, who was German and largely unperturbed by these Austrian concerns, worked assiduously to create a truly nationwide Heimwehr army and by late 1924 had worked out an ambitious scheme for one. His plan, obtained by American military intelligence from "a reliable Italian source,"[42] envisaged a hierarchy of units roughly coinciding with the country's subprovincial administrative areas. The Heimwehr's *Kreis-*, *Bezirks-*, *Gau-*, and *Ortsgruppen* were to correspond respectively to brigades (45 of them), regiments (180), battalions (720), and infantry companies (2,880). The companies were, in turn, to be composed of 4 platoons of about 20 men each. On this basis it was hoped ultimately to establish an army of 240,000 men, with a reserve half again as large—in a country where by treaty the army and police forces combined were limited to one-sixth the size of the Heimwehr's projected main force.

The following table indicates the "actual strength" in each province claimed by the Heimwehr as of January 1925:

	Kreis- (brigades)	Gau- (regiments)	Bezirks- (battalions)	Ortsgruppen (companies)
L. A. & Vienna	7	23	69	207
Upper Austria	5	14	54	216
Styria	5	20	80	340
Carinthia	5	20	80	280
Tyrol	5	20	80	240
Vorarlberg	2	6	18	54
Salzburg	2	8	24	72
Totals	31	111	405	1,409

However, even if the claimed number of brigades and regiments existed, it is highly unlikely that the proportionately low number of companies were close to being fully, or even effectively, manned. Significantly, there were no data for the Burgenland, indicating that the Heimwehr and the Schutzbund were still honoring an agreement not to organize in that province, although the American reporter did note that the Front Veterans' Association, which had about twelve thousand "effectives" around Vienna, was trying to expand into that province.[43]

Such grandiose plans notwithstanding, the years from 1924 to 1926 were really a time of testing for the Heimwehr's faithful membership. The active core was primarily composed of *Freischärler*, the free booters so romantically described by the soldier-poet Guido Zernatto: the degraded and maligned professional officers and aristocrats, left with a small pension or luckily—if they but realized it—most of their lands; reserve officers who were not content to become merely school teachers or white-collar workers; and disillusioned youth who wondered at the military exploits of their bitter elders and who saw no future in a society that tolerated economic depression and unheroic politics. In the eyes of these angry and restless men the socialists were responsible for the drabness and uncertainty of their lives. To these injuries the socialists added the insulting slogan, "No more war!" which brought their heroic years—or dreams—into disrepute.[44]

With such notable exceptions as Steidle and Pfrimer, both lawyers and both typical representatives of provincial hostility toward "Red Vienna," the men who year in and year out conducted Heimwehr operations were mainly retired officers and disentitled aristocrats. From their ranks came the staff men, the adjutants, and the local officers who built and maintained widespread organizations in rural provinces, a job that often had to be done two or three times in the course of the decade and one that required, as Revertera expressed it, the direction of a general staff. It was the perseverance of these men and the financial support they managed to procure from the provincial governments and industrialists that kept the Heimwehr alive during this period.

There remains considerable uncertainty about the size and composition of the Heimwehr's rank-and-file membership. Throughout the 1920s the most faithful following came from the peasants and the lower middle classes of the mountain provinces. The peasants probably had less reason than anyone else to fear the Social Democrats, who adopted a moderate agricultural program in 1925. But the Church, whose priests were mostly peasant sons, railed against the irreligious socialists, and propagandists cried that these enemies wanted to put to the torch the farms of this most-independent peasantry in central Europe.[45] Depending on the political climate of the moment, the peasants were joined by tradesmen, lawyers, and bureaucrats from the towns and villages. In June 1928 observers assumed that about 70 percent of the Heimwehr members were peasants; 20 percent, students and townsmen; and 10 percent, workers, most of these recruited only after July 1927 mainly in the industrial areas dominated by the German-controlled Alpine-Montan Gesellschaft.[46] In the mid-1920s Heimwehr membership fell from a high of perhaps one hundred thousand early in the decade to probably somewhere between thirty and fifty thousand.[47]

Trying to overcome the notion of most rank and file members that their task was primarily defensive, Steidle and others worked hard to arouse support for a Heimwehr initiative in political affairs. In 1926 the tempo of its activity picked up considerably and was noticed by a few keen observers. The leaders sought to exploit the anxiety kindled by both the massive socialist demonstrations in May and July 1926 and the approach of the quadrennial parliamentary elections. About the time that Chancellor Ramek blandly assured the British minister in July 1926 that the Heimwehren were gradually dissolving of their own accord, the new German consul in Innsbruck, H. Saller, expressed his alarm over the growing belligerence of the Tyrolean Heimatwehr, with its frequent mountain maneuvers and especially with its noticeably harder line

towards the Social Democrats. Citing two occasions when the Heimatwehr had threatened to use force against government measures, Saller
warned that the movement posed a real danger to the provincial
government.[48]

The controversial programmatic statement adopted by the Social
Democratic party in Linz late in October 1926 provided the Heimwehr
leaders a welcomed new means of seeking support. Although the main
thrust of the program was revisionist in that it pledged the socialists to
operate within the democratic republican framework "to abolish any
and every class rule," the socialists sought to hold their left wing by
insisting that to prevent the bourgeoisie from provoking counterrevolution the working class had to control sufficient military strength
to defend the republic and to "conquer the power of the state in a civil
war . . . and break resistance . . . by the instrument of dictatorship."[49]
With Steidle in the van, Heimwehr leaders promptly seized upon these
quoted passages to arouse fears that the socialist leaders intended to
use violence to establish a dictatorship of the proletariat. In mid-
November Steidle called for a "dictatorship of healthy common sense
[Diktatur des gesunden Hausverstandes]," whatever that meant. He
contrasted the "taught" democrat Otto Bauer (then chairman of the
SDP) with the "born" democrats of the mountain provinces. In still
other speeches Steidle developed with renewed vigor his favorite
theme: that Austria's Social Democrats were the most radical Marxists
outside Russia and its bourgeoisie the most passive in Europe. Crying
that "we have entered a decisive stage in the struggle for power," he
asserted that only active self-help, not passive self-defense, could clean
up the mess created by Austria's stillborn version of foreign parliamentarism. The necessity of the hour called not only for sacrifices by the
bourgeoisie but also for trust in the Heimwehr leaders, discipline, and
unconditional obedience by the members.[50]

Steidle and Pabst also intensified their efforts to form a military-
political movement that would embrace all the provinces. By the end of
1926 they got the two major paramilitary leagues in Styria to join their
loose Alpine confederation, which they renamed the Selbstschutzverbände (Self-Defense Leagues). They also drew the Front Veterans'
Association under Colonel Hiltl into close collaboration with them.
Although recognized as "federal leader" of this enlarged league, Steidle
was really only the chairman of its executive committee without having
any special powers.[51]

By the first week of 1927 disquieting tension permeated the Heimwehr camp.[52] According to Consul Saller, the Heimwehr leaders of

Styria and Carinthia, as well as Colonel Hiltl, declared that they were no longer able "to keep their men in check." They were concerned about the forthcoming elections and, more immediately, about prospects that the southern provinces would become a theater of conflict if Italy and Yugoslavia went to war over Albania. Once again Heimwehr leaders began to give serious consideration to a coup d'état and to speak of a march on Vienna. Saller heard that they were making plans to seize control of the government and to establish a directory, in which "naturally Federal Chancellor [-aspirant] Steidle would play a leading role." The consul also reported that Pabst had received tacit assurance that Italy would maintain benevolent neutrality in the event of a struggle between the Heimwehr and the Schutzbund.

However much the Heimwehr leaders harbored putsch dreams, they soon decided that the moment was not propitious. In the first place their financial backers did not share their readiness to take such risks. Saller, who felt that only lack of financial support prevented immediate action, reported that the president of the Tyrolean Manufacturers' Association, a generous contributor to the Heimatwehr, opposed carrying out a putsch plan "at present." Heimwehr solicitors encountered similar restraint in Germany; there the government urged potential supporters, especially the Stahlhelm and Georg Escherich, not to rock the boat in Austria. Other considerations gave further cause for pause. A putsch would have little chance of success in the face of the consolidated strength of the Schutzbund in Lower Austria and Vienna, and there was always the possibility of intervention by the Little Entente. Undoubtedly intramural rivalries also made concerted action difficult. And, when facing reality, most Heimwehr leaders, with the notable exception of the representative from Styria, doubted that their men would march on Vienna even in an "emergency."[53]

Beginning in the second week in 1927 the idea gained ground that Seipel's new cabinet, in office only since October 1926, should be allowed to run its course and that plans for action should be made only if election results were unacceptable. At an important conference held in conjunction with a public rally in Klagenfurt on January 30, the leaders finally decided to shelve offensive plans for the time being. In his public address Steidle flirted with the prospect of civil war and again called for self-help instead of self-defense; but in the leaders' private discussions, which dealt primarily with matters of internal organization, about which there was growing confusion, the moderate wing carried the day. Governor Vinzenz Schumy of Carinthia in particular discouraged adventures of any kind, while Colonel Hiltl surprised observers by agreeing to go along with the majority.[54] "Positive" action was to be deferred until after the national elections in the spring. Overshadowed by the events of July 1927 and after, these machinations have gone unnoticed. But they indicate that the paramilitary leaders did not view their task merely as defensive, that they in fact did want to acquire political power.

On the very day of the Klagenfurt rally, events occurred in Schattendorf, a small village in the Burgenland, that were to have major repercussions on the republic's history. During a clash between the Front Veterans and the Schutzbund a worker and a boy were killed by gunfire. The incident was symptomatic of the growing political tension in Austria as well as of socialist fears of collaboration between Austrian and Hungarian reactionaries. After the murders at Schattendorf, workers expressed their outrage in protest demonstrations throughout the country, although Heimwehr threats forced them to cancel plans for a demonstration in Innsbruck. In general, workers heeded the admonition of Social Democratic leaders that they should await justice at the trial of the accused men scheduled for July.

Even as calm seemed to return for a while, things remained tense beneath the surface. Although precisely what happened during early 1927 remains obscure, there can be no doubt that the Heimwehr had showed its true colors. German diplomats felt that it clearly "carried the seed for surprise" and should be watched carefully.[55] In a long report dated February 22, the German minister in Austria, Count Hugo Lerchenfeld, made the point perfectly clear. Many in the Heimwehr preferred a "rip-snorting" war to the "foul" peace, he wrote, and rumors were still circulating of plans to march on Vienna, of German and Hungarian support for the Heimwehr, and of schemes to arrest prominent Social Democrats. To the perhaps self-serving appeals for disarmament made by leading socialists, especially Deutsch, who impressed Lerchenfeld favorably, Chancellor Seipel repeatedly replied that the disarmament of the Heimwehr was not within the power of the federal government. Seipel gave Lerchenfeld a further indication of his attitude when he said that the government did not object to "disciplined self-defense men" serving as border patrols; he was sure that in the event of trouble "the people would certainly find the necessary ammunition somewhere."[56]

As spring came, popular attention across the country began to focus on the parliamentary elections. Finally set for April 24, they were hailed as an important contest between the bourgeoisie and the proletariat. By and large the Heimwehr supported the unity list formed by the Christian Socials and the Pan-Germans. Just ten days before the elections the nationalistic, anti-Semitic Carinthian Heimatschutz began publishing the *Heimatschutz-Zeitung*, which became the longest-lived of the Heimwehr weekly newspapers. The two numbers appearing before the elections warned that disunity, "election fatigue," and indifference on the part of the bourgeoisie would forfeit victory to the Social Democrats. Although disenchanted with parliamentary government, the editors explained, "We must support the bourgeois parties in parliament as we would strengthen a dam against a threatening flood." Once there was no longer any danger of a "Red overflow" in parliament, it would be possible to "have a serious word with the parties" and "convert them to our views." The editors seemed to think that this could be done without the use of force, but, in any event, for the moment the duty of patriots was to cast a vote for a nonsocialist party.[57]

The outcome of the elections did not bring a Red overflow, but it did justify the apprehension of the Heimwehr leaders. Seipel's unity list proved to be a tactical blunder, and the number of coalition supporters in the Nationalrat fell from ninety-two to eighty-five. The distribution of seats gave the Christian Socials only two votes more than the Social Democrats, who won 42 percent of the popular vote and increased their representation from sixty-eight to seventy-one. The government was badly shaken. But Seipel managed to achieve after the election that which had eluded him earlier: he persuaded the nationalistic, basically anticlerical Agrarian League, which had been in opposition and had increased its strength from five to nine seats, to join forces with the governing parties. This enlarged "bourgeois" coalition gave the cabinet ninety-four votes in the Nationalrat, two more than in the previous legislative period.

Had the crisis of mid-July 1927 not upstaged them, the April elections might well have become known as the turning point in Heimwehr history. Faced with the prospect that the socialists might win in the long run, the Heimwehr leaders concluded that if antisocialists could not win in parliament they would have to prepare to fight outside it. Only three days after the elections Saller reported new signs of vigorous Heimwehr activity.[58] Its publicists appeared visibly upset by the election returns, although they probably welcomed the new fuel for propaganda. The young *Heimatschutz-Zeitung* began to hammer away with an antidemocratic bombardment. In a series of postelection articles entitled "What Now?", it demanded that the "costly" second chamber, the Bundesrat, be changed into a functional corporative council (Ständerat), and called for an unequal balloting system to give greater influence to the privileged and the landed. Announcing that "the battle is begin-ning"—a reference to obstructive tactics employed by the Social Demo-crats in the new Nationalrat—the paper asserted that the government should send the lawmakers home and govern without them.[59]

On the eve of the trial of the men accused of murder at Schattendorf, Steidle publicly announced that the Heimwehr was again active and eager for battle. In a long "programmatic" speech to an assembly at Wels, Upper Austria, he provided additional evidence of the spirit which prevailed in the Heimwehr just before the riots in Vienna that followed the trial. After complaining that Austria was "a state that was forced upon us and that we do not want," Steidle devoted most of his time to condemning the Austro-Marxists. These adversaries always cried that the Heimwehr was threatening the republic solely as an ex-cuse to maintain their Schutzbund, which to Steidle was only a party militia for their "Red fascism." Any attempt to work with the Socialist party was equivalent to committing suicide, for the party "wants to rule; it wants to expropriate." Excoriating the bourgeoisie for leaving the "creation of a nonparty power" in the hand of such a few, Steidle announced that the Heimwehr was ready to support a strong govern-ment that would work for all—one that "leads and governs and not merely staggers from one compromise and embarrassment into another." The Heimwehr did not want to fight the patriotic workers but intended only to free them from class warfare, terror, and hate; it did not want civil war but only civil peace. To achieve these goals, Steidle thought it necessary to have "an organized force, and that is what the patriotic defense leagues desire to be." Agreeing with a recent statement by Deutsch that "the deciding battle lies ahead," Steidle warned that if a revolution were to break out, the socialists would control Vienna, and the provincial governments would be the only ones in Austria capable of maintaining order. It would be the task primarily of the Heimwehr to unite the opposition against the socialists. "We will also resort to force if necessary," he promised.[60] It was fair warning on the eve of the storm.

When Steidle spoke on July 3 he could not have wished for more than the unintended socialist "revolution" that followed the acquittal in Vienna on July 14 of the defendants from Schattendorf. The pivotal events from July 15 to 17 tragically sharpened the republic's political polarization. The burning of the justice building; the massive riots whose brutal repression left about ninety people dead, most of them working-class civilians; and the nationwide strikes called by the socialist leadership to retain the confidence of the angry workers and to force the government to bargain—all this shocked and frightened many of the nonsocialists whom Steidle had earlier tried to arouse. As the country ground to a standstill on the sixteenth, people who could find out almost nothing about what was happening in the capital could readily believe that a revolution was underway. (Either it did not matter to them or else they did not know that the socialist leaders had tried to prevent all street demonstrations and had forbidden the Schutzbund to use arms.)

The situation provided a golden opportunity for the Heimwehr to act forcefully and "defensively." Steidle's forecast was realized. Heimwehr actions in the provinces, unexpectedly vigorous in the Tyrol and Styria, saved a badly shaken cabinet from having to make meaningful concessions to the Social Democrats, who were demanding its resignation.

On the morning of July 17 a representative of the federal government flew to Innsbruck. The cabinet needed the support of the provinces to stay in power and asked the Tyrolese government to take all measures necessary to remain in complete control of the province and if possible to force an end to the strike there. The Tyrolean officials promptly enlisted the Heimatwehr as auxiliary police to maintain order, while the governor of Vorarlberg used the Heimatdienst for similar purposes. On the night of July 17/18 these forces joined the regular police in occupying most of the important railroad stations against only token resistance. The strike committee felt compelled to withdraw to Salzburg. Although the Heimatwehr's effort to restore emergency rail traffic met with only limited success, some trains did move and communications were partially maintained. Consul Saller reported that "to a certain extent" the Heimwehr helped make the strikes in the Tyrol and Vorarlberg "illusory."[61]

In Styria there was even greater danger of violence than in the Tyrol, in part because there were more strikers and in part because the Heimwehr acted without the official sanction enjoyed by the Heimwehr in the western provinces. Repeating his exploits of November 1922, Pfrimer mobilized his Heimatschutz on the morning of July 16, and between six and ten thousand men armed with rifles and machine guns soon had most of the strikers in the Mur Valley confined to their home towns. Alarmed at this show of force, the socialist leaders in upper Styria first asked for negotiations and then yielded to Pfrimer's demand that the strikes be called off unconditionally and that all "acts of terror" be stopped. Pfrimer then hurried to Graz, where he threatened to march on the capital if the strike was not immediately ended throughout the province. Hoping for a compromise, Governor Hans Paul began talks with the socialists on the night of the sixteenth, but Pfrimer, in "a most uncompromising mood," told them that if they remained adamant the talks would be renewed in the streets the following morning. The threat of force was given greater substance by the arrival in Graz of Nationalrat Deputy Rintelen, who threw his weight behind Pfrimer. Provincial socialist leaders saw no choice but to give way. In "hysterical messages" to Vienna, they urged the central directorate to call off the strike in order to prevent either its total collapse or the outbreak of civil war.[62]

Pfrimer was exceedingly disappointed that the victory was not complete. He later claimed that when Seipel thanked him for being the "savior of Austria" he replied that if he had his way the "Reds would have absolutely nothing more to say." He really wanted to march on Vienna, but he realized that he could not undertake such a venture without the acquiescence of the government. Rintelen, who had sought Italian aid for a similar purpose two years earlier,[63] joined in imploring Governor Paul to support a Heimwehr campaign with Styrian troops. Pfrimer and Rintelen thought that they could surround Vienna with 150,000 men, control the city's water supply, force the socialists out of political affairs, and then call a plebiscite to sanction their actions. But the governor refused to cooperate, whereupon Pfrimer lamented that the country had missed its best chance to rid itself of the "bolshevists."[64]

The Heimwehr did not play as spectacular a role in Upper and Lower Austria as it did in Styria, the Tyrol, Vorarlberg, and Carinthia, where the well-organized Heimatschutz also helped occupy railroad stations and intimidate the strikers. However, so strong were the emotions aroused by the strikes that in Upper and Lower Austria several thousand antisocialists mobilized spontaneously in towns where there had previously been no Heimwehr organization. In Upper Austria Peter Revertera and Major Friedrich Mayer urged Governor Josef Schlegel to take energetic measures against the strikers. They offered to assist him with twenty thousand unarmed men and threatened to act on their own if the strike were not ended by the next day (the eighteenth). Although Schlegel did not avail himself of the volunteered manpower, Franz Langoth, the province's security director, asked the men to remain on alert, and the Heimwehr's technical emergency auxiliary (Technische Nothilfe) there, as elsewhere, was called into action to restore vital communications.[65]

At the height of the crisis Austria stood on the brink of civil war and possibly of foreign intervention in its wake. Neither would have been to the advantage of the Social Democrats. In Vienna the socialist leaders tried to negotiate with Seipel, but the chancellor, emboldened by Heimwehr support, would not commit himself in any official statement. Feeling that they would have to be content with Seipel's private assurances that he would not use the tragic events of July 15–17 as an excuse for a general assault on existing social legislation, the Social Democrats called off the strikes. At midnight on July 19 transportation and communications employees resumed work everywhere in the country except in the Tyrol, where there was an eight-hour delay—whether through a misunderstanding or as a last gesture of defiance is not clear.

Thus, the catastrophe of July 1927 thrust the Heimwehr into a consequential role in national affairs. Their intervention against the strikes brought them to the favorable attention of the frightened nonsocialist public in a way that would hardly have been possible otherwise. No socialist denials and no attempt to laugh off the Heimwehr's appearance on the political scene as "ridiculous and cowardly"[66] could alter the fact that the situation in Austria had changed greatly. The workers' party found itself on the defensive, while the Heimwehr immediately assumed a broad political offensive. Having long waited for such an opportunity, the Heimwehr set about to make life as miserable as possible for the socialists. Moreover, as Consul Saller observed, the Heimwehr now seemed to threaten the federal and provincial governments as much as to support them against the socialists. In a telegram on July 22 Steidle publicly warned Seipel that it would not tolerate socialist participation in a coalition of reconciliation (since socialists had "caused" the riots), and promised "unyielding resistance" to the government if it made life easy for the Marxists. And the *Heimatschutz-Zeitung* asked, "Will Seipel act, or will he give the Reds time to regroup?" If order were not restored in Vienna, then the Heimwehr would move against Vienna.[67]

Never again would the Austrian public fail to be aware of the Heimwehr's existence. With help from numerous sources it was finally able to sustain a political offensive. Appearing united and pledging to renew the country, it burgeoned for two and a half years after July 1927 into something approaching a popular movement. Chancellor Seipel encouraged its activity in hopes of forcing the socialists to make concessions on bitterly contested legislation, including a revision of the constitution that he hoped would pave the way for a more authoritarian form of government (though not a Heimwehr dictatorship). Equally significant, the Heimwehr leaders also renewed their contacts with the Hungarian government and, through it, with Mussolini, who began to support their antisocialist and dictatorial goals. The Heimwehr reached the peak of its power during the crisis over constitutional reform in the fall of 1929, only to suffer a severe reversal of fortune because of its contemptuous and counterproductive reaction to the failure either to gain power or to force its extreme proposals through parliament.

For all the developments after July 1927, however, the history of the Heimwehr in the 1920s was essentially of one piece when viewed with regard to leadership, aims, and activities. There was greater continuity in all of these than has been acknowledged by scholars concentrating on the period after 1927. Nor was there a sharp ideological break at any point in Heimwehr development in the 1920s. Its leaders had one over-riding goal throughout: to attain political power for themselves. They were dedicated to the notion of establishing a military-type dictatorship based, if possible, on mass participation in a political army. Always proponents of vague and varied notions of an organic society, they easily moved to the emphasis on corporatism that marked them in 1929 and after. Even then they remained more concerned with gaining power than with the fine points of theory. In that respect they remained true to their pre-July outlook. Thus, while their chances for success were greater after July 1927, their impatience with anything short of total success was as much the product of aggressive ambitions nourished in the years before that date as of their heady expansion in 1928 and 1929.

3
March to Political Prominence
July 1927 to December 1928

As a result of the crisis of July 1927 bitter class warfare soon dominated Austria's political life. Instead of seeing the July days as a warning to reconciliation, extremists fanned the passions and hatreds aroused by that tragedy. Those in the antisocialist camp were determined to weaken their opponents further and to revise legislation they deemed inimical to the interests of the moneyed and the Church. Socialists responded with verbal vituperation against Schober, Seipel, and the Church, which they urged their adherents to leave. Where the Austrians might have temporized, the Italian and Hungarian governments used the Heimwehr to keep the country in turmoil. In all the political tumult that lay ahead, the Heimwehr played a driving, if at times a manipulated, role. By November 1927, when there circulated mysterious putsch rumors, it seemed clear to moderate observers, such as the liberal *Oesterreichischer Volkswirt*, that the Heimwehr had purposes other than merely supporting the official armed forces; they warned that it meant to carry out a rightist coup or to destroy the civil rights of the workers and provoke a leftist uprising.[1]

The *Volkswirt*'s editors were reading the Heimwehr's aims correctly, even if its preparations were not yet so far along. Through the winter of 1927/1928 the Heimwehr leaders attempted to use the opportunity provided by the July days to consolidate an organizational base from which to launch a political offensive that they hoped would result in the creation of an authoritarian regime. Determined to make the most of their opportunity, Heimwehr leaders hastened to recruit followers for a so-called *Volksbewegung* that they claimed would renew the country's political and social life. In meetings throughout the countryside, propagandists exaggerated the danger of a "bolshevist" revolution and urged the government to crush the weakened opponent. Early in January 1928 the German minister in Vienna reported, "not without worry," to his superiors that the Heimwehr was recruiting members in the provinces with the slogan of a "march on Vienna."[2] Its spokesmen also began to advocate what the *Volkswirt* called "a genuinely fascist corporative

constitution."[3] As a result of this campaign, supported at first by Austrian industrial and financial circles, Heimwehr organizations spread
into new areas and increased their membership through 1929. Still mix-
ing patriotic enthusiasm and antisocialist resentment, they also began to
welcome people who for one reason or another could not be militarily
active and provided for them a category of political membership distinct from the military units. By this means the Heimwehr could swell
its numbers and respectability as a political pressure group. In the last
analysis, however, its ability to influence political developments depended almost entirely upon its potential for armed action.

By the same token, in the eyes of many Austrians the power—or
threat—of the Social Democrats depended upon the same potential. If
anything, however, the events of July had shown that the official armed
forces, especially the Viennese police, would shoot workers and, more
importantly, that the socialist leaders, who realized the precariousness
of their situation, would have to be provoked to the utmost before they
would actually take up arms against the government. Repeatedly retired
General Theodore Körner, the military commander of the Schutzbund,
admonished his troops to do everything possible to avoid clashes with
the official armed forces of the state and to keep from giving the Heimwehr an excuse for taking armed action.[4] But much of the nonsocialist
population, still not sure of the reliability of the small federal army, in
which over half the soldiers still voted socialist in elections to their
councils,[5] argued that apart from the Schutzbund the concentrated
workers formed an army unto themselves and could be mobilized more
quickly than the scattered provincials. Moreover, Catholics were incensed by the socialists' barrage of "leave-the-Church" propaganda
directed against the priest-chancellor,[6] and the vitriolic tirades, led
by *Arbeiter-Zeitung* editor Friedrich Austerlitz, against Schober for
having given the order to murder workers in Vienna alienated many
who stood for "law and order." Such people were simply unable to
believe that the July days were not a preview of the coming revolution
that they thought Otto Bauer had promised in the Linz program. With
a vengeance the Heimwehr played upon the fears that the socialists
sought to destroy by violence private property, what was left of the
traditional social order, and the Catholic Church. In such an atmosphere many nonsocialist politicians were willing to tolerate and even to
support the Heimwehr, as uncomfortable as it was for those who basically did prefer order to strife and who realized that the Heimwehr
might someday get out of hand.

Fortunately for the Heimwehr, both of the country's two leading politicians, Chancellor Seipel and Police President Schober, sought, each in his own way and for his own purposes, to establish close relations with it. The Heimwehr could use these connections to enhance its image and to gain a hearing for its aims. More importantly, the connections opened the way to greater supplies of money and equipment, even if not nearly enough fully to satisfy the insatiable Heimwehr leaders in their unceasing efforts to become the dominant force in Austrian politics. For additional aid they looked abroad, chiefly to Hungary and Italy. The resulting double and triple games of ambitions and personalities, of temporary alliances and general duplicity, of expectations aroused and hopes dashed, wove an intricate political story.

Finally bringing his support for the Heimwehr into the open, Seipel spoke publicly in its favor for the first time in Munich on 5 October 1927. After criticizing the socialists' "terror," he said that the Heimwehr was necessary to protect the majority from a minority that wanted to force its will on the country. Before an Austrian audience two weeks later Seipel repeated his encouragement of the Heimwehr somewhat more circuitously: "When we see the enemies of Jesus Christ marching in better organized and armed groups, then we must do everything to eliminate the deficiencies of our own armaments and organization. The true love for the people must manifest itself in our not shirking the decisive battle within the people and for the people."[7]

Behind the scenes Seipel played a more direct role in Heimwehr affairs. Once again, as in 1922, he urged the Heimwehren to forge a united front and promised in return to secure adequate financial aid. It was more than a coincidence that the leading Heimwehr leagues of Lower Austria, Vienna, and the Burgenland joined Steidle's loose Alpine confederation, already renamed the Bund österreichischer Selbstschutzverbände (Federation of Austrian Self-Defense Leagues), in Baden on 16 October 1927, and that a week later Austria's bankers' and manufacturers' associations put fifty-five thousand Austrian schillings (AS) at the Heimwehr's disposal,[8] marking the beginning of domestic assistance that may have totaled 1.5 million schillings by the middle of 1930. Although the several Heimwehr organizations retained their autonomy—Steidle was only the chairman of the Heimwehr's "federal command," as the provincial leaders were known collectively—and although the distinctions between the Tyrolean and the Styrian wings remained obvious, the patronage of Seipel and the moneyed interests helped forge the appearance of Heimwehr unity, which in turn gave it the appearance of greater weight than it in fact carried.

Seipel's contemporaries, even those close to him, interpreted his relationship to the Heimwehr in various ways. *Reichspost* editor Friedrich Funder, who was a close personal friend of Seipel's, thought the chancellor embraced the Heimwehr as "the awakening of the slumbering bourgeois masses," and another admirer called him a "symbol of the movement." Leopold Kunschak, the Christian Social labor leader in Vienna, thought that Seipel saw in the Heimwehr a welcome, if unsought, partner in his antisocialist policies and hoped to make it his tool. More skeptical observers, however, assumed that Seipel espoused the Heimwehr chiefly to keep it in hand.[9] Considering Seipel's relationships with Austria's antisocialist paramilitary organizations throughout the 1920s, it seems certain that he sought out the partner, naturally with the expectation that as long as he could control its support he could keep it in hand. Even so, Seipel may not have proceeded on this course without some misgivings. He must have sensed, just as there were those who warned him, that it was possible for him to become a prisoner of his own creation.[10]

In Schober the Heimwehr thought it had a patron who was a dependable man of action, one who would respect the military nature of the Heimwehr and who would hold politicians like Seipel firmly to the antidemocratic course. Schober probably thought the same, but he better understood the fact that he was both an ally and a rival of Seipel. Thus, he wanted influence over the Heimwehr not just to crush the socialists but also to enhance his power in Austrian politics. The relations between the Heimwehr and Schober became perhaps more intricate than those between the Heimwehr and Seipel; in the end they certainly created greater animosities. But for a while the Heimwehr expected much from the police president, with whom Steidle and Pabst and other Heimwehr leaders were frequently in personal and written contact. Frequently they pestered him for helmets, spikes, and other paraphernalia. But the ties were closer than that; early in 1928 Steidle apparently agreed to place the Heimwehr under Schober's command in "serious emergencies" (although some Viennese Heimwehr leaders objected that Schober was not sufficiently anti-Semitic or trustworthy).[11] Schober always promised more than he could or would deliver, but through mid-1929 the Heimwehr leaders continued to hope that he would be their man, the one who would open their way to power. At the same time Schober, playing them along and perhaps even letting Steidle know that he did not think much of his abilities,[12] hoped the Heimwehr would serve him; even more than Seipel, he seemed not to fear that it might some day get out of hand.

In the fall of 1927 something was afoot that might have given Seipel and Schober second thoughts. But perhaps they saw in the rumors not an indication that the Heimwehr might someday get out of hand but the possibility that it was being taken in hand by an Austrian rival. Early in November the German press reported both that a fascist organization headed by Anton Rintelen and supported by Mussolini existed in Austria and that a communist putsch would take place there within two weeks. The public never learned much more about the affair than these original allegations, but diplomatic correspondence indicates that the perennial plotter Rintelen was up to his old tricks. The German ambassador in Rome, Baron Constantin von Neurath, reported on October 26 that Italian money and arms in large quantities were going to Austria for an undertaking apparently against, not the Viennese socialist regime, but the federal government and *Anschluss*. Soon thereafter Gustav Stolper, the liberal and nationalistic economist who had moved from Vienna to Berlin and who published the *Volkswirt*, had a friend in Vienna inform Police President Schober that Rintelen had received a large subsidy from Italy and would probably attempt to transform Austria into a fascist province within a year, a message that Schober relayed to Seipel. Heimwehr leaders disclaimed any aggressive intentions, and Seipel told the German minister in Vienna that the socialists were probably using their international connections to create pressure against the Heimwehr, hence the rumors. He claimed to doubt that there was any tie between Italians and the Heimwehr, or at least that any "serious persons" in Austria were involved. However, according to the American minister in Vienna, A. H. Washburn, Seipel was disturbed enough to confront Rintelen, who swore that the rumors were without foundation. In addition, Schober told Washburn that he did not think that Rintelen had gotten much from Italy, since in September Rintelen sought funds for the Heimwehr from Austria's banking association, which in turn asked Schober's advice. Although Schober apparently did not tell Washburn what his advice was, the American felt certain "that the bankers and industrialists are furnishing the sinews of war" to the Heimwehr. This mysterious episode provided a preview of several autumn crises that were to assail the republic in the years ahead.[13]

As far as the public was concerned, the Heimwehr's most potentially disruptive activity in the fall of 1927 and throughout 1928 was the effort to "organize" in the industrial cities concentrated in the eastern part of the country. There the Heimwehr leaders launched a campaign to gain control of the street and workbenches. The Heimwehr *Aufmarsch*, which was a rally preceded by a parade, or march, of the participants in various degrees of uniform dress and closed ranks, was by no means an innovation in Austrian politics. The socialists had long been experts at staging massive demonstrations on the days celebrating labor (May 1) and the republic (November 12) and on other special occasions. However, even though both sides used the device to attract attention and to intimidate as well as to provoke their opponents, the socialists generally limited such activities almost entirely to the cities that they helped govern, whereas the Heimwehr hoped ultimately to deny them the right to demonstrate anywhere. Unfortunately, the Social Democrats considered Heimwehr rallies in industrial cities invasions of their rightful domain and seemed to accept the Heimwehr's claim that its appearance in such cities was a victory for the foes of Marxism and a setback for the workers' party. Since most Heimwehr marchers had to be imported from the countryside, the socialists might well have let them parade and go back home without making much ado about it. But their own demagogic tradition required that they put up a show of opposition to the "fascists." Accordingly, the location and size of Heimwehr demonstrations took on great symbolic significance.

The person who stood in the forefront of the Heimwehr campaign in the cities was Dr. Walter Pfrimer, the persevering leader of the Styrian Heimatschutz who was most noted for his German nationalism, anti-Semitism, and eagerness to do battle—literally—with the socialists. Born in 1881, like Steidle in an area that was detached from his native province after the war, the young Protestant attended school at Marburg on the Drava, where he early became active in nationalistic societies. He earned his law degree at the University of Graz in 1906 and worked as an official in the bureaucracy for several years before beginning his own practice in upper (northern) Styria. Pfrimer had but slightly more military experience than Steidle, and just as bare a chest afterward. Late in 1917 he was elected chairman of the newly formed German People's Council (Volksrat) in upper Styria, and it was in this capacity that after the armistice he supervised the formation of several local self-defense associations around Judenburg. He enhanced his reputation as a militant leader by mobilizing several thousand of his men for an armed confrontation with striking workers at Judenburg in November 1922. After that show of force, he seemed convinced that he would one day vanquish Social Democracy in an armed showdown, a myth strengthened by his role in July 1927. His rise was furthered by the merger of the smaller Styrian Heimwehr, which had been oriented toward the Christian Social party, with his nationalistic Heimatschutz in November 1927, a strengthening of the Heimwehr movement in which Seipel almost surely had a hand. At the same time Pfrimer made the concession of toning down his German nationalism by dropping the swastika from the Heimatschutz insignia, but he also asserted that the Heimatschutz would not protect the interests of any political party and that it would continue to demand the fulfillment of its program. Even more than his Tyrolean colleagues, Pfrimer deeply hated the political party that represented labor, an aversion deriving in part from his detestation of parliamentary democracy in general as something "un-German." A man with a plodding, uncompromising intellect, he neither understood nor wanted to understand modern industrial and social change. He got along well with the peasants and villagers of Styria and faithfully expressed their provincial outlook. In this view, the socialist workers had been led astray by alien (i.e. Jewish) leaders, and Pfrimer felt it his mission to reclaim the workers for Germandom, "to win the soul of the German worker," as he put it.[14]

Pfrimer was well situated to lead the assault against the socialists. His base of operations around Judenburg bordered on the heavy mining and metallurgical complexes of the Alpine Montan Gesellschaft. Controlled after the mid-1920s by German steel magnates, the Alpine Montan was the largest industrial enterprise in the country and dominated the central part of upper Styria, especially the cities of Donawitz and Leoben. The Alpine Montan became a powerful opponent of labor unions and political socialism and heavily subsidized the Heimwehr's assault on street and workbench.

It was not until late in 1927 that the Heimwehr was ready to risk meeting the socialists in the streets. An earlier rally attempted by the Styrian Heimatschutz on September 18 in the Lower Austrian city of Gloggnitz, which lies just north of the mountain pass (Semmering) that divides the two provinces, lacked the magnitude first planned. In the face of a Schutzbund "alert," provincial authorities forbade the Heimatschutz to march in closed ranks, and the Styrians sent only two—instead of the planned eighteen—truckloads of men.[15] But that was in Lower Austria, where Heimwehr influence was still minimal.

In Styria Pfrimer could expect better cooperation from the officials. Indeed, while he was getting ready to stage large-scale demonstrations, the governor issued a three-month injunction against all political parades by any paramilitary organizations, a ban intended to prevent socialist rallies until the Heimatschutz was ready. Soon after the prohibition expired, Pfrimer's Heimatschutz signaled its readiness for combat with a successful *Aufmarsch* in Bruck on the Mur on November 27, a demonstration that probably would have been impossible before July.

Bruck had great emotional significance beyond its importance as a major rail junction in the heart of the upper Styrian industrial region. Overwhelmingly socialist, it was dominated by Koloman Wallisch, who was anathema to Austria's rightists because of his ties with the soviet regime in Hungary in 1919 and because of his proclamation of a dictatorship of the proletariat in Bruck in July 1927, an action regarded even by most Social Democrats as precipitous. Varying accounts of the Heimwehr rally and the Schutzbund demonstration the following Sunday provided a mild example of the disparity of partisan reporting typical of the time. The *Neue Freie Press* reported that 7,680 Heimatschutz men were there; but the *Arbeiter-Zeitung* counted only 5,208 men. When the Schutzbund gave its "mighty answer" the socialist paper claimed that over twelve thousand men participated, to which the *Heimatschutz-Zeitung* retorted that there were only 6,084 marchers, proof of socialist weakness and the beginning of the Red *Götterdämmerung*.[16]

After 11 March 1928, which saw Heimwehr rallies at Gloggnitz and Klagenfurt, hardly a Sunday passed throughout the spring and summer without demonstrations by one side or the other, sometimes taking place on the same day in the same town. An exchange of taunting epithets and a few fisticuffs usually accompanied these Sunday strolls, and on occasion there were more serious incidents. By and large, however, each group seemed content to let speakers warn the other side that it was playing with civil war. Heimwehr spokesmen repeatedly asserted that their organization was necessary to prevent the misuse of the public transportation system, to prevent terror against the workers, and to support the government in securing constitutional reform. They accused the Schutzbund of being a "party guard," while their supraparty Heimwehr represented a true "movement of the people." The Social Democrats turned this argument to their advantage: the party exercised control over the socialist military formations, while the Heimwehr leaders were responsible to no one. Not without justification, moreover, the socialists charged that Heimwehr rallies in industrial centers were intended to provoke their followers into giving the Heimwehr an excuse to start a civil war. As Pabst later acknowledged, the Heimwehr was always prepared—at least after mid-1928—"to take advantage of a socialist provocation" and to turn any major *Aufmarsch* into a putsch.[17]

While waiting for such an opportunity to come, the Heimwehr, in conjunction with its industrial backers, began a systematic effort to weaken the socialist unions. In May 1928 industrialists provided the Heimwehr with AS 6,000 and office space to initiate the formation of "independent" factory unions (unabhängige Gewerkschaften). The nominal founders of the Heimwehr union were locksmith Fritz Lichtenegger, metal worker Josef Lengauer, and blast furnace foreman Sepp Oberegger, all of whom were employed by the Alpine Montan and eventually became Heimwehr delegates to the Nationalrat. Rising unemployment in upper Styria tempted radical malcontents, who had once formed a communist front against the Social Democratic unions, to succumb to Heimwehr blandishments.[18] Everywhere the Heimwehr attempted with growing success to "protect" strikebreakers and renegades and to help nonsocialist workers find jobs, if possible at the expense of SDP members. Both Steidle and Pfrimer tried to assure workers that the Heimwehr was not antilabor and did not oppose good working conditions and just wages, so long as they did not go beyond the point of harming the employers' earning power. The Heimwehr was simply against class warfare and against the "terror of the worst sort" that forced a worker to join a socialist union in order to hold a job.

As a result of the Heimwehr offensive, there was a notable increase in the number of strikes stemming from organizational disputes. In the Alpine Montan company the "independent" unions succeeded in breaking the predominance of the socialist unions in many of the factory councils.[19] Not content just to secure the guarantee that nonsocialist workers would not be "terrorized" into joining a "free" union, the Heimwehr unions tried to create their own closed shops, thereby opposing also the Christian unions, which early in June 1928 responded by forming their own paramilitary units known as the Freiheitsbund. The *Arbeiter-Zeitung* complained repeatedly about factories that would hire only nonunion or Heimwehr men, especially in Styria. Even Stolper's liberal *Volkswirt* expressed grave concern at this weakening of the old unions. Nonetheless, claiming that wherever its union was in control industrial peace replaced class warfare, the Heimatschutz ultimately boasted of a collective contract with the Alpine Montan company that included ten thousand employees. Heimwehr unions spread among the industries on the southern railway line in Styria and then into Lower Austria and Carinthia and more slowly into Vienna and Upper Austria. They also began to organize groups representing transportation and communications workers, occupations deemed extremely important in any showdown with the socialists and thus having symbolic significance.

By the summer of 1929 the Heimwehr claimed that there were twenty-
five thousand workers in its labor organizations in Styria alone, though
this figure was probably somewhat inflated.[20]

The extension of Pfrimer's activities into the neighboring industrial
areas of Lower Austria, the country's largest province, led not only to
clashes with socialists but also to rivalry with the province's older Heimwehr organization, which tended to be oriented more toward the peasants than the workers. The population of Lower Austria, slightly less
than that of Vienna, was almost evenly divided between an industrial
proletariat and an independent peasantry. Industry was concentrated in
the cities—Mödling, Wiener Neustadt, Neunkirchen, Gloggnitz—along
the southern railway, which connected Vienna and upper Styria, and in
a few cities, notably St. Pölten and Amstetten, along the western railway. By and large the western and northern reaches of the province,
the latter called the Waldviertel, were agricultural and Christian Social.
The old party-oriented Selbstschutzverband under Julius Raab and
Baron Karg-Bebenburg was largely limited to these areas. After July
1927 Pfrimer's Heimatschutz seized the initiative in the cities along the
southern railway. From the time Pfrimer supervised the organization of
a local group in Gloggnitz in September 1927 until the historic *Aufmarsch* in Wiener Neustadt on 7 October 1928, the Styrians controlled
Heimwehr expansion in the southern part of Lower Austria, and their
influence remained strong thereafter. In addition, Styrian organizers
were active in Vienna, where they competed with several other Heimwehr groups, in the Burgenland, and also in a small enclave in Upper
Austria. The Styrians also exercised strong influence over the Carinthian
Heimatschutz.

In view of their overwhelming predominance in the eastern part of
Austria, the nationalistic Styrians soon began to demand a greater voice
in the Heimwehr Bund. Undoubtedly Pfrimer would have liked to dis-
place the dominant Tyroleans. But primarily because the Hungarians
decided to channel their support through Steidle and Pabst, the Styrians had to collaborate with their rivals, who for their part made concessions to Styria's weight in the east. At a conference in Innsbruck in
mid-July 1928 the top leaders from all the provinces agreed to the formation of a dual leadership. Pfrimer became the "second" federal
leader, with the same rights as Steidle to make emergency decisions.
Thereafter the directives and communiques of the federal command
were issued over their joint signatures, often along with those of the
first and second military leaders, former Lieutenant General Ferdinand

Pichler and former General Heinrich Lustig-Prean. It was a cumbersome arrangement, satisfactory to neither Steidle nor Pfrimer, but it did suffice to preserve the appearance of Heimwehr unity for an important two years.

Behind this facade, however, the different provincial organizations remained largely independent. Nor was the Heimwehr as supraparty as its propaganda would have its followers and others believe. According to a lengthy report on the Heimwehr by the American military attaché, Major W. W. Hicks,[21] there existed within each province a Heimwehr "executive committee" composed of Christian Social and Pan-German politicians in proportion to the strength of each party in the provincial diet. Hicks understood that these committees made all decisions of any importance, appointed leaders of the larger units, and approved direct elections of leaders of the smaller units. The politicians were in turn advised by a military committee of retired officers. The central executive committee (federal command), which consisted of the provincial leaders and their top military advisers, was further assisted by a staff consisting of nearly a score of prominent ex-officers and advised by about the same number of big industrialists and large landowners. But the federal command had little authority over the provincial associations and could not do much more than urge uniform policies and training methods and try to work out a national mobilization plan for a combined use of all their forces.

In early summer 1928 the Heimwehr claimed to have 150,000 members. It was thought that peasants and others from the rural areas comprised about 70 percent of the membership, that students and tradesmen (which presumably included men from the professions and civil service) contributed about 20 percent, and that workers accounted for only 10 percent. The members varied in age from sixteen to sixty, and allegedly over 70 percent of them had had military experience during the war. However, Hicks thought that only fifty-two thousand members were organized and trained militarily. Of that number only twenty thousand men were prepared for action away from their home localities, while twenty-two thousand were equipped for local military duty and ten thousand for auxiliary noncombat service. These fifty-odd thousand men, of whom about three hundred were trained officers, were organized into fifty infantry battalions of approximately eight hundred men each, who were further divided into four companies of four platoons. In addition there were seventeen machine gun platoons, each of which had ten guns and ammunition, and two or three field batteries with a total of fifteen howitzers and five hundred rounds per gun. Hicks reported the distribution of Heimwehr strength as follows (number of men in parentheses):

Province	Infantry battalions	M.G. platoon	Field batteries
Tyrol & Vbg.	11 (8,800)	3 (150)	—
Styria	10 (8,000)	3 (150)	1 (100)
Salzburg	10 (8,000)	3 (150)	—
Upper Austria	8 (6,400)	3 (150)	—
Carinthia	8 (6,400)	3 (150)	1 (50)
L. A. & Vienna	3 (2,400)	2 (100)	—
Total HW combatants	50 (40,000)	17 (850)	2 (150)

Hicks understood that the Heimwehr infantry had ready access to ten thousand Mauser rifles of German origin, most of which had come from Bavaria in 1920 and 1921, and thirty thousand Austrian Mannlicher rifles, for all of which there were ammunition and bayonets. The Heimwehr armory also included hand grenades, gas bombs, and a few armored cars. Undoubtedly thousands of additional rifles were privately owned by Heimwehr members. The Heimwehr strength was supplemented by the members of the FKV, liberally estimated at twenty thousand in December 1927.

The Heimwehr's normal operating expenses amounted to about AS 100,000 (or $14,255 in 1928) a month. The governments of Tyrol and Carinthia defrayed most of the Heimwehr expenses in those provinces, while in the others funds came from the industrialists and large landowners. The officers of the larger military units, all staff officers, and military advisers received small salaries as paid professionals to supplement their pensions. The political leaders were supposedly paid, not by the Heimwehr, but from the funds of their political parties if they had no other source of income. At this time the "enlisted men" received remuneration or subsistence only when they were called into service by the provinces.

Hicks was concerned with the Heimwehr primarily as a potential auxiliary of the federal army. He knew of no formal liaison between the Heimwehr's federal command at Innsbruck and the ministry of war in Vienna, but on the provincial level the Heimwehr military advisers maintained close if unofficial ties with the army's brigade headquarters and had worked out plans for the use of the Heimwehr as relief and auxiliary troops. There had also been occasions, especially in the Tyrol, Carinthia, and Styria, in which the Heimwehr had participated in maneuvers with federal troops. The Heimwehr's own training methods consisted generally of target practices, lectures and map problems, and during the summer minor terrain exercises and practice marches. However, as the federal army, which at the time numbered about 20,800 men and officers, became more efficient and lost its socialist cast, participation in Heimwehr exercises began to slump, for it was felt by some officers that any urgent military necessity for the existence of the Heimwehr was waning. In summary, Hicks thought that generally speaking the Heimwehr resembled the American Legion from the standpoint of the federal government, which provided only moral support for it, whereas from the standpoint of the provinces it represented a reliable national guard without legal federal recognition. Hicks thought the Heimwehr could be useful against internal disorders, which he apparently thought would come from socialist inspiration.

What Major Hicks and most observers did not realize was that the Heimwehr was about to become more an Italo-Hungarian "foreign-legion" than a defender of the peace in Austria. It was already launched on an adventure that its leaders hoped would make them the arbiters of Austria's destiny rather than merely an auxiliary military and police force for a weak parliamentary regime. As Steidle wrote the premier of Hungary in May 1928, it was time for the Heimwehr to become a "state-political organization" that

wants to and must force the so-called bourgeois parties to alter the half-bolshevik constitution that came into being under the pressure of the red streets of Vienna, regardless of the resistance or events unleashed thereby.

The 150,000 men organized in the ranks of the Heimwehr, who are prepared to risk [everything] for the victory of their Weltanschauung, cannot and will not be content with the role of a barking but chained watch dog, crouching until the owner, in this case the bourgeois parties, releases it, as on July 15, 1927, only to chain it again immediately after it has done its job against the threatening thief. On the contrary, these men want to have a voice in the shaping of the state.[22]

Steidle's contact with Bethlen had clearly revived his old ambitions.

Count István Bethlen sparked the renewal of foreign support for a Heimwehr putsch against the government of Austria's democratic regime. It was a revival of a favored old conspiratorial alliance, and this time Bethlen secured the backing of the government of a major power instead of that of a separatist province. The Hungarian premier desperately wanted to see established in Austria an avowedly rightist and antidemocratic government that would back his claims for reclamation of formerly Hungarian lands, especially in Czechoslovakia and Romania. He found Austria's friendship and trade treaties with Czechoslovakia abhorrent, almost another link in France's Little Entente, which he knew that Mussolini, too, wanted to undermine. To Mussolini Bethlen held out the prospect that an Austrian government dependent on them would cease to make an issue of the Italianization of the south Tyrol. It was a timely approach, for Chancellor Seipel's criticisms of Italian policy in the south Tyrol led Mussolini to recall his minister to Austria from February to June 1928. In addition, Bethlen suggested to Mussolini that a rightist government in Austria would steer away from *Anschluss* with the new socialist-dominated government in Germany.[23]

The Hungarian documentation of this three-way cabal published by Lajos Kerekes indicates that Steidle and Pabst asked Premier Bethlen for weapons and money (AS 300,000) as early as August 1927. He gives no details of these contacts before the spring of 1928, but he suggests that the Hungarian government never entirely stopped its financial aid to the Heimwehr, and he also states that Pabst maintained his contacts with rightist groups in Hungary throughout the 1920s. Even so, it must have been only after the July days and the Heimwehr's request for money that Hungarians once again became intimately involved with Heimwehr conspiracies to establish an authoritarian regime in Austria. Kerekes makes it clear that some time after that request Bethlen sent General Béla Jánky, whom he attached to the legation in Vienna, to Austria to study the Heimwehr carefully. The Hungarians also received overtures from Pfrimer's entourage, but for several reasons—primarily their suspicion of Pfrimer's pro-*Anschluss* sentiment—they decided to work through Steidle and Pabst.

In May 1928 Steidle informed Jánky that the Heimwehr now needed AS 1,494,000 ($212,000 in 1928), nearly one-third of it immediately and the rest soon thereafter. He planned to give AS 740,00 in two installments to the provincial organizations for outfitting their men, allotted as follows: Lower Austria, AS 200,000; Upper Austria, AS 160,000; Salzburg, AS 100,000; Carinthia, AS 80,000; Styria, AS 70,000; Vienna, AS 60,000; the Tyrol, AS 50,000; Vorarlberg, AS 20,000. Of the remaining funds he would apply AS 60,000 to the Heimwehr press and to propaganda calling for a constitutional revision, AS 30,000 to acquire gas grenades and blowers, and AS 64,000 to acquire eight short-wave transmitters; create a "special formation" with AS 100,000; and, finally, keep

AS 500,000 in a "mobilization fund" to meet the emergency needs of a military campaign. In addition Steidle asked for 18,000 rifles with 300 rounds each and for 190 machine guns.

For several weeks the Hungarian premier worked to arrange an agreement between the Italians and the Heimwehr. Mussolini, who in April had already promised to provide the AS 300,000 originally requested by Steidle, was still ready to follow Bethlen's lead, but his foreign minister, Dino Grandi, insisted that the putschists pledge in writing that they would not make an issue of the south Tyrol. Twice, early in June and late in July, Steidle visited Bethlen and assured him of the Heimwehr's determination to find, or if necessary to create, an excuse to demand that the government accede to its wishes. While Steidle cautiously stated that the socialists would have to provide a provocation before the Heimwehr could afford to march on the capital, he clearly hoped that events connected with a daring *Aufmarsch* that the Heimwehr planned to hold on October 7 in the socialist citadel of Wiener Neustadt would lead to a showdown. To be ready for that day Steidle needed Italian money, so on August 1 he sent Bethlen a signed statement pledging that the future Austrian government (in which Mussolini expected Steidle to participate) would regard problems in the south Tyrol as an Italian affair and that it would not seek *Anschluss* with "leftist" Germany. Finally, after further delay in Italy, on August 23 Jánky gave Steidle AS 600,000. Shortly thereafter the parties began making arrangements for the shipment of arms into Austria, but at this time they failed to work out a satisfactory scheme.

Through his talks with Steidle and from other sources Bethlen gained the impression that the leading figures in Austrian politics and industry were eager to force the Social Democrats out of public life. He knew that the Heimwehr enjoyed close ties with Police President Schober and his staff, and in June Steidle implied that ties with Army Minister Vaugoin would insure success for the Heimwehr's undertaking. In July Steidle somewhat proudly reported to Bethlen that Seipel had recently drawn closer to the Heimwehr (which other observers also noted)[24] and might even join the "action." In any event, the chancellor was again pressing Austrian industrialists to provide the Heimwehr with the assistance it needed to maintain, if not to expand, its strength. Assuring the Heimwehr leaders that he would not allow their *Aufmarsch* to be prohibited by provincial authorities, Seipel also led them to believe that he, too, hoped that the socialists would offer resistance, in which case he would use federal forces in support of the Heimwehr. If only the socialists would play their allotted role in Wiener Neustadt on October 7!

Located about thirty miles south of Vienna, Wiener Neustadt is Lower Austria's second largest city. It was solidly socialist and regarded by the SDP as impenetrable. For those reasons the Heimwehr had to "conquer" its streets. The Styrian Heimatschutz announced that the *Aufmarsch* was intended to celebrate the union of Lower Austria's two Heimwehr organizations under Julius Raab's leadership. As a final tribute to their work in Lower Austria, the Styrians wanted to sponsor and join this first united appearance of the new organization and—in a warning intended to sound ominous—to show all Austria, "especially the alien Red leaders," that the Heimwehr is "already before the gates of Vienna."[25]

The Social Democrats seemed to rise to the bait. Claiming to see in the Heimwehr's plans the beginning of a great fascist offensive, in mid-July they announced plans to hold a "workers' convocation" in Wiener Neustadt also on October 7, and explained that such a meeting was necessary to keep the irate citizens from obstructing the Heimwehr gathering. In addition, the socialists undoubtedly used their contacts with foreign parties to bring pressure on the Austrian government, which they hoped would eventually forbid both demonstrations.

For two months before the appointed date the prospect of a violent confrontation at Wiener Neustadt dominated the country's news and caused concern in many European capitals. While the Social Democrats tried to find some means to prevent the Heimwehr *Aufmarsch,* the Heimwehr kept up a barrage of ominous, if not always consistent, propaganda. One press release early in August suggested that "Since the legal power has proved itself too weak and the parliamentary system unable to enact the most urgent legislation, extraparliamentary possibilities . . . of unraveling the Gordian knot must be considered. If necessary by brute force." And in an interview a few days later Steidle stated that a civil war—an act of self-defense—that brought order to Austrian affairs would only raise the country's prestige in the capitalist world. Such bombast elicited expressions of alarm from cabinets, financiers and newspapers in England, France, and the Little Entente. In the face of such reaction the Heimwehr press bureau, speaking for Steidle, announced that the Heimwehr would send only part of the Styrian and Lower Austrian formations to Wiener Neustadt and toned down its promise of a forceful solution to all the country's problems. Nevertheless, the Heimwehr continued to insist that it would ignore any prohibition of its rally and would win for nonsocialists the "right to the street" and "freedom of opinion." Moreover, early in September Pfrimer, who

did not see eye to eye with Steidle and who wanted to proceed more
recklessly, asserted that his men would appear in full force and blus-
tered that "today, at least in the Alpine provinces, the Heimwehr is the
people."[26]

Whether by accident or design, Seipel handled the situation master-
fully to his own advantage. It is not certain that he was fully aware of
the Italo-Hungarian role in the Heimwehr agitation (Kerekes intimates
that he was not)[27] or, for that matter, that he was committed to the
Heimwehr's goal of instituting a rightist government. In fact, in view of
the foreign complication revealed by Kerekes, it is not likely, as Gulick
charges, that Seipel engineered the whole affair simply to get the socialists to make concessions on the rent control issue, even if he did use the

The first federal leader, Dr. Richard Steidle,
at the *Aufmarsch* in Linz on 14 October 1928.

The second (co-) federal leader, Dr. Walter Pfrimer,
speaking at the *Aufmarsch* in Innsbruck on 12 November 1928.

situation to that end.[28] But by his stubborn defense of the Heimwehr's "right" to march in Wiener Neustadt, he induced the socialists, who convened their annual congress earlier than usual because of the crisis and who still hoped for a law prohibiting all paramilitary demonstrations, to offer to discuss a change in the rent control law. The most that Seipel would promise during what the *Neue Freie Presse* called an "ugly" parliamentary debate on October 3 was to open negotiations on internal disarmament after October 7, but even then he hedged the offer with enough conditions to make it obvious that he was not eager for successful talks. While before parliament the chancellor defended the Heimwehr and Pabst, he also managed to keep the Heimwehr leaders somewhat off balance. He warned them privately not actually to begin hostilities against the socialists, and he suggested that they bring fewer men into Wiener Neustadt than they had first planned. Moreover, by a one-sided prohibition of the socialists' formal rally, Seipel compelled his opponents to announce that workers would occupy the streets and main square of Wiener Neustadt throughout the weekend, and thus drove the Heimwehr leaders to demand that official armed forces protect their meeting "from Marxist attacks or other hindrances." However, the socialists, whose ploy might have worked (some business circles and almost all the independent press were urging the government to pro- hibit the Heimwehr rally) had they not flinched in the game of nerves, felt the risk of calling Seipel's bluff too great and appealed for a reci- sion of the ruling against their rally. With both sides giving way, Seipel saw to it that Heimwehr and socialist negotiators agreed on a plan to parade at different hours so that both groups could use the coveted main square. They further agreed that large contingents of army and gendarme troops should form a buffer betwen the rival political armies. These arrangements took the edge off the mounting hysteria, but with reporters from most of the world's great press pouring into Austria, an air of dreadful expectancy still pervaded the country.[29]

On October 8 Count Lerchenfeld reported that the 380 journalists at Wiener Neustadt on the previous day had found little work. The sev- enth had passed peacefully. Eight thousand strategically placed govern- ment forces kept about nineteen thousand Heimwehr marchers (mostly from Styria) apart from the socialists' fourteen thousand Schutzbund members and twenty-one thousand civilian demonstrators. Across the country thousands of Heimwehr men stood on "alert," armed and ready to march—to Wiener Neustadt or to Vienna?—at the first sign of social- ist "resistance." But Seipel had provided too much "protection," and the disciplined socialists gave no pretext for action. Steidle and Pfrimer made the principal speeches for the Heimwehr, Deutsch for the social- ists. Their pronouncements, hardly out of the ordinary, were largely in- tended to convince their followers of the significance of the occasion and to give them a feeling of importance. The impressive size of the socialist rally afforded the SDP some consolation and helped veil the fact that they had not prevented the Heimwehr *Aufmarsch*. After all its great expectations, the Heimwehr had to content itself with the boast that it had demonstrated its "right to the street" and that its "victory" had strengthened the Seipel government.[30] Two weeks later, however, a Styrian Heimwehr member, the baron who in May had approached the Hungarian government for Pfrimer, published an open letter to Steidle expressing his impatience with such victory claims; he wanted to put an end to the party system altogether (and to Seipel in the process).[31]

Indeed, despite their claims, the Heimwehr leaders were disgruntled, their Hungarian and Italian patrons even more disappointed. They had all expected different results on October 7, witness the fact that for two days before the demonstrations Pabst had enjoyed the use of the whole communications apparatus of the federal police to coordinate his enter- prise.[32] Yet for neither the first nor the last time the Heimwehr leaders reneged on a bold plan for action. Why? In general, from this and other experiences one must conclude that their ambitions were greater than their resolve. They had a healthy fear of failure as well as cautioning respect for authority. In this case, it seems likely that for all their ties to Seipel, Schober, and Vaugoin, they were not absolutely convinced that these officials, who were keenly aware of Austria's dependence on France and England, would permit them to establish an open dictatorship (even one including these respected figures) unless the socialists clearly provided a pretext. Failing that, the Heimwehr leaders would have to keep hoping for better luck next time and promising their foreign backers that they would do better in the future. In fact, it required both continued *Aufmarsch* activity and Hungarian intercession to persuade the Italians to resume their support for the Heimwehr after a lapse of a year.

Meanwhile, apparently believing that he had the Heimwehr securely under his control, Chancellor Seipel attempted to use his victory at Wiener Neustadt to weaken the Social Democrats. His invitation to the parliamentary parties to discuss internal disarmament, in accordance with his pledge in the Nationalrat on October 3, was but a cynical formality. As he told the German minister, he considered disarmament at the time a hopeless dream but still "his most important personal mission" (on his own terms, it may be surmised). Here again the chancellor backed the Heimwehr's conditions and added some of his own, whose acceptance, as Steidle candidly observed, would mean "the end of Austro-bolshevism."[33] Against the criticism of more moderate members of his party, especially the spokesmen for the Christian labor unions, Seipel championed the Heimwehr with increasing obstinacy. He was clearly growing impatient with the longevity of socialist power in the life of the republic and evidently intended to use the Heimwehr as a strong arm to force major constitutional changes. His unsuccessful agitation for enlarged presidential powers so soon after Wiener Neustadt supports such a contention. Then, in mid-December, Seipel confessed his "solidarity" with the Heimwehr movement, in which "the longing for true democracy is one of the strongest driving forces." He was not willing to have the Heimwehr restricted "for the sake of a sham peace," even if its permissible activities did not please the socialists, who abused their privileges to the street, to parades and other demonstrations "as a means of exercising terrorism in matters of freedom of opinion and organization." Later remarks in the same vein led the moderate *Volkswirt* to fear that Seipel was proclaiming a "kind of personal union" between the Heimwehr and the armed forces that held an ominous portent of future conflict.[34] Nevertheless, if, as Gulick contends, the truth of the "democracy" for which Seipel began to campaign in the fall of 1928 was its identity with dictatorship, he intended it to be a clerical-industrialist and not a Heimwehr-fascist one.

Cheered by Seipel's encouragement, the Heimwehr leaders continued their march activities and propaganda efforts throughout the winter of 1928/1929 and worked especially hard to strengthen their movement in Vienna. If the Heimwehr could appear in force in the capital it might convince the country that it was indeed a formidable popular movement capable of confronting the socialists on their home ground. There, where the militant antisocialists were so thoroughly outnumbered, their organizations had been most divided. But under the prodding of Seipel several groups agreed in mid-December to "unite" as the Selbstschutz Wien, affiliated with the confederation under Steidle and Pfrimer.[35] Although Steidle delivered a bellicose speech to a large Heimwehr audience in Vienna on December 17 ("Red Vienna must become German Vienna"), it was to be several months before the Heimwehr created much of a storm in the capital. Nevertheless, the Viennese opposition to the Social Democrats began at least to look more imposing. The Heimwehr had begun its last step in the march to political prominence.

4

First Peak of Power

Nineteen-twenty-nine

It was the year of the Heimwehr. During 1929 the Heimwehr reached
its first peak of power, and its only one as anything like the *Volksbewegung* it liked to picture itself. With its formal membership swelling
to nearly four hundred thousand by late summer, it appeared to have
succeeded in creating a "renewal" movement combining antisocialists
and nondemocrats of all hues in demands for fundamental changes in
Austria's political institutions. From the time it conducted its first big
Aufmarsch in Vienna on February 24—a demonstration which threatened for a while to create a crisis reminiscent of the Wiener Neustadt
affair[1]—the Heimwehr set the pace of political developments through
most of the year. It promised a "fight without quarter" in which either
it or the SDP would "remain alone in the field." Although it failed to
achieve its most extreme demands, it did play a major role in the making of a chancellor and in a revision of the constitution.

In reality, the Heimwehr marched to the beat of two, and at times
three, different drums. The most regular ones were beat by Ignaz Seipel
and István Bethlen, whose tempo much of the time was the same; then
at crucial moments their rhythm was disturbed by Mussolini's big boom
and by the discordant notes coming from the west. Both Seipel and
Bethlen aimed at developments that would destroy the SDP and create
a dictatorship in Austria by the autumn of 1929. Seipel hoped to realize
that goal by his own political maneuvering and by the threat of force,
whereas Bethlen pushed throughout for an armed putsch that would
put the Heimwehr in control of Austria. Mussolini was as eager as the
other two men to destroy the socialists' power, but he disliked Seipel
and distrusted the Heimwehr leaders. He correctly sensed that they
talked a much tougher line than they were willing or able to back up
with deeds. In fact, time and again the Heimwehr leaders solemnly
promised actions, both implicitly to the public and explicitly to their
patrons, that they never carried out, partly because of the alarm expressed in financial and governmental circles in the west when civil war
appeared imminent in the late summer, and partly, one suspects, be-

cause of cold feet. Nevertheless, at the peak of the crisis over constitutional revision, Mussolini did provide the Heimwehr with another large
subsidy. At that time, the fear that the Heimwehr meant indeed to
launch an armed attack on the capital prompted the Social Democrats,
who were aware of the international intrigues, to allow a moderate reform of the constitution in December.

While in most cases such extremism accompanies severe economic
crisis, the Heimwehr actually benefitted from the relative prosperity in
central Europe during most of 1929. Largely because of this the extreme
German nationalists in Austria had less cause to look to Germany for
economic salvation than they had had earlier or would have after the
onset of worldwide depression. The fact that throughout 1929 Germany
had a socialist chancellor also contributed to the willingness of Austria's
German nationalists to go along with those backed by Italy and Hungary. Undoubtedly Pfrimer and others chafed at the Hungarian veto on
Heimwehr participation in the Stahlhelm festivities in early June and at
the lukewarm response by Mussolini and Bethlen to proposals from
German rightists for a "white international."[2] On these and other
grounds Steidle and Pfrimer clashed behind the scenes throughout the
year. Before the public, however, they always managed to speak with
one voice, thus lending great force to their campaign for constitutional
reform. The harmony of their vocal clamor heightened the fears of turmoil that gave the late summer's crisis such urgency.

A series of violent incidents between Heimwehr and socialists, especially in Styrian and Lower Austrian communities, marked the early
months of 1929. The most dramatic skirmish in the early part of the year
was the "battle" in the socialist party building in Gloggnitz on February
3. The vice-mayor of Wiener Neustadt, Josef Püchler, planned to speak
on "The Lies of the Heimwehr." Such a "provocation" could not go unanswered. Invited by the socialists to hear the "truth," local Heimwehr
adherents turned out in force and claimed that, as the majority in the
hall, they should control the meeting. When despite their shouts
Püchler proceeded to speak, the Heimwehr leader, Stocker, hauled him
from the stage and a royal fray ensued. Püchler, who himself wielded a
wicked flag pole, was hospitalized for three weeks by a spade's blow to
the head and was but one of many injured that day.[3] While one cannot
contend that the socialist ranks were free from ruffians and hotheads, it
is nevertheless clear that such incidents were part of a Heimwehr campaign to raise the political temperature and to create a feeling of dreadful crisis in which the voices of moderation on both sides could not be
heard. To intensify the conflict, the Heimwehr federal command an-

nounced in late March that it was time to take more drastic measures to "put an end to the Red terror." A much-publicized directive instructed all local leaders no longer to wait until the "foe" had actually attacked their men, but at the first sign of provocation to use the "sharpest means" to protect them. If anything, the number of incidents increased in April and May.[4]

Kerekes links this order from the federal command directly—and perhaps correctly—to a four-hour conference between Seipel and Steidle on March 23. Steidle reported to his Hungarian contacts that the chancellor told him it was time for the Heimwehr to become more active after the fashion of the *fascio*. Seipel intended to direct a broad offensive from the background and would attempt to use the press as a means of preparing public opinion for major changes, which he thought would have to come about no later than the autumn.[5] The record of this conversation is the clearest evidence to date in support of the contention that by this time Seipel was committed to the total destruction of social democracy. It certainly throws additional light on the chancellor's unexpected resignation on April 3, which does indeed appear part of a well-conceived political campaign in which the Heimwehr was to play a major role. Seipel did not alone create the Heimwehr of 1929 (he had almost certainly learned of the Italian subsidy, if he had not known about it all along), and probably his vision of the good society differed from that of the Heimwehr leaders. But they were willing to work in close collaboration in setting the stage for the establishment of some kind of authoritarian government, even while each saw in the other a tool.

One of the hallmarks of the Heimwehr of 1929 was its espousal of the corporatist doctrines associated with Professor Othmar Spann. It has also sparked a controversy over interpretation: namely, when did the Heimwehr become "corporatist"? A number of scholars have tried to show that Adam Wandruszka was wrong when he asserted that only in 1929 and 1930 was there a disastrous attempt to graft a "positive" ideology onto the Heimwehr, but these scholars in turn bog down in their efforts to find the exact date on which the Heimwehr first called for a corporative state. This, too, misses the point. Along with many related theories, Spann's notions of the universally "true" state had been common property in rightist circles ever since the early 1920s, and the Heimwehr had always been vaguely corporatist. But in a sense Wandruszka is the more accurate, for only in connection with Seipel's campaign for "true" democracy did it try to formulate and propagate an official and inherently exclusive ideology based on Spann's teachings.[6]

Othmar Spann was an irascibly intolerant pedagogue who aspired to be a counter-Marx in both theory and practice. He not only claimed to understand all the errors of Marxism, which he abhorred, and the truth of how society should be ordered, but also he sought to direct the political activities of groups intended to bring a hierarchical corporative order into being. He drew about him an elitist circle of young academicians who fell under the spell of his search for certainty while studying at the University of Vienna, where Spann was professor of economics and sociology from 1919 to 1938. Foremost among his disciples were Dr. Walter Heinrich and Dr. Hans Riehl, both of whom devoted much of their time in 1929 to instructing Heimwehr audiences throughout the country in the "positive" aspects of anti-Marxism. By this they meant the creation of an authoritarian state, rooted in tradition and religion and organized on the principles of hierarchy and functional corporatism.[7]

Exactly when and how the Heimwehr established close ties with the *Spannkreis* are intriguing, yet unanswered, questions, as are those concerning Seipel's relationship with Spann. Seipel's biographer Von Klemperer cites his diary to show that Seipel first mentioned meeting Spann in February 1927, but then not again until 2 October 1929. It is clear that the *Spannkreis* was drawing close to the Heimwehr before the latter date. It may be that Pfrimer first established ties with the Spann circle sometime in 1928; Hans Riehl himself later recalled that in February 1928 the Heimwehr groups in the Tyrol and Styria united for the purpose of bringing about a corporative reorganization of the state. But the relationship probably did not become an intensive one before 1929. During that year the Styrian Heimatschutz published several pamphlets by Spann and his disciples, and in mid-June Spann appeared with Pfrimer at a Heimatschutz rally. A significant development in the relationship came when Walter Heinrich, who spent four months early in 1929 studying fascism in Italy and then began lecturing before Heimwehr audiences in July, was designated as an advisory general-secretary of the Heimwehr chiefly responsible for its ideological propaganda, a post he held through the first half of 1930. If, as Heinrich and Pabst both recalled, his appointment came about at Seipel's prodding, it must have taken place late in 1929, by which time Seipel seemed personally committed to corporatism. For a while Heinrich got along well with the Heimwehr leaders; Pabst liked him and later called him his "right-hand man," in many ways "better than Spann."[8]

Spann's pamphlet, *Die Irrungen des Marxismus*, published by the Styrian Heimatschutz in 1929, was representative of the oversimplified propaganda and the conspiracy theory directed at Heimwehr members. Spann condemned Marxism as the result of the unfettered individualism caused by capitalism. He believed that Marxism would disappear once its intellectual leaders were convinced of their errors; hence, Marxist theory must be opposed by a "constructive" one. Meanwhile, what made Marxism so dangerous was the fact that, through control of Russia, international communist leaders—among whom Spann included the Austro-Marxists—had behind them a means of power, thus making it possible for hordes of people to take to the streets of Vienna and for the Palace of Justice to burn (15 July 1927) "at the push of a button in Moscow." Spann feared, therefore, that theories alone would not be sufficient to counter the Marxists and that it would take what he called "work—incessant, hot work in the service of the truth"—to avoid disaster.[9]

Such calls to action served to heighten an already tense situation in Austria. The keynote of the political conflicts of 1929 was Seipel's resignation from the chancellorship on April 3. The whole country was surprised by this move, for there was no pressing political crisis at that moment. Whatever the reasons for his resignation, which have been warmly debated ever since, it removed an element of continuity and predictability from the government and opened the way for a more passionate clash of interests. There was something ominous about the suggestion of a Catholic analyst close to Seipel that, since the resignation indicated the failure of parliamentarism, the Heimwehr should be enlarged as a reliable support for the Catholic leaders who would be called upon to lead Austria out of chaos.[10]

In the ensuing month-long cabinet crisis the Heimwehr played what diplomatic observers called its first significant role in federal politics. In conferences with party leaders in Vienna, Steidle and Pfrimer demanded a continuation of the Seipel course, and the three coalition parties agreed on April 11 that the new government would pledge to work with the Heimwehr. As the *Neue Freie Presse* noted, "Doubtless the Heimwehr today represents a force that is in a position at least to hinder much that parliamentary democracy would like to achieve." While the negotiations dragged on behind the scenes, Heimwehr propaganda kept tension high. Making threats typical of his unimaginative oratory, Pfrimer asserted at Villach that "our struggle is really directed against the corrupt democratic parliamentary system"; promising that "the Styrian panther will spit fire," he urged his listeners "on to Vienna with weapon in hand!" In like vein the *Heimatschutz-Zeitung* proclaimed,

This parliamentary system must go! We need men at the head of the state who will compel the Social Democrats to cooperate in emergency measures or else push them aside. That is not a putsch. One simply shoves aside fanatics who would want to prevent putting out the fire—and any who call these firemen "violators" belong in an asylum. So it is in Austria. We have no more time to wait. The Heimwehr will not simply stand by and watch the destruction of the state; the people see in us the last hope of salvation.[11]

Despite all the dire threats, however, the Heimwehr leaders were not yet ready to initiate armed action. While demanding thorough constitutional changes, Steidle drew in the extended lines of Heimwehr bombast; to those who could not understand "why [it] had not already acted in a different way," he explained that the leaders had a "tremendous responsibility to carry and could never answer for it if they got into a conflict with the power of the state, which the Heimwehr really supports." By the time of a tense *Aufmarsch* in St. Pölten on May 5— another encounter that saw heavy police patrols, strictly delineated agenda, prohibition of weapons and alcohol, and an alerted Schutzbund—a new chancellor had been selected.[12]

Upon taking office at the head of a cabinet representing the three previous coalition parties, Ernst von Streeruwitz pledged to uphold the constitution and to leave the settlement of "pending" difficulties to "those who have been elected by the people." The fifty-five-year-old former cavalry officer had been a prominent spokesman for industrial interests in the Nationalrat since 1923, and he had earlier channeled subsidies to the Heimwehr. But he was not viewed as an irreconcileable partisan in Austria's ideological cold war, and his election sparked hopes that a hotter war could be avoided. British financiers held out the lure of a substantial loan if Streeruwitz were able to dissolve the private armies. The Social Democrats, hoping to foster moderation on all sides, let it be known that they would meet the new chancellor part way. True to their word, the socialists allowed the speedy passage of several important measures representing major concessions, foremost among them the easing of the controversial rent ceiling and a program of federal assistance for private housing construction.[13] But the honeymoon was soon over, for the Heimwehr leaders did not intend to fall victim to moderation.

Streeruwitz soon discovered that he was not master in his own house. At the outset of his administration he came into conflict with the Heimwehr, which he evidently viewed as an outfit of strikebreakers or, at most, as a defensive army. When its leaders tried to act like backroom bosses at his inauguration, Streeruwitz complained that he had expected

help, not pressure from those whom he had once aided. Soon thereafter
Steidle publicly asserted that Seipel would return to office within a few
months, and Pabst moved his headquarters from Innsbruck to Vienna to
be at the center of action.[14] The chancellor was irritated by their continued efforts to provoke the socialists, but he found that the Heimwehr
was protected by his two ministers who controlled the state's armed
forces and that there was really little he could do to defuse the ticking
time bomb. In what Kerekes calls a kind of treaty, Army Minister
Vaugoin and Police President Schober assured Steidle in mid-May that
they were sympathetic with the Heimwehr's campaign and agreed together "to take the fate of Austria into their hands and to determine its
further development." Streeruwitz felt compelled to agree to consult
with the Heimwehr in preparing for constitutional reform and, further,
not to undertake any regulations that would weaken the Heimwehr's
position.[15] It was only his vanity that prevented Streeruwitz from fully
realizing the interim nature of his appointment, and he hoped to master
the situation by playing a waiting game, partly in hopes that internal
rivalries would weaken the Heimwehr.[16]

With Austria so dependent on tourist business, government officials
vainly attempted to prevent a tense summer of demonstrations and
violent incidents. Although socialist authorities in Vienna were forced
by Minister of Interior Schumy to permit a Heimwehr *Aufmarsch* long
scheduled for May 12, they decreed a summer-long injunction against
outdoor rallies effective May 13, and Governor Buresch, a Christian
Social, announced a similar prohibition for Lower Austria. Then, in a
directive affecting the whole country, Schumy forbade the use in
demonstrations of anything that might be considered weapons, including steel helmets, spades, and pickaxes. To turn attention away from
these injunctions, the Heimwehr announced that it would discontinue
marches in major tourist centers throughout Austria until the fall. But,
protected by Governors Stumpf of Tyrol and Rintelen of Styria, the
leaders protested strongly the prohibition of defensive weapons, especially helmets ("How shall we protect our heads against Social Democratic stones?"), and they instructed their subordinates to do their
"unquestionable duty" in protecting all participants in Heimwehr
demonstrations from "attacks by incited compatriots."[17]

Except in Vienna, the march moratorium meant little. Not only was
the Heimwehr allied with the men who controlled Austria's armed
forces, but also Church officials, despite some criticism from youthful
reformers, provided both a means of circumventing the moratorium on
marches and a platform from which to condemn any who wished to

preserve a modus vivendi with the Social Democrats.[18] With this support the Heimwehr continued its demonstrations in the guise of flag dedications and blessings under Church auspices. The most blatant infraction occurred at Aspang on May 26, when two hundred men, many with spades, ignored the district official who told them they were infringing upon the regulations.[19] Thus, any hopes that the summer of 1929 would be peaceful proved illusory.

Everywhere the tempo of the Heimwehr offensive picked up as the summer began. The ferocity with which its spokesmen attacked the "system" concealed the underlying rift between Steidle and Pfrimer over new advances by the Stahlhelm. Traveling in Germany, Seipel worked from afar to keep the leaders together and to intensify the campaign for a complete alteration in Austria's governmental system. In his famous "Critique of Democracy" delivered at Tübingen, Seipel championed the Heimwehr as "a strong popular movement that wants to liberate democracy from the rule of parties." He thought its militarism necessary to maintain discipline and to prevent it from itself becoming a party (of which there was widespread talk among Heimwehr circles in Styria and Carinthia).[20]

The rise of nationalistic young Prince Starhemberg in Upper Austria added a new element of urgency to the Heimwehr campaign. People saw in it further radicalization of the whole movement rather than a stage in its internal leadership struggle. Starhemberg used his family fortune to create units of *Jäger* responsible to him personally and then pushed aside the three coleaders representing the major nonsocialist parties.[21] He soon joined other Heimwehr personalities in speaking at a series of well-attended indoor meetings in Vienna, where the American minister perceived a "great awakening" among the antisocialists.[22] In July came the announcement that on September 29 there would be demonstrations in four large towns on three sides of Vienna, with the east left open "for the flight of those who came from the east." The implication was clear. Meanwhile, the *Arbeiter-Zeitung* ran a serial exposé of the Heimwehr's connections with government and industry that further polarized opinion in Austria and was used for anti-Heimwehr propaganda abroad. Again the foreign press began to express concern about the possibility of civil war in Austria.[23]

Throughout the summer the Heimwehr's Hungarian backers worked to procure the rest of the Italian subsidy promised in 1928. Mussolini showed himself impatient with what he considered the Heimwehr's foot-dragging and demanded that its leaders sign a written promise to carry out the sharp swing to the Right within the near future. In response, on August 10 Steidle, Pfrimer, and Pabst signed a statement pledging "to carry out the decisive action for the change in the Austrian constitution" no later than 15 March 1930. Of course, the sooner they received the "promised cooperation" the sooner they could act: "The federal command will do everything in its power to undertake the action in the fall" of 1929. For some reason this letter reached Mussolini only two weeks later, and it was a month after that, at the height of another cabinet crisis, that the first of the further two installments of Italian subsidy reached Steidle.[24] But, as if to prove to the *Duce* its determination, the Heimwehr provoked a bloody clash with its opponents in mid-August.

The news of a big street battle in a small Styrian town on Sunday, August 18, seemed to herald the outbreak of civil war and evoked consternation in the western press. At St. Lorenzen about two thousand men led by Hans Rauter and Konstantin Kammerhofer, the fiery little Heimatwehr leader of the upper Mürz valley, deliberately forced a fight with socialists who gathered to hear a speech by Koloman Wallisch, whose appearance anywhere was a great provocation to the Heimwehr. After first agreeing to hold a counterdemonstration in a nearby town, Heimwehr leaders changed their plans at the last moment (supposedly because the local socialist press had called them cowards). On the morning of the eighteenth the Heimwehr distributed leaflets warning women and children not to come to St. Lorenzen, where there would be a "settling of accounts." After that, both sides expected an encounter. Wallisch attempted to avoid a clash by holding his rally at the town's church square instead of at the wine gardens that Heimwehr men had already occupied. This change, however, was a technical infraction of the registered plans, and Rauter persuaded the local authorities to prohibit the socialist meeting. Wallisch refused to heed the injunction, and a regular civil war in miniature broke out. Fence slats and stones gave way to revolvers and rifles and finally to machine gun fire. Of the approximately two hundred wounded, more than half were Heimwehr men, but of the four killed, three were socialists.[25]

There remain some perplexing mysteries about the battle of St. Lorenzen. The *Deutschösterreichische Tages-Zeitung*, a stridently nationalistic sheet that had sympathies with Pfrimer, claimed to have documentary evidence that the socialists planned to teach the Heimwehr a lesson at St. Lorenzen, and in a cabinet meeting Army Minister Vaugoin blamed the socialists for luring Kammerhofer's men to St. Lorenzen and for shooting first. Some observers, such as Vice-Chancellor Schumy, blamed both sides as well as the gendarmery. But even

Schober's office did not believe that the socialists would willingly give the Heimwehr an excuse to take armed action.[26] Indeed, an overall view of the situation leads to the conclusion that the Heimwehr was chiefly responsible for the clash. Still, it is possible that its leaders did not act in concert, that instead Pfrimer may have planned an incident that would boost his own power or hoist Rintelen into the chancellorship.[27] In any event they, or he, hoped further to polarize the political life of the country in order to hasten a final confrontation.

But in thus resorting to violence and flirting with a putsch, the Heimwehr invited stiffened resistance from bourgeois moderates as well as from the socialists, who showed that they would fight back and announced that they would resist a march on Vienna. More significantly, Schober, while still taking the antisocialist line in public, privately warned the Heimwehr leaders that an unprovoked putsch would meet the resistance of official forces. Although the government took no measures against either of the paramilitary opponents, it did, partially under the pressure of foreign opinion, instruct security officials to forbid all simultaneous counterdemonstrations and to enforce rigidly the prohibition of weapons at public assemblies. All in all, the Heimwehr leaders appeared to have been thrown momentarily off balance, and St. Lorenzen may have tempered their plans for a putsch as such.[28]

The prospect of civil war so frighteningly illuminated at St. Lorenzen also prompted some CSP leaders to seek means of curbing the Heimwehr's extremism. In an ambiguous gesture, the one hundred thousand members of the Lower Austrian Peasants League (Bauernbund), an economic interest association, corporatively joined the Heimwehr in a union whose technicalities and conditions are unfortunately not known. Peasant leader Josef Reither strongly implied that the purpose of the union was to support the moderate leadership of the province's Heimwehr against the radical elements close to Pfrimer. The *Volkswirt* suggested that the CSP intended thus to cover a tactical retreat by providing the Heimwehr an apparent boon. As it noted, such unions added exactly nothing to the Heimwehr's military formations, a fact that the Heimwehr leaders recognized. When a couple of economic groups in Tyrol merely "declared their solidarity with the goals of the Heimwehr," the Heimwehr praised such methods that did not threaten to disrupt its tight organization.[29]

The Heimwehr attempted to make the most of the situation with an intensive propaganda barrage. In this it was aided by the murder of a Heimwehr man in a scuffle on the outskirts of Vienna on the night of August 19/20 which it linked with St. Lorenzen. Heimwehr propaganda accused the Marxists of trying to lure it into striking at an inopportune moment and indignantly accused its enemies of cowardice for introducing the use of firearms into their struggle. On August 24 the *Neue Freie Presse* published an interview with an unnamed Heimwehr leader who announced that beginning in September the Heimwehr would hold rallies until late autumn. He denied that Schober had advised the leaders to be more cautious and stated that they had not even talked with Chancellor Streeruwitz; he also denied that a rift existed between Steidle and Pfrimer. When asked if the Heimwehr contemplated decisive action, the spokesman replied, "Our plan for a reform of the constitution can be realized only by a fundamental change of the system. The appropriate time for our action will depend largely on the resistance which the Marxists will employ. If they will not resign voluntarily, we will force them to. He who is against us will be swept away by the development." The man concluded by comparing the Streeruwitz government with the Facta regime in Italy just before Mussolini's march on Rome in 1922.[30]

Intensifying its propaganda campaign as fall approached, the Heimwehr welcomed the constitutional amendments formally proposed on August 25 by Landbund leaders Winkler and Schumy. The proposals projected an authoritarian presidential system in which a single "economic" chamber would supersede parliament. Winkler and Schumy recommended that the amendments be adopted by a simple majority in parliament (not by the required two-thirds) and then in a referendum, an unconstitutional procedure previously suggested by Seipel. The Heimwehr, warning against a "series of negotiated concessions" to the socialists, boasted that it would be the "other means" promised by Schumy and Winkler if the Social Democrats prevented parliamentary passage of the proposals. The *Reichspost* exulted, "The whole people is awakening. . . . The Heimwehr is the attitude of the people embodied in an organization, the will of the people in force and deed." In several interviews Seipel emphasized his support of the demands of the Heimwehr, which he now called an "irresistible movement." In the same vein, a small book by a "friend of the Heimatwehr" appeared in Innsbruck and created a sensation. Purporting to show, as its title insisted, the "Way to Austria's Freedom," the author compared Austria with old Rome, where not the senators but the dictators saved the state from threatening dangers: "A government of the strong hand creates more credit than a parliament of weak heads." As representative of the majority of Austrians, the Heimwehr justifiably claimed the "power in the state" and would become a "roaring storm" if it did not get its way.

What appeared to be an ultimatum published in the Heimwehr press in mid-September had an even greater impact. In this "last warning" the Heimwehr demanded total reform instead of half measures. If the government felt too weak for such, it should give way to a strong cabinet in which the Heimwehr would have its rightful influence. In a comment laden with sinister implications, it warned that the marches scheduled for September 29 had not been planned "without a deeper meaning." The hands of the clock pointed to five minutes before twelve![31]

Time had indeed run out on the Streeruwitz government if not yet on Austrian democracy itself. As the Seipel-Heimwehr campaign approached its climax, a combination of imminent civil war at home and financial pressures from abroad made Streeruwitz's position untenable. Western financiers demanded that to retain their confidence the Austrian government must restrain the Heimwehr, and Britain's foreign minister privately expressed his concern about putsch rumors to Streeruwitz. On the other hand, however, Mussolini had made it clear that his approval of a loan—required because of Italy's treaty claims against Austria—depended upon its changing its constitution to suit him. Indeed, in early September a high official in the Austrian foreign ministry told the German chargé d'affaires that Austria might have to install a pro-Heimwehr cabinet in order to win Mussolini's approval for a loan.[32] About the same time, Seipel's man in the cabinet, pompous Army Minister Vaugoin, who was not without higher aspirations for himself, frankly told the Hungarian military attaché that on September 29 the Heimwehr would drive the socialists from Vienna's city hall. Backed by Vaugoin's vain boasting, Hungary's foreign minister, Lajos Walkó, saw Mussolini on September 10, and, despite Mussolini's skepticism that the Heimwehr would actually attempt a putsch on the twenty-ninth, won his promise of more money for it by the end of the month. The *Duce* hoped that the change of government would soon take place, but, in a fateful assertion, told Walkó that he wanted neither Seipel nor Rintelen to be the next chancellor and would prefer to see Schober head the government.[33] Thus it was largely Mussolini, still stepping cautiously, who determined that his would-be emulators did not succeed Austria's Facta. He wanted a friendly but stable government in Austria that would weaken the Social Democrats more than he wanted the Heimwehr to imitate his march on Rome.

With the Heimwehr leading the agitation against Streeruwitz and calling for Schober, wide sections of the Austrian population began to demand that the police president assume the chancellorship. Perhaps Schober would be sufficient guarantee of order to bring home the international loan that Streeruwitz was seeking in Geneva. Even the socialists, who preferred a correct bureaucrat to a more partisan politician, effected a reconciliation with the "strong man" of 15 July 1927, through Canossa-like apologies by Mayor Seitz.

The critical decisions about the cabinet change were reached during Walkó's visit to Vienna on September 19 and 20, when he had long but separate talks with Seipel and Steidle. Both men felt that the socialists were on the ropes and that the time had come for a push to the right. They were sure that the Heimwehr could be brought into the cabinet legally, without its being necessary to risk a putsch on the twenty-ninth. It was clear that both Seipel and Steidle thought that Schober was too "correct" to head what they wanted to be another interim cabinet that might have to use force in preparing the way for the ultimate authoritarian regime. They preferred Vaugoin or Rintelen. Nevertheless, Walkó urged Steidle to settle for Schober because of his reputation abroad, even if he might not make a clean sweep of the socialists all at once. That could come later, after the constitutional revision to which Schober also seemed committed. Steidle assured Walkó that on that score he would not allow any compromises that would only delay the final solution demanded by the Heimwehr and its backers. Steidle expected to have a Heimwehr representative, probably Baron Arbesser of Styria, in the transitional cabinet soon to be formed. Apparently satisfied that events would now move along swiftly, the Hungarians let Steidle have approximately AS 380,000 of Italian money on September 21.[34]

Walkó's conferences with Seipel and Steidle took place in secret, but the atmosphere of crisis weighed heavily throughout the country. On September 19 Count Lerchenfeld, just returning to Vienna from his vacation, telephoned Berlin that a cabinet change was imminent and that Schober would probably be the next chancellor. The unfortunate Streeruwitz, not sure of the support of his own party and beset by old acquaintances to do "it" with "them," stirred himself too late to avert his fall. When he returned from Geneva on the twenty-fourth, he had a reform bill ready to present to parliament and wanted desperately to hold on. By then, however, Seipel had convinced the president of the National Bank and the provincial governors that a change was necessary. It hardly required Pabst's announcement the next afternoon that Streeruwitz would fall before dark to topple the government. Although the parliamentary club of the CSP supported the chancellor, the Agrarian League deputies, who were working hand-in-glove with Seipel, instructed Schumy to leave the cabinet, whereupon Seipel, still the chairman of the CSP, advised Streeruwitz to nominate Schober as his successor. In reporting these events, Lerchenfeld thought the only thing not somewhat obscure about Seipel's attitude was his support of the Heimwehr's goals "from a to z"; it seemed that "internal political developments are essentially determined by the Heimwehr movement." However, Lerchenfeld still stood by his prediction of the nineteenth that Schober would not allow the Heimwehr the decisive influence to which it aspired.[35]

Here at the peak of their influence the Heimwehr leaders viewed the emerging Schober regime with both hope and misgiving. To be sure, Vaugoin and Schumy retained high posts, and Minister of Justice Franz Slama was one of the Pan-German Party leaders of the Upper Austrian Heimwehr forced out by Starhemberg in July 1929. But Schober found an excuse not to give a prominent Heimwehr leader an important position in the financial uncertainty that the crisis had brought about. To save face the Heimwehr announced that it had refused two cabinet posts offered to it in order to retain full freedom of action. Loudly proclaiming Schober "their man," Heimwehr leaders pledged their support for his efforts to pass sweeping constitutional revisions.[36] In talks with Heimwehr leaders just after his appointment, Schober apparently convinced them that he would indeed hold out for a reform acceptable to them and asked them to intercede with Mussolini in behalf of the international loan. This they did, but still urged Mussolini to make his approval conditional upon satisfactory reforms. They were uncomfortably aware of the facts that, despite what they took to be his solemn promises to them, Schober was not entirely of their making and that he had much more freedom of action than they. When the Hungarian minister congratulated Schober on his appointment and said that his government hoped that he would make a tabula rasa of the Social Democrats, he replied merely that he felt it desirable for Austria to pursue policies oriented toward Hungary and Italy and pointedly added that the socialists had indicated their willingness to discuss proposed constitutional changes in parliament.

This statement sufficed to give the Hungarian leaders serious second thoughts about Schober. In an urgent entreaty on the twenty-seventh, Bethlen warned Steidle against placing too much confidence in Schober and urged the Heimwehr to drive the socialists out of Vienna before the movement lost its momentum and its enemies recovered their balance. Steidle assured Bethlen's representative that he and his colleagues would see to it that thorough changes were made and that, if necessary, they would replace Schober with Vaugoin.[37] For the moment, however, they were not prepared to believe that Schober, with whom they had long had contact and who had joined them in opposing Streeruwitz, would really let them down. They could only await further developments.

In his introductory remarks before the Nationalrat on September 27, Schober took an ambiguous and somewhat distant position vis-à-vis the Heimwehr while strongly endorsing most of the Landbund's reform proposals. He spoke of the "blameless men of honor from all strata of the population" who were in the Heimwehr and thought that their demands for "thoroughgoing reforms in the constitutional and administrative fields" were fully justified. He would seek to "maintain an adequate contact with the Heimwehr and to direct the movement in those paths which lead toward a fulfillment of its demands, so far as they are justified, in a legal fashion." Finally, in a sharp warning directed implicitly at the Heimwehr, Schober made a forthright assertion of his determination to maintain peace and order. In response SDP spokesman Robert Danneberg left an opening for a peaceful resolution of the crisis. By asserting that some reforms envisaged by Schober were absolutely unacceptable to the socialists, Danneberg implied that his party would negotiate the others—except under threat of a putsch.[38] Two days later the Heimwehr's long-heralded demonstrations in four towns near Vienna, as well as numerous socialist counterrallies, took place without undue incident. Thus, while trying to prove their determination, both sides expectantly waited to see what direction Schober would take in the question of constitutional reform.

However, before he could turn his attention to the constitution, Schober faced a serious bank failure. Just after he took office the large Boden Credit-Anstalt Bank, already in a vulnerable position because of overinvestment and of heavy support of the Heimwehr, failed under the run on Austria's banks by both foreign creditors and internal investors. Its president later admitted that it collapsed "just at the moment when, because of fears of a Heimwehr putsch, the political tension in Austria had reached its climax."[39] Schober took the quickest way he could find to overcome the crisis: he badgered Baron Louis Rothschild, head of Austria's other major financial house, the Credit-Anstalt, into taking over Sieghart's bank without allowing time for any real investigation of its obligations. Although Schober's speedy action helped set the stage for the more dramatic crash of Rothschild's bank a year and a half later, it temporarily averted a major financial disaster and an unsavory political scandal and had a calming effect on the country.[40]

After acting decisively to allay fears on one front, the new chancellor set about to prepare the constitutional legislation that he had promised. The Heimwehr leaders had their own conception of what it should be. On September 30 Steidle and Pfrimer handed Schober a draft of "fundamental" changes, the main points of which were greatly increased powers for a popularly elected president, the termination of Vienna's autonomy and its subordination to federal officials, unequal voting rights, and the creation of an "economic" legislature. Once again Schober, who was fully aware that Vaugoin was standing in the wings, assured his importunate supporters that after he had pushed through changes such as they envisaged he would form a new cabinet containing Heimwehr representatives and then proceed to disarm the socialist army. Schober referred their constitutional proposals to a ministerial commission composed of Vaugoin, Schumy, and Slama, who were to prepare a bill for him to submit to parliament.[41]

However, the Heimwehr leaders also had a more radical scheme in mind, which presumably they would institute should the socialists block "legal" reform or try to prevent the accretion of Heimwehr power by armed force. In October 1930 the Landbund press agency released what it alleged to have been Heimwehr demands in the fall of 1929 for a "provisional constitution," a temporary dictatorship while the Heimwehr corporative state was being created. The Landbund claimed that the document was presented to "three leading Austrian politicians," who may have been the ministerial commission appointed by Schober. The scheme, which the *Neue Freie Presse* compared to the fascist regime in Italy, probably emanated from the *Spannkreis*. It showed how far the Heimwehr leaders had gone in their dreams of a dictatorship that completely excluded all vestiges of democratic practices. Pending the enactment of a new basic charter the Heimwehr wanted all legislative and administrative powers vested in a supreme leaders' council composed of three to five men. There would be two advisory bodies, a "small" and a "great" state council. The small council would consist of the members of the supreme council, the ministers and state secretaries, two representatives of the self-defense leagues, the provincial governors, the police president, and the federal commissioner of Vienna—a total of twenty-two to twenty-four men. The great council would be more nearly a corporative body composed of representatives of the self-defense leagues, occupational groups, the Church, appointed members, and occasionally experts called in for specific problems—a total of about fifty persons. The supreme council would appoint the ministers, governors, and members of the state councils, although the Heimwehr, the Church, and the economic groups would nominate their own appointees. Should it seem necessary to allay apprehensions of foreign governments and the home population while the new constitution was being worked out, then a carefully selected assembly would be convened to discuss proposals and suggest improvements.[42]

Even for the Heimwehr leaders it took considerable audacity to propose such a regime. They were assuming much greater political power —and military power, for that matter—than they in fact controlled. The conservative parties had considerable vested interests that the Heimwehr scheme would destroy. From these interests even Seipel met opposition to changes that were less fundamental than these would be. As intimidators of the socialists, the Heimwehr was welcomed by conservative industrialists and big landowners; as rulers, its leaders were hardly needed or desired. Most parliamentary politicians realized that such a frontal assault on democratic practices would not be accepted by the socialists without civil war and that any attempt to institute them would jeopardize the financial support from abroad on which Austria depended.

On October 18 Schober presented his reform bill to the Nationalrat. The proposal went far toward meeting Heimwehr demands concerning the powers of the presidency and the status of Vienna, and would even disallow socialist participation in provincial and local governments where they were in a minority (but not that of nonsocialists in reverse situations). The bill so pleased Mussolini that he let the Heimwehr leaders know that the AS 512,240 they received in mid-October would be the last subsidy, since he expected things soon to evolve to the point that the Austrian government would support them adequately.[43] The Heimwehr greeted the proposal with restrained satisfaction; while praising it as a great success for the movement, the leaders, prompted by Seipel and the *Spannkreis*, warned that it was but a first step toward a corporative state, for it promised only the eventual transformation of parliament's upper house into a chamber representing economic interests. Only as it became clear that Schober, who was permitting committee debates to drag along, might settle for a compromise did the Heimwehr and its foreign backers begin to express anxious impatience. But by then counterpressures were building up.

From late October through early December Austria was wracked by bitter political warfare that at times threatened to erupt into civil war. The Heimwehr held rallies throughout the country and disrupted meetings in which moderates pleaded for compromise with the socialists. At mass demonstrations in Vienna on October 27 and in Graz and Innsbruck on November 12, Heimwehr leaders called for "complete work" with the reforms that they were ready to force through with all the means at their command. While the Heimwehr thus relied upon the threat of violence, the socialists, anxiously on the defensive, made a good show of their determination to guard their interests. They called for compromise and utilized all their connections with sympathetic parties abroad, especially Britain's ruling Labor party and the German and Czech socialists. In a move that appealed to Schober and the foreign press, the socialists threw the onus of aggression on the Heimwehr by proposing complete internal disarmament, any attempt at which Steidle said the Heimwehr would resist by force of arms. Meanwhile, promising resistance if a coup were attempted, the socialists kept the Schutzbund on alert night after night and conducted numerous meetings to explain the situation to their followers and to urge discipline and self-restraint.

By early November the threat of civil war in Austria held the attention of much of Europe. Newspapers in the west made it clear that government and financial circles there deplored the rantings of the Heimwehr and expected moderation and, if possible, disarmament, to prevail in Austria. Although the British government was reluctant to make a démarche directly to the Austrian government, Foreign Minister Arthur Henderson told the House of Commons on November 4 that a "breakdown of the present Parliamentary negotiations, if followed by any attempt to deal with the problem by other means, would naturally cause His Majesty's Government grave concern as constituting a serious menace to international stability." Two days later the French foreign office announced its agreement with Henderson's statement and urged the Austrian government to initiate internal disarmament.[44]

Schober, whose government was still financially dependent on these powers, had no choice but to let their attitude affect his policies. He deftly played his hand well on all sides. While promising the British and French envoys that he would keep the Heimwehr in check, he also sought to soften Mussolini with assurances that he wanted his government to be on the best of terms with Italy and Hungary. He then called the Heimwehr leaders to him early in November and, referring to the country's growing financial uncertainty, cautioned them to exercise restraint.[45] At the same time he began private negotiations with Robert Danneberg, a socialist of moderate views, about a compromise on the constitutional reform issue. The conservative parties were apparently too intimidated by the Heimwehr to work openly in committee with the Social Democrats. By the middle of November Schober and the socialists had reached an agreement, which was not immediately made public.[46]

By this time the Heimwehr and Schober were sharply at odds, and in its propaganda the Heimwehr continued to assert that it would not tolerate a compromise. In desperation the Heimwehr leaders wavered on the brink of action. Visiting Berlin, a leader of the Heimwehr's civilian affiliate in Vienna, the Heimatbund, told officials in the foreign ministry that the Heimwehr leaders, recognizing that they had passed the zenith of their appeal and not wanting to lose all influence, were ready to topple Schober's cabinet if he were unwilling to create a fascist regime. Wavering antisocialists like Minister of Interior Schumy and Kurt von Schuschnigg, a parliamentary deputy, were asked to support a coup d'état. And Steidle once again told Bethlen's liaison that the Heimwehr might have to put Vaugoin in Schober's place.[47]

However, when matters came to a head on November 18, Vaugoin decided to support the chancellor.[48] He realized that a putsch would have but slight chance of success in the face of financial pressure and possible military intervention from abroad. The flight of capital had become so serious that Austrian bankers urged moderation in the reform issue,[49] and Schober was able to get the industrialists to cut their support for the Heimwehr to a trickle.[50] On the afternoon of the eighteenth, Vaugoin informed a cabinet meeting that the Heimwehr in the provinces planned to strike that evening. Pabst had just issued an alarm warning Heimwehr men that it was even possible that they would come into conflict with the state's forces. Ordering large police contingents to occupy all government buildings in Vienna, Schober and Vaugoin summoned the Heimwehr leaders to the chancellory and in a stormy session warned them that a putsch would be met with force. Moreover, Schober threatened Pabst with a close examination of his citizenship status, thereby implicitly threatening the German with expulsion.[51]

Whatever the Heimwehr leaders may have had in mind, their bluff had been called. Vaugoin had given unexpectedly strong support to Schober, and in parliament the three coalition parties, dismayed by Schober's threat of resignation, rallied behind him. Publicly the Heimwehr continued its bombastic opposition to any compromise, but in the face of such opposition, its leaders decided, partly on Seipel's advice, not to attempt a putsch. For about three hours on November 20 Seipel conferred with Steidle, Pfrimer, Pabst, Rauter and Heinrich. Frustrated, they decided to bring pressure on Schober to exclude Schumy from the cabinet and to name Steidle and Pfrimer as ministers of the interior and social administration respectively; they hoped in this way to carry out a putsch from within.[52] Meanwhile, they called off their alert, and the threat of civil war in 1929 began to recede. The chancellor thus gained the upper hand. But he did not actually move against the Heimwehr, for he needed its pressure to get the Social Democrats to agree to any constitutional revision at all.[53]

Until the eve of the passage of the compromise reform bill, the Heimwehr maintained its belligerent stance. Its leaders publicly denied that their relations with Schober were at all strained and boasted that there would be no compromise—while quietly reducing the list of points on which compromise would be unacceptable.[54] Nevertheless, their version of acceptable concessions did not coincide with that of the nonsocialist deputies in parliament. On December 6 Schober informed the Heimwehr chieftains of the contents of the compromise legislation that he would present to the Nationalrat the next day. The measure was a great disappointment to them.

Throughout the night of December 6/7 a large group of angry Heimwehr leaders deliberated on the policy they should adopt toward the pending legislation. They considered trying to topple Schober during the parliamentary debates, but Seipel advised Steidle against such an effort on the grounds that public opinion had not been sufficiently prepared for it either at home or abroad. They grudgingly concluded that they had no choice but to allow the reform bill to pass. At the same time they agreed to continue to campaign for an authoritarian state regardless of the wishes of the parliamentary parties. They were sure that some of the controversial legislative issues coming up in 1930 would lead to the final reckoning with the socialists.[55]

The Nationalrat passed the constitutional revision in only one day. The major effect of the revisions was to end the sovereignty of parliament by balancing it with a presidency having considerable political powers: the president was to be elected by popular vote; he could appoint and dismiss the cabinet, which still had to enjoy the confidence of parliament; he became the commander-in-chief of the armed forces; he received the right to dissolve the Nationalrat, but not indefinitely and only once for the same reason; and when approved by a permanent parliamentary subcommittee, he could issue emergency decrees, which within four weeks the whole Nationalrat had to affirm, amend, or repeal. The status of Vienna as a province was left basically unchanged, as was the system of government in the provinces and smaller communities, where the socialists retained the right to participate in coalition governments. In a ruse made as a gesture to the Heimwehr, the upper chamber was replaced by the "provincial and occupational-estates chamber," but its composition was reserved for a future constitutional amendment and the Bundesrat remained as a "provisional" institution.[56]

The compromise left the Heimwehr leaders dispirited and embarrassed. After all their bombast, their failure was obvious. Their primary goal of fundamentally weakening the SDP, especially in Vienna, had not been realized, and by their excessive demands and threats they had lost the good will of the nonsocialist parties. The ill-fated campaign soon produced bitter dissension and recrimination among the Heimwehr leadership and defections from their following as emotional exhaustion checked the momentum of their "popular" movement. Although Schober tried to assure the Heimwehr leaders of the temporary nature of the reform and of his plans for their organization in the future, they bitterly resented his default on what they took to be definite commitments to them, including backing for a coup d'état. Indeed, Pabst later called Schober "the greatest liar he ever knew."[57] The Heimwehr leaders were also miffed with Mussolini, whose vacillation they partially blamed for ruining their chance for a "forceful solution."[58]

Nevertheless, the Heimwehr refused to admit defeat. If anything, it tried to conceal its quandary with more radical bombast through the rest of December and into January. Together with Seipel, who launched his own drive for further limitations on the Nationalrat and the autonomy of Vienna, it immediately proclaimed the commencement of the "second stage" of their campaign for the "transformation of the state." The "patriotic population" could never be satisfied "with this constitution so mangled by the Austrian bolsheviks."[59] As it turned out, however, the catalytic role that the Heimwehr played in producing the constitution of 1929, an effective instrument that was revived in 1945, marked the high point of its influence in Austrian politics until the Pan-German party defected to the Nazis in 1932. This weakening of the governing coalition finally made Heimwehr support indispensable to a Christian Social party afraid to face the electorate. In the meantime, however, the Heimwehr, still trying to push extreme demands, lost what little cohesion it seemed to have during 1929 and found its wings clipped, first by Schober and then by the voters.

5
Desperate Gambles
Nineteen-thirty

In a New Year's address to the CSP members of the Vienna City Council, Seipel warned that 1930 would be a year of continued unrest in Austria. Because "people are dissatisfied with the old forms of democracy and parliamentarism," further reform was an urgent necessity and could not be accomplished without turmoil.[1] Neither Seipel nor his Heimwehr allies had any intention of letting Austrians rest from the political war against the Social Democrats. They planned to keep tension high by demanding that parliament deal with a succession of controversial issues, culminating in another revision of the constitution. If they could drive the socialists into desperate intransigence the non-socialist majority might be willing to attempt the complete destruction of their political and ideological enemies. But Seipel and the Heimwehr leaders found themselves faced with nearly insurmountable obstacles and were unable to take advantage of the initial effects of the world-wide economic crisis that might otherwise have strengthened their radical movement.

In the first place, Chancellor Schober's preeminence was such that for several months his position was virtually unassailable. As a result of his handling of the constitutional reform in 1929, Schober enjoyed respect and admiration both at home and abroad. At a conference in The Hague early in the new year the parties to the Treaty of Saint-Germain, including Italy, formally renounced their claims to reparations and also to their general lien on Austria's wealth, thereby clearing the way for an international loan. This diplomatic victory was the high point of Schober's career. More important for Schober's position at home was Mussolini's decision to try to influence Austrian developments more through the chancellor than through the Heimwehr. Early in February Schober traveled to Rome to conclude a treaty of friendship and arbitration with Italy and also to convince Mussolini that he could be more efficiently antisocialist than the Heimwehr could be. While Mussolini expressed his protective "sympathy" for the Heimwehr, he asserted that it should remain united and disciplined behind the government, gave

Schober leave to manipulate it as he thought necessary, and did not cavil at Schober's implicit hint that he might have Pabst expelled from Austria.[2] Standing thus at the crest of his powers, Schober could confidently expect to keep the Heimwehr in hand by controlling its finances and replacing its leadership with a more pliable one, in which latter regard he seemed already to have his eye on young Prince Starhemberg, the new leader of the Upper Austrian Heimwehr.[3] Although fearing that he intended to use the Heimwehr merely to extract enough minor concessions from the SDP to keep him in good graces with the bulk of the antisocialist population, the Heimwehr leaders felt that for the moment they had no choice but to go along with the chancellor. In the meantime Seipel, backed by Vaugoin in the cabinet, began to lay the bases for gradually undermining Schober's position.

For some time, however, the general weariness with crises and alarms allowed relatively moderate spokesmen to dominate the political life of the country. Seipel's warning not to demand a year of peace and quiet stirred a storm of disapproval even among large segments of his own party who were suspicious of corporatism, fearful of civil war, and opposed to a Heimwehr dictatorship. In such an atmosphere the Heimwehr leaders, trying to nourish the political antagonisms needed to sustain their extremist movement, found themselves at odds not only with Schober but also with most leaders of the nonsocialist parties. The Heimwehr's unseemly vendetta against Vice-Chancellor Schumy, a Landbund leader from Carinthia, dramatized its difficulties with the parties. Schober supported Schumy vigorously by threatening to withhold financial support from the Heimwehr and by demanding of its leaders, especially Pabst, that it "regulate its position vis-à-vis the government" by "unconditional subordination."[4] When the Heimwehr later tried to force the nonsocialist parties to pledge their support to its "corporative" principles, its new emphasis on ideology only provoked stiffer resistance. Such differences in turn bolstered those elements in the Heimwehr, especially strong in Styria and Carinthia, who wanted to enter election lists in open rivalry with the coalition parties instead of urging their members to vote for any nonsocialist party in the traditional "supraparty" policy. The two big setbacks suffered by the Heimwehr during 1930 occurred when during the spring it pushed its ideological demands to the point of cleavage with the government, and when during the autumn it split over the issue of how to campaign in national elections.

A third obstacle to Heimwehr effectiveness proved to be the dramatic

loss of the cohesion that had given it the appearance of a popular movement. The radical phrase-making about a "second stage" of reform could
not conceal the extent to which the failure of its campaign for a more
extensive revision of the constitution left it weakened and divided.
Early in January Heimwehr spokesmen admitted that a reorganization
involving "some friction" was underway and claimed that a leadership
crisis was desired as a "healing and cleansing process." But they vigorously denied that either of the two federal leaders or Pabst, who was to
seek Austrian citizenship and "sacrifice" his German officer's pension,
would be replaced (though Pabst was then in the process of appealing
the German government's decision to stop his pension). Especially discredited by the unsuccessful campaign of 1929, Pabst had to wend his
way carefully among the contending factions. He did not entirely trust
Seipel because of the latter's clericalism; but, thinking little of Pfrimer's
leadership ability, he reluctantly saw in the old alliance with Steidle
and Seipel the means to his own ends, the creation of a Heimwehr-led
military dictatorship—first in Austria, then in Bavaria, and finally in the
whole German Reich.[5]

Thus, while Pfrimer moved steadily closer to the Nazis, Steidle and
Pabst sought desperately to exert predominant authority in order to
keep the Heimwehr at the disposal of Seipel's program.[6] At a leaders'
meeting late in January it was decided to bring conformity into the
structure and statutes of the different provincial organizations, to give
more attention to economic matters, and "in principle" to create a
corporative constitution. In a long lecture Dr. Walter Heinrich made
his supreme effort to instruct the assembled leaders in "our organic idea
of the state." "The goal is the national, Christian, and social German
state, the bases of which are indicated in German history." The community of the people should be organized around the "major functional
groups [Lebenskreise], the corporations [Stände], which do not, as do
the parties or classes, operate against each other, but live together and
are mutually essential." Although he assured his listeners that the corporative state would be built from the bottom up, he asserted that it "is
only possible if on the corporative foundations one erects a strongly
authoritarian structure." Heinrich was confident that the political elite
in such a system would govern in the interest of all. Thus in his view the
corporative state would overcome class warfare, expertly promote the
economy, advance the common welfare, and be the guardian of social
justice. "It must be attempted, because we will not let ourselves be
annihilated without resistance." The idea and the deed must go to-

gether. A few days later Seipel spoke for the first time before a Heimwehr audience as such and called for the creation of a corporative
chamber as part of the legislature.[7]

By early February the proposed restructuring was largely complete,
at least on paper. Reporting on the changes made during the "lull in the
fighting," Steidle's *Alpenländische Heimatwehr* announced vaguely that
councils of "trusted comrades"—especially the economic and corporative bureau—were to "advise" the federal leadership on political, economic, and military matters. An extensive German intelligence report
gave a more thorough picture of the changes. The purpose of the reorganization was to increase the power of the federal command vis-à-vis
the provincial leaders. The federal headquarters in Innsbruck now
operated in conjunction with a smaller and a larger leaders' council.
The latter was composed of the provincial leaders and chiefs-of-staff
and the directors of six newly created advisory bureaus. Heinrich, as
director of the economic and corporative bureau, had the assignment of
working out the details of the new constitution called for by the Heimwehr program; Secretary of Legation Georg Alexich, who was still in
government service, directed the bureau on foreign policy. The new
storm troops, composed of the earlier "mobile formations" of each province, were now under the federal command of Captain von Prankh, the
Bavarian baron living in Styria, and his deputy Guido Jakoncig, the
lawyer who had created a *Jäger* battalion in Innsbruck. Starhemberg
became the leader of the youth groups; propaganda was directed by
Dr. Hans Riehl, a disciple of Spann; and the press bureau did not yet
have a leader. These changes, never fully instituted, failed to bring
peace to the Heimwehr camp.[8]

The continuing collaboration with Seipel proved to be more divisive
than unifying, and the cracks in the Heimwehr's leadership continued
to widen. The nationalistic elements showed a growing distrust of
Seipel's influence over Steidle as well as increasing irritation at the ties
with Italy. As early as mid-December Eduard Pichl, the nationalistic
leader of the Viennese Heimwehr union, resigned with complaints that
Steidle had ordered him not to preach anti-Semitism and *Anschluss*.[9]
On February 1, at a time when Steidle and Pabst hoped to consolidate
all provincial Heimwehr papers into one daily organ, Starhemberg, who
still stood close to the Nazis and hence to Pfrimer, launched his own
weekly paper, the *Starhemberg-Jäger*.[10] Pfrimer's Styrian and Carinthian following seemed increasingly inclined to make a complete break
with the parliamentary parties. Steidle wanted to continue the policy of
supporting a united front of the established nonsocialist parties but

early felt constrained to indicate that they would have to satisfy Heimwehr wishes in order to prevent it from becoming a separate party.[11]
In March Austrian Nazi leaders decided to try to reach an agreement
with Pfrimer's wing of the Heimwehr for the next parliamentary elections, then expected in the spring of 1931; the following month Pfrimer
entered into a secret compact with the Nazis in which he recognized
Hitler's leadership.[12] In the face of all this dissension, the only way to
maintain any semblance of Heimwehr unity was to revive the antisocialist campaign.

Accordingly, Seipel and the Heimwehr launched the so-called antiterror campaign that dominated the national scene during March and
early April. Just as Schober was moving toward an economic armistice
with the socialists and succeeding in negotiations for a commercial
treaty with Germany, the CSP insisted on the passage of labor legislation that would restrict the influence of the "free" trade unions, which
antisocialists accused of using terror to maintain closed shops. The
Heimwehr cloaked its internal dissensions in the loud demand for a law
to guarantee "freedom of opinion and organization in the shops." The
measure it wanted would make it possible for an employer to extend to
all employees the terms of a contract accepted by a minority of workers.
Naturally, the Social Democrats opposed such extreme aspects of the
bill, and for a while it appeared likely that a stalemate in the negotiations would bring down the Schober government. Finally, however,
moderate elements in the CSP prevailed, and on April 5 the Nationalrat
passed a compromise measure. The law explicitly forbade closed shops,
but a majority of affected workers had to approve any collective contract. There was also a clause that protected employees from exclusion
from work by intimidation or force. The chief impediment to union
activities was the prohibition of the deduction of dues and fees from
wages. The law fell far short of Heimwehr expectations, but by the time
of its passage the leaders were so beset with internal problems that they
accepted it as a victory over bolshevism.[13]

By late March a serious three-way fight for the leadership of the
Heimwehr had developed. Starhemberg began assiduously to seek a
stronger voice in the federal council. Not only did he continue to build
up his forces in Upper Austria, but also he began to play a direct role in
Heimwehr affairs in Vienna and Lower Austria. Although still tending
to side with Pfrimer, Starhemberg at times seemed to direct thrusts
against both federal leaders, and the ideologues complained that his
activities disrupted the educational work of the Heimwehr.[14] Following
a series of shake-ups in the Viennese Heimwehr during which strong-

willed Emil Fey emerged as leader of the union affiliated with the federal command, several of the more radically nationalist groups asked
Starhemberg to assume leadership over them. The resulting muddle
almost toppled Steidle and Pfrimer, but at a leaders' meeting on April 9
and 10 they recognized Starhemberg's new *Jägerfreikorps-Wien*, composed of the dissident groups, as a constituent part of Fey's umbrella
association. By this tortuous route they managed to preserve the façade
of unity, correctly labeled by the *Arbeiter-Zeitung* as a "truce in Viennese affairs."[15]

More important was the dispute over the leadership of the Lower
Austrian Heimwehr, where Julius Raab was also caught in the clash
between the antiparty nationalists and those who favored working with
the bourgeois parties. Early in the year Pfrimer and Starhemberg attacked Raab, who was close to Seipel, for his subservience to the CSP,
but they did not force a showdown then because of the Bauernbund's
support of Raab. Nevertheless, Starhemberg continued to jockey for
influence in Lower Austria and early in April asserted that he should be
allowed to take charge there, "since he had done such a good job in
Upper Austria." When Raab protested that he wanted to remain independent of both the Upper Austrian and Styrian associations, the federal leaders promised to settle the leadership question at a general
assembly of Lower Austrian leaders on May 18. Starhemberg then
joined Steidle and Pfrimer in issuing a statement urging people not to
"be misled" by rumors of discord among them, but never explicitly
stating that the three were in basic agreement.[16] On May 4 there were
two Heimwehr rallies in Lower Austria, a well-attended one for Starhemberg's adherents at Laxenburg and one for Raab's followers at St.
Pölten, whose poor attendance his friends in government, Governor
Buresch and Army Minister Vaugoin, tried to conceal by an unnecessary use of federal troops against the alerted Schutzbund, by which
action Vaugoin may also have wanted to embarrass Schober, who was
then in London.[17]

Throughout this period the Heimwehr continued its feud with
Schober, especially over a modest proposal to regulate the possession of
arms. Still trying to procure an international loan, Schober sought western sympathy by reiterating in a confidential letter to the League of
Nations his pledge to regulate civilian armament. Through a chancery
official Schober assured the Italian and Hungarian governments that he
did not intend actually to disarm the Heimwehr. But the Heimwehr
leaders feared further treachery by the chancellor, and on March 27
Steidle and Pfrimer jointly addressed a letter to Bethlen requesting a

large supply of weapons and ammunition to provide arms to the Heimwehren of Vienna and Lower Austria so that they could then refuse to
surrender. For the moment, however, Mussolini convinced Bethlen not
to make further difficulties for Schober, whose fall the *Duce* feared
would be followed by a new Seipel regime. Until Schober's letter became public knowledge in late April, the Heimwehr continued its pre-
tense of support for the chancellor. Thereafter they broke sharply with
Schober and adamantly opposed the slightest gesture toward "disarmament."[18] As a result of the conflict with Schober, the Heimwehr leaders
tried to resolve their rivalry and sought a means to force sympathetic
politicians to do their bidding. They hoped thereby both to defeat
Schober's "disarmament" bill in the Nationalrat and to accelerate their
drive toward a corporative state.

In pursuit of these goals the Heimwehr stumbled into the so-called
oath of Korneuburg at the meeting of Lower Austrian leaders on May
18. The meeting was originally planned to settle the dispute over the
provincial leadership, and the *Neue Freie Presse* had detected no hint
of plans for anything more extraordinary than that. It was generally
expected that the vociferous and radical nationalist forces, backed by
Pfrimer and Starhemberg, would overthrow Raab. But Steidle, who
only the week before had made a vague prophecy of an antidemocratic
"cultural deed that can have decisive significance perhaps for all of
central Europe,"[19] worked feverishly to keep the Lower Austrian Heimwehr in his camp. He hoped that victory in Lower Austria would force
the whole CSP, and not only Raab, who was a Christian Social deputy
in the Nationalrat, to support corporative principles as well as to oppose
Schober's "disarmament" legislation. In a long speech at Korneuburg
Steidle rejected the idea prevalent in Styrian and Carinthian circles that
no Heimwehr leader should hold elective office as a party member, but
he asserted that party discipline should be subordinated to Heimwehr
interests, that party politicians owed their primary allegiance to the
federal Heimwehr leaders. The fateful question for the politicians was
whether or not they wanted to declare themselves for the fascist system,
"a clear and simple formula." If Raab would make that choice, they
would all go further together, but if Raab insisted that the Heimwehr
was to be solely the servant of the parties, they would go separate ways.
Steidle asked for a clear yes or no to the "confession" that he then read
to the unsuspecting assembly. The programmatic allegiance to dictatorship read by Steidle left his audience in great confusion. Steidle gained
an ephemeral victory when Raab somewhat ambiguously declared that
he was "also today . . . in accord with the goals of the federal com-

mand." Moreover, all but one of the twenty party politicians present expressed their agreement with Steidle's statement, although many later claimed that in the confusion they did not know what was happening. Steidle clearly stole a march on those who wanted the Heimwehr to become what amounted to an adjunct of the Nazi party. With Raab's pledge of allegiance to Steidle's dictatorial, corporative program, the nationalists lost their excuse to overthrow him. Pfrimer felt constrained to cheer the turn toward "fascism" as a "historic moment" in the movement; he hoped that it would lead the Heimwehr to sever its ties with the CSP and to move toward a seizure of power. But he and his followers were nonetheless angered at the lack of a clear pledge to anticlerical and *völkisch* principles. Steidle, who pushed the meeting along quickly, adjourned it before Starhemberg, who first had to attend a rally in Upper Austria, could arrive.[20]

Exactly what Steidle read as his confession is not known. There are several reports to the effect that what he actually said differed considerably from what later became the official version. According to one account that has the ring of authenticity, Walter Heinrich composed the statement in great haste just before the meeting began, and Steidle did not know its exact contents before he read it to the assembly. Only after he and Pabst, together with Pfrimer, had reworked Heinrich's draft, which Pabst later called "too sharp," did they release a written text to the press. By then Starhemberg, too, had been persuaded by Steidle to go along with their statement of principles, despite the fact that he felt tricked by the whole affair.[21] The *Neue Freie Presse* of May 19 omitted parts of the controversial Heimwehr oath, but on May 20 the government's *Wiener Zeitung* quoted the final version of the text, which reads as follows:

We want to renew Austria from the ground up!

We want the people's state [*Volksstaat*] of the Heimatschutz.

We demand of each comrade: indomitable faith in the fatherland, indefatigable zeal in serving, and passionate love of homeland.

We want to reach for [*greifen nach*] the power in the state and to remold the state and economy for the benefit of the whole people.

We must [completely] forget individual advantage, must unconditionally subordinate connection with, and demands of, the parties to the objective of our struggle, for we want to serve the community of the German people!

We reject western democratic parliamentarism and the party state.

We want to put in its place the self-administration of the corporations [*Stände*] and a strong state leadership, which will be formed, not by party representatives, but by the leading persons of the large corporations and by the most capable and most proven men of our popular movement.

We fight against the disintegration [*Zersetzung*] of our people by the Marxist class struggle and the liberal capitalistic economic order.

We want to realize the self-administration of the economy on an occupational-corporative basis. We will overcome the class struggle and establish social dignity and justice.

We want to improve the welfare of our people by a fundamentally sound [*bodenstark*] and commonly shared economy.

The state is the embodiment of the whole people; its power and leadership see to it that the corporations remain subservient to the needs of the whole people.

Every comrade should feel and confess himself to be a bearer of the new German conception of the state [*Staatsgesinnung*]; he should be prepared to risk possessions and life; he should recognize [*erkenne*] three powers: faith in God, his own hard will, and the command of his leaders![22]

All commentary at the time emphasized the spontaneity of the Korneuburg oath.[23] It was at once a desperate measure to reestablish Heimwehr unity, a reckless challenge to the nonsocialist parties and the government's proposed arms legislation, and a statement of principles. The *Neue Freie Presse* of May 20 called it a surprisingly offensive "political accident." Indeed, what caught the country by surprise and provoked a storm of controversy within the CSP and of opposition from the Landbund and Pan-German Party was Steidle's explicit political challenge rather than the contents of the Heimwehr ideological confession, which had been generally known for several months if not for several years.[24] It was also surprising that the Heimwehr would attempt to promulgate a formal creed in view of the divergent outlooks of many of its members. In this regard Steidle may have been perturbed by charges that the Heimwehr had the capacity to destroy the existing system but no plans—not to speak of ability—for constructing something new (in his prophetic speech on May 10 Steidle had spoken of a "dictatorship of reconstruction"). Moreover, he was pushed toward adopting an exclusive corporative program by Heinrich, Riehl, and Spann. They had already done considerable work on an explicit statement of Heimwehr aims. Heinrich surely envisaged his version of the oath as a solemn step toward the creation of a corporative state, not as a tactical weapon for settling an internal Heimwehr dispute or for fighting a minor piece of legislation. Pabst, influenced by Heinrich but not having much personal interest in the notion of corporatism, primarily hoped to institute in the Heimwehr the *Führerprinzip* to end its provincial particularism and thus hasten a putsch to transform Austria into his healthy kernel of Germandom—in other words, a militaristic dictatorship pure and simple. Steidle was thus pulled between the corporative and dictatorial views of Heinrich and Pabst on one hand and pressured by Pfrimer's antiparty feelings on the other. All in all, seen as a proclamation of principles, the Korneuburg oath served only to inject greater bitterness and petty partisanship into the political life of the republic. As an effort at maintaining Heimwehr unity, it provoked further discord; and as an attempt to exert pressure on the government, it only stiffened resistance.

This Korneuburg oath immediately became the subject of fierce controversy within the Heimwehr and throughout the country. For the moment Steidle retained the major voice in the federal command, since as a CSP delegate to the Bundesrat he was trying to gain control of that party. But Starhemberg kept alive the rivalry for leadership by criticizing the oath and by threatening to keep the Upper Austrian Heimwehr from pledging allegiance to it, a pledge which was demanded from all provincial associations. The nonsocialist parties felt compelled to take a position regarding the oath, and the ensuing controversy nearly tore the CSP apart. The whole issue became more critical in the face of an even sharper and more immediate challenge to the governing parties issued by the Heimwehr on May 21.

On May 20 Schober, who did not react publicly to the events at Korneuburg, and Vaugoin discussed "recent events" and the arms legislation they planned to introduce with Steidle, Pfrimer, Pabst, Starhemberg, and Rauter. As Schober told the cabinet later that day, there was no meeting of minds whatsoever, although he tried to explain to the Heimwehr men that he had to carry a minimal arms control law to satisfy the British government.[25] The next day Steidle and Pfrimer published an open letter that amounted to a demand for Heimwehr control of the country's police forces. Implicitly acknowledging that their displeasure with the "disarmament" bill—which insultingly "equated" the Heimwehr with the Schutzbund—might jeopardize an international loan, they claimed to speak for all the patriotic population and to accept responsibility for the fate of the fatherland. Peace in Austria was possible only with the Heimwehr, not against it. Men enjoying the Heimwehr's confidence should administer the interior portfolios at both the federal and provincial levels while Heimwehr and government forces worked together in disarming and disbanding the Schutzbund, the real cause of all the unrest in the country. Unless these conditions were met, the Heimwehr would oppose any disarmament legislation, no matter how innocuous.[26]

This ill-advised ultimatum left the Heimwehr in a very exposed position and invited a rebuff from the government and the parties even more than did the Korneuburg oath. The *Neue Freie Presse* attacked it as a serious mistake: nothing would be more humiliating for the Heimwehr than the impression of a lack of earnestness, and "their document deserves only a shrug of the shoulders, for even the Heimwehr leaders cannot believe it realizeable." The cabinet met on May 22 and, after a lengthy discussion of Heimwehr policy, unanimously rejected the demands. In presenting the truly innocuous disarmament bill to the Nationalrat the next day, both Chancellor Schober and Vice-Chancellor Schumy addressed the Heimwehr in "language hitherto used only by socialist speakers." The chancellor "regretted" to have to reject outright the recent demands, but he explicitly warned the Heimwehr not to endanger public law and order. Schumy, whose interior portfolio was the main target of the Heimwehr demands, challenged his opponents to prove their following through the "legal democratic way" of elections; he also renounced his disputed membership in the Carinthian Heimatschutz.[27]

In this case the Heimwehr was true to its word. The legislation merely stipulated that the federal chancellery instead of the provincial governments would be competent to regulate the possession of arms, and said nothing about disarmament. Nevertheless, the Heimwehr's opposition to the bill remained adamant. It publicly objected that someday a socialist chancellor would use the law against the Heimwehr, but feared that Schober himself might do so. In typical extremist fashion, Steidle pressed the attack ad hominem: he accused Schober of "protecting the bolsheviks" by trying to weaken the militancy of the "indigenous folk." Had the government accepted the Heimwehr's disarmament "suggestions," it would have been embarrassing, because then the Heimwehr would have had "further to protect the present system." But now it was "free of all obligations to put itself at the disposal of a system that has proved itself wrong." Steidle's breach with Schober was complete.[28]

Coming on top of the Korneuburg oath, the Heimwehr's intransigent opposition to the disarmament bill further provoked hostile reaction from all sections of the moderate nonsocialist population. Both the Landbund and the Pan-German Party decided to make no accommodation whatsoever with the Korneuburg program. Numerous figures in the CSP spoke out against the Heimwehr, including labor leader Leopold

Kunschak, peasant leader Josef Reither, who abruptly severed the Lower Austrian Bauernbund's union with the Heimwehr, and Governor Otto Ender of Vorarlberg, who as leader of the province's Heimatdienst warned Steidle that a separate Heimwehr party in his province would secure little following.

The national CSP, however, with Vaugoin as its new chairman and Seipel still an influential voice, proved less able to withstand Heimwehr pressure than its branch in tiny Vorarlberg. Representatives of the party held a series of talks with several Heimwehr leaders—with the notable exception of Pfrimer—that culminated on June 4 in an ambiguous compromise permitting mutual toleration. Steidle at first offered to support the CSP in the approaching elections (required by April 1931) if the party would promptly overthrow Schober. Seipel also spoke out against Schober, but, because Vaugoin wanted to wait until the chancellor had appointed the CSP's candidate to head the federal railways, the conferees refused to grant Steidle's extreme demands. The final compromise, proposed by Governor Ender, stated that "even a Christian Social deputy can pursue also the battle aims of the Heimwehr, as they were defined in conversations between the leaders of the Heimwehr and representatives" of the CSP. It was understood, however, that the Heimwehr would not undertake anything against the "legal conduct of the affairs of state," that party interests would take precedence over those of the Heimwehr, and that the leaders of the two organizations were to exchange opinions about politics. Even this mild concession to the Heimwehr represented a weakening of the CSP's ability to control it.[29]

Although the federal command hastened to announce that they had made no changes in the text of the Korneuburg oath, it was obvious that their power grab had failed. Steidle's inability to push through his extreme demands made an open split within the Heimwehr even more likely. By early June Lerchenfeld heard from various sources that the days of Steidle and Pabst were numbered and that Starhemberg, at this time still closely associated with radical nationalist policies, would probably succeed them. Heimwehr subordinates in Upper Austria announced that they would give their allegiance only to Starhemberg, and the *Tagespost* (Linz) asserted that Steidle would have to go if the Heimwehr was to be held together.[30] On one side Steidle was criticized for having brought the Heimwehr into open conflict with the bourgeois parties, and from another side he was upbraided for not being radical enough. In another indication of the split, an unnamed Heimwehr representative approached the German People's Party for funds in support of the moderate "bourgeois" wing against the "militant" wing.[31] Behind the scenes both Schober and Seipel worked toward a change in the Heimwehr's leadership. Each of them expected to be able to control its policies through the impressionable and inconsistent Starhemberg. Schober, in conjunction with his colleague Schumy, continued to make plans to deport Pabst, and he won Italian approval for his intervention in the Heimwehr leadership during a secret visit to Vienna by Foreign Minister Grandi. The chancellor also arranged a meeting between Grandi and Starhemberg, apparently the prince's first contact with Italian fascism. Grandi informed Starhemberg of the wasted financial "sacrifices" Italy had made for the Heimwehr, thus giving the prince a weapon to use against Steidle and Pabst. Grandi also advised Starhemberg to try to keep the Heimwehr united and to expend its energy against the socialists, not against Schober and the bourgeois parties, a line that Starhemberg soon reflected in his attacks against Steidle.[32]

With the Heimwehr thus disoriented, the government was free not only to push its disarmament bill through the Nationalrat, but also to strike a more direct and disruptive blow at the "irresistible movement." Neither the fulminations of the Heimwehr leaders, especially Pfrimer and Fey, nor five Heimwehr meetings held throughout Vienna on June 13 prevented the Nationalrat from passing the bill in its second reading on that day, after rejecting all socialist efforts to put real teeth into the law.

Then, almost before the Heimwehr leaders could denounce the bill's passage, Schober had Pabst arrested in Vienna on the fourteenth. Accusing him of impermissible interference in Austria's internal affairs, federal authorities deported him—he chose to go to Italy—as an undesirable alien on the next day.[33] The government carried out its well-prepared stroke against the Heimwehr swiftly and unexpectedly. The official communique attributed the responsibility for the decision to Schumy, while Schober "supported" the action of his minister of the interior and in the Bundesrat told Steidle that, until Korneuburg, he had been able to prevent Schumy's having Pabst expelled. But the initiative for the arrest really lay with Schober, who had become completely estranged from Pabst and feared his organizational ability and determination to seize power for the Heimwehr. The government's statement attacked Pabst's role in recent "unpleasant incidents" in the Heimwehr, such as the Korneuburg oath and the opposition to the disarmament law. But apparently Schober was much more concerned about the evidence that Pabst had been trying to subvert Austria's army and police forces, which may have been one reason why Vaugoin, albeit somewhat reluctantly, approved the arrest and deportation. Schober was also irritated by Pabst's continued efforts to sabotage an international loan.[34]

The almost passive way in which the Heimwehr took this affront demonstrated the impotence of the movement, and the Social Democrats cheered this reaction as the *Heimwehrdämmerung*. The Heimwehr leaders, already at odds with each other, were left dazed and perplexed by the loss of the one real unifying personality in the national organization, although some may not have been sorry to be rid of Pabst, whose overbearing authority was somewhat resented and whose policies, especially since Korneuburg, were seen as unfortunate, even in the Tyrol. Nevertheless, the Tyroleans appeared genuinely upset about the expulsion. The Tyrolean government issued an official protest, and Governor Stumpf hastened to Vienna to seek competence for granting executive clemency, but to no avail. There were protest demonstrations in Innsbruck throughout the weekend, and the *Alpenländische Heimatwehr* called the deportation a "stab in the back." However, the call by Guido Jakoncig, a friend of Pabst's and the leader of the Innsbruck storm companies, for a mobilization of the entire Heimwehr as a demonstration against the deportation went unheeded.[35] Outside the Tyrol the country remained calm. In Upper Austria Starhemberg decried such treatment of a loyal German compatriot while corrupt non-German immigrants went unmolested, but at the same time he ordered "all comrades" to maintain strict discipline and not "to undertake anything without my express command." Trying to strike a tough pose, Pfrimer accused Schober of having gone back on all the assurances he made to the Heimwehr before he took office. As Lerchenfeld noted, however, all the Heimwehr pronouncements seemed somewhat restrained; caught off guard in a weak moment, there was not much its leaders could do.[36]

As Schober had calculated, his insulting blow, far from giving the Heimwehr a rallying cry for concerted action, actually accelerated its disintegration. At a conference in Leoben on June 16 its leaders boasted that they would not—"as hoped"—allow themselves to be provoked by the government's action. Later reports alleged that in vain Othmar Spann urged the conferees to take up arms in defense of their idea. Instead, they merely protested the deportation and announced that they would try to secure its recision. Behind a shield of secrecy there raged a turbulent struggle for control of the organization. Steidle bore the brunt of the anger at the Heimwehr's severe setback and was taken to task for the way he and Pabst—who had received personal funds from Germany in addition to a large Heimwehr salary—had squandered their resources. Steidle agreed to restrict his activities for a time chiefly to Vorarlberg, the Tyrol, and Salzburg. Other personnel shifts made at Leoben indicated that Pfrimer, who was less publicly associated with the ill-fated policies, would be the rising Starhemberg's strongest rival: Pabst would remain the nominal chief-of-staff, but Pfrimer's lieutenant, Hans Rauter, temporarily assumed his duties; another Styrian, Sepp Hainzl, a farmer from the upper Mur Valley, was added to the inner council; and the central offices were transferred from Vienna to Graz. Besides these realignments, one German intelligence agent reported a "fundamental change" in the Heimwehr: the leaders agreed to sever the close ties with the Spann circle and return to the "original mission" —which was "to create a chiefly military formation." Heimwehr papers indeed began to downplay and to reinterpret into harmlessness the Korneuburg oath. Observers saw the Heimwehr now at a crossroads, where it had to decide whether to remain a supraparty supporter of the coalition government or to go its own way as a separate party.[37]

A Heimwehr party was again being mooted, but the discussion merely proved the degree of confusion and uncertainty within the movement. Shortly after he arrived in Venice Pabst told a correspondent of the *Corriere della Sera* that he would withdraw from Austrian politics, but that the Heimwehr would continue to pursue its goals by seeking seats in parliament. The Heimwehr press agency immediately denied such intentions. Then on June 25 Rokitansky, editor of an extremely prodictatorial journal, announced the creation of the "Austrian Heimatschutz Party, economic-political community of the creating estates." He contended both that he acted in conjunction with the dissident Viennese Heimwehr fascist, Fritz Heger, and that Starhemberg did not object to his move. At a meeting in Leoben on June 30 the Heimwehr leaders denied any connections with the new party; and the *Heimatschutz-Zeitung* asserted that Heger's new venture had nothing to do with Starhemberg's Viennese Jägerfreikorps. But Rokitansky retorted that Pabst also was for his party and desired a union between it and the Heimwehr: "Pabst . . . could not always do what he wanted, but always knew what he wanted." Soon thereafter, an anonymous Styrian "labor leader" called for the Heimwehr to send a revolutionary vanguard into parliament to serve as a means to an end, not as an end in itself as a party would.[38] These exchanges were but agitated flurries while the Heimwehr leaders were trying to find some means of recovering their lost influence.

During the remainder of the summer Schober worked to bring the chastened Heimwehr safely under his control. He allowed Governors

Stumpf and Rintelen to smooth the way for publicly announced talks
between him and representatives of the Heimwehr, chiefly Starhemberg
and Rauter, and made a few meaningless concessions to their face-
saving efforts, such as agreeing "in principle" to allow Pabst a brief visit
to straighten out his personal affairs and appointing the honorary treas-
urer of the Viennese Heimwehr, an elderly industrialist named Dr.
Friedrich Schuster, as minister of commerce. By early June the Heimwehr press saw "an improvement of relations" and announced that it
would do "everything possible" to maintain the unity of the anti-Marxist
front. In a more meaningful intervention, however, Schober continued
to manipulate the Heimwehr leadership, while at the same time keeping
the Heimwehr leaders under close surveillance.[39] He persuaded Austrian industrialists to suspend payments to Steidle and to channel them
instead through Starhemberg, while industry in Styria continued to
support Pfrimer. Through private talks Schober also cultivated ties with
Starhemberg,[40] who became an even more serious contender for Heimwehr leadership after personal visits with both Bethlen and Mussolini
in early summer. The two premiers were at the time assiduously wooing
Schober away from a new diplomatic initiative in central Europe recently undertaken by France and were hopeful, moreover, that Schober
would soon cleanse the Austrian railways of socialist personnel in order
to facilitate trans-shipment of arms. Hence they desired the Heimwehr
to be a dependable instrument in the chancellor's hands and advised
Starhemberg accordingly. Mussolini, who apparently impressed Starhemberg greatly and promised him financial support, urged him to seek
sole leadership of the Heimwehr, to strengthen its military capacity, and
to build a united front with the government parties to oppose the
socialists at the next elections.[41]

Thus backed by heads of government at home and abroad, and at the
same time on good terms with Seipel, Starhemberg jockeyed for the
Heimwehr leadership. He continued his attacks on Steidle and demanded, albeit not before the public, that the Tyrolean account in
detail for his expenditures of the earlier Italian aid; indeed so impa-
tiently did he complain that the Italian minister in Vienna, Auriti, im-
plored him to keep the matter quiet. Starhemberg demonstratively
absented himself from a leaders' meeting in Innsbruck at the end of
July, at which Pfrimer and Steidle further weakened each other by en-
gaging in more mutual recriminations. Nevertheless, for the moment
agreeing to continue their collaboration, they publicly adopted a moderate line free of any attack on Schober. While they asserted that the

Heimwehr would have the decisive word in the next elections, it was obvious that the two men disagreed on the extent to which they would work with the existing parties. Steidle, who still looked to Seipel for guidance, had backed far away from his Korneuburg demands and was willing to support the clerical wing of the CSP, while Pfrimer, steadily moving closer to Hitler's camp, wanted to campaign independently of the coalition parties. There existed a sufficient rift between the two federal leaders for Starhemberg to thrust his wedge. On September 1 Schober told the British minister, Sir Eric Phipps, that he expected early and favorable developments in the Heimwehr situation.[42]

The next day Starhemberg won election as the sole federal leader during a stormy conference at a private villa in the northwestern Styrian town of Schladming. From the divergent accounts of the meeting, it is clear that the old leaders did not give up without a fight, both against Starhemberg and against each other. Apparently Steidle won some sympathy with revelations of "intrigues" against him, but he found himself isolated after Julius Raab, the Lower Austrian leader, nominated Starhemberg in such a manner as to make it seem that the CSP opposed Steidle. Pfrimer remained in contention, but his lackluster personality was not able to command the allegiance of his disenchanted colleagues; even the Styrian delegation could not agree unanimously to support him. Although none of the several accounts of how the eleven votes— representing the nine provinces, the Railroad Guard, and the Turnerbund—were cast give the same picture, they make it clear that several ballots were taken and that the proceedings must have been acrimonious.[43]

A change in Heimwehr leadership had long been in the offing, but both the timing of the switch and the fact that the youthful Starhemberg emerged as sole leader caught the public by surprise. Only thirty-one years old, Starhemberg was in many ways still a boy-soldier, albeit one of ancient aristocratic lineage. Named after the illustrious count who commanded the defense of Vienna through the siege of 1683, he was trained by his officer-father in the arts of knighthood. He went off to war in 1916, served two years on the Russian and Italian fronts, and experienced as a "personal shame" the collapse of the Habsburg Empire in which his world "broke completely apart." He had developed a thoroughly military mentality, although in his preference for the comradeship of the fighting unit to the aloofness of his rank he was a disappointment to his father. After trying for two years to escape his postwar disappointment and boredom—often "in city amusement places"—Star-

hemberg enrolled in political science courses at the University of
Innsbruck. His studies were soon interrupted by the excitement of the
Heimatwehr shooting match late in November 1920 and by Steidle's
oratory, which awakened in him a desire "to become a good speaker
some day." Following the adventure of smuggling and stealing arms in
the winter, he joined the group of nationalist students under Ludwig
Draxler who fought as part of the Freikorps Oberland in upper Silesia
in the summer of 1921. When he returned to Innsbruck in October, he
felt that the Heimatwehr had already become unimaginative and ultra-
conservative; he impulsively helped found a revival of the Oberland and
moved to Munich, where he became an admirer of Hitler. Although he
marched in the rear ranks during the putsch on 9 November 1923, and
later helped Göring escape to Austria, he did not join the Nazi party,
since he disdained political parties "and everything that goes with
them." For two more years Starhemberg remained in Munich, becoming
active in student politics at the university and, in the middle of 1924,
training for six months with the "underground" German Reichswehr.
Early in 1926 he returned to Upper Austria, where he intended to
devote himself "to civilian activity and useful work."[44]

The Social Democratic *Linzer Programm* of November 1926 re-
awakened Starhemberg's interest in the Heimwehr movement, and after
July 1927 he began to organize the farmers of his native district (the
Mühlviertel) into active local groups. The death of his father in November 1927 left him a princely title, responsibility for the family estates,
and a large personal inheritance. The excitement connected with the
Aufmarsch at Wiener Neustadt in 1928 called him back to the green-
white banner. With an impromptu speech—a "rip-snorting patriotic
wringer"—to a gathering at an inn following the first provincial Heimwehr convocation in Upper Austria on 14 October 1928, he convinced
himself of his ability to sway men: "On that evening began my fight for
Austria." The *Heimatschutz in Oesterreich* made much of the fact that
Starhemberg's "magnificent leadership qualities and his significant
political abilities" let him climb quickly from local to regional leader.
His assets were considerable: a famous name, lithe youthfulness, brash
nationalism, and—far from least—his family fortune. Starhemberg used
the latter to organize the rural citizenry into Jäger, in effect feudal
armies, many of them mobile and all of them well armed and loyal to
him personally. With the backing of these groups and with the support
of Pfrimer, he was able to push aside the collegium of party-connected
leaders and become sole provincial leader in July 1929. In the following
year he brought the Heimwehr of Upper Austria to its height: forty

thousand activists, one-half of whom were organized into twenty-three
Jäger battalions.[45]

From his Upper Austrian base Starhemberg successfully spread his
Jäger formations and his bid for power into Vienna and portions of
Lower Austria and Salzburg. He claimed to view the Heimwehr as a
support for the state's weak military forces, not as a political party.
There is no reason to doubt his assertion that he "came into the political
arena . . . as a soldier," and that he generally held politicians in contempt.
Until he acquired a position of national responsibility, his political in-
experience and inconsistency—if not ineptitude—were not exceedingly
noticeable or detracting. All too suddenly, however, Starhemberg found
himself in the spotlight, not only in Austria, but also in the struggle for
Austria between her southern and northern neighbors.

It was clear from the various comments on Starhemberg's elevation
that the country did not know what to expect from him, especially with
regard to the upcoming parliamentary elections. Although most observers viewed him as an extreme nationalist, they also knew that he was
very erratic and impressionable. It was known that Starhemberg, who
visited Hitler late in the spring of 1930, was sympathetic with the Nazis,
but also that he had ties with the officers and aristocrats in the CSP. At
the same time he seemed to remain aloof from all parties, relying on his
private military units to force a hearing. Under him the Heimwehr
could move in one of several directions: collaborate with the Nazis, become the partisan tool of the CSP, support any bourgeois government in
power, or attempt to establish itself as a separate paramilitary party.
The *Volkswirt* caustically concluded that since Starhemberg could mean
anything to anybody he was "certainly the right leader for the unified
Heimwehr movement."[46]

Behind the scenes the country's two most prominent nonsocialist politicians sought to dominate the new Heimwehr leader. Phipps called the
shelving of Steidle and Pfrimer a "distinct feather in the Chancellor's
cap," and Lerchenfeld assumed that Schober, who clearly thought the
change would mean less Heimwehr hostility toward his cabinet, sent
directions to Starhemberg through a third man. Although Schober contributed greatly to Steidle's fall, it is doubtful that he was in a position
to dictate the selection of Starhemberg over Pfrimer. Starhemberg's ties
with Bethlen and Mussolini probably had more to do with his election
than those with Schober. Moreover, from what is known of Julius
Raab's role at Schladming it is quite likely that Seipel, who still hoped
to make the Heimwehr suitable coalition material for the CSP, also had
a hand in influencing pro-CSP provincial leaders to vote for Starhem-

berg. But no one was sure who would control Starhemberg after his election or, for that matter, whether he would be able to hold the confederation together.[47]

Starhemberg immediately issued a proclamation calling for unity and pledging himself to pursue the old goals of the Heimwehr, the "hope and future of our people and fatherland." For a few days it was not certain whether either Steidle or Pfrimer would cooperate with the new regime; in one speech Steidle stopped just short of declaring the Tyrolean Heimatwehr "independent." In the end Starhemberg was able to hold the confederation together for a few more months, just as Steidle had earlier done, by making concessions to the Styrians. Pfrimer agreed to become deputy leader, and Rauter remained chief-of-staff, with Mayer of Upper Austria as his deputy; Oberegger, the labor leader from Donawitz, took over the administration of the central office. In addition, Starhemberg must have made some political commitments to the Styrians, but they remain unverified. Franz Winkler, the Landbund leader in Styria, asserted that Starhemberg pledged in writing—with his "princely word of honor"—to lead the Heimwehr "in the greater German sense without compromise against the parties of the parliamentary system," to destroy the existing Marxist and Catholic labor unions, and to establish Heimwehr youth and women's auxiliaries against the Christian Socials, which, in fact, the Styrians had already begun to do. On the other hand, Raab later claimed that Starhemberg promised not to lead the Heimwehr against the CSP. Starhemberg did not cast any light on the matter when he announced that he would not make any programmatic declarations, that he would think everything through and then act rather than talk.[48]

At first Starhemberg himself was probably more concerned with the organization's striking force than with its partisan alignments.

Out of a narrow-minded and rather inert movement I hoped to create an active political fighting force. I did not intend that it should lose its indigenous peasant and bourgeois character. Yet, within this large and somewhat immobile force, I aspired to create a formation on the lines of a Free Corps, which would impart to the Heimwehr the necessary mobility and dynamism. . . . I wanted to pick out from the 200,000 Heimwehr about 40,000 to 50,000 able bodied men to form storm battalions. This would provide the force necessary to back up our political ideology.

To acquire sufficient arms for such a force he collaborated with Julius Gömbös, Hungary's minister of war and an occasional hunting partner. They hoped to get from Mussolini and divide between them the one hundred thousand Austrian rifles captured by Italy in the war, with Starhemberg to be responsible for arranging their shipment into and through Austria. However, before Starhemberg could act on these plans, which were later to create an international scandal, the unexpected fall of Schober's cabinet on September 25, as he put it, "upset all my plans and made me concentrate my efforts in other directions."[49]

In one of the least defensible acts of his public career, Vice-Chancellor and Minister of War Vaugoin, who was also chairman of the CSP, withdrew his party's support of Schober's coalition. For some time the CSP —still influenced by Seipel—had been trying to oust Schober. But the unsavory issue Vaugoin used to force his resignation helped produce an irreparable split among the parties which had ruled together since 1927. For over a year the administration of the federal railway system, in which the Christian Socials sought to reduce the influence of the Social Democrats, had been a potentially explosive issue. Early in 1930 Schober tentatively agreed to the appointment of the CSP candidate for the general directorship, controversial Dr. Franz Strafella, who had "reorganized" Graz's streetcar system to the detriment of the socialists. But Strafella carried the taint of corruption. When the Social Democrats, in an effort to defeat his candidacy, accused him of profiteering and tax evasion, Schober insisted that the appointment to which he had already agreed now be contingent upon the outcome of Strafella's libel suit against the *Arbeiter-Zeitung*. The divided verdict, part acquittal and part conviction, was a moral condemnation of Strafella, and Schober refused to proceed with the appointment. At this juncture Vaugoin resigned and was immediately asked by President Miklas to form a cabinet.

The consequences of this maneuver made it more than an ugly episode. In fact, this cabinet crisis and its immediate sequel marked the beginning of that prolonged governmental instability to which the republic eventually succumbed. Had the CSP used some excuse other than Strafella to depose Schober, they might have saved the coalition. However, in view of the heavy Nazi vote in the German elections on September 14, the CSP was probably less concerned with saving the coalition than with holding elections as the governing party—hopefully in conjunction with the Heimwehr—before Nazi sentiment in Austria became much stronger. Given the worsening economic conditions and the growth of German-nationalist opposition, Austria could hardly avoid the threat of tumult and instability. But, especially in view of the fact that long-term collaboration with the socialists was hardly a feasible option for them, the Christian Social leaders were very unwise in thus risking the estrangement of the parties loyal to Schober and in setting the precedent of a minority government. Moreover, in opening to the Heimwehr the opportunity to become something more than an armed troop outside the political arena their tactics bordered on the irresponsible.

At first the Heimwehr, which had earlier loudly pushed Strafella's candidacy but had seemingly remained out of the final controversy, was of divided counsel over the policy it should pursue. After Starhemberg, surprised by the not unwelcome news of Schober's fall, returned from Hungary, the federal command greeted Vaugoin as chancellor designate and called for a continuation of the coalition, which was necessary "to hold Marxism in check." When, however, the Landbund and the Pan-Germans demanded the retention of Schober as chancellor, the coalition collapsed. Under the tutelage of Seipel, who hastily returned from Norway, Vaugoin asked the Heimwehr to join the CSP in a minority government, this in spite of the fact that the Heimwehr was not yet a parliamentary party. The two CSP leaders had great difficulty in persuading Starhemberg and especially Pfrimer to join the cabinet and helped arrange a mutinous ultimatum: Steidle, Fey, and Raab told Starhemberg that if he did not enter the cabinet one of them would. Late on September 30 Vaugoin's cabinet was sworn into office with Heimwehr men in two of the most important cabinet posts: Starhemberg as minister of the interior, and the Salzburg leader, Dr. Franz Hueber, as minister of justice. Seipel became the foreign minister. As conditions for its cooperation with the CSP, the Heimwehr allegedly demanded a sharper fight against Austro-Marxism and "effective" measures for the amelioration of unemployment and of the economic crisis in agriculture.[50]

The new government soon showed its colors. At Vaugoin's request President Miklas dissolved the Nationalrat and set new elections for November 9. The cabinet named Dr. Engelbert Dollfuss president of the federal railways, and he promptly appointed Strafella to the more important post of general director. Vaugoin discontinued the activities of the permanent parliamentary committee for military affairs, whose socialist members had long criticized his administration of the war ministry.[51] Starhemberg's ministry stopped the proceedings against Pabst because of "lack of evidence," and on October 29 the cabinet rescinded his expulsion, an issue it had discussed earlier in the month.[52] And under Hueber the government began a campaign of rigorous and usually petty censorship against opposition newspapers. In such ways the minority government flirted with unconstitutional authoritarianism.

The Heimwehr leaders were unable clearly to define their electoral policies. Pfrimer opposed elections altogether and later claimed that Starhemberg promised to prevent their taking place.[53] But as early as October 1 a meeting of the provincial leaders resulted in the announcement of a "political fighting group," the Heimatblock, for those "who do not want to cooperate with the existing parties." Still, only in Styria and Carinthia was it certain that the Heimatblock would campaign independently.[54] The next day Starhemberg and Pfrimer jointly announced that the Heimwehr took the "rudder of government" not to support the CSP and also determined "not to have it wrested from our hands even by a red majority." Crying "Putsch-Proclamation" the *Arbeiter-Zeitung* led an excited reaction to this ill-advised rhetoric that redounded against the Heimwehr. Starhemberg hastily and unconvincingly explained that since the tactics of the Heimatblock had yet to be worked out, only those prejudiced against the Heimwehr could have read into the statement an attack against the chancellor or an intention not to observe the result of the elections. Nevertheless, by following Pfrimer's radical line, Starhemberg destroyed the rationale of the coalition with the CSP and also lost the support of several other provincial Heimwehr groups, for the pro-CSP leaders were bolting the Heimatblock, just as the latter was bolting the new coalition. Fey and Rabb decided to campaign on the CSP lists in Vienna and Lower Austria, and the Heimatdienst in Vorarlberg agreed not to put up a separate list. Steidle reluctantly followed the lead of Starhemberg and Pfrimer.[55]

Starhemberg's flirtation with the Nazis complicated the Heimwehr's confusion over electoral policies. Since early in 1930 the Austrian Nazis had been working toward an electoral alliance with the nationalistic wing of the Heimwehr, and indeed were close to both Starhemberg and Pfrimer. But while Pfrimer was already virtually in their camp and thus unhappy with the Heimwehr's support of the CSP in the minority government, neither Starhemberg's outlook nor his political methods were as well defined as Pfrimer's. Starhemberg was still emotionally attached to German nationalism and to Hitler's slogans, but both his personal ambition and his reverence for Habsburg tradition began to pull him away from the Nazis. He would be happy to work with Hitler in Austria, but he would not agree to work under the Nazi leader as long as he had any prospect of attaining power independently of him. Starhemberg's personal relations with Bethlen and Gömbös, his still expedient ties with Mussolini, and the possibility of working with the authoritarian

wing of the CSP all opened what seemed to be a more promising avenue to power than did subordination to the Nazi *Führer*. Significantly,
all of his powerful mentors and backers wanted to keep him away from
Hitler and to use him to offset the Nazi appeal. Nevertheless, early in
October Starhemberg and his colleague Hueber, who was a brother-in-
law of Hermann Göring, negotiated at some length with Nazi leaders in
Austria and Germany—Hitler saw Hueber in Munich—about an electoral alliance. Both parties demanded the prominent spot on a joint list,
however, and it was largely their inability to arrive at a compromise
over the division of the spoils rather than any ideological differences
that led to the breakdown of the talks. Starhemberg may have been
truthful in contending that he never seriously considered an alliance
with the Nazis except on his own terms. But it is more likely that, once
assured of financial support from Italy and Hungary for a separate campaign to compete for the Nazi vote, Starhemberg felt overly confident
that the Heimatblock would play the same role in Austria as the Nazis
in Germany and enter the Nationalrat in force as a "fighting" antiparliamentary vanguard, as he put it. According to Starhemberg's account, Vaugoin did not appreciate his reasoning, but Seipel "completely
understood the situation" and, along with Mussolini, gave his blessing
to the separate ticket.[56]

By the middle of October the lines for the election were drawn, and
the campaigns became bitter and hard fought. The SDP stood strongly
and confidently against a badly divided antisocialist camp. Starhemberg
insisted on running separate Heimatblock lists even in those areas where
the Heimwehr leaders had made alliances with the CSP, especially in
Lower Austria and Vienna, where relations between Fey and him
rapidly deteriorated. The Nazis also campaigned throughout the country. The fact that the Pan-Germans and the Landbund, except in Upper
Austria and Salzburg, formed an electoral bloc under Schober added to
the confusion among the antisocialists. Early in the campaign the Landbund published what it claimed had been the Heimwehr's demands for
a new constitution in the fall of 1929 and a "revelation" of Pabst's
machinations against the Schober government. When Hueber, as was
his manner, had the latter censored, the Social Democrats convened the
Viennese diet in order to immunize the material for publication, a move
that the pro-Seipel *Reichspost* lambasted as propagandistic "frivolity"
at the expense of the taxpayer. Meanwhile, in hopes of provoking the
socialists into armed resistance so that he could wage war on them,
Minister of Interior Starhemberg ordered numerous searches for Schutzbund weapons. More significantly, he and other impatient Heimwehr

leaders tried to induce Vaugoin to call off the elections and govern by decree.[57]

Once again, as during every autumn since 1928, Pfrimer's Styrian Heimatschutz began to prepare for a *Marsch auf Wien*, at first with the approval of Starhemberg. Although Starhemberg constantly asserted that the Heimwehr opposed the use of force, he himself later claimed that he entered the cabinet "with the object of bringing about a coup d'état." On October 16 he informed the Hungarian counselor of legation that on the twenty-sixth Styrian Heimwehr troops would undertake a putsch designed to make him dictator, Steidle nominal chancellor, and retired General Otto Ellison, who was in charge of military preparations in Styria, the head of the army. Pfrimer also sent a representative to ask the same Hungarian official about financial and military assistance from his government for the undertaking. While Premier Bethlen and Minister of War Gömbös, the latter of whom wanted to support a Heimwehr putsch, sought further information and tried to decide what course to follow, rumors of a pending putsch began to spread throughout Austria and into the foreign press. On a visit to Styria, Upper Austria's Lieutenant Governor Franz Langoth heard open talk of a march on Vienna and observed preparation for battle under General Ellison's direction and in close accord with the gendarmery. At a parliamentary committee meeting on October 21 the SDP formally protested activities in Styria: Heimatschutz men received weapons, instructions to prepare a pack with food for two days, and assurance that if anything happened to them their families would receive pensions. These preparations formed the most serious threat of a putsch yet faced by Austria, for this time the more cautious Pabst was not in control, and, as Seipel told John Gunther —actually by way of trying to discount the rumors—the people in Styria were more "primitive" than in other parts of Austria. Pfrimer took his putsch plans seriously, as apparently did Ellison, a legitimist in a strange alliance with Styria's nationalistic Heimatschutz leader.[58]

While Starhemberg equivocated, too many important people expressed opposition to a Heimwehr putsch to make it possible to attempt one. The federal military leader of the Heimwehr, retired Marshal Hülgerth, disparaged both Pfrimer and Ellison and opposed their plans in reply to a query from Hungarian officials, to whom Seipel also somewhat ambivalently advised caution. Thus faced with divided counsel, the Hungarians got Mussolini to join them in urging Starhemberg and Pfrimer not to undertake a putsch. They also had Vaugoin, whom bankers were already imploring to oppose illegal action, warned of the seriousness of the threat from Styria. The chancellor quickly obtained assurances from Starhemberg that he would suppress all attempts to disturb order and then sent a high-ranking general to Graz to keep things under control.[59]

Although all chances for success were thus foiled, the putsch threat did not subside immediately. Starhemberg later claimed that he intended to lead a coup and prevent elections only in collaboration with the chancellor and the army, and that when Vaugoin, confident of victory at the polls, would not countenance such a risk he ordered Ellison —under threat of detention—"to do nothing without my express command." Nevertheless, it seems clear that he desperately hoped for a forceful denouement with the socialists before the elections. In part out of revenge and in part as further preparation for a putsch, Starhemberg secured control of the federal police after an indiscretion by its acting president, Dr. Ignaz Pamer, who opposed a putsch and suspected Starhemberg of complicity with Ellison. At the time the putsch was predicted, Pamer reported to Seipel instead of Starhemberg, who held the interior portfolio, and energetically alerted his forces. Starhemberg at once dismissed the man from federal service and forced—at the threat of withdrawing from the cabinet according to Ludwig—the appointment of Franz Brandl, a nationalistic police administrator whom Schober had shunted aside, as the permanent president (thus closing Schober's avenue for returning to his former position, which Pamer had been holding for him). Although Starhemberg ambiguously assured one group of policemen in Vienna that as minister he would never request anything that could bring them into a conflict of conscience, Brandl had the impression, he later claimed, that "decisive steps" were at hand, and that Starhemberg wanted to establish a dictatorship before the elections in conjunction with Vaugoin and Seipel. Eight days before the elections Pfrimer, who kept his men ready to march for over a week, went to Vienna to encourage Starhemberg, who Pfrimer later claimed gave assurances that "We'll do it," only to go back on his word.[60]

As voting day neared the tension mounted. Nazis and Heimwehr men frequently disturbed political rallies of the SDP and of Schober's National Economic Bloc, and there were a few rough encounters. The Heimwehr candidates allied with the CSP concentrated their campaign on the necessity of driving the Reds out of Vienna, but the Heimatblock candidates, who insisted that they were not a party but would be the "fighting troop" of the Heimwehr in parliament,[61] directed their venom chiefly against the other non-Marxist parties. The Reichspost, which of course supported the Heimwehr candidates allied with the CSP, tried to hold the Heimatblock under its wing also but often had difficulty in doing so, especially when on October 29 Starhemberg asserted that regardless of the outcome of the elections the Heimwehr would never let the reins of government out of its hands. This statement caused such alarm that he hastily denied its implications.[62] Only a few days before the elections, however, Starhemberg intensified the searches for Schutzbund weapons. But forewarned of Starhemberg's police action, the socialist leaders relocated their weapons and counseled their followers to answer with their votes on November 9.[63] At the same time the *Neue Freie Presse* again detected a putsch psychosis in Styria, with officers and aristocrats especially active. One Heimatblock candidate exclaimed, "It's revolting . . . to speak in an election meeting; I would be much happier, if with a weapon in my hand I could make order in this pigsty," and Count Czernin assured some Heimatschützer that their action would be supported by Hungarian and Italian troops. On the eve of the elections Starhemberg and Pfrimer called on Vaugoin to discuss possible action in case the results were not favorable. They found that the chancellor thought it unnecessary to plan for such a contingency, for he was confident that they would be pleased with the outcome of the voting.[64]

Contrary to Vaugoin's expectations, the voters clearly indicated popular disapproval of the minority cabinet. The coalition partners could draw little consolation from the fact that there were more "anti-Marxist" votes in 1930 than in 1927, for these were spread widely among the contending antisocialist lists. Indeed, despite a loss of several thousand votes the SDP was returned as the largest party in the Nationalrat with seventy-two seats, a gain of one, whereas the CSP emerged with sixty-six seats, seven fewer than before. Schober's union of Pan-German Party and Landbund won nineteen seats, a loss of two; and the Heimatblock, winning 6.2 percent of the vote, trailed with eight seats. The Nazis won 3 percent of the vote but no parliamentary representation. Putting up a brave front, the *Reichspost* claimed a victory for the government, because together the CSP and Heimatblock had one more seat than the CSP previously, and the Heimwehr boasted of the setback given to the SDP, especially in view of the fact that the Heimatblock won its basic seat in the Alpine Montan area of upper Styria.[65] The governing coalition still represented a minority in the Nationalrat, however, and the smaller parties—now the Schober bloc—continued to hold the balance of power. Unless the CSP were to countenance a dictatorial coup, a new compromise would be necessary, for it was most unlikely that Schober

would serve under Vaugoin or with the Heimatblock. On the evening
following the voting, Starhemberg urged Vaugoin "to take measures,"
which "would have been possible," but the chancellor "objected";
Mussolini's liaison with Starhemberg also advised against a putsch.[66]
Nevertheless, the cabinet did not resign—supposedly it wanted to
present itself to the new Nationalrat, a step it did not take before it dissolved the previous legislature—and there remained the threat of unconstitutional action. The Heimwehr press spoke menacingly of sending
its group into parliament to "control" the parties and to force the fight
against the Reds. In response the socialists held a massive demonstration in Vienna on November 12, the Day of the Republic, to express
their satisfaction with the outcome of the voting and their demand that
the minority government, especially its Heimwehr members, had to
go.[67]

On the same day at the Brenner Pass the Tyrolean Heimatwehr welcomed Major Pabst back to Austria. With the Italians treating him as an
honored guest, there were numerous expressions of sympathy for Mussolini and for Austrian fascism. Later in Innsbruck Pabst told a Heimatwehr meeting, "Two things are necessary, firm unity and the realization
that no people can get to the top by means of ballots and elections.
These things must be done away with. Only a strong armed movement
can lead the Heimwehr to its goal—the seizure of power in the state.
And to this it must come in the immediate future." Once again he expressed his hope that when the green-white Heimwehr flag waved over
Austria, the "impulse" would spread to the "great German fatherland,"
and he again called for a "white international" to oppose the "red international."[68]

Within a week Pabst's presence created serious tension both within
and without the Heimwehr. His return was viewed with mixed feelings
not only among members of the Tyrolean government but also among
the Heimwehr leadership, among whom he immediately tried to reassert
his authority. But there soon developed a bitter dispute between Starhemberg and him over both leadership and policies. Shying away from
a putsch policy without the support of the leading politicians, Starhemberg seemed prepared to seek Heimwehr fortunes in parliament; to
make his bargaining position appear stronger, he claimed that the Nazi
votes increased by half again the Heimwehr's electoral base and predicted—to cries of "Heil Hitler!"—that "sooner or later" the two movements would unite. Pabst, disappointed with Vaugoin's cautiousness
and convinced that antidemocrats should not seek success in the laby-

rinth of parliament, made the creation of a completely unified leadership capable of pushing through political and economic demands a prerequisite to his resuming active participation in the organization. A blustering statement by Steidle, warning against a coalition with Schober, demanded "necessary" reforms from the existing minority government; in the absence of such reforms, the Heimwehr would have to become more radical or fall apart. On November 18 the Heimatblock announced the conditions under which it would support a new cabinet, both of which were unacceptable to Schober: a sharp swing to the Right and control of the interior ministry.[69]

Meanwhile, not only the ferment within the Heimwehr but also the course of negotiations for a new cabinet put the Heimwehr menace in a truer perspective and showed that its wishes were out of tune with both the populace and the political parties. The Tyrolean Bauernbund, objecting to Pabst's and Steidle's friendly relations with the oppressors of South Tyrol, expelled the latter from its membership but remained corporatively in the Heimatwehr and demanded that it return to its original goals and subordinate itself to the governor. With many other Christian Socials, especially Upper Austria's Governor Schlegel, Princess Fanny Starhemberg, Leopold Kunschak, and prominent peasant spokesmen, urging a moderate course, Vaugoin's cabinet agreed to resign when given assurances that a coalition of the Schober bloc and socialists would not follow; and Vorarlberg's Governor Ender began negotiations with the groups led by Schober and Starhemberg. Displeased at the prospect of an Ender Government, Starhemberg continued to demand the interior portfolio. However, Schober, who was slated to become vice-chancellor and foreign minister, refused to enter a cabinet with the Heimatblock on the grounds that its presence would handicap his diplomacy. By November 27 Lerchenfeld considered highly unlikely not only Heimatblock participation in the new cabinet but also any dangerous military adventures, because the Heimwehr's internal split was so far advanced, Pabst was quiet again, and Steidle was visiting in Switzerland. On the twenty-eighth Starhemberg, possibly hoping one last time to provoke resistance, carried out a search for Schutzbund arms in Linz, but the workers "found it a joke." After Vaugoin's resignation the next day, Starhemberg tried desperately to keep some Heimwehr representation in the cabinet, first renouncing his own claim to the interior ministry and then expressing willingness to accept any portfolio and to seek changes only in a legal way. Nevertheless, despite Seipel's last minute intercession on Starhemberg's behalf, an Ender-

Schober government took office on December 4 without Heimwehr representation. Carl Vaugoin remained the minister of war, Franz Winkler of the Landbund received the interior portfolio, and Pan-German Hans Schürff that of justice. In concluding a report on the new cabinet Lerchenfeld observed, "Thus democracy remains in Austria," on which point he quoted Seipel as saying to him with a smile, "Sometimes nothing is made more difficult for one than to be a good democrat."[70]

The failure of the minority government and the inauguration of the new cabinet supported by the former coalition of Christian Socials, Pan-Germans, and Landbund, seemed indeed to herald a reprieve for the parliamentary system in Austria. The Social Democrats appeared as strong in opposition as ever, and the right wing of the CSP under Seipel, who was in failing health, was momentarily eclipsed. The Heimwehr, which "had undergone the transformation from an 'irresistible' military movement to a parliamentary midget party" of eight deputies, joined its bitter enemies in opposition to the new government.[71]

Starhemberg's participation in the cabinet and electoral campaign had proved an almost unmitigated fiasco. The poor showing at the polls clearly disproved the Heimwehr's claims to be a popular movement of renewal in which all patriotic Austrians saw their only hope for deliverance, and the peaceful surrender of its ministerial portfolios drove the wedges of division deeper between its radical putschists and its advocates of restraint. Starhemberg was discredited on all sides in the Heimwehr, thus leaving the entire movement without any figure capable of keeping it united and effectively restoring a significant influence in Austria's political affairs. Old Heimwehr hands could find some consoling factors, however. There was still more to the Heimwehr than its "midget party," which itself would help restore Heimwehr influence and ultimately play a fateful role in the republic's history. Many dependable Heimwehr troops had simply voted for the old parties while still marching in the *Doppelreihen,* ready to take down their hunting rifles, if, as the American military attaché put it, "they can be shown what Marxists look like." Too, the Heimwehr's foreign backers, though disenchanted, had not entirely lost interest in keeping the movement alive and united, as shown by an emergency conclave of Hungarian and Italian officials in Budapest in mid-December. Moreover, even the new Austrian government hoped to use a chastened Heimwehr as a threat to hold over their more formidable opponents, the Social Democrats, and more concretely to use its provincial groups as police reserves under legal authorities, as was already the case in Chancellor Ender's Vorarlberg, expected from Raab's groups in Lower Austria, and anticipated from a Tyrolean Heimatwehr without Steidle. Nevertheless, if the political situation at the turn of the year was one of relative quiet, as it seemed to Lerchenfeld, it was largely because of the widening fissures appearing in the Heimwehr movement following its second disruptive setback of 1930.[72]

6

Division, Debacle, Endurance

Nineteen-thirty-one

Just as Austria began to experience the full weight of the depression, the Heimwehr leaders found themselves so weakened through successive blunders that they were unable to take advantage of it for their own ends. As Gulick suggested, with sham sympathy, it seemed as if the Heimwehr had risen too early, during a period of relative improvement in economic conditions, and as if it were in ways responsible for the economic crisis and hence obviously incapable of curing it. Although activity within the Heimwehr became fervid, the general public paid little attention to its internal struggles, and many followers, including the Turnerbund, a constituent part of the Heimwehr, drifted over to the apparently better organized and more dedicated Nazis. Wandruszka saw the once popular movement now as only scattered groups of politically homeless private guards of individual leaders, both the products and the tools of the "Balkanization" of Austrian politics. The Heimwehr was inconsequential in national political affairs during the seventeen months in which the old three-party coalition continued to hold together.[1] But the competition of the Nazis, and to some extent their attacks on Austria's independence, spurred segments of the Heimwehr to renewed vigor and eventually won for it again the patronage of Mussolini and the CSP.

Ironically, the key factor on which the significance of the Heimwehr would later hinge was the entry of the eight Heimatblock deputies into the Nationalrat, ridiculed by their opponents and regretted by their leaders. Besides Starhemberg and Hueber, the Heimatblock deputies were Max Werner (Tyrol), Sepp Lengauer and Sepp Hainzl (Styria), Hans Ebner (Carinthia), and Johann Auinger and Fritz Lichtenegger (Lower Austria). Only at the last moment did Starhemberg finally decide to lead his delegation, and even then with such reservations that his early resignation was foreseen, partially because his successor on the list, Odo Neustädter-Stürmer, represented the Heimatblock in economic matters during the cabinet negotiations.[2] Their appearance in full uniform and feathered cap at the opening session of the fourth parliament caused a mild stir, and later their rowdy behavior enlivened the sessions, but by and large they had little influence on legislation until a realignment of the coalition early in 1932 gave their votes the balance of power.

On the day on which the government presented its program to the Nationalrat, Starhemberg set the tone for the Heimatblock's participation in parliament, both by his antics and his programmatic speech. He caused an uproar early in the proceedings when, during a speech by Karl Renner, he drew his hand under his chin in the sign of a noose and then, when the socialists protested vociferously, reached quickly for his hip pocket. His adversaries cried that he was reaching for a revolver, whereupon, with a flare for drama, he smilingly produced his cigarette case. His maiden speech was both a brusque and impolite attack on the parliamentary system and the Social Democrats and also an appeal for support to the moneyed interests, with but slight attention to the concerns of the poor and unemployed. Instead of using the customary salutation to the "Esteemed House" or "Ladies and Gentlemen," he addressed his colleagues as "Comrades! Women and Men!" and stood before them as the leader "of that popular movement on which are fastened the hopes of the entire Austrian people for all future. For we know that only we are capable of leading the Austrian people toward a new and better future. . . . The main troops come later; the vanguard is here." Starhemberg devoted most of his speech to political economy. He called for the enactment of an economic four-year plan, which would include central control of all financial transactions at all levels of government (i.e., socialist dominated municipalities); the simplification (reduction) of taxation; protection of domestic production; control of the grain and livestock markets; assistance to agriculture through transformation of the land tax into one on proceeds, creation of a forestry council, an end of the tax on lumber exports (his own principal source of income); effective measures to reduce unemployment, including a compulsory labor service designed so as not to lower wage levels or to compete with private enterprise. He concluded with the hope that he had convinced his hearers "that the day is not far off when this house and the whole state will belong to us. Heil!"[3]

From the beginning, however, Starhemberg failed to enforce consistency and unanimity in his parliamentary faction. Heimatblock members voted first with the government and then against it, and frequently divided, with Lengauer and Lichtenegger—"workers"—most often voting with the SDP. On one socialist resolution, which would require government approval for the closing of large factories, six Heimatblock men voted with the SDP, one with the government, and one abstained. Such betrayal led industrialists temporarily to suspend payments to the Heimwehr. The Heimatblock's own legislative proposals were merely suggestions, without any details, that the government should draft and introduce measures for combating unemployment through the protection of domestic production, for a program of economy in government, or for the relief of the agricultural crisis.[4] Parliament took little notice of these resolutions.

Moreover, Starhemberg's group was almost from the first without electoral bases, for the movement of which it claimed to be the vanguard found itself in an advanced state of disintegration. Large segments of the Heimwehr practically disavowed their parliamentary "party" as inconsistent with their nonparty character. Especially was this so in the Tyrol and Lower Austria, where before the end of 1930 there were already open splits. It was already unlikely that the Heimatblock could survive another election. This was especially true in view of the fact that labor unrest threatened the unity of the Heimatschutz in upper Styria, where the Heimatblock had won its basic mandate. With employment controlled by German capital, there was a distinct possibility that the workers would soon become Nazi. In the face of this threat Pfrimer and part of the Heimatblock tried to protect the workers' jobs and wages even at the risk of losing entirely what little subsidy Austrian industry was still able or willing to provide the Heimwehr.[5] It was probably the only time that Pfrimer crossed his Alpine Montan patrons.

The most serious splits in the Heimwehr ranks occurred in the Tyrol and in Lower Austria. Following his unsuccessful campaign on the Heimatblock ticket, Steidle had to struggle to retain his position even within the provincial association. His position was seriously jeopardized by his expulsion from the Tyrol's pro-CSP Bauernbund and from the CSP club in the Bundesrat. Even Pabst forsook him by trying to maneuver Guido Jakoncig into the Tyrolean leadership. It was thought that Starhemberg would support Jakoncig and that in the subsequent split the more pious peasants would secede and place themselves under the Christian Social governor. Steidle, confident that he could "certainly survive a little palace revolution," made the dramatic gesture of "withdrawing from public life"—with the promise that at the suitable moment he would resign his political offices—in an open letter to Governor Stumpf. However, support for Jakoncig proved to be weak, and Steidle managed to mend his fences within the Heimatwehr sufficiently to hang on to his post. His position was strengthened when Pabst moved to Munich in mid-December. For the next several months Steidle worked assiduously to restore his ties with the CSP, a step made more difficult and necessary by the formation of a purely Christian Social armed guard called the Ostmärkische Sturmscharen (East Mark Storm Troops) under the aegis of Kurt von Schuschnigg, who hoped to extend his organization throughout the country.[6]

A lasting division occurred in the Lower Austrian organization. As the only prominent leader to be returned to parliament as a Christian Social, Raab decided to abstain from Heimwehr activities until matters could be clarified. After the exclusion of the Heimatblock from the new government a complete break came quickly between those groups who, as Starhemberg put it, had confessed the goals of "pure fascism" and would give fealty to the federal command, and those who wanted to adhere to "the original program of cooperation with the legal elements." Early in December Starhemberg's adherents elected Count Albert Alberti, district leader of Amstetten, to head a new Heimatschutzverband of Lower Austria. Claiming a following of ten thousand men, the new HSV then set about to form its own peasant association under Dr. Herbert Faber, the radically nationalist leader of the district in Lower Austria called the Waldviertel. Raab, accusing Starhemberg of breaking the agreements made at Schladming and appealing to popular prejudice against aristocrats, organized approximately half of his former following of almost forty thousand into the Lower Austrian Heimwehr, which claimed continuity with the pre-Korneuburg goals and received the blessings of the *Reichspost* and the Bauernbund. Raab also founded his own newspaper, the *Niederösterreichische Heimwehr*, which first appeared in late January 1931 and expressed the antinationalistic clericalism that clearly differentiated his group from the "wildest Catholic haters" who followed Alberti.[7]

Splits in other provincial Heimwehr groups soon threatened to lead to an open cleavage on the national level. Early in December the Vorarlberg Heimatdienst informed Starhemberg that it would not take part in any councils of the federal command until its composition and nature had been clarified. Nor was Pfrimer following Starhemberg unreservedly. He dismissed Hainzl and Lengauer from their positions as his deputies in Styria because they had entered the Nationalrat, and appointed fiery little Konstantin Kammerhofer as the single deputy leader. At the same time he carried out a reorganization so that the district leaders were responsible directly to him, not to their followers.

Starhemberg, still proclaiming "the complete unity and determination of the great supraparty Heimwehr movement," attempted both to appease his radical followers and to placate his more cautious critics, to be both rashly threatening and responsibly conciliatory. On December 14 he said he was more sympathetic with forceful action than with sitting in parliament, but that such action had to be prepared: "The state is easily conquered, but to hold the state is difficult, is a great problem. The future must be built by serious, responsible work." He continued in this conciliatory yet "positive" vein a week later before about eight hundred of his followers in Lower Austria: "Marxism must be fought with an idea, not merely by having an army to counter the Schutzbund or by beating up the incited followers." To Raab's charges he answered that his Heimatschutz was not anticlerical, but asserted that religion and religious institutions should not be used for party purposes. But his power base continued to crumble. At a meeting on January 11 the Tyroleans unexpectedly retained Steidle as their permanent leader, proclaimed the organization "unified and independent," and announced that for the time being the Heimatwehr would restrict its activities to the province.[8]

The formal division in the national organization finally occurred at a meeting of the provincial leaders in Vienna on 27 and 28 January 1931. Instead of allowing one vote for each province, Starhemberg wanted to make the votes relative to membership, which, so long as Styria and Upper and much of Lower Austria remained loyal, would assure him of a majority. To secure these changes, he wanted to take the vote from Vorarlberg, which he claimed had forfeited its voice in the council by its announcement of early December, and give it to the leader of his Viennese Jäger, thus shifting the voting alignment from five to five to six to four. Steidle, however, insisted on recognition of autonomy for the Heimatwehr. Then Emil Fey, spearheading the opposition, called on Starhemberg to resign in favor of either Steidle or Hülgerth, the federal military leader and the new provincial leader of Carinthia; Fey further demanded clear delineation of authority, Heimwehr withdrawal from everyday politics, and separation of the "militant movement" from the parliamentary Heimatblock. He also criticized Starhemberg for not leading the fight against the film *All Quiet on the Western Front*. When Starhemberg in turn demanded the ouster of Fey and Stocker because they had bolted the Heimatblock in the fall campaign, those two, joined by Steidle, Matt of Vorarlberg, and Vas of Burgenland, left the meeting. They promised to return when their viewpoint was given due consideration. From those remaining Starhemberg demanded and received dictatorial powers over the entire organization with the right to remove provincial leaders, on the basis of which he pronounced the deposition of Fey and the dissolution of Stocker's Railroad Guard. Thereafter voting in the federal command, on the basis of one for each ten thousand active members, would take place only in the following cases: the election of a new federal leader, a vote of confidence, or at the leader's request. Starhemberg also decreed that no leaders could be allowed to exercise a political mandate and announced that he would resign his seat in the Nationalrat in order to demonstrate his nonpartisanship. Those leaders remaining with him claimed to represent four-fifths of the total Heimwehr membership concentrated in the geographic heart of the country as opposed to the dissident minority at its western and eastern edges. Thus the lines were clearly drawn, although by leaving the Nationalrat (to be succeeded by Odo Neustädter-Stürmer, a "specialist" in corporatism), Starhemberg clearly made a concession to his opponents.[9]

The secessionists, proclaiming that they would have nothing to do with an association in which the most primitive rights were ignored, confederated themselves loosely as an *Arbeitsgemeinschaft* (working community). At their news conference Steidle especially criticized the election adventure of the Heimatblock, against which he had warned but with which he had cooperated as a matter of discipline. After that fiasco it seemed necessary either to liquidate the movement or to reorganize it, an effort to be undertaken by Fey, since Steidle was busy in the Tyrol. Appointing Fey to receive any communications from Starhemberg's group, the five rebels stated their willingness to reconsider after the withdrawal of the dictatorial decrees, which "may be allowed the Italian minister president, but not for long to the Federal Leader Prince Starhemberg." The latter replied with a news conference of his own: his entry into the cabinet and the Heimatblock's participation in the election were forced on him against his better judgment; exactly because such was possible the federal leader had to have more authority.

As a result of this open split in the federal leadership, the division in the Tyrolean Heimatwehr took on new intensity. The dissidents in the Tyrol, including Jakoncig and the Heimatwehr's military leader, began to organize directly under Starhemberg, and according to the *Neue Freie Presse* there were about a thousand men in such groups. Addressing three hundred of his subordinates, Steidle gave further indication of the extent of the split in the province by saying that it was better to have twelve thousand men in agreement than fifteen thousand badly divided. Steidle charged that the scheme to allow one vote for each ten thousand members was but a Styrian plot to take over federal leadership, and he suspected that only one-half of the fifty-five thousand members claimed by Pfrimer were active in the Styrian Heimatschutz. He further complained that the Heimwehr's basic idea, anti-Marxism, was being shoved aside in favor of the personality of Starhemberg, who wanted absolute power to march with his Jäger without anyone's knowing exactly where he wanted to go. Steidle suggested that the national organization should be united militarily under one leader, Hülgerth, and politically under a collegium of provincial leaders, and that it should withdraw from daily politics.[10]

Distressed at this internecine warfare, Seipel once again attempted to take the Heimwehr's fortunes in hand. From his convalescence in Vorarlberg he conducted a lively correspondence and entertained a parade of visitors, including Jakoncig, the Tyrolean dissident, in behalf of Heimwehr unity.[11] More importantly, Seipel, supported by Rintelen, persuaded Austrian industrialists to renew some assistance to Steidle, who at the moment seemed more likely to support CSP authoritarianism than did the unpredictable Starhemberg.

The Central Association of Manufacturers, long disturbed by the Heimwehr's erratic course, was upset both by the split in its ranks and by the Heimatblock's support of the socialists' attempts to stop factories from closing and to hold wages up. Working through the FKV, which offered its mediation, the CAM initiated negotiations between Starhemberg's federal command and the Steidle-Fey groups, but publicly remained neutral in the dispute. There followed the formation of a committee on arbitration composed of Rauter and Karg-Bebenburg for the federal command, Schweinitzhaupt and Reichl for the secessionists, and Lustig-Prean as neutral chairman. Behind the scenes, however, the industrialists expressed their preference for Steidle's methods and put pressure on Starhemberg especially to recognize Hülgerth as military leader of all Heimwehr forces.[12]

From the beginning the deliberations of the new committee were hampered by the sharpening feud between Starhemberg and Steidle. Concerned for his "prestige," Starhemberg responded to Steidle's challenge with a speaking tour in the Tyrol on February 18–20, despite pleas that he wait until after the unity talks. Provincial officials forbade public assemblies to avoid clashes, but speaking before invited groups of the FKV and Bund Oberland, Starhemberg played up the differences in goals: some wanted to take the Heimwehr back to 1927, to make of it a watch and protection of society for the bourgeoisie, while he and his followers wanted to continue the "renewal movement" and the fight against the current system. Turning Steidle's weapon against him, Starhemberg called for the implementation of the oath of Korneuburg. Steidle answered that his Heimatwehr would restrict its activities solely to the Tyrol—although always ready to cooperate militarily under Hülgerth—until it would be possible for a larger community to fulfill its original mission. Schweinitzhaupt, whom Steidle recalled from the arbitration committee, added that "the time of a unified organization is temporarily at an end." The differences began to appear irreconcilable. Nevertheless, perhaps to counter charges that he had capitulated to the government and CSP of the Tyrol and to make a gesture of compromise with Starhemberg, Steidle finally resigned his seat in the Bundesrat.[13]

Briefly at the beginning of March it appeared that Starhemberg's position might improve. Following Stocker's resignation from the leadership of the Railroad Guard, Starhemberg appointed a respected engineer, Hofrat Nouakh, to lead it on his terms. And then at a meeting of the Burgenland Heimwehr the lesser lights, influenced by Rauter and Morsey from Styria, repudiated Vas's secession—the "provincialization" of the Heimwehr—and accepted Starhemberg's claim to sole leadership; they reelected Vas when he agreed to follow their wishes. The *Panther* boasted that Steidle and Fey were now isolated, but it soon became clear that Starhemberg had not generally got the upper hand. In the Burgenland the determined Christian Social advocates led a splinter secession, and in Vienna the leader of Starhemberg's Jäger had to be removed because he offended the CSP too openly. Moreover, Starhemberg's sad financial plight was becoming a matter of general knowledge, especially after his newspaper appeared for the last time on March 5.[14]

With his fortunes thus declining Starhemberg defiantly adopted a policy whose failure was to force him into semiretirement from Heimwehr activities for several months. Early in March he announced that the Heimatblock under Neustädter-Stürmer would campaign independently in the Upper Austrian elections in mid-April, because the parties had rejected his plea (i.e., his terms) for a unity list. Hardly explainable, this decision rent Starhemberg's home base, forced him to make wildly contradictory statements, and led to an open denunciation by the Christian Socials (in the face of which Princess Fanny, herself mildly critical of her son, gave up her posts in the CSP). He asserted that the Heimatblock and the Heimwehr were separate and that the latter would not campaign for the former or guard its assemblies. In the voting on April 19, the Heimatblock was humiliated, receiving twenty-one thousand fewer votes than were cast for it in Upper Austria in November, not a single provincial mandate, and but slight representation in the city council of Linz.[15]

Coupled with his personal financial problems, this disaster rendered Starhemberg's position untenable. He tried to regain some influence by

unifying all the organizations in Vienna loyal to him as the Heimatschutzverband Wien, a step he had been planning for some time. If he
hoped thereby to subdue Fey and force him to join the new organization, he was disappointed: Fey replied by declaring his Viennese group
completely independent of the federal command and by accusing Starhemberg of being the one who refused all suggestions for unity and
nonpartisanship.[16]

Finally, at a meeting in Linz on May 2, the provincial leaders still
associated with Starhemberg prevailed on him to take an extended
"leave of absence" in order to resolve his financial problems. Pfrimer
"temporarily" assumed the federal leadership. Both Starhemberg and
Pfrimer issued public statements, the first entrusting responsibility to
the other until he could resume his activities, and the second promising
to lead the organization according to old, proven principles. In contrast
to the *Reichspost*, the *Neue Freie Presse* assumed—as did Raab's weekly
—that Starhemberg's vacation would be permanent: "That which had
to come has happened." Pfrimer had the unenviable task of trying to
stop the Heimwehr's disintegration.[17]

The breakdown of the Heimwehr movement, due both to poor leadership that antedated Starhemberg and to continuing differences over
goals and methods, was almost complete. A paramilitary pressure group
is not typical, in that it has no economic base or constituted channel
through which it can exercise influence. Depending on its aims, it must
effect its wishes either by physical intimidation or by actual seizure of
power through military force. If intimidation proves unsuccessful and
rebellion can or will not be attempted, then such a pressure group must
either bide its time, risking dissolution while hoping for new opportuni-
ties, or try to compete with other political groups in the constituted
process. The Heimwehr leaders were too divided in outlook and allegiance successfully to carry out the transformation—begun before
Korneuburg and accelerated by the electoral campaign—from a nonpartisan paramilitary support group to a so-called renewal movement
that was in effect a separate party. During his first period of leadership,
Starhemberg did not pursue either approach consistently or deter-
minedly. In the resulting confusion he antagonized important Heimwehr colleagues as well as most party politicians. Only the debacle of
Pfrimer's putsch later in 1931, coupled with the growing radicalization
of politics as a result of the economic crisis, rescued Starhemberg from
oblivion.

Pfrimer took over the direction of those Heimwehr groups still loyal
to Starhemberg at a time when the furor over the customs union be-

tween Germany and Austria that began on March 21 was at its height
and when Austria's economic plight, dramatized by the collapse of the
Credit-Anstalt on May 12, was daily growing worse. The internal woes
of the Heimwehr could not compete with these crises for national attention, and it seemed that the days of that organization were numbered.
Indeed, the new German minister in Vienna, Kurt Rieth, thought that
Starhemberg's withdrawal indicated the "fact" of the Heimwehr's complete "collapse."[18]

Undaunted, Pfrimer entertained other hopes, nourished by the
nationalistic passions enflamed by French opposition to the customs
union. There is strong evidence that when Pfrimer succeeded Starhemberg he was again planning a putsch by the Styrian Heimatschutz.
Convinced that all other ways by which the Heimwehr could come to
power would fail, he thought that only a decisive deed could stop its
disintegration and restore its influence in the country. The deepening
economic crisis and the mounting army of unemployed in the winter of
1931—over three hundred thousand—led him to believe that the Heimwehr's hour would soon come. He hoped to hasten that hour.[19]

Pfrimer began his long-desired tenure as sole leader with a proclamation that he intended to lead a "revolutionary renewal movement" in
opposition to the old democratic parties, to which Heimwehr activists
must no longer belong. He did not intend to wait for the "so-called
evolutionary development" and invited those who felt too weak or discouraged to go the way of battle and renewal to lay aside their uniforms, since he needed a completely loyal following. As if to indicate
what he hoped would be a break with the past, Pfrimer changed the
name of the national organization from Oesterreichische Selbstschutzverbände to Heimatschutzverband Oesterreich, a change which also
reflected the greater Styrian influence.[20]

The sentiment prevailing at numerous peasant rallies held throughout
Styria and Lower Austria on May 3 further showed that Pfrimer had
already begun to chart his course before he succeeded Starhemberg the
previous day. In each province about fifteen thousand men demanded
drastic economies in public administration, higher protective tariffs for
agricultural products "against Russian dumping," tax reductions, and
easier credit for agriculture. At the rally in Gröbming, Styria, attended
by Count Othmar Lamberg, who was to play a major role in coming
events, the peasants called for a march on Vienna,[21] the sort of "popular"
cry that Pfrimer wanted to hear.

In dreaming of his coup Pfrimer was greatly influenced by Raimund
Günther's *Diktatur oder Untergang*, which appeared in 1930, and by

Günther himself, an ardent nationalist and antisocialist. The book was a polemic not only against republicanism and democracy but also against undue emphasis on corporatism. Extolling "heroes" and the *Führerprinzip*, Günther contended that Austria was still legally a monarchy, since the republican constitution had never been submitted to a popular vote, as instructed by Kaiser Karl in his resignation. The situation had become so bad that a transitional dictatorship was unavoidable, but, in the interest of the general welfare, the reformers should try to realize their aims by means of political negotiations before undertaking a coup. Pfrimer's scheme followed closely this pattern of thought.[22]

Late in March 1931, Pfrimer established an Economic and Corporative Bureau of the Styrian Heimatschutz to work out plans for governing after he seized power. One of its leading members was Olaf Petri, who frequently contributed articles to the *Panther* and *Heimatschutz-Zeitung* calling for a dictatorship to combat the economic crisis.[23] The bureau produced an economic and political program of five typed pages, the *Program der Ständeorganisation Oesterreichs*.[24] Its avowed goal was "the economic and cultural rebirth of Austria on religious, social, and patriotic foundations" through a complete reconstruction of the social order, the pillars of which were state, economy, and people. By and large the points of the program were only vague and general desires, with no indication of how they would be achieved or of how the new state would be organized. But, in keeping "with German tradition," government should be nonpolitical, authoritative, and corporative.

For a while Pfrimer removed references to the use of force from the front page of his weekly newspaper, the *Panther*. Apparently he hoped thus to prepare the way for trying to reach his goals via negotiations. His idea was to win widespread approval of specific demands on the government; if they were not granted he could then claim that a coup was justified. This was one of the objects of the peasant rallies on May 3, although some of the speeches that day clearly indicated that the Heimatschutz hardly expected such demands to be met.

The government's hasty support of the Credit-Anstalt provided Pfrimer an explosive theme for demagogy. Not without justification he demanded a complete investigation of the bank's collapse. Olaf Petri, Pfrimer's self-styled economic expert, called the emergency bill to meet the crisis a "*Diktat* of the House of Rothschild" and decried the government's support of Jewish bankers at the expense of Austro-German taxpayers. Taking advantage of widespread public wrath, Pfrimer began in mid-June to circulate a petition calling on the government to investigate the bank failure, to arrest those responsible for it, to impound the directors' private fortunes, to require the return by all the bank's leading officials of the amounts by which their monthly income had exceeded two thousand schillings since 1928, and to impound the assets of all legislators who voted for the government to guarantee the obligations of the Credit-Anstalt. The headline of the *Panther* on July 11 proclaimed that the petition was meant dead-seriously. Apparently Pfrimer thought that he could either force the government to accept these demands or, if not, that he could simply insist that he be given power.[25]

The cabinet crisis of mid-June further incensed Pfrimer. The continuing difficulties of the Credit-Anstalt and the accompanying collapse of all hopes for the establishment of a customs union with Germany prompted Winkler to resign his cabinet post on June 17, thus toppling Ender's government. In the ensuing negotiations, in which the Heimwehr leaders had no part, Ender agreed to form a new cabinet only if the Nationalrat granted him extensive power to meet the economic crisis by decree for a limited period of time. The legislators refused to confer such authority. In a dramatic reversal Seipel tried to form a government of national concentration for a limited period in which all the parties in the Nationalrat except the Heimatblock would be represented, with the SDP to control almost half the cabinet posts. The offer seemed evidence of the seriousness with which Seipel viewed the national and international situation. But the socialist leaders decided not to take upon themselves any onus for the austerity measures which they knew had to come. In what appears in retrospect to have been one of their most grievous mistakes, they persisted technically in opposition while indicating their willingness to permit speedy passage of necessary legislation. They hoped thereby to keep the party united and to prevent, especially with the Heimwehr in shambles, a Communist-Nazi polarization as in Germany. Ultimately they hoped to win over enough of the "masses in motion" to gain a majority in the next national elections. Seipel apparently toyed briefly with the idea of another minority— "dictatorial"—cabinet, but could not win over enough of his party to attempt it. Finally, Governor Karl Buresch of Lower Austria managed to bring together the old Ender cabinet with only minor changes; Winkler returned to the interior ministry and Schober to the foreign ministry. Chancellor Buresch seemed dedicated, despite his past support of the Heimwehr, to a continuation of constitutional government and evidenced a willingness to meet the Social Democrats half way.[26]

But, although political peace was temporarily restored on the surface, economic conditions steadily worsened. While the budgetary deficit grew rapidly, prices tumbled and industrial production declined to 70 percent of its peak in 1929. Unemployment in June 1931 stood 28 percent higher than in June 1930 and for 1931 as a whole averaged 20.3 percent of the work force. Wages, salaries, pensions, and unemployment benefits had to be reduced, and agricultural debtors were badly hurt by the drop in prices. In August 1931 Chancellor Buresch requested an emergency loan of 250 million schillings from the League of Nations.[27]

Pfrimer used these developments to rouse his followers against the government "of the weak hand" that allowed such economic misery. On the day the new cabinet took office he called on it to "clean house or get out." A week later he said that if those "patent democrats" could get away with breaking the constitution by prohibiting rallies[28] and by collaborating with the Reds, then for the Heimatschutz the constitution was only a scrap of paper that it would shred to pieces. On August 2 he warned the ministers to turn the government over to patriotic people if they wished to avoid bloodshed and violence, adding, "I am ready to defray the costs of the emigration of the members of the government if they will promise not to return." By this time the Hungarian minister to Austria, Lajos Ambrozy, was convinced that Pfrimer was finally determined to undertake some kind of forceful action without, he thought, much prospect of success.[29]

Throughout the summer Pfrimer tried to consolidate his control of the Heimatschutz and to bring the secessionists back into the national organization. He conferred from time to time with Starhemberg and publicly ignored the prince's assertion that he had no intention of letting his leave of absence become a permanent abdication from the federal leadership. In mid-June Pfrimer named the new leader of the Jägerfreikorps-Starhemberg, Josef Smercka, as the provincial leader of the Viennese Heimwehr groups loyal to the federal command, a step that still left Fey's followers outside the pale. In fact, throughout July Pfrimer and the secessionists remained as far apart as ever. In mid-July the groups under Fey, Steidle, Raab, and Vas joined the Freiheitsbund of Kunschak's Christian labor unions and the FKV under Major Kopschitz in establishing a more formal "patriotic" *Kampfgemeinschaft* (fighting alliance) that replaced the earlier "working alliance." By early August both Steidle and Fey, however, seemed to want to restore relations with the federal command, primarily as a means of securing control of a reunited organization for themselves. Steidle and Pfrimer conferred at Zell am See on August 7, but despite Pfrimer's announcement that they had reached "complete agreement on goals and means" and had thus created the basis for reunion, they failed to settle their differences, for the Kampfgemeinschaft still rejected Pfrimer's *Führerprinzip* and his proposals for a coup d'état. In mid-August Fey proposed a restoration of the dual leadership of Steidle and Pfrimer for political matters and the recognition of Hülgerth as the sole military commander of a reunited Heimwehr. Pfrimer let the suggestion pass without a reply. Steidle's newspaper, betraying a longing for the good old days of 1927–1929, commented that even if organizational unity were still a long way off, unity of purpose was necessary in the face of hard times and Marxist gains.[30]

Either Pfrimer thought reunion on his terms nearer than it was or he considered it unimportant, for he proceeded with his putsch plans, which began definitely to take shape when Count Karl Othmar Lamberg became his close adviser and "adjutant general" on August 18. Lamberg, a minor aristocrat whom many of his peers regarded as conscienceless and incompetent, was an advocate of immediate action. Apparently Pfrimer sought a dependable partner for his adventure, since his chief-of-staff, Hans Rauter, himself a condottiere type, was opposed to a putsch. Rauter, whom Pfrimer managed to dissuade from resigning with the promise that Lamberg would not become a military or political leader, receded into the background for the next weeks. In frequent discussions at Lamberg's castle, Pichlarn by Stainach in the mountains of northwestern Styria, men such as the gendarmery commandant Meyszner, who was now also a member of the provincial government, several civil servants, and Raimund Günther all advocated a putsch, while aristocrats Baron Egon Berger-Waldenegg, Baron Andreas Morsey, and Count Kunata-Kottulinsky opposed military action against the government. In these talks Pfrimer always insisted that something had to be done to dispose of the existing system and prevent the enslavement of Austria by international finance, but he also stated that he had no thought of acting in defiance of the federal executive. Apparently it was Lamberg who devised the scheme of using a socialist rally, to be addressed by Koloman Wallisch at Liezen in the Enns valley on Saturday, September 12, as a pretext for calling out the Heimatschutz to keep order in that area: Schutzbund "disorders" would then lead to a general mobilization and a march on Vienna.[31]

On September 4 Pfrimer met the top leaders of the Heimatschutz including Starhemberg in Leoben. He was angered that the government was ignoring his petition, which he claimed had already received 620,000 signatures,[32] and he seemed to be determined to establish a dictatorship before the pending presidential elections. There are conflicting accounts regarding the debate that followed. Hofmann, following Winkler's report to the Nationalrat, accepts the contention that

Pfrimer and Lamberg openly called for action to prevent a black-red coalition, that particularly Hülgerth opposed anything but a purely defensive use of the Heimwehr military forces in support of the government, and that Starhemberg and the others agreed to action (not an outright coup) only at the "obviously most opportune moment." Afterwards Pfrimer assured both Hülgerth and Starhemberg that he would undertake nothing other than "a big campaign of economic propaganda" without their knowledge and consent, and agreed to discuss further developments with Starhemberg on September 14, by which time Pfrimer hoped to rule Austria.[33]

Notwithstanding his later defense, it is very difficult indeed to determine Starhemberg's role in the days before the putsch. Only two days after the conversations on the fourth, he declared to peasants near Linz that the Heimwehr would "soon, perhaps very soon, have to undertake a difficult assignment." Saying that a dictatorship of common sense was necessary, he pledged that he would be found wherever Pfrimer was and that no one would succeed in separating them. And on the eighth he resumed the active leadership of the Heimwehr in Upper Austria.[34] He must have suspected, if he did not know, that Pfrimer was not to be denied his putsch; and, while probably doubtful of its success, he wanted to be prepared for any eventuality.

Pfrimer and Lamberg proceeded with their plans. On the seventh they instructed a subordinate to create a disturbance at Wallisch's meeting on the twelfth. Then on the tenth, in the presence of Berger-Waldenegg, Hülgerth offered to resign as federal military leader. Pfrimer assured him that a strike against the nation's executive forces was not contemplated. When Hülgerth and the Carinthian leaders repeated that they would not support a putsch, Pfrimer cloaked himself in silence. The next day he again assured several Carinthians that he would not do anything without Hülgerth's consent, and he told Konstantin Kammerhofer, who distrusted Lamberg, that leading politicians, including Rintelen, were privy to the affair.[35] The *Panther* that appeared on September 12 carried a lead article by Olaf Petri with the banner headline, "Something Must and Will Happen."

What happened was the result of subterfuge by Othmar Lamberg, who presented Pfrimer with a fait accompli. When the subordinates who had been instructed to create disorders on the twelfth learned that the socialist rally was directed against the Nazis instead of the Heimwehr, they sought Pfrimer at Lamberg's castle to get new instructions. In the absence of Pfrimer, Lamberg told the men that it was no longer necessary to bother the socialist rally, because there was already fighting in Bruck on the Mur and the Heimatschutz must mobilize immediately. He assured them that the disagreements between Pfrimer, Starhemberg, and Hülgerth had been settled and that Rintelen would join the enterprise with Styrian troops. Plans were already made to arrest Governor Schlegel of Upper Austria and Ministers Winkler and Vaugoin at 11:00 P.M., at which time Pfrimer would assume governmental power. Lamberg also ordered the mobilization of the Heimatschutz in the Enns Valley at 11:00 P.M. When Pfrimer arrived on the afternoon of the twelfth Lamberg convinced him also that there was fighting in Bruck, and Pfrimer, already talking about seizing power, readily concurred with the earlier commands. Lamberg then dictated a report of disorders for one of the subordinates to give Pfrimer ("for appearances," Pfrimer said at his interrogation), and Pfrimer gave a courier letters to Starhemberg and Puchmayr in Linz, calling on them to follow his lead. He also ordered the courier to alarm the Heimatschutz unit in Kirchdorf, a small town in southern Upper Austria that was directly under Styrian command. Final preparation included delivery of a note from Meyszner to the commandant of the gendarme academy in Bruck: "The Heimatschutz has been called out for a large maneuver, and I request, should the Reds attempt to interrupt it, protection for the Heimatschutz," and the distribution of two placards, bearing Pfrimer's signature, which announced that Pfrimer had taken over the government and decreed a provisional constitution. Thus the events of the tragicomedy were set in motion.[36]

Pfrimer's proclamation to the people of Austria informed them that they had called him in time of direst need to save them and be the supreme protector of their rights. In order to prevent the complete collapse of the state, the Heimatschutz had seized power in accord with its fundamental principles. The new "state leader" declared the constitution illegal but, with important reservations, left it in force until the people had a chance to decide on the final form of government. Actually, the "constitutional patent" posted throughout upper Styria tore the law of the land into shreds: Pfrimer decreed that Austria was now a federal state instead of a republic and that Vienna was to be reincorporated into Lower Austria; he assumed ultimate legislative and executive power in both the central government and the provinces as well as command over the armed forces; he suspended trial by jury and proclaimed martial law; and he abrogated the articles concerning the national legislature. He also called to auxiliary police duty all the "patriotic" paramilitary organizations. Pfrimer saw as his goal the "harmonious development of the rich resources of the Austrian people in a folk com-

munity built on a corporative basis." There can be no doubt also that
had Pfrimer succeeded he would have put an end to the SDP. It is not
known what steps he planned to take next. In fact, at his trial in December he suggested that these placards were prematurely posted and that
the immediate goal of the exercise had been to force the government to
grant certain economic demands of the Heimatschutz.[37]

Operations began according to schedule before midnight on September 12. The basic military plans were worked out by General Ellison,
probably as early as 1929, certainly by the fall of 1930. Styria was to
form the heart of the enterprise, with the Lower Austrians joining after
the Styrians crossed the Semmering Pass late in the afternoon of the first
day. Heimwehr units in Salzburg, Upper Austria, and Carinthia were to
stay on alert to increase the pressure on the government. The plans
assumed the neutrality of the official armed forces, with only the Schutzbund as a possible obstacle. There is evidence that Pfrimer expected
help from right-wing volunteers from Hungary, but the Hungarian
government played no role in the affair.[38]

The Heimatschutz was early robbed of the element of surprise.
Carousing workers in Bruck noticed the activity and notified Wallisch,
who in turn contacted the offices of the *Arbeiter-Zeitung* and Julius
Deutsch. Threatening to mobilize the Schutzbund, Deutsch called
Minister of Interior Winkler and Robert Danneberg called Chancellor
Buresch and urged them to take immediate counteraction. It took the
government several hours to admit that a widespread, coordinated military campaign was underway, but finally the competent ministers gave
orders for their forces to prevent the advance of the rebels. At mid-
morning on Sunday, the thirteenth, probably as many as fourteen thous-
and Heimatschutz men were ready for action, and for several hours they
controlled most of upper Styria and for a while Graz itself. The putschists arrested several socialist mayors and legislators, took over police
duty (where they were not supported by Meyszner's gendarmery),
interrupted traffic, and fired into socialist headquarters in Kapfenberg
killing two men. But they were not effective revolutionaries, especially
in that they made no effort to seize control of the state's communications system. And, according to Berger-Waldenegg, some of Prankh's
men marched in the wrong direction.[39]

Pfrimer soon realized that he stood alone. The Heimwehren of the
other provinces were not following his lead, and the official forces, except for scattered police units in Styria, moved against the putsch.
Under Meyszner's influence in the temporary absence of Lamberg,
Pfrimer had earlier issued the self-contradictory order for his men to

avoid clashes with government forces but to hold their positions and continue to march toward Vienna. Then, somehow mysteriously incapacitated, between 9:00 and 10:00 in the morning Pfrimer gave the order to liquidate the action, after which he began his exodus and paid no more attention to what was going on.[40]

At about the same time the socialist leaders called on Chancellor Buresch with the demand that the government move resolutely against the insurgents, or else the Schutzbund would go into action. Buresch, supported by Schober and Winkler, promised to keep matters under control. Around noon the government issued a proclamation to its "Fellow Citizens" in which it promised severe punishment to those who had led the uprising against the fatherland in a time of dire economic crisis.[41] By telephone Rintelen, who remained passive as long as he could without badly compromising himself, suggested that Buresch could bring the affair to a quicker end, freeing the chancellor to depart as scheduled for Geneva, if he would offer an amnesty to the guilty Heimwehr leaders.[42] But Schober and Winkler balked at this proposal and persuaded Buresch to send troops into upper Styria. Due to unusual and unexplained mechanical troubles the army advanced very slowly, however, and the retreating Heimatschutz men had plenty of time to abscond with nearly all their weapons and equipment—including several machine guns and even a few light cannon—safely intact. Reports appeared in an Innsbruck newspaper that the putschists were promised twenty-four hours to see how the populace reacted before government troops would actively intervene.[43]

When events turned against the Heimatschutz in Styria, Starhemberg tried to limit the uprising. After a hurried talk with Revertera and Neustädter-Stürmer he mobilized his Upper Austrian troops—in case of Schutzbund attack—but gave explicit orders to avoid conflicts with government forces. At the same time he sent word to district authorities that he would not join Pfrimer unless the Styrians were engaged in defensive action against the Schutzbund. In the early afternoon Rauter called him to relay Pfrimer's order to move on Vienna in full force, although by this time the Styrian leader had completely withdrawn; Starhemberg countered with the demand that the enterprise be terminated. He later claimed that he called Vaugoin and promised to have all Heimwehr men withdrawn and demobilized by 10:00 P.M. if only the army would advance slowly enough to prevent clashes, to which proposal Vaugoin drawled, "I can't make any promises, but see that you get away." Starhemberg boasted that it was after this conversation that the mechanical difficulties began to plague the convoys.[44]

In the other provinces there was very little action. Pfrimer sent a letter to Alberti in Lower Austria asking him to take over the provincial government and to contain Vienna. The letter was given instead to Karg-Bebenburg, who refused to participate in the venture and only alerted the men of his home district of Amstetten and Waidhofen/Ybbs. Only one district leader in Salzburg, Elshuber of Pongau, whom Pfrimer had contacted directly, obeyed the orders without asking his provincial command, which otherwise merely called an alert. In Carinthia, Hül-gerth would have nothing to do with the affair and only alerted his men. Tyrol and Vorarlberg remained quiet; Steidle assured Buresch of his loyalty on the afternoon of September 13.[45]

The ludicrous rebellion lasted less than twenty-four hours. Pfrimer resigned "to avoid bloodshed," asked Berger-Waldenegg to succeed him (about noon on Sunday), and fled to Yugoslavia. Though not a leading putschist, Rauter also resigned. After talking with Starhemberg on the telephone about 4:00 P.M., Berger-Waldenegg gave orders for the Heimatschutz in Styria "to disband under the cover of darkness, to avoid clashes with the executive, and to save the weapons." By 10:00 Sunday evening Styria was completely quiet.[46]

Exactly who instigated the putsch has never been clarified. Whether Pfrimer was used by men who wanted to weaken the Heimwehr or whether he looked for assistance to those who would help him do what he wanted to do anyway is simply not known. The Austrian scholar who undertook an intensive investigation of the putsch concludes that Nazi intrigues were behind it and that Lamberg, the man who actually set the events in motion, was, in fact, a Nazi agent. Hofmann bases this conclusion largely on the testimony of both Revertera and Starhemberg. Revertera claimed that Lamberg, whose escape into Bavaria he assisted, left behind a package of Nazi literature. Starhemberg later protested that the Nazis wanted to bring the Heimwehr into conflict with the government in order to discredit it—or to use it in the event that the putsch succeeded. According to this interpretation, Pfrimer, who for years had agitated for a march on Vienna, was but a willing dupe of more incisively insidious figures in the background. That may or may not be. A rather simple man (his defenders would call him straightforward), Pfrimer was passionately pro-German and clearly hoped that his putsch would serve the cause of *Anschluss*. In all likelihood Pfrimer did receive extra money from the Alpine Montan company, which was controlled by German capital, and perhaps also from other German sources, as Kerekes assumes on hearsay evidence. But the fact that Pfrimer was supported by German interests does not mean that his backers only wanted him to engage in a fiasco that would leave the way clear for the Nazis. More likely they were all, including Lamberg, moved by a furious indignation at the failure of the customs union and by the determination to prevent Austria's becoming any more financially dependent on France and her allies. Starhemberg and Revertera had their own reasons for blaming the disaster on the Nazis, and their charges need not be taken at face value.[47]

In any event both the Nazis and the socialists sought to reap advantage from the Heimwehr's predicament. Stepping up their propaganda, the Nazis ridiculed the Heimwehr's "nth" seizure of power and argued that only their better philosophy, not force of arms, would defeat "Jewish Marxism" by legal means. Both they and the socialists tried to discredit Starhemberg by loudly charging that he betrayed Pfrimer and was but an untrustworthy dilettante. But where the Nazis called on Heimwehr adherents to join their camp, the socialists vociferously demanded the dissolution of all Heimwehr associations. Their campaign had more political power behind it and, given their fear that the next Heimwehr putsch might be allowed to succeed, was understandable. However, under the circumstances, when it appeared that the debacle would anyway weaken the Heimwehr, it might have been wiser for the socialists merely to have laughed the venture to scorn rather than to provoke sympathy for their opponents. As it was, the socialists' anti-Heimwehr vehemence soon drove to the Heimwehr's defense the "bourgeois" journals that had supported their first demands for dissolution, with the national-liberal *Volkswirt* almost sympathetically viewing the putsch as the result of understandable frustration at the failure of the customs union project.[48]

To demonstrate that it was in control of the situation, the government immediately undertook wholesale arrests of Heimatschutz members and suspended from duty all bureaucrats who participated in the insurrection.[49] Starhemberg was also taken into custody, although as Buresch told the German foreign minister, in Austria "one did not go about arresting a prince so quickly." The government also announced that it would use the army in a "renewed, very energetic disarmament action" against the Heimwehr. But its zeal was of very brief duration, and there took place only a token seizure of weapons (according to the Hungarian minister perhaps one-fifth of those held by the Styrians). The cabinet refused to dissolve any Heimwehr organizations, as demanded by the socialists, partly because the ministers feared it would be politically inexpedient to cater to their opponents, who at this juncture were not willing to give up their Schutzbund, and partly because they did not want to antagonize further a group that seemed to pose no immediate threat and that might someday provide crucial support, especially in the Nationalrat, where an important vote was pending. An opposite procedure (i.e., the arrest of only the top Styrian leaders and a thorough disarming) would probably have been more effective, especially since the numerous arrests and charges of treason transformed "ridiculous putschists" into "heroes and martyrs" receiving widespread sympathy.[50]

The *Panther* did not miss an issue. Government officials seized the first run of eighteen thousand copies of the issue for September 19, but the publisher printed another twenty thousand copies without the objectionable passages but with a reprint of an article by Raimund Günther summarizing his arguments that the republican constitution was illegitimate. The paper demanded the release of the arrested men, an end to punitive action against government officials who aided the putschists, and the cessation of newspaper attacks against the Heimwehr. Reminding its readers of the Red revolt in July 1927, the paper defended the putsch as the action of a people in need. Pfrimer acted solely out of love for the Austrian people; sadly he was influenced by bad counsel and a "mystification." The *Panther's* demands were supported by demonstrations all over Styria and by celebrations at the release of some of the "heroes," as at that of Count Stürgkh, who helped Pfrimer escape through his estate on the Yugoslav border.[51]

Thus, despite the ridicule it invited, the putsch itself, the socialists' reaction to it, and the government's inept handling of its "liquidation" awakened new interest in the Heimwehr in much of Austria. If anything there was temporarily a growth rather than a decline in its following. In mid-October a short-lived, pro-Pfrimer weekly, *Der Heimatbote*, appeared in Wiener Neustadt. Nevertheless, it was with good reason generally assumed that for the foreseeable future the Heimwehr would hardly be in a position to influence governmental policies, at least not on its own initiative. That it could survive such a debacle and remain a potential political factor was mainly due to the animus and fear that most nonsocialists felt toward their opponents and to the eight Heimatblock votes in the Nationalrat. It was also due to the anger and frustration engendered by the country's economic conditions. Furthermore, energetic competition from the Nazis for the allegiance of the dissatisfied spurred Austrian traditionalists and anti-*Anschluss* foreign backers to sustain the Heimwehr as a political factor.

For the remaining months of 1931 the Heimwehr was primarily occupied with readjusting its internal affairs in the wake of Pfrimer's folly. The putsch did not jeopardize its existence as much as call its loyalties into question, and there ensued a vigorous contest for its allegiance between the Nazis on one hand and those political leaders who favored the maintenance of an independent Austria under an authoritarian government on the other. There was never much likelihood of completely healing the breach between the Heimwehr groups that seceded from the federal command earlier in the year and Pfrimer's impatient followers. For a while it appeared likely that the latter might carry the bulk of the Heimwehr into the Nazi camp, and hence entirely into opposition to the government and into support for *Anschluss.*

In determining which direction the Heimwehr would take, Starhemberg held the key position, for as Pfrimer's "deputy" the leadership of the federal command almost automatically reverted to him. During his well-advertised four-day stay in a Linz jail, the upper Styrian leaders who were still free pledged their loyalty to the Heimatschutz idea and "its purest and most unselfish champion, Federal Leader E. R. Starhemberg."[52] While Steidle and Fey refused to proclaim their solidarity with Starhemberg, they did agree with other members of the federal command that all would stand together under Hülgerth in the face of a socialist attack on the Heimwehr.[53] The charges against Starhemberg were soon dropped on the grounds of his early message of loyalty to the district authorities and of lack of evidence that he was a party to the conspiracy. He formally resumed command of the national organization, insofar as it still existed, immediately after his release.[54] His most pressing concerns were to keep the Styrians in the fold and at the same time to bring the Tyroleans and Viennese back into it.

Starhemberg faced an important option when parliament considered the government's economies bill early in October. At first the chancellor believed he would need the votes of the Heimatblock to pass the unpopular measure, which was requisite for the new loan that he had requested at Geneva. On a night that Gulick calls "famous in the annals of the republic," Buresch offered Starhemberg ministerial posts in return for the Heimatblock's support of the bill. For several reasons, not least the fact that the measure would cut the salaries of many of the bureaucrats who sympathized with the Heimwehr, Starhemberg refused to cooperate. Buresch then turned to the Social Democrats. While declining an invitation to join the cabinet, Otto Bauer expressed willingness to vote for the reform if several points were first revised. During the night the provisions dealing with salary cuts in the lower brackets, a more steeply graduated income tax, collective bargaining rights, and the retention of unemployment benefits were hammered out to the satisfaction of the socialists. On the afternoon of October 3 only the Heimatblock voted against the emergency legislation—fine thanks for Buresch's mildness after the Styrian uprising.[55]

Starhemberg thus showed his unwillingness to play the parliamentary game. Instead of joining the government, he all but dared it to disband the Heimwehr and called for the ouster of Winkler and Schober from the cabinet. On a speaking rampage he denounced democracy and the parliamentary system, capitalism, and socialism, and adopted Pfrimer's contention that the constitution was illegal: "What is there in this state to betray?" While disclaiming knowledge of Pfrimer's putsch plans, he praised the Styrian comrades for trying to combat the country's economic crisis and pitched his appeal to the growing grievances of the peasants. Starhemberg saw the decisive campaign "to conquer the state by revolution" just beginning and demanded blind obedience from every single *Heimatschützer*. The socialists complained in parliament about these "provocative" speeches, but the government ignored them.[56] Schober, however, took Starhemberg's insults more seriously and brought suit against him—eventually winning a token settlement of AS 200.

By his bombastic belligerence Starhemberg not only gave vent to his own inclinations, but also, more importantly, hoped to keep open his options vis-à-vis the Nazis. He was alarmed at Nazi inroads into the nationalist ranks of the Heimwehr and impressed by the celebrated Harzburg alliance between Hitler and the leaders of the Stahlhelm and of the conservative German National People's Party on October 11. For several weeks he was torn between a similar association with the Nazis and collaboration with the right wing of the CSP. His personal financial circumstances made him subject to CSP influence, and in mid-October Steidle and Fey began to make public, if cautious, approaches to his camp.[57] On the other hand, shortly after the Harzburg agreement German nationalists provided some money for the Heimwehr in an effort to lure Starhemberg into an alliance with the Austrian Nazis, who were now led by Theodor Habicht, a German whom Hitler appointed as Nazi leader for Austria in July 1931.[58] With the announcement of plans for a large joint rally at which both Habicht and Rauter would speak in Graz on October 31, Austrian newspapers of all colors expectantly discussed the question of whether the Heimwehr would, or should, opt for "Harzburg or Habsburg": to align with the Nazis or remain aloof from them and hence Germany in favor of Austrian particularism and possibly a Danubian confederacy under a restored monarchy. Starhemberg was hard pressed by Heimwehr nationalists like Rauter and Faber, both of whom entered loose local alliances with the Nazis early in November to the cheers of Olaf Petri in the *Panther* that "We belong together!" Although the extent to which these agreements actually subordinated the Heimwehr groups to Nazi control was not clear, they nevertheless made it urgent for Starhemberg to reach a comprehensive understanding with the Nazis or to gain support from other quarters.[59]

At this point Starhemberg could have gone either way, since he was neither an opponent of most Nazi doctrines (anti-Semitism notably excepted) nor a proponent of Catholic corporative theories. His concern was more practical than ideological: the realization of the great ambitions he now entertained for himself in Austrian politics. To that end he would have welcomed the Nazis into his camp, but, no longer committed to *Anschluss,* he saw no greater advantage in subordinating himself to them late in 1931 than at election time in 1930. In his only meeting with Habicht the two men's ambitions clashed uncompromisingly.[60] At the same time it was made clear to Starhemberg in talks with Seipel and several industrialists, including his old friend Fritz Mandl, who had important ties in Italy, that a clear break with the Nazis would again make the Heimwehr suitable coalition material for the CSP, which from pan-German perspectives remained particularist, or rather pro-Habsburg and pro-Danubian (more than pro-Italian). More important, Mussolini, who hoped to draw Austria into his orbit, would provide funds and also let Starhemberg play *Duce* north of the Brenner Pass, the role for which Hitler now backed Habicht in the Nazi camp. Starhemberg had little choice but to take another step away from a group with whom he had once had close ties.[61]

Nevertheless, to be able to negotiate with the Tyroleans and Viennese with some cards still in his hand, Starhemberg sought to placate his nationalist wing. According to Franz Winkler, Starhemberg gave the Styrians his word of honor that together with the army he was preparing a coup that would install an anti-CSP government dominated by the Heimwehr. Diplomatic observers also knew that Starhemberg wanted to create a right-wing cabinet.[62] Holding out such hopes, his principal subordinates proposed a truce with the Nazis, in which the two groups would refrain from attacking each other, while remaining independent. At a meeting of provincial leaders in Linz on November 17, Rauter and Meyszner, the spokesmen for the Styrian dissidents, temporarily acceded to the wishes of the majority and acquiesced in this formula.[63]

Thus apparently in control of his organization, Starhemberg felt that he could risk the public dissociation from the Nazis that was requisite for support from Seipel's circle and Mussolini and for cooperation from Steidle and Fey. He took the step before an assembly of his Lower

Austrian followers on November 22. In a speech that became standard Starhemberg fare over the next two years, he boasted of Heimwehr accomplishments before the Nazis ever appeared in Austria and accused the latter of wanting to subordinate Austrian problems to German policy. The Heimwehr would probably have to act to save Germandom in Austria from the bolshevik danger and to create a healthy state there before the ultimate goal of *Anschluss* would become diplomatically feasible. But, while asserting that the Heimwehr was invincible as long as it remained united, he admitted that it was no longer in a position to determine the place and time for coming to power and thus would have to be ready for any eventuality. The next day with Seipel's backing Starhemberg conferred with Steidle and Fey. The three men agreed, according to press releases, on the goals of the Heimwehr and on a form of cooperation for "specific cases," although the latter were not defined and the impression was left that Steidle and especially Fey still had serious reservations about working with Starhemberg.[64]

To these developments the Nazi press replied with such virulence that any hope for a truce between the two right-wing groups was largely ended, at least outside of Styria. It accused Starhemberg of having opted for the Habsburg extreme. On November 26 Habicht's office announced that the Nazis were no longer interested in any alliance with the present Heimwehr federal command, and as if to emphasize the enmity there was a brawl at a Nazi meeting in Linz, where the Upper Austrian Nazi leader spoke against the Heimwehr and then would not allow a rebuttal. In Styria two days later Starhemberg dissociated himself from the legitimists but angrily asserted that Austria's needs could not be met by a retroactive salvation through a Third Reich, especially since Hitler could not guarantee that he would seize power in Germany and effect an *Anschluss* before the complete collapse of Austria.[65]

Starhemberg soon realized, however, that he could not oppose the Nazis with such vehemence and at the same time retain the allegiance of the entire Styrian Heimatschutz. This was made clear by the secession of Styria's Bund Oberland and a student organization in Graz. In an effort to hold the largest provincial organization intact, Starhemberg once again felt forced to moderate his position somewhat and to try to walk the tightrope between Harzburg and Habsburg. At a day-long meeting with 150 Heimatschutz leaders in Graz on November 30, he accepted an ambiguous nine-point statement of principles that vaguely supported *Anschluss* and opposed both restoration and a Danubian federation: the Heimatschutz "is a militant, racial, and patriotic revolutionary renewal movement" and "demands the organically built, corporatively structured racial state . . . that can be respected and accepted someday as a valuable branch of the greater German fatherland, to which we aspire." While the last point asserted that "a comradely relationship" and "a mutual understanding" with the Nazis was "quite possible," Starhemberg nevertheless stated that a nationwide political alliance with the Nazis was not possible because of international considerations.[66] In the long run this highly touted agreement failed to hold the Styrian Heimatschutz together, especially since the following week Starhemberg again sounded his anti-Nazi, pro-Austrian theme. But for the time being the Styrian Heimatschutz leaders resisted the Nazis' insistence that they demand more binding commitments from Starhemberg. On the national level a meeting between Franz Hueber, the Heimwehr leader in Salzburg, and Theo Habicht did nothing to bring a real truce between the Heimwehr's federal command and the Nazis any nearer.[67]

Unexpectedly, the first lasting Heimwehr defection to the Nazis was in Lower Austria. Provincial leader Alberti removed Herbert Faber from his post in the Waldviertel for continuing to seek an alignment with the Nazis against Starhemberg's instructions. At an unruly meeting in Krems on December 12, Starhemberg and Alberti met cool receptions and heard demands both for Faber's reinstatement and for a Nazi alliance. When they rejected the demands, Faber proceeded to organize a separatist Deutschen Heimatschutzverband Oesterreichs linked with the Nazis.[68]

At this point Seipel moved quickly to counter Starhemberg's losses to keep him from yielding completely to nationalist pressures. Behind the scenes he brought about a reconciliation between Starhemberg, Steidle, and Fey, and at a meeting of the provincial leaders on December 11 the latter two agreed to associate their organizations with Starhemberg's federal command. On the fourteenth the three men publicly demonstrated their rapprochement by speaking from the same platform before four thousand people in Vienna.[69] The Heimwehr would again become coalition material for the CSP's right wing, a prospect that Seipel deftly held out to Starhemberg.[70]

But also on the fourteenth began an event that tested the newly found harmony in the federal command: the treason trial against Pfrimer and seven others in Graz. A week earlier Pfrimer had slipped into Austria from Germany and surrendered himself to the state prosecution in Graz, which hastily drew up an indictment of high treason against him so that he could be the chief defendant at the trial already scheduled. It may well have been, as Starhemberg later charged, that Pfrimer returned only when he was assured that there was no longer any danger of conviction. Even so, Starhemberg surely knew at the time that the government was not eager to create any more nationalist martyrs. Indeed, he got Fey and Steidle to join him publicly in assuring Pfrimer of their "true and lasting comradeship" and in calling for his acquittal.[71] And it was Starhemberg, more than Steidle or Fey, who was moved by the outpouring of nationalist as well as antidemocratic sentiment at the trial.

Given the widespread sympathy for the putschists that existed throughout Styria, there was never much doubt about the trial's outcome. Pfrimer argued his own defense, and the prosecution permitted the trial to be conducted largely on his terms. Other counsel emphasized the idealism and unselfish patriotism of the defendants, and one of them cried, "To oppose the rule of parties is not high treason." Finally, Governor Rintelen's testimony that he had in no way been restricted in the performance of his official duties by the Heimwehr on September 13 seemed calculated to lead "with forceful logic to the conclusion that those who stood before the bar were innocent" of treasonous intent or deed. On December 16 a tragic clash in which local gendarmes killed two socialists and wounded three others during a search for Schutzbund arms at the town hall of Voitsberg, a small Styrian industrial town, enabled the counsel for defense to warn the jurors in lurid terms of the threat of Red revolution. The jury needed only forty-five minutes to acquit Pfrimer and his codefendants. The socialists, who had feared and predicted such an outcome of the trial, hastily issued a proclamation urging their followers to remain calm in order not to repeat the disaster of July 1927 and rather lamely warning that the next time they would defend their freedom themselves and not rely on such justice.[72]

Starhemberg was present for the celebration that followed the acquittal, which Pfrimer cheered with the remark, *Salus publica suprema lex.* Pledging themselves to what they called the "Pfrimer-course," the two men tried to present a picture of unanimity and comradeship. Starhemberg agreed that the verdict of patriotic men was the "most annihilating judgment" against the government and formed a new step in the Heimwehr movement. But the comradely gestures hardly moved Pfrimer, who always remained extremely bitter toward Starhemberg and within a few days began to express pro-Nazi sentiments. Although he did not resume active leadership of the Styrian organization, Pfrimer undoubtedly exercised a pro-Nazi influence on his friends in it.[73]

Nevertheless, partly because of its putsch mystique the Styrian Heimatschutz held its followers, many of whom did not like the Nazi emphasis on elections and "legality." At the end of December the loose political alliance between the Nazis and the Heimatschutz, which dated from early November, was dissolved. For the time being the Heimatschutz maintained its connection with the federal command. But it was a tenuous one largely dependent on the extent to which Starhemberg pushed the German nationalist over the clerical-legitimist cause.

As the year came to a close Starhemberg still stood, as he would for the next two years, between the Nazis and the right wing of the CSP. By temperament he continued to lean toward the Nazis, with whom he hoped to work out some means of cooperation. But he did not like their ridicule of Austria's Habsburg traditions or, more importantly, their insistence that he subordinate himself to Theo Habicht. He felt that a sufficiently radical posture on his part against both the socialists and Austria's moderate cabinet might bring about Nazi acceptance of him. In the meantime such policies made him unacceptable to all but the most authoritarian wing of the CSP. Although Seipel seemed to want to form a cabinet including the Heimwehr—and may have had Mussolini's encouragement[74]—he could not swing enough of his party behind the plan to make it possible without a coup d'état. In the view of most members of the CSP, Austria was too dependent on France and England for financial assistance to permit an open assault on the socialists. It was this deference to the western powers and to the socialists that Starhemberg attacked in his effort both to flirt and to compete with the Nazis. He fought hard not to be outdone in radical demagogy.

7

Rescue and Revival

Nineteen-thirty-two

As 1932 began, Starhemberg commanded an uneasy organization that could do little more than bluster on the sidelines. Hoping to defuse the Nazi threat to the very existence of the Heimwehr and of Austria, he and his followers intensified their demands for a forceful assault against the socialist positions of political and economic power. In a sense the government stood half-heartedly between the Heimwehr and the socialists, who for their part resolutely refused to provide a pretext for civil war. Thus, while still engaged in its internecine feud with the National Socialists, the Heimwehr continued to probe the government's defenses, hoping that by somehow breaching them it would finally be able to storm the bastion of the democratic socialists. The break did not come until May, when ironically the parliamentary Heimatblock became the means by which the floundering Heimwehr could again play a key role in Austrian politics.

The Heimwehr leaders hoped to find in the despair of the peasantry, lower bureaucracy, and small entrepreneurs—all hard hit by the deepening economic crisis—an opportunity to recoup some of their lost influence. On January 12 Starhemberg publicly addressed several economic demands to Chancellor Buresch and warned that there would be a popular storm, a mass *Aufmarsch* in the face of any "illegal" prohibitions, if they were not put into effect. Most of them rather naively assumed that any "patriotic" government could simply do what it wanted to do about trade and finance vis-à-vis other countries and financiers. Starhemberg called upon the government to correct the unfavorable balance of trade, if necessary by renouncing all its commercial treaties and entering new ones only on the basis of strict quotas; to reduce the state's role in the social welfare system; to create for one year a compulsory labor service of about sixty thousand unemployed men; and to repeal the Credit-Anstalt laws while continuing to support its industrial dependents until they could be left entirely in private hands. If the bank's foreign creditors would not agree that its debt be halved and changed into noninterest-bearing obligations which would be retired over twenty years beginning in 1935, the Austrian government should simply declare a moratorium on these payments.[1]

Starhemberg's ultimatum was not well received. The cabinet prepared to keep government forces on alert, and Vice-Chancellor Winkler even wanted Starhemberg arrested. The *Volkswirt*, accusing him of using Nazi economic thought, saw little practicality in the demands. The *Arbeiter-Zeitung*, which jeered that *Robot*—forced feudal labor—was a tradition with the Starhembergs, scorned them as childish economics; they were intended only as an excuse for another putsch, by which Starhemberg, deeply in debt, hoped to regain his solvency. Once again the socialists saw Seipel as the real villain of the piece. The *Neue Freie Presse* paid little attention to it all. But the *Reichspost*, without mentioning the threatened insurrection, showered praise on Starhemberg's "statesmanlike memorandum" of "serious, discussable proposals for saving the economy," which showed that the Heimwehr had "again found the path of positive political cooperation."[2]

The proposals were undoubtedly part of a scheme to create difficulties for the government. The *Neue Zürcher Zeitung* reported that they were drafted in the Industrialists' Club and approved by "a politician of the right"—surely a reference to Seipel, whom the British minister saw as wanting an early return to power. The Swiss newspaper saw the Heimwehr as more than ever the tool of political groups who hoped by awakening latent discontent in the provinces to compel President Miklas to prorogue parliament and appoint a government of the extreme right.[3] Such speculations proved alarmingly accurate. The Heimwehr's official history states that early in 1932 the Tyrolean Heimwehr began "a great propaganda campaign against the corrupt party system and demanded the formation of an authoritative government of technical experts . . . and the disarmament of the Schutzbund."[4] Indeed, the commercial and trade organization of Innsbruck, a corporate element of the Tyrolean Heimatwehr, sent a telegram to Miklas requesting that he call Seipel to head a government that excluded parliament. From Styria, the Heimwehr leaders, including Pfrimer, announced that they would consider a *Volksaufmarsch* a second putsch, with Heimwehr men from all provinces to converge unarmed on Vienna, where they would receive weapons and overthrow the Buresch government. Before an audience in Wels on the seventeenth Starhemberg shouted that if anyone should try to hinder his *Aufmarsch*, "then let the revolution begin." He was careful, however, to add that the Heimwehr's enemy was not the executive forces, but the Schutzbund, whose revolutionary intentions had again been made clear by the recent discovery of another cache of arms.[5]

Starhemberg must have hoped that the unannounced police search of the socialists' party building in Ottakring, the working-class district on the west side of Vienna, might provoke retaliation. The sanctimonious *Reichspost*, "horrified" at the discovery of an arsenal that included eight machine guns, eight hundred rifles, and a thousand hand grenades, tried to keep the public aroused. Socialist leaders, enraged at the search and seizure after the Styrian Heimatschutz had been allowed to march home with its weapons the previous September, called on the workers to show them their determination to defend the republican constitution and liberty as long as the Heimwehr remained armed against them. Julius Deutsch boasted that the lost weapons would be replaced tenfold, and the *Arbeiter-Zeitung*, trumpeting the slogan "battle against fascism," spoke of a growing "defense fund" and many enlistments into the Schutzbund. At the same time, however, in a formal proclamation the SDP simply admonished the faithful to restraint and readiness and warned their antagonists that in certain situations they would call a general strike.[6]

In retrospect, all this seems like much excitement about nothing or at the most only rehearsals for what would come later. The private armies did not clash, and despite the fact that for all practical purposes the government ignored its demands, the Heimwehr did not march. While some higher officials again urged the disarmament of all paramilitary groups, the chancellor let the opportunity for an impartial step in that direction pass with the remark that it required great patience to take Starhemberg's threats and insults calmly.[7]

About all the Heimwehr accomplished during the uproar was the unification of the Viennese Heimwehr groups. In return for Major Fey's acceptance of his claims to the national Heimwehr command, Starhemberg recognized Fey as sole leader in Vienna. Major Fritz Lahr, the self-proclaimed fascist leader of a large, formerly independent Heimwehr group, became Fey's deputy, and Starhemberg's former lieutenant in Vienna, the able Baron Arbesser, was removed to the federal staff. In his public acknowledgment of the occasion, Fey indirectly deferred to Starhemberg by recalling the glorious ancestor who had "alone saved Europe from Asiatic barbarism [*Unkultur*]." Then, again seeming to claim for himself the role of savior, Fey pledged to fight all the dark and antinational powers—embodied by the Social Democrats—and not to surrender a foot of German soil.[8]

Emil Fey's new position and developments later in 1932 proved great boons in his rise to national political power. Born the son of an imperial councillor in Vienna in 1886, he became a professional officer and the epitome of the proud, obdurate veteran of the vicious fighting of World War I. When he joined the crack Deutschmeister regiment early in 1915, he was officially described as having a "self-possessed, thoroughly stable character of noblest convictions. In all places and under all conditions calm and sensible. A conscientious, highly ambitious, elegant officer and thorough soldier,"[9] Fey earned his country's highest honors during his years along the Isonzo, where he was wounded four times and lost an eye (his glass eye contributed to his cold, impassive appearance of staring haughtiness). He testified to his own courage by applying for the Maria-Theresa Order, awarded only to men who requested it themselves on the basis of a heroic military accomplishment carried out without specific orders and on personal responsibility. After repeated supplications to the new republican officials, who were not sure of the validity of the award after the fall of the monarchy, Fey received the coveted decoration, which he nearly always wore, but not membership in the knighthood; undaunted, he allowed himself to be called *Theresienritter* Major Emil Fey.

Fey was another of the many men in the German world who never got over the war. Unable to adapt himself to civilian life, he adopted Austria's Social Democrats as his lifetime enemies. One reason for his lasting hatred of the socialists was the thankless humiliation inflicted on his regiment when it returned as an orderly unit to Vienna at the end of the war; almost twenty years later Fey still wrote with anger of the "unkempt civilian official of the new government" who met them at the station and told them that the renowned Deutschmeister were disbanded. As he became involved in veterans' and political affairs, Fey acted as if the same qualities that had brought him honor at the battlefront were efficacious in politics. He had little faith in any form of persuasion other than that of military force; to him, "every detour is cowardice."[10] He became the general secretary of the Association of Professional Officers, a position in which he was able to make himself known to influential personalities and to sponsor the earliest "self-defense" groups in Vienna. Among the leaders of Colonel Hiltl's Frontkämpfervereinigung, he remained unobtrusively active throughout the 1920s and became prominent during the dramatic proliferation of Heimwehr organizations in Vienna after July 1927.

A nationalist, Fey was nonetheless shrewd enough always to cast his lot with the conservative Christian Social leaders. As they moved away from democratic government, his star rose and his outlook became more and more Austrian and less German. This association with the CSP, his own ambitions and those of his wife, whose pretensions kept him constantly in debt, as well as personal jealousy, led to rivalry between Starhemberg and him that endured throughout their association in the Heimwehr and also affected the fate of the republic. When at the beginning of 1932 Starhemberg found himself forced to make concessions to his rival in order to strengthen his own position, Fey intended to make the most of the situation. He saw to it that his speeches and interviews, repetitious in their antisocialist vituperation, received advertisement equal to that given other Heimwehr leaders.

Meanwhile a cabinet crisis of great significance hastened a lasting transformation of the country's political alignment. After the long-deferred burial of the customs union project, Schober's position as foreign minister became extremely tenuous in a government financially dependent on the western powers. Whether the crisis growing out of this situation was the result of French pressure, as generally thought, or of Seipel-Heimwehr machinations, as the British minister in Vienna seemed to think, is not clear. In any event Buresch, claiming to want to shift Schober to some other ministry while maintaining the existing coalition, resigned on January 27. But the Pan-Germans, who were actually looking for an excuse to leave the cabinet in order to retain their political identity vis-à-vis the Nazis, refused to cooperate unless Schober were allowed to pursue his "German course" as foreign minister. Their refusal to remain in the cabinet ended the ten-year collaboration between them and the CSP and plunged the republic into the parliamentary crisis from which it never recovered. On the twenty-eighth Buresch conferred with Hueber and Neustädter-Stürmer about tolerating a minority government of Christian Socials and Landbund, but the Heimatblock delegates said they would continue their previous policy, which was largely one of opposition, perhaps with the expectation that they could thus force Seipel's return to power as the country's savior. Faced with this obduracy, Buresch found it necessary either to secure socialist acquiescence in a minority government that controlled only 75 of 165 seats in the Nationalrat or else to dissolve parliament and call new elections. The SDP did not press the issue, and on the twenty-ninth Buresch, as chancellor and foreign minister, formed a minority cabinet which included Franz Winkler and Hans Bachinger, Landbund leaders from Styria and Upper Austria, as vice-chancellor and minister of the interior. The only other notable change in the cabinet was the appointment of the young Tyrolean lawyer, Kurt Schuschnigg, a favorite of Seipel, as minister of justice; his inclusion was partially an attempt to mollify Buresch's critics in the Tyrol, both in its autonomous branch of the CSP and in the Heimatwehr, which put its men on alert and warned that it might not be able to keep its dissatisfied members under control if Buresch did not step aside.[11]

The new cabinet, generally recognized as a caretaker government, was primarily concerned with economic problems. Buresch's warning to the great powers on February 16 that Austria must be allowed to expand its area of trade or protect its domestic market by restricting imports set the stage for the abortive Tardieu Plan and eventually for another major international loan for Austria through the League of Nations. Before the early adjournment of the Nationalrat, the Social Democrats permitted it to grant Buresch emergency powers to meet the economic crisis, a gift they had denied the more capable Ender in June 1931.

During the relatively quiet weeks of late winter Starhemberg, Steidle, and Fey, now demonstratively if unconvincingly reconciled, continued their threatening demands tempered by cautious qualifications. At this point they kept the Heimwehr alive and noticed more by sheer bravado than by any earnest prospect of success. In a belligerent tirade on February 18, Starhemberg said he would prefer "to cut loose today rather than tomorrow" but added that "the great decisive act must be thought over by the leaders," who were not so dumb that they would give "the system" a chance to strengthen itself by the defeat of the Heimwehr: "We are waiting until the men of the executive [military] together with us chase the parasites of this system to the devil." A few days later Steidle repeated his demand that President Miklas appoint a cabinet of nonparty experts.[12]

In a sense Interior Minister Bachinger's new proposal for general internal disarmament merely provided grist for the Heimwehr's propaganda mill. How dare the government "equate" patriots with the Schutzbund! From the beginning the socialists suspected a ruse to get them to disclose the locations of their hidden caches, especially when the chancellor expressed his "complete understanding" for the Heimwehr's contention that nonsocialists could not afford to lay down their arms until their opponents were completely harmless. And when Steidle referred to the disarmament talks as "monkey business," the *Arbeiter-Zeitung* answered with a picture of an armed Heimatwehr march—despite the continuing prohibitions—in Lienz, the East Tyrol: that was the real *Affentheater*. Only Raab among the Heimwehr leaders told Bachinger that his organization was ready to cooperate in a "just and

general disarmament." Thus faced with the collapse of his plans, Bachinger chose to postpone admission of defeat by appointing a committee
to study the problem. At the same time the Tyrolean diet enacted a
measure that would make any disarmament of the Heimatwehr ineffec-
tive. It rejected the finance control office's recommendation that it stop
support of private armed formations and instead empowered the executive to activate such organizations as emergency police and to supply
weapons for their use.[13]

About the same time that the disarmament issue was shelved, Starhemberg's financial problems began again to cause him public embarrassment and to weaken his position within the Heimwehr. In mid-March
his office felt it necessary to explain that he was staying at a ski resort
in Vorarlberg not to resign but to convalesce from an attack of tonsil-
litis. The *Arbeiter-Zeitung* reveled in his financial predicament (he allegedly owed 3 to 4 million schillings), and even the *Neue Freie Presse*
waxed unusually caustic in its criticisms of "Dilettante" Starhemberg's
"political and financial immoderation and immaturity." By the end of
the month there was widespread talk that he would resign, and, following new disputes with Steidle, there were signs that the Heimwehr's
newfound unity was again in jeopardy. Starhemberg worked hard to
mollify the Tyroleans, and early in April the leaders made a public
statement of their support for Starhemberg "at this time of attacks
against him because of his financial difficulties," incurred because of his
"idealism and sacrifice" for the Heimwehr.[14] Nevertheless, such affirma-
tions of loyalty could not conceal the fact that the strains of electoral
campaigns then getting underway in several provinces and municipalities were intensifying the divisive tendencies in the Heimwehr.

Although the Heimatblock did not dare enter a list for any of the
elections, Starhemberg again tried unsuccessfully to work out an accommodation with the Nazis. He had conferred with Pabst and Hitler in
February, when he went to Berlin to address the National Club, and
had mistakenly gained the impression that Hitler was prepared to acknowledge his demands for leadership and for Austrian independence.
Late in March Pabst, apparently invited by Starhemberg to resume his
old job, came to Austria to attempt to mediate between Habicht and
Starhemberg. Habicht, however, fearing that Starhemberg posed a
threat to his leadership of the Austrian Nazis, would not consent to an
alliance. Hitler stood by Habicht, and the Nazis conducted a vigorous
campaign on their own.[15] Pabst played a very ambiguous role in the
following weeks, and was probably responsible for keeping most of the
Heimwehr behind Starhemberg at this time. Thereafter he appeared in

Austria at frequent but irregular intervals, both to try to mediate between the Heimwehr and the Nazis and to prod the Heimwehr to action against the Social Democrats.[16]

In the voting on April 24 the Nazis made astounding and alarming gains and confronted Austria with a new political equation. Altogether about three-fourths of the country's registered voters went to the polls, and the returns made it clear that the composition of the Nationalrat no longer accurately reflected the relative strengths of the parties. In the provinces of Vienna, Lower Austria, and Salzburg, the Nazis received approximately 336,000 votes, a sum which exceeded the combined Heimatblock-Nazi total for the whole country in the parliamentary elections of November 1930. They completely wiped out the Pan-German People's party representation in the three diets and severely weakened both the Landbund and the CSP, who lost their majorities in Salzburg and Lower Austria and had to rely more than ever on the sufferance of the Social Democrats to govern in those provinces. In Vienna the Nazis increased their votes from only 27,500 in 1930 to over 200,000, which won for them nearly half of the nonsocialist representation. They also made respectable showings in municipal elections in Styria and Carinthia. These National Socialist victories also changed the complexion of the Bundesrat, which reflected the relative party strength in the provinces. With the entry of the Nazis, the parties of the governing coalition lost their majority in the upper chamber, where the combined socialist and Nazi opposition could now force the lower house to pass legislation over a suspensive veto.[17]

As an anti-Marxist vehicle for protesting the country's economic misery, the Nazis threatened to sweep all before them, including the old Heimwehr. Now any accommodation between the feuding cousins would be on Nazi terms, and in the coming weeks Heimwehr groups in Styria, Carinthia, and Lower Austria moved to join what they took to be the bandwagon.[18] More importantly, the CSP's confidence was severely shaken. Clearly unnerved by the new situation, Starhemberg hoped to prepare for any eventuality by mending his fences in Germany, although on the day of the elections he received encouragement from Mussolini to take up the cudgels against *Anschluss*.[19] Within a few days of the voting, Starhemberg again traveled to Berlin, this time more quietly than in February. Only his unreliable account of his conversations with Röhm and Hitler is available. He claims that he was invited by Röhm, who along with several German Nazis hoped to gain prestige by fishing in Austria's troubled waters. However, Heinrich Himmler's presence at Starhemberg's talk with Röhm prevented any meaningful

negotiation between them. Starhemberg then had what he called an unexpected and secret conversation with Hitler, who arranged the meeting
through Pabst and Prince Waldeck-Pyrmont. In what was to be their
last personal encounter, Hitler used architectural allegory in advising
Starhemberg to make his policies fit the new building that the Nazis
were constructing. In his memoirs Starhemberg pictured himself as
adhering faithfully to an anti-Nazi line, but at the time he must have
equivocated. As it turned out, however, he soon faced a more immediately promising opportunity.[20]

While still in Berlin, Starhemberg received word from Neustädter-
Stürmer that the eight Heimatblock votes had become decisive and
that "an agreement . . . had already been reached with the chiefs of
the Christian Social party, and a stronger government, capable of solv-
ing immediate problems, could be set up."[21] Starhemberg's memory of
the chronology of this period was weak, but his decision to support the
government formed by Dr. Engelbert Dollfuss in May 1932, although
it led to a lasting division between the Heimwehr's "German" and
"Austrian" wings, saved the organization from general dissolution and
insignificance for several years. What it meant for the republic was
something other than salvation.

At issue was the opposition parties' demand for new national elections in the wake of the Nazi victories on April 24. On April 28 the
Social Democrats, who had held their own in the elections, the Pan-
Germans, and the Heimatblock moved dissolution and the calling of
national elections. Buresch's minority cabinet, which opposed elections
during the economic crisis and negotiations for an international loan,
collapsed. But indications that deals were in the making came on May
3, when both the Heimatblock and the Pan-Germans agreed to delay
consideration of dissolution from the sixth to the tenth. When Starhemberg returned from Berlin, he and the provincial Heimwehr leaders
decided that the Heimatblock would withdraw its support of dissolution if the CSP met their conditions for the formation of a cabinet that
would adopt a clear-cut rightist policy. The Christian Socials, never
seriously considering accommodations with the socialists, had to choose
between national elections and a coalition with the Heimatblock.[22]
Austria's political future stood at a crossroads. It was a time of decision that was to seem increasingly momentous as from there the country turned gradually from democratic procedures toward dictatorial
rule. A key determinant was the attitude of the Heimatblock, for it held
the balance of power in the Nationalrat, and this at a time when its
old mentor Seipel already lay on his deathbed.

The cabinet negotiations lasted through the first three weeks of May. Starhemberg's policy was jeopardized by the Styrian Heimatschutz's opposition to support of the "system parties"; on May 9 it announced that it would remain a "renewal movement based on the Korneuburg program." Furthermore, Starhemberg and his colleagues were not sure that Minister of Agriculture and Forestry Dollfuss, whom President Miklas named chancellor-designate on May 10, promised "sufficient guarantee for their demands." While the Heimwehr vacillated, the threat of dissolution was ended on May 12 when a compromise resolution calling for the Nationalrat to set the date for elections in its autumn session carried with the votes of the CSP, the Landbund, and the Pan-Germans, who thus in theory supported dissolution but in practice postponed the day of reckoning with their Nazi competition. Thereafter Dollfuss's efforts to form a majority government were vexed by the Pan-Germans' opposition, the Landbund's refusal to support a cabinet of administrators instead of politicians, and the uncertainty of the Heimatblock's policy. Finally, hoping to stave off a Styrian secession that might deprive it of two important votes, the Heimatblock in effect demanded that Rintelen become chancellor, but Rintelen, who did not want to bring himself into disfavor with the Nazis, vetoed his own candidacy. When the Styrian Heimwehr leaders nonetheless decided to declare themselves politically independent, Starhemberg persuaded Hainzl, who resigned as provincial leader, and Lengauer to remain in the Heimatblock's parliamentary club. Thus, about midnight, May 19/20, Starhemberg was able to assure the CSP that the Heimatblock would remain united under his direction and that they would support a Dollfuss government.[23]

Starhemberg thus tied his fortunes, or at least his hopes of salvaging some political influence, to the CSP and, as it turned out, to the person of Dollfuss. Early in the negotiations he exclaimed that by a rightist government he meant "no Dollfuss government,"[24] but this may have been a reaction to Dollfuss's statement at their first meeting that he intended to ask the socialists to enter the government. Starhemberg need not have been worried about a grand coalition, however, for the chasm between Austria's two major parties was already too great for reconciliation to be possible, especially since everywhere else in Europe political polarization was becoming more pronounced. What he did have to worry about was losing his last chance to gain a toehold on power while he still had a separate political identity. He had little choice but to take advantage of the opportunity at hand, although the Heimwehr was not yet in a position to play a significant role in policy-

making. Indeed, some followers protested that he was delivering the
Heimwehr into Dollfuss's hands. Starhemberg claimed that he supported the cabinet without making any "conditions of a political nature," except that Dollfuss and he "should collaborate loyally and
frankly, and that neither should take any decisive step without informing the other."[25] However, at the time a Landbund paper reported that
Dollfuss promised to kill a bill that by abolishing hereditary entails
would open much of Starhemberg's wealth to his creditors.[26]

Throughout their collaboration Dollfuss and Starhemberg treated
each other with respect and a frankness that eventually bordered on
grudging admiration. But theirs was never an easy relationship. Each
man justifiably suspected the other of trying to make a deal with the
Nazi leaders, especially after Hitler became German chancellor. Their
relationship was also strained after the exclusion of parliament in
March 1933 gave the Heimwehr more opportunity to set the pace of
the offensive against the Social Democrats.

The cabinet list that Dollfuss presented Miklas gave the Heimatblock much more influence than their number of seats or their support
throughout the country warranted. They formally named only the minister of trade, Guido Jakoncig, the freebooter turned lawyer who be-
friended both Pabst and Starhemberg. But Rintelen became minister
of education, and Hermann Ach, a bureaucrat who became minister of
security, was known to be pro-Heimwehr. For the Landbund, Vice-
Chancellor Winkler and Bachinger, now the head of an interior ministry deprived of its police functions, remained in the cabinet, as did
Christian Socials Schuschnigg, Vaugoin, Resch, and Weidenhoffer, who
continued to direct the ministries of justice, army, social administration,
and finance. Besides the chancellorship, Dollfuss held the portfolios of
agriculture and foreign affairs. In the lower house this new cabinet
controlled a slender majority of only one vote,[27] a doubly precarious
margin in view of the fact that the Bundesrat began to force the Nationalrat to pass legislation over its suspensive veto.

With such uncertain support Dollfuss was not expected to maintain
a government any longer than had his predecessors or to pursue a vigorous and independent course. However, he bravely let it be known
that he considered his administration a sacred Austrian mission.[28] For
over two fateful years—the worst ones of the depression—he clung to
his position and did much to change Austria's bankruptcy into near
stability and her despair—at least that of most nonsocialists—into hope.
At the same time he became one of the most controversial figures of
the First Republic, when with the support of Mussolini and the Vati-

can he engineered the transformation of Austria from a democratic republic into an authoritarian dictatorship.

Dollfuss, the devout son of Lower Austrian peasants, first trained for the priesthood. But, as a youth of unusually small stature, he seemed to need to prove himself in other ways. Because of his size he needed special permission to join the army. As a lieutenant in the renowned Tyrolean Kaiserschützen he served with distinction throughout much of the war on the Italian front. Afterwards he continued secular studies in Vienna and Berlin, where he received the doctorate. During the 1920s he distinguished himself in administrative positions in the agricultural organizations of Lower Austria and entered the national arena by his elevation to the presidency of the federal railroads. When he became chancellor in his fortieth year, he had never held an electoral mandate, and he remained less a politician than a somewhat opportunistic administrator with immense personal ambition. He had developed an authoritarian nature, tempered by a strong humanitarian impulse and in most situations a jovial personality. He became chancellor without any grand scheme other than a vague commitment to Catholic social doctrines and to "Austria." Sensing that he was inheriting Seipel's mantle, although he was not yet as doctrinaire as the dying statesman with whom he had a long conference on July 10, Dollfuss would cooperate with anyone who would acknowledge these priorities.[29]

From the beginning the Social Democrats responded negatively to the prospect of a Dollfuss ministry. Even if Dollfuss did approach them during the cabinet negotiations, it is most likely that he posed terms unacceptable to them. With currents throughout Europe running against democracy, the socialist leaders feared that entry into a conservative-led cabinet from a weakening position might destroy their independence and undermine their principles to such an extent that a radical separatist movement would destroy their ranks. Once Dollfuss took office the socialists viewed him as a prisoner of the Heimwehr, regardless of how reluctant he had been to ally with it. Although for a while Dollfuss had proper relations with socialist leaders such as Deutsch, with whom he once agreed to discuss future problems, the tension in parliament soon transformed political opposition into personal animosity, especially as the influence of the Heimwehr grew.[30] While appreciating the socialists' position, one cannot help wishing that they had risked the concessions that might have strengthened parliamentary institutions before the onslaught from a Nazi-dominated Germany. Given the disposition of forces and the fact that Dollfuss was still (and at the other end of the political spectrum remained) malleable, they missed the last possible chance to avert what in retrospect often seems inevitable. Even if eventual absorption by Nazi Germany might not have been averted, Austria could have been spared the bitter anguish of civil war. Once the Heimwehr gained, or was given, the balance of power, it was able, with Mussolini's support, to force the destruction of Austria's Social Democrats.[31]

Thus, the entry of the Heimwehr into the ruling coalition in May 1932 proved to have lasting significance. The forces had now joined which, pressed by the Nazis on one side and alienated from the socialists on the other, would provoke civil war, jettison the republican constitution, and bring Austria into Mussolini's political orbit. Once these changes had taken place there was to follow under the regime of "Austro-Fascism" nearly two years of apparent stability and even a growing "Austrianism," almost, as it were, a long calm between storms. In the meantime two turbulent years still lay ahead. As long as the government operated within a parliamentary framework, its position was precarious in the extreme. During the next ten months the Heimwehr clung desperately to its small share in the government, and, despite the fact that it almost slipped when its parliamentary delegation lost its unanimity at a critical moment, it gradually managed to increase its power, not so much numerically as functionally.

At the outset Starhemberg's decision to enter the cabinet was made at the cost of the defection of the Styrian Heimatschutz. On May 19 its radical nationalists, led by Kammerhofer, Rauter, and Meyszner, declared their political independence but, following the fashion of such dissident factions, announced their willingness to cooperate militarily with General Hülgerth. They elected Kammerhofer the new provincial leader and claimed control over Styria's two Heimatblock deputies, Hainzl and Lengauer, who decided for the moment, however, to support the government.[32] At the same time there was secession within the secession. Pfrimer, who had already announced his withdrawal from the Styrian Heimatschutz on May 8, formally assumed the leadership of Herbert Faber's German Heimatschutz. He immediately concluded an agreement in Frankfurt that subordinated his small Austrian following to Hitler, although he imagined that he retained his political autonomy.[33] At first the Styrian Heimatschutz was extremely critical of Pfrimer's defection and pledged itself to its "unalterable course," which for the moment meant a middle line between Starhemberg and Pfrimer. But the Styrians soon reached an agreement with the Nazis mutually to stop propaganda attacks and to discuss all differences. On May 27

Kammerhofer published a twelve-point statement of principles, much more Nazi in tone than the nine points of the previous November, which helped pave the way for the eventual union of the two groups.[34]

Thus unable to hold his pro-Nazi following or to work out a satisfactory agreement with the Nazi leadership, Starhemberg again sought support in Italy and Hungary during travels early in June. According to his own account, he assured Mussolini, who seemed willing even to countenance a Habsburg restoration in order to prevent *Anschluss*, that the Heimwehr would indeed oppose the Nazis, of whom he had only recently spoken solicitously. However, Starhemberg wanted help against Dollfuss as much as against the Nazis, for he feared that Dollfuss might feel compelled to coalesce with the socialists in order to procure a new international loan for Austria. Starhemberg proposed a remedy with a familiar ring: the Heimwehr should seize power, both to prevent a CSP–SDP coalition and to weaken the Nazi appeal. Whether or not Mussolini actually favored a putsch, he did agree to revive a plan that Starhemberg and Gömbös had concocted in 1930 and which Starhemberg claimed Dollfuss now approved. Old Austrian weapons captured in 1918 were to be sent to an Austrian army factory for repair; however, instead of being returned to Italy, some of them would be shipped to Hungary and some would be kept for the Heimwehr. Regent Horthy and Minister of War Gömbös again gave their whole-hearted support to the scheme,[35] which in January 1933 was to gain notoriety as the Hirtenberg Weapons Affair.

Back in Austria Starhemberg found public excitement over Austria's new appeal for a loan so great, even before any terms were known, that events threatened to outrun his plans. The Heimwehr leaders, fearing French pressure on Dollfuss to make peace with the Social Democrats, agreed to consider acting in conjunction with the National Socialists in ousting Dollfuss and placing Rintelen in the chancellorship. On June 24 Starhemberg and Jakoncig discussed alternate plans for action with Pabst, who hoped to mediate a Heimwehr-Nazi agreement, and with officials from the Italian and Hungarian legations. Leaving their policy toward a loan unclear, the Heimwehr leaders momentarily decided to erect an authoritarian government under Rintelen, immediately if Dollfuss offered concessions to the Social Democrats, later if he managed to avoid that step. In any event they expected that armed resistance from the Schutzbund would lead to a brief civil war.[36]

But this vague script was soon discarded. After a long meeting with Seipel on July 10, Dollfuss seemed committed to carrying on his illustrious predecessor's work against the socialists.[37] Then in Lausanne five days later he won terms for a loan of 300 million schillings that were hardly more onerous than those for the Geneva loan of 1922. Britain and France did not try to force a reconciliation with the socialists. In view of these developments Starhemberg once again pulled away from a collaboration with the Nazis that threatened his political influence. The implications inherent in Nazi gains in German elections on July 31 hardened his resolve. Support for Dollfuss seemed to be the only way to maintain the Heimwehr's tenuous hold on governmental power, a view that Minister of Trade Jakoncig also adopted.

For these reasons Starhemberg and Jakoncig gradually came to support the loan protocol. But because the renewed prohibition of *Anschluss* made the treaty highly unpopular with the nationalists, Starhemberg did not have the solid backing of his parliamentary deputies, whose votes were crucial. Thus, the battle over the ratification of the Lausanne Protocol proved to be a critical test both for him and for Dollfuss. To what extent advice from Mussolini may have influenced Starhemberg's policies is not known, but even if the dying Seipel called upon him to support the loan, as Kerekes alleges without citing evidence,[38] Starhemberg must have been guided primarily by his own assessment of his political situation.

The debate on the first reading extended over three sessions, with a weekend intervening between the second and the third, at which a Pan-German motion of no confidence would determine the fate of the bill and of the government. This delay gave Starhemberg time to bring most of his men into line. Four of the more nationalistic Heimatblock delegates—Hueber, Hainzl, Ebner, and Werner—seemed determined to oppose the loan. However, the promise of continued participation in political affairs as well as the Nazi threat led the provincial leaders to give Starhemberg a vote of confidence on July 29. It was then expected that he would be able either to carry the recalcitrant deputies with him or to force their resignation. Indeed, on the next day Hueber gave up his seat in the Nationalrat; he was succeeded by August Elshuber, an early Heimwehr member from Salzburg. Werner's opposition faltered after Steidle called the loan a necessary evil.[39] Still, the votes of the Styrian and Carinthian deputies remained in doubt.

The first test of the government's position came on August 2, when at the conclusion of debate on the first reading there was a vote on the Pan-German motion of no confidence. Speaking for the Heimatblock, Neustädter-Stürmer contended that acceptance of the loan would not represent betrayal of the nationalist goal: "There is only one kind of national policy in Austria: to create work and bread." He argued cogently that it was not the conditions attached to the loan that would prevent *Anschluss*, but rather Article Eighty-eight of the Treaty of Saint-Germain and the relationships of the European powers. In balloting that came as near as possible to overturning the government without actually doing so, only two Heimatblock deputies, Ebner and Hainzl, joined the socialists and Pan-Germans in opposition. The tie vote, eighty-one to eighty-one, meant that the motion was defeated. It was, however, not only Starhemberg's success in holding most of the Heimatblock in line which made possible this narrow victory for the government, but also the death early on the morning of the second of Ignaz Seipel, which enabled the CSP to fill a seat that otherwise would have been empty. The Lausanne Bill was then sent to the committee.[40]

It had been a close call, and, although the competent committee acted on the protocol on August 4, Dollfuss decided to delay the last readings on the Lausanne Bill in hopes of getting a safer margin, for a tie vote on a government measure would mean defeat. Thus, on the sixth it was announced that the next session of the Nationalrat would consider the economic demands that had been raised by the Heimwehr, since especially the creation of a voluntary public works labor army seemed necessary to secure the Heimatblock votes. Dollfuss was also watching the struggle for the soul of a Pan-German deputy who, to avoid a painful decision, took sick leave before the next vote on the loan. Meanwhile, Starhemberg worked to keep his men in line. Even while the *Arbeiter-Zeitung* was jeering that his home base of Lower Austria was crumbling because of opposition to the protocol, Starhemberg won a vote of confidence from Carinthia's subleaders, which temporarily stirred hopes that Provincial Leader Ebner would rejoin the government camp.[41]

When the bill was placed before the house again on August 17 it was still a risky venture. Although the opposition had lost the delegate on leave, Werner announced his withdrawal from the Heimatblock club. But Jakoncig won over the wavering delegate by promising him that he could speak for the Heimatblock in the debate and thus state his reservations before voting affirmatively. The government had calculated correctly, and the bill passed by the narrow margin of eighty-one to eighty, with Ebner and Hainzl again joining the opposition and soon thereafter requesting a room for their own "club."[42] But the ordeal was not yet over. On August 19 the Bundesrat not unexpectedly rejected the measure, thus forcing the Nationalrat to act on it again. With a last flurry of delegate manipulation, the loan protocol squeaked through this final reading by a vote of eighty-two to eighty. Following the passage of this and several other controversial measures, including the creation of a limited volunteer labor service, the Nationalrat, which theoretically had already dissolved itself, adjourned until October 20.[43] After Dollfuss's harrowing parliamentary trial, France continued to punish Austria for the customs union scheme by delaying the loan despite the fact that the Austrian Social Democrats, who for domestic political reasons had opposed the protocol, urged their French counterparts to ratify the treaty.

While most political groups quietly enjoyed the brief respite in the country's political wars that followed adjournment, the Heimwehr continued to seethe. The parliamentary crisis strengthened Starhemberg's ties with the government, but at the same time it weakened the movement behind him. In most of the provinces various groups were continually declaring themselves for or against Starhemberg's support of the government. Winkler reports that Alberti, Hueber, and Ebner seemed to be swinging toward Kammerhofer, the separatist leader in Styria, although the positions of the first two remained ambiguous. An indication of the final split between Starhemberg and the major Styrian organization was the publication of a new pro-Starhemberg weekly newspaper to compete with the *Panther* and the vacillating *Heimat-schutz-Zeitung*. Printed in Vienna, the first issue of the *Oesterreichische Heimatschutzzeitung* appeared on September 10. Since Starhemberg was still in financial straits, there was some question of the source of the paper's backing. It may well be that the government lobbied in its behalf with industrial sources, since a month later the now pro-Nazi critic of Starhemberg, Rokitansky, charged that the Heimwehr was rewarded for its support of the Lausanne Treaty by a subvention of AS 800,000.[44]

It was not long before all the political groups claiming the sole right to speak for the masses returned to the fray. With violent incidents occurring more frequently, the Nazis, who imported Goebbels and Göring to spark their demonstrations, began to steal the Heimwehr's thunder, and the socialists dropped the Heimwehr in favor of the Nazis for their major propaganda attacks. Early in September a fracas in Styria left one Nazi and one socialist dead.[45] When such clashes began to occur in Vienna, they became the pretext by which the Heimwehr was able to gain greater power in the government.

The focal point of the Heimwehr's drive to power was the control of the police and gendarmery. Hermann Ach's resignation as minister of security on September 27 opened the door to another critical phase in the decline of the republic—or the rise of the Heimwehr. The struggle over the succession showed that Dollfuss was desperately trying to maintain some freedom of action vis-à-vis the Heimwehr. When rumors that Emil Fey would succeed Ach prompted bitter expressions of opposition to such an appointment on the grounds that the Heimwehr's parliamentary strength did not warrant another powerful portfolio, Dollfuss gained time to try to find another combination—albeit still in an antisocialist context. His only chance was to bring the Pan-German Party again into the governing coalition. Meanwhile, Dollfuss contemplated reuniting the security portfolio with the vice-chancellorship under Franz Winkler, but the Heimwehr demanded that a man in whom it had confidence receive the post in keeping with the agreement made in May. To put off such a weighty decision, Dollfuss himself temporarily assumed the responsibility for security affairs. One of his first steps was to name Franz Brandl the permanent, instead of acting, police president of Vienna. Although Brandl was appointed by Starhemberg (in the fall of 1930), he had drifted away from Heimwehr circles; thus Dollfuss secured Brandl's position before a new Heimwehr minister had a chance to remove him.[46]

The issue hung fire for three weeks, while Dollfuss frantically and unsuccessfully sought to draw the Pan-Germans into the coalition in order to reduce his dependence on the Heimwehr, who were threatening to leave the coalition if Fey were not appointed minister of security. Dollfuss even sent a representative to beseech German Chancellor Papen to bring pressure on the Pan-Germans to enter the Austrian cabinet. Dollfuss assured Papen that he would try to arrange special concessions in the matter of the Lausanne Protocols to satisfy the Pan-Germans and that he would appoint a minister to the vacant legation in Berlin acceptable to, or rather selected by, the German government. Through his emissary, who talked with Papen in Munich on October 12, Dollfuss told Papen that the situation in Austria was so serious that the use of emergency decrees, as in Germany, was becoming unavoidable (unabweisbar),[47] and he warned that, should the Pan-Germans not cooperate, Austria would be forced to draw closer to Italy and Hungary, a course which he thought would be uncomfortable for Germany. Papen, pressed by the Nazis in Germany, did not wish to intervene in Austria's internal affairs, but he finally instructed his diplomats in Vienna cautiously and indirectly to inform the Pan-Germans that the German government would be pleased if they supported Dollfuss.[48] All these approaches to the Pan-Germans proved unavailing. Some of them —Langoth, for example—earnestly opposed Dollfuss.[49] Others assured the new German minister, Kurt Rieth, that they did not wish to over-throw the Dollfuss cabinet, which they might enter later, but they simply could not openly support Dollfuss or the Lausanne Protocol for fear of losing their remaining constituents to the Nazis. Thus rebuffed by the Pan-Germans, Dollfuss had to yield to the Heimwehr's pressure or lose his slender parliamentary majority.

Anticipating their new accretion of power, the Heimwehr leaders gathered in Vienna. From all reports the meeting on October 15, at which Steidle was named Starhemberg's deputy leader, was an ami-cable display of unanimity. All seemed to agree that participation in the government was necessary to prevent a slide to the Left, especially when Neustädter-Stürmer assured them, in what was probably a refer-ence to Fey's pending appointment, that the "course is going to the Right," and when Starhemberg pronounced the political program to be for the "government to make itself as independent of parliament as possible." Starhemberg added that the ultimate mission of the Heim-wehr was to exercise alone the leadership of the state.[50]

This internal accord and outward ferociousness carried over to the public rally on the Heldenplatz on the sixteenth. The real significance of the occasion was the participation of Chancellor Dollfuss and of Auriti, the Italian minister in Vienna. Dollfuss, whose "official appear-ance" Starhemberg said the Heimwehr knew how to value, thus signi-fied his capitulation to Heimwehr demands. Reminding Dollfuss that the Heimwehr stood at his side—whether as an encouragement or a warning was not stipulated—Starhemberg publicly urged the chancel-lor to stand hard and fast against the socialists and to become indepen-dent of parliament. He also announced tentative plans for a massive Heimwehr rally in Vienna during the coming spring.[51]

Fortuitously, other events on that same Sunday provided the Heim-wehr a chance to force Dollfuss's hand in the matter of the security office. During a well-publicized Nazi procession through Vienna's out-lying workers' district of Simmering, Schutzbund members guarding the local party building fired into a group of marauding Nazis, killing two of them and a policeman and seriously wounding four other men.[52] This grim event marked a climax to an increasingly violent series of incidents between the socialists and the Nazis. On the next day Doll-fuss appointed Fey state secretary in charge of public security affairs, a post formally subordinated to Dollfuss as minister.[53] Coming when it did, in the wake of violence and on the eve of a session of parliament that was certain to be a continuous crisis, Fey's appointment was in-deed ominous. Now he, too, had a power base from which he could

Major Emil Fey (left) speaking at the Heimwehr rally on Vienna's Helden-platz on 16 October 1932, the day before he became state secretary for secu-rity; Prince Starhemberg looks on. (Bildarchiv der österreichischen National-bibliothek.)

effectively exercise his rather morbid hostility toward the socialists and pursue his enigmatic ambitions. His first step was to issue an order temporarily prohibiting in Vienna all open air demonstrations by those political groups involved in the Simmering affair (i.e., the SDP, the Nazis, and the Communists); this left his own Heimwehr free to parade wherever it desired.[54]

However much against his wishes it might have been, the chancellor was reversing Seipel's policy of keeping the Heimwehr dependent on the government. But he seemed driven into a position in which he had no choice. One "democratic" solution to his predicament—coalition with the Social Democrats—was not open to him, both because of the socialists' insistence on remaining formally in opposition and because of the outlook of his own party. The more traditional "democratic"

procedure in the situation would have been national elections, which
the Nazis loudly demanded. But the result of elections would have
been disaster not only for Dollfuss and the CSP but also for the system
of parliamentary government, given the attitudes prevailing among
major political groupings. Nazi gains would have made it impossible
for the nonsocialist majority to form a cabinet without the Nazis, and
popular attitudes would have made it difficult for the conservatives to
accept a coalition dominated by the Social Democrats, who would
probably have emerged as the largest single faction; by the same token
the socialists would have been reluctant to enter a coalition as a junior
partner of a battered CSP.

It was a sad dilemma. The tragedy of Dollfuss's having to rely on the
Heimwehr for his majority was that he had to allow them to drive a
growing wedge between him and the socialists, who before Fey's appointment had tacitly tolerated his government. As Dollfuss told German Minister Rieth, he had been able to maintain himself in office only
by coming to terms on each issue with the Social Democrats, who then
adopted methods that prevented his fall. But the Heimwehr was insisting that he break completely with the socialists, who supposedly got
the advantages but not the responsibilities of coalition. He well understood that Fey's appointment would be a step toward breaking the
bridges with the socialists.[55] It was, in fact, that appointment rather
than Dollfuss's bitter exchanges with Otto Bauer in the Nationalrat on
October 20 and 21, as Gulick contends,[56] that represented a turning
point in the parliamentary history of the First Republic. The latter
events reflected the Heimwehr's preferment—and Dollfuss's growing
exasperation with the harrowing parliamentary process.

It was in a very tense atmosphere that the Nationalrat convened on
October 20. The most pressing business was the interpellation brought
by the socialists, who protested the government's "misuse" of the War
Economy Enabling Act of 1917, the appointment of a "putchist" as state
secretary, and the one-sided prohibition of demonstrations. Karl Seitz's
speech to the house on these questions provoked considerable turbu-
lence, with Dollfuss by his interjections frequently acting a rather ridiculous, if unwitting straight man for the keener repartee of Vienna's
mayor. Seitz directed the brunt of his attack at the ruling coalition's
dependence on the eight—or rather six—votes of the Heimatblock,
which he charged no longer had any popular basis for existence. Evok-
ing the picture of the little chancellor standing between Starhemberg
and Jakoncig on the Heldenplatz, Seitz must have stirred in Dollfuss a
conscience already troubled by the realization that he was becoming a

prisoner of the Heimwehr. After one particularly heated exchange, the chancellor led the ministers and their supporting delegates from the chamber, not to return until Seitz had finished his speech with motions of no confidence in the government and for new elections in November. Rather than answer the interpellation immediately, Dollfuss irately announced to the house that he found it beneath his dignity to reply at that time and would do so the next day.[57]

The session of October 21 demonstrated even more the sad plight of the government's position in parliament. Dollfuss defended his appointment of Fey by calling the house's attention to Fey's honorable citations in the defense of the homeland and his oath—"so help me God"—to uphold the constitution. Then Fey, in his first appearance before parliament, concocted a ludicrous technicality to justify his disputed directive: the constitution guaranteed that equality before the law would not be denied explicitly on grounds of birth, sex, rank, class, and religious confession; his injunction, however, concerned only certain political parties which had recently disturbed the peace. But the really dramatic events followed a bitter personal exchange between Otto Bauer and Dollfuss, in which Bauer took Dollfuss to task for yielding to the Heimwehr and Dollfuss sputtered something about Bauer's being a bolshevik. There ensued another of those undignified missile-throwing, name-calling, fist-flying brawls for which Franz Josef's multinational Reichsrat had become so renowned and with which the Nationalrat had already had some experience. This time the Heimatblock's Lichtenegger was in the vanguard, at least until Jakoncig's quick clearing of the ministers' desks deprived him of further ammunition. The chair recessed the session for one hour and forty-five minutes. It may have been this occasion that Gedye had in mind when he recalled that Dollfuss once angrily declared in the halls of parliament that he would never again sit in the chamber when Bauer was speaking. At the conclusion of the debate the house defeated opposition motions of no confidence in the government. By the same division, eighty-three to seventy-eight, it then accepted a CSP resolution requesting the cabinet to lay before the house proposals for elections at the beginning of the spring sitting. This emotional experience undoubtedly left Dollfuss disposed to move against an institution over which he did not enjoy safe political control and to the methods of which he could not personally adjust.[58]

Dollfuss soon suffered further exasperations in parliament. Although no Heimatblock deputy voted against the government on October 21 (Hainzl was evidently not present), that vital delegation was still not united, for Hainzl and Ebner at once renewed their request for a separate "club" room. The defection of Hainzl robbed the government of its one vote majority in the budget committee. For over two weeks the work of the house and nearly all its other important committees came to a standstill. Rather than bring in its budget as a minority report, the government demanded and got a change in the rules to deprive a member who bolted party discipline of his committee assignments. In the complete reappointment of the fourteen working committees, Hainzl and Ebner received no assignments for the Heimatblock, thus completing their breach with that delegation.[59] Relying on the six loyal members of the Heimatblock, the government could still with luck command a one vote majority in the Nationalrat. But it was a precarious hold on governing power.

Meanwhile, newly appointed State Secretary Fey continued his provocative disregard of the constitution and his discrimination against the socialists. Although he did suspend his prohibition of socialist parades in Vienna for one day (November 12), that concession was certainly the prudent part of valor. Not long afterward he announced a Christmas peace, a prohibition of all public assemblies, indoors and outdoors, from December 11 to January 8. The sweeping nature of his injunction, which this time seemed to include the Heimwehr, violated constitutional guarantees of assembly rights. Mayor Seitz addressed a long letter to Dollfuss in which he challenged the constitutionality of Fey's action and said that he did not feel constrained to enforce it in Vienna on the grounds that only federal ministers, not state secretaries, could issue directives to provincial governors. Dollfuss hastily replied that he took responsibility for Fey's action and ordered Seitz to comply. Reminding Seitz of his prohibition in the spring of 1929, Dollfuss overlooked the distinction that it forbade only private military processions, not all assemblies.[60] Either in spite of or because of Fey's arbitrary peace, the Christmas season passed without serious incident. It was the lull before the storms that were soon to break.

By a cruel irony of timing, the Hirtenberg Weapons Affair further widened the gulf between the Heimwehr and the socialists only three weeks before the event that dominated the crisis-ridden year of 1933— Hitler's accession to the chancellorship in Germany. Early in January Austrian socialists discovered that about forty carloads of rifles and machine guns, preceded at the end of December by ten cars of "iron wares," had recently come from Italy to the Hirtenberg Munitions Factory owned by Starhemberg's friend Fritz Mandl, where they were being reloaded on trucks for shipment to Hungary. On January 8 the

Arbeiter-Zeitung demanded that the shipments be stopped. Two days later it reported that Starhemberg and Mandl had recently traveled to Budapest on political business. Starhemberg began a long series of public denials of any involvement in the affair. But when reporters from France and Britain began to give it intensive coverage and to link the Heimwehr with it, the scheme long planned by Starhemberg and Gömbös produced a veritable tempest in diplomatic affairs that soon threatened the Dollfuss cabinet. In view both of the revisionist aspirations of Hungary and of the tense relations between Italy and Yugoslavia, the Little Entente, led by the Czech government, assailed the Austrian government and pressed the governments of France and Britain for diplomatic support. Awkwardly yet haughtily explaining that Italy had commissioned the Hirtenberg factory to recondition the old Austrian weapons, the Dollfuss cabinet publicly rebuffed the western powers, whose governments finally professed themselves satisfied with Italy's reluctant notification that it was prepared to take the weapons back as soon as the contract for their repair had been completed. The western governments then hastily dropped what seemed a distracting and peripheral concern in comparison with the potential challenge to the international order threatened by the Nazi seizure of power in Germany. Only days after it became known that the general director of the Austrian railways had attempted to bribe the head of the socialist railworkers union into allowing the weapons to be diverted into Hungary,[61] the French foreign minister, Joseph Paul-Boncour, announced on March 1 that France considered the matter closed, as did Anthony Eden late in July, when, without adequate proof, he told parliament that "the entire Hirtenberg war material has been taken back to Italy."[62] In the face of Hitler, it matters little whether the French and British governments were gullible or cynical.

The Austrian socialists congratulated themselves on having revealed to the world the Heimwehr's efforts to bring Austria into the Italo-Hungarian orbit. But, even if they were scarcely hurt by the disingenuous charge that they wanted to deprive Austrian workers of employment in order to hasten revolution, they might have been wiser to have said nothing about the matter. Granted, they surely would have acted differently had they foreseen Hitler's accession, and it is possible, though not likely, that France and Britain might have jerked Austria away from the Italo-Hungarian connection had Germany avoided that fate. It must also be acknowledged that even in the absence of the bitterness left by the Hirtenberg Affair, Dollfuss and the Heimwehr would not likely have sought socialist aid against the Nazi threat instead of competing with the Nazis in antisocialist vehemence. All that said, it remains true that by their interference the socialists greatly increased the antipathy of Dollfuss toward them and also hardened the Heimwehr's and Mussolini's determination to see them destroyed. Moreover, the socialists failed to realize even the elementary goal of blocking the gun-running. Starhemberg assured Mussolini in the spring of 1933 that the arms "were in a safe place in Austria at the disposal of the Heimwehr, if needed." In fact, some of the weapons were sent to Hungary at that time. The rest (84,400 rifles and 980 machine guns), still on Austrian soil, were divided between the Heimwehr and Hungary by a secret clause in the Rome Protocols signed by Mussolini, Dollfuss, and Gömbös in March 1934,[63] a time when it was no longer possible for Austria's socialists to interfere in such matters.

8
Between Dollfuss and Hitler
Nineteen-thirty-three

Hitler's accession to the chancellorship in Germany had immediate and far-reaching significance for Austria. It strengthened the political appeal and emboldened the opposition of Nazis in Austria, who began to receive great quantities of supplies from across the border. Moreover, in its wake formal diplomatic relations between the two governments soon deteriorated to a point approaching enmity, and by late spring nearly all economic intercourse between them had come to a halt. The net effect was to make Dollfuss more dependent than ever on foreign support. Although there was a high price to be paid for it, he felt that he could more surely rely on Mussolini than on the western powers. Britain seemed to be interested only in "good economy and finance," and France tended to appraise Austrian affairs from the viewpoint of the Little Entente and to some extent of the Social Democrats, without, however, backing these friends to the hilt. In fact, the western powers wanted Italy to be the chief protector of Austria's independence, and, while from time to time they admonished Dollfuss about this or that, for all practical purposes they gave Mussolini a free hand in Austria's domestic affairs. For his part, Mussolini hoped to get along with Hitler and was urged by the Hungarian government not to let Austria prevent an accommodation among the fascist and prorevisionist powers. But at this point Mussolini did not intend to defer to Hitler or to tolerate "Prussians on the Brenner."

There could be little doubt about Hitler's personal attitude towards Austria: his goal, stated on the first page of *Mein Kampf*, was *Anschluss*. Writing in the mid-1930s, Konrad Heiden sensed that of all Hitler's international ambitions Germany's relationship with Austria was his most personal concern, an expression of perverted nostalgia, concepts of nationalism or power politics notwithstanding.[1] But Hitler also clearly perceived the importance of Austria's strategic location in the heart of central Europe. Although the foreign ministry, which Hitler did not fully subdue for nearly two years,[2] counseled caution and the Hungarian government begged him to tolerate the Dollfuss regime,[3] such were his personal ambitions and the dynamics of his political movement that he could not long pause in his drive toward European hegemony, to which he undoubtedly aspired all along. Since for the moment it was necessary to observe the formalities of Austrian independence, Hitler set about to help Nazis gain governmental power there, a development that he felt sure would give him de facto control of the country. Annexation could wait until the Austrians had been properly indoctrinated and the international community had acquiesced in a fait accompli.

Besides Germany's economic importance to Austria, Hitler had two weapons at his disposal: the power of the German government and the dynamics of the Nazi movement. Within two weeks after his accession, the intelligence agency of the Reichswehr ministry granted a subvention to the Styrian Heimatschutz, largesse for which it had had no funds only a month earlier.[4] But it was chiefly the Nazi party that wielded the propaganda and terrorism intended to bring about the collapse of the Dollfuss government. The head of the Austrian section of the Nazi party, with headquarters in Linz, was Theo Habicht, a short, puffy, thick-bespectacled German whom Hitler sent to Austria in July 1931 and who fervently devoted himself to his assignment. Hitler allowed Habicht considerable freedom of action in his efforts to effect a Nazi seizure of power in Austria. They hoped to force Dollfuss into calling national elections, the results of which they were sure would make it impossible to maintain a right-center cabinet without the Nazis, who would demand control of the police and judiciary. Hitler made it clear that Dollfuss, to whom he evidently had a personal aversion, would have to go.[5]

None of the coalition partners ruling Austria welcomed the conflict with the Nazis that Hitler and Habicht forced on them. Many people in and out of the government, and certainly most Heimwehr leaders, tried to look upon the Austrian Nazis more as kindred rivals with whom some modus vivendi should be possible than as bitter enemies. But mounting terrorism and Habicht's intransigent refusal to compromise on any except his own terms caused the government and the Heimwehr leaders, still mistrustful of and often at odds with each other, gradually to conclude that they would have to fight the Nazis. The ruling partners were determined not to allow elections in which the Heimatblock would almost certainly disappear and the CSP suffer considerable losses. Entirely aside from what in retrospect may seem to have been the injustice or the foolhardiness of their position, especially with regard to the socialists, they increasingly felt that they were waging a two-front struggle against the Marxists, who would destroy private property and the traditional social order, and the Nazis, who would destroy Catholic Austria. But against the former they fought doggedly and fanatically, against the latter reluctantly and circumspectly.

Chancellor Dollfuss had very ambivalent feelings about *Anschluss*. During the war he had expressed wholeheartedly an Austrian rather than a German patriotism, a sentiment that later revived, but during the disillusionment of the 1920s he advocated union with republican Germany. This sympathy for Germany was probably strengthened by his marriage to a Prussian whom he met in Berlin, a woman who was later disowned by her Nazi sisters.[6] In his maiden speech before the Nationalrat, while reaffirming Austria's independence, the chancellor emphasized the close connections between Austria and Germany, countries bound by ties of race, tradition, and geography. Soon after Hitler took office, Dollfuss approached him indirectly with the proposal that Germany assume France's portion of the Lausanne loan—still not floated—in return for which Austria would pursue an all-German policy. But Hitler scornfully responded with the demand that Dollfuss resign and that national elections be held in Austria.[7] Under the pressure of vicious Nazi attacks on his government and person, Dollfuss began to expound on Austria's qualities of cultural uniqueness and on her European mission, concepts that became a part of his political creed during 1933. Even so, Dollfuss hoped for over a year that he could reach an accommodation with Hitler that would both preserve Catholic Austria and at the same time relieve him of dependence on the Heimwehr and its Italian patron.

Hitler's accession placed great strain on the Heimwehr's unity and self-assurance. Not only was it engaged with Dollfuss in a two-front struggle against Marxists and Nazis, but also it found itself maneuvering for position between Dollfuss and Hitler. Many Heimwehr leaders, sensing that pro-German nationalism threatened to carry everything before it, thought of trying to come to face-saving terms with the Nazis in order to be on the winning side. During the spring several of them worked on schemes to replace Starhemberg with someone less associated with the Italian connection than he and then to adopt policies that would make the Heimwehr *bündnisfähig* with the Nazis. Pabst once again sought to play the role of gray eminence in such a transformation, though he apparently first gave Starhemberg a chance to lead the Heimwehr into the Nazi camp. Starhemberg, without electoral base and fearful that Dollfuss might after all make a deal with the

Nazis, wanted to keep his options open, but Habicht refused any kind of truce that would have left Starhemberg even the appearance of equality.[8] He therefore had to rely on Mussolini and work with Doll-fuss. Pabst then turned again to the Tyroleans and found Steidle and Jakoncig receptive, as well as men like Alberti and Hueber elsewhere. Moreover, there are grounds to assume that he also drew Fey, who was parlaying his cabinet post into a position of power, into an anti-Starhem-berg plot. Among other indications, it seems clear that Fey attempted to take Steidle under his wing.[9] The conspiracy, if such it could be called, smoldered throughout March and came to a head in mid-April, as will be seen. In the long run, however, its various lines tended to cancel each other out; few proved willing to make the abject surrender —or sell-out—demanded by Habicht, if not by Pabst. Although un-doubtedly many individual members of the Heimwehr, impressed by the Nazis' activism and optimism, changed uniforms, only the Styrian Heimatschutz under Konstantin Kammerhofer moved corporately to-ward the Nazis. On March 9 he changed the organization's name to "German-Austrian Heimatschutz," a move that Starhemberg countered by entrusting Baron Egon Berger-Waldenegg with the interests of the loyal "Austrian Heimatschutz," which according to official reports suc-ceeded in creating an effective if relatively small organization.[10]

All factions of the "loyal" Heimwehr continually pushed Dollfuss to the right. The rhetoric at the well-attended convocation of the Heim-wehr in the Vienna Konzerthaus on February 20 provides a case in point. Starhemberg warned the government that his followers would support it only if it stood strongly against the socialists and the western powers. There must be no new elections, which would only produce a black-red (i.e. CSP-SDP) coalition as a result of the Nazi danger. Aus-tria should be run in the manner of Germany, Hungary, and Italy: the cabinet and the president must determine to "make order" without par-liament. In less public circumstances Starhemberg and other Heimwehr leaders demanded that the government place Vienna under the control of a federal commissioner.[11] They increased the pressure on the govern-ment to strike hard against the socialists during the weeks following the exclusion of parliament.

The government's chance to make order without parliament came sooner than Starhemberg, or probably anyone else, expected. Through a now famous comedy of errors, as it were, the Nationalrat provided the cabinet with an excuse to claim that parliament had immobilized itself. The crisis began during a tense special session on March 4, in which the Christian Socials refused to accept passage of a Pan-German

proposal on the grounds that one socialist vote was an invalid dupli-
cate, thus creating a negative tie. In the ensuing tumult, all three presiding officers of the Nationalrat resigned. There being in the rules of
procedure no provision for such an exigency, the delegates simply dis-
persed without a formal adjournment.[12] They exhibited considerable
confusion, but little awareness of the import of their departure.

After a short period of indecision, Dollfuss seized this unexpected
opportunity to suspend parliamentary activities. Several considerations
influenced his decision. First was his own exasperation with a body that
he could not control. Second was Hitler's victory in the German elections on March 5, which led all observers to expect the Nazis to make
an impressive showing in the event of elections in Austria. Finally, of
course, was the pressure exerted by the Heimwehr as well as by the
governments of Hungary and Italy.[13] In the War Economy Enabling
Act of 1917 Dollfuss had at hand an instrument with which he could
run the country without parliament, and once he began to govern by
decrees based on that law he never earnestly sought a chance to turn
back. On March 7 the cabinet announced that temporarily it would
function, without parliament, as "the legal government appointed by
the federal president." By decree it banned all unauthorized meetings
and processions (theoretically those of the Heimwehr also) and provided for more stringent censorship of the press.[14]

The crux of the crisis came on March 15. In an effort to rectify his
error in resigning so precipitously, the third presiding officer, Pan-
German Josef Straffner, summoned the Nationalrat for 3:00 that afternoon. He would not be dissuaded, and the cabinet set the stage for a
dramatic conflict by announcing that it would prevent an "unconstitutional" meeting by force if necessary. Furiously debating their predicament, the Social Democrats finally decided not to resort to arms at this
juncture, and let slip probably their last chance to rally their followers
in massive resistance to the government's manifest breach of the constitution.[15] The opposition delegates did manage to hold a hurried convocation at 2:30 P.M. on the Ides of March, but Straffner had hardly
declared the session of March 4 closed before police began to enter the
building. With the ruling parties denying the legitimacy of the rump
session and ignoring resolutions of no confidence passed by the less
powerful Bundesrat, the impasse remained.[16]

The real danger of armed action on that fateful day came from the
Right, not the Left. To what extent the Heimwehr leaders acted in concert is not clear, but it is probable that Fey, and others in league with
him, took the lead not only in opposing Straffner's meeting of the Na-

tionalrat but also in trying to gain complete control of the country's police and gendarme apparatus. Concentrations of armed Heimwehr men in Vienna and in several of the provinces once again prompted putsch rumors. About twenty-five hundred men assembled on Vienna's Judenplatz and in the adjacent building that once housed the ministry of agriculture. Police President Brandl, who had become pro-Nazi and anti-Heimwehr, placed the men under heavy surveillance and may have moved to disperse them. Brandl's zeal aroused Fey's wrath and brought about his dismissal on the evening of the sixteenth. The next day Dollfuss, taking full responsibility for Brandl's dismissal, told the cabinet that Brandl had moved too slowly in occupying the parliament building and had spread alarmist rumors about the Heimwehr actions on the fifteenth even though Fey had assured him—Dollfuss—that the mobilization was purely precautionary. Despite the public defense of Fey by Dollfuss, there remains the possibility that on the fifteenth the two men were sparring and that—as Goldinger contends—Dollfuss tacitly encouraged the police action, which enabled him both to check Fey and to dismiss Brandl.[17]

In the provinces the Heimwehr's pressure on the government to take further measures against the socialists was more effective than in Vienna. On the fifteenth the Tyrolean government made the Heimatwehr an auxiliary police detachment, and Fey then ordered the police to search the socialist headquarters and press building in Innsbruck. The next day the Tyrolean government ordered the dissolution of the socialist Schutzbund throughout the province, and on March 23 Steidle became the director of security for the Tyrol, a preferment sponsored by Fey.[18] In Lower Austria Heimwehr troops exchanged fire with some Schutzbund men on the heights above Waidhofen on the Ybbs during the night of March 15/16. The provincial council promptly dispatched a special commissioner and army troops to keep order; they arrested several socialists while leaving the Heimwehr unmolested. On the twentieth the provincial officials dissolved the Schutzbund in the districts of Waidhofen and Amstetten.[19] Heimwehr hopes met greater resistance in Upper Austria, however. On March 15 both Governor Schlegel and Franz Langoth, the Pan-German security director, thwarted Fey's plans to mobilize as auxiliary police the provincial Heimwehr forces, whose provincial leaders, Wenninger and Puchmayr, announced that twenty-six hundred men were already on alert and only needed weapons before they could begin serving.[20] Amidst reports that large groups of Heimwehr men, who were to be supported by Hungarian legionaries already on the border, were preparing to move toward

Vienna or had already begun to do so,[21] tension remained high during the following weeks. Because of official censorship, all this Heimwehr activity—or threat—was never advertised very widely. But the rumbling from the provinces carried a message to Dollfuss: move more forcefully against the Social Democrats.

In this demand all the Heimwehr leaders could concur. A long letter that Steidle addressed to Dollfuss on March 30 indicates the relationship between the chancellor and the Heimwehr leaders, who severally and individually maintained great pressure on him. Steidle warned that if the Schutzbund were not dissolved he could no longer remain the deputy leader of an organization that supported such a weak government and would withdraw his Heimatwehr from the national front. Recalling the deceit of Schober, Steidle complained that his rank and file had forced him reluctantly to support Schober's cabinet; but with Dollfuss, just the opposite was the case, and if the government should again leave the Heimwehr to public ridicule he would be doubly grieved at the inevitable disaffection of his followers, most of whom would go over to the Nazis. In supporting Dollfuss the Heimwehr had suffered the loss of their Styrian comrades and the hatred of the Nazis, and since March 15 their faith had been badly shaken by the half measures and indecisiveness of the government, which apparently moved to the Right but still leaned to the Left. It was to be feared that decisive action would come too late to prevent Austria from becoming a bolshevik island in an anti-Marxist Europe. Steidle closed with another demand for proof of Dollfuss's good intentions: the chancellor should sever his ties as quickly and completely as possible with the Landbund, "corruptionists and silent partners of the Reds," especially Vice-Chancellor Winkler. As much as he would hate to see the end of their friendly relations, Steidle foresaw the collapse of the regime if Dollfuss did not demonstrate his good faith in fourteen days.[22]

Steidle's charges, if seriously meant, were unfounded. By allowing the dissolution of the Schutzbund in the Tyrol and in part of Lower Austria, the government had already tested the socialists' reflexes and had set the pattern for the piecemeal way in which it would slowly undermine the ability and the will of the socialists to resist its transgressions. Fey had already hinted publicly that the Schutzbund was about to be destroyed, and several days before Steidle dispatched his letter the cabinet had decided to discuss the matter.

The blow fell on March 31. With another decree the government dissolved the Schutzbund throughout the country and prohibited the wearing of its uniform and badges. In a hopelessly vain gesture, Seitz responded the same day by outlawing the Viennese Heimwehr on the same grounds (i.e., it had disturbed law and order, overstepped its statutes, prepared a coup d'état, and endangered the republic). Dollfuss immediately approved the Heimwehr's appeal and reversed Seitz's edict.[23] Once again the socialist leaders chose not to respond violently to the challenging blow. In some measure they circumvented it by transforming the Schutzbund into an underground army on the model of the formally decentralized Ordnerschaften that existed before 1923. But every such setback for the socialists put them in a weaker position to defend their political and economic achievements in Vienna and other industrial cities. Unable for various reasons to work politically with the "bourgeoisie," they were rapidly losing the ability to fight them militarily.

The destruction of parliament and the dissolution of the Schutzbund were significant milestones in the history of Austria between 1918 and 1938. By these steps the Christian Social rulers and their Heimwehr allies not only destroyed the political institution through which their opponents could legally challenge them but also arbitrarily and one-sidedly removed the publicly and officially sanctioned counterweight to the antirepublican paramilitary legions of the Right. As a result, the position of the government did appear less perilous than when it faced a hostile parliament and the threat of national elections; at least it could now conceal much of its opposition and also act with less restraint than previously. The democratic republic as such ceased to exist.

Thus, while still maneuvering for dominant position in their partnership, the right wing of the CSP and the Heimwehr supported each other in establishing a dictatorship controlled by a minority and based ultimately on the threat of force. The result neither of a march on the capital nor the electoral strength of any political party, even an antidemocratic one, the transitory regime between March 1933 and May 1934 was nevertheless in some ways analogous to that of 1923–1924 in Italy. But there was greater continuity between Austria's parliamentary and dictatorial regimes than between those in its larger neighbors to the south and the north, and there was never an authentic single-party dictatorship in Austria, despite efforts to create one. Although at crucial moments it allowed the Heimwehr, backed by Mussolini, to push it faster and further than it wanted to go, the authoritarian wing of the Christian Social party remained the dominant partner in the regime that gradually took shape. Encouraged by the Church, these conservatives were seeking to restore Austria's traditional social order. Only gradually, as he came under bitter attack by the Nazis from outside the

government and as he strove to fend off the challenge by the Heimwehr from within, did Dollfuss become committed to the traditionalist
course. In March 1933 he hardly intended to revise Austria's political
life as much as or in the way that he did.

That Dollfuss would be able to retain his position throughout the
transformation was not a foregone conclusion. Aside from the country's
grave economic problems, Dollfuss's greatest weakness—in an age of
political armies—appeared to be that he did not have troops of his own.
Once the need for a parliamentary majority was ended, it was more
than ever the military aspects of the Heimwehr that gave it its strategic
influence, that and the fact that Mussolini used the Heimwehr as his
chief means of influencing Austria's internal affairs. As long as it was impossible to bring together a coalition of the moderate middle, and as long
as the Austrian government was determined to resist the Nazis—and
could get the backing from Mussolini to do so—the Heimwehr could
maintain its influence and could remain a threat to the conservatives.
Dollfuss's position as chancellor was seriously challenged by both
Prince Starhemberg, the Heimwehr's federal leader who remained outside the cabinet until the spring of 1934, and Major Emil Fey, the
Heimwehr's powerful leader in Vienna whose cabinet position gave
him control of the federal police and gendarmery forces. Until Dollfuss's death in July 1934 these three men formed a kind of dictatorial
triumvirate, although they remained jealous rivals for predominance
and for survival given the ever-present possibility that the regime might
collapse under the weight of the country's tremendous unemployment
(which averaged over four hundred thousand for the whole of 1933)
and the Nazi onslaught.

It was, then, a team rent by mutual suspicions and uncertain of its
popular backing that undertook the two-front struggle against the rising brown and the receding red tides. Neither the CSP nor the Heimwehr could be sure of its own cohesiveness or of the dependability of
its partner vis-à-vis the Nazis. The Heimwehr, rather more than the
CSP, still saw in the socialists a detested, if weakened, adversary whom
Dollfuss, or others in the CSP, might try to keep as an alternate junior
partner; thus, its leaders were determined to force the government to
destroy the SDP. With Austrian politics marked more than ever by
violence and conducted largely through clandestine channels, the multiple currents soon became more complicated than ever, and the year
following March 1933 was a period of great fluidity.

While the government was busy dealing with the socialist "menace,"
the Nazis escalated their attacks until by late spring terrorism reached

epidemic proportions. Moreover, Hitler began to use openly the power of the German government in trying to force the Austrian government into submission. Over Bavarian radio came vitriolic attacks that incited Austrians to sedition against their "illegitimate" government. Worse, Hitler used economic pressure. During his first month in office his government raised sharply the tariffs on Austrian wood, cattle, and dairy products. In late April he terminated negotiations, begun before he entered office, toward a bilateral preferential trade treaty of the sort approved by an international conference at Stresa in September 1932. A month later Hitler moved to stop the large flow of German tourists who provided a major source of income for Austria's mountain provinces. In these ways Hitler showed his determination to topple Dollfuss.

Its threatened position forced the Austrian government to strengthen its military and police preparedness. But since neither of the coalition partners trusted the other with control of additional armed manpower, considerable infighting took place over the next year. The army was still only about three-fourths the size permitted by the peace treaty. Dollfuss and Vaugoin hoped to gain permission from the treaty powers to fill it out with short-term conscripts as a step toward transforming the army into a drafted force. But Starhemberg and Fey knew that universal military service would destroy the basis of their political power and forced Dollfuss to give up the idea. They tried to follow up this victory with a scheme to put their followers on the federal payrolls. Fey began to demand the creation of an auxiliary police corps—a Hilfspolizei—to be composed of "loyal" paramilitary troops. The issue of the creation and control of such auxiliary forces became a source of bitter conflict between Fey on one hand and Vaugoin and Vice-Chancellor Winkler, the Landbund leader, on the other.[24] The latter two feared, surely not without justification, that Fey would use control of a large half-official yet politicized armed force in behalf of his own political advancement. Indeed, the suspicion grew that Fey aspired to control all the state's armed forces, including the federal army, which Dollfuss was determined to keep out of Heimwehr hands. While together with Schuschnigg Dollfuss tried to mediate the conflicts within the cabinet, the chancellor nevertheless tried to strengthen his own hand by encouraging the growth of other paramilitary groups, especially Schuschnigg's Sturmscharen.

But once again the Heimwehr scored a limited victory. On April 10 the cabinet tentatively approved the creation of a "voluntary" auxiliary force,[25] and Fey made the first official announcement of the plan during a radio address on April 18. The Assistenz-Korps, to be trained by the army but to be counted as emergency police, would consist of five thousand short-term volunteers from the "patriotic" associations and would represent a necessary low-cost reserve for the state's executive forces in fighting the Marxists and in defending Austria's "special mission." It was not until May 4, however, that the French government, which in the wake of the Hirtenberg Weapons Affair in January had threatened to count the Heimwehr as part of the military establishment allowed Austria by treaty, agreed in view of developments in Germany to ignore the Heimwehr and to permit Austria to supplement its official forces for emergency use. It seems likely that the creation of this assistance corps, which was not formally decreed until May 26, was a compromise, since Fey and Starhemberg had originally demanded that all their followers be declared auxiliary police and since the army retained basic control of the volunteers.[26]

Meanwhile, the government continued to direct its repressive measures more against the socialists than the Nazis. Fey, who was personally more hostile toward the Social Democrats than anyone else in the cabinet, zealously followed up the dissolution of the Schutzbund with frequent searches for weapons. Also, the censorship of socialist publications reached ridiculous extremes. But there was more. On April 20 the government prohibited the traditional May Day celebration by the workers, while at the same time announcing that in mid-May the Heimwehr would assemble for a patriotic demonstration. The next day the government forbade all strikes faintly political and even those with clear economic motives in public or public-service undertakings (a decree that did not apply to white-collar public employees). Such measures represented both anti-Marxist competition with the Nazis on the eve of municipal voting in Innsbruck and also concessions to the Heimwehr, which was just then experiencing an internal crisis because of the Nazi appeal. Dollfuss had not yet clearly taken up the cudgels against the Nazis, and indeed campaigned for his party in Innsbruck with an essentially antisocialist appeal.[27]

These one-sided policies notwithstanding, it proved difficult for the governing coalition to hold its own against the Nazis. Only a few days before the important elections in Innsbruck, the leaders of Kammerhofer's "German-Austrian Heimatschutz" in Styria, the recipient of subsidies from Germany, signed an agreement to act in military and political concert with the Nazis. Although the organization technically retained its separate identity, it recognized Hitler as leader of the German nation and agreed to wear, "as once before," a small swastika. The allied organizations called for new parliamentary elections to create a strong government of "national concentration." Pro-Austrian rightists in and out of the Heimwehr drew some consolation from the fact that at least a third of Kammerhofer's Heimatschutz (between fifteen and eighteen thousand men had paraded in Graz in November 1932) would not follow him and rejoined the small faction still affiliated with Starhemberg's national organization and led since March by Berger-Waldenegg.[28] At the moment, however, such consolation meant little, for on April 25 Nazis won election to the Innsbruck City Council in impressive numbers.[29] Dollfuss responded to heightened agitation for parliamentary elections with a prohibition of elections at any level of government for at least six months. When there followed rumors that a Nazi uprising was imminent and that Bavarian Nazis were preparing for an armed invasion, Dollfuss reinforced the border guard, called on some Heimwehr units to help patrol, and prohibited the wearing of uniforms and the display of political symbols except by "patriotic" societies.[30]

Such unexpected enthusiasm for the Nazis produced widespread despondency and another crisis of command in the Heimwehr camp. Starhemberg later admitted that some leaders tried to oust him and that several had misgivings about the big demonstration planned for May 14, which Starhemberg felt necessary to restore Heimwehr morale. Starhemberg himself undoubtedly wavered momentarily. But following Dollfuss's first visit to Rome in mid-April, there seemed to be more promise for Starhemberg in the Dollfuss-Mussolini connection, where he hoped to have some independence of movement, than in a surrender to the National Socialists. If the *Arbeiter-Zeitung* had the correct information (it usually oversimplified its reports but often had surprisingly intimate knowledge of Heimwehr affairs), Franz Hueber of Salzberg, who visited his brother-in-law Göring in early April, Count Alberti from Lower Austria, and Major Matt from Vorarlberg were the men most eager to overthrow Starhemberg and come to an agreement with the Styrians. Steidle and Minister of Trade Jakoncig sympathized with the dissidents but did not push the matter, which occupied Heimwehr circles through the end of April, to a showdown. No informative communique was ever published, but Starhemberg managed to weather the storm—according to his critic, Rokitansky—only with the help of Dollfuss's threat to have Steidle removed as security director of Tyrol. Be that as it may, the British military attaché reported that according to Fritz Mandl, who called Jakoncig a "permanent grouser," the leaders "had rallied round well in support of Starhemberg," partly because defections in Styria and elsewhere proved less massive than originally thought and partly because of realization of what an open split in the Heimwehr would mean in the face of the Nazi threat.[31]

Starhemberg's recommitment to the present course and the crisis in the Heimwehr led to reconstruction of the cabinet on May 10. Despite its internal dissensions the Heimwehr continued to increase its influence. Although the disloyal Jakoncig left the ministry of trade and was succeeded by Dollfuss's Christian Social friend, Fritz Stockinger, Fey became full minister of public security with independent control over the country's police and gendarmery, and Starhemberg's friend, Odo Neustädter-Stürmer, entered the cabinet as state secretary for "work creation" and tourism in the ministry of social administration. Dollfuss tried to offset the Heimwehr gains by giving Schumy of the Landbund, an old critic of the Heimwehr, charge of the economic affairs in the foreign office with the rank of minister. But the fact remained that one Heimwehr man controlled the police and another was in a position to influence the use of public funds.[32]

Another demonstration of Heimwehr influence was the long-awaited *Aufmarsch* in Vienna in the guise of a celebration of the two-hundred-and-fiftieth anniversary of resistance to the Turkish siege. Starhemberg had long dreamed of such an event. He wrote that Dollfuss wanted to make the CSP congress in early May a great demonstration for the "Austrian front," but that he talked the chancellor into using "a massed rally of the Heimwehr, if possible fully armed," as a "really big patriotic demonstration in Vienna." Since it was "imperative that the Heimwehr should not be hampered by a lack of money," Starhemberg went to see Mussolini, who promised 2 million schillings and diplomatic support. Skeptical colleagues told Starhemberg that he would not get even one thousand men to appear. He admitted that "it was impossible to say with any certainty how strong my following really was. . . . All the same, I was determined to take the risk. If I failed, there was no hope anyhow of saving Austria."[33]

Surely Starhemberg knew that sound preparations had been made, the men recruited and provided for. On May 12 the cabinet had taken action that would make the grand demonstration seem legal; it authorized the chancellor and Fey to permit carefully selected exceptions to the decrees of March 7, if the proposed meeting was patriotic and helpful to the state. Less formally, the prince and the chancellor rehearsed their roles at a birthday celebration for Starhemberg. The prince assured Dollfuss of his complete loyalty, and the chancellor replied that from the first the person of Starhemberg had bound him to the Heimwehr and that he knew how to value such friendship and confidence from one who had always dealt with him in complete openness and honorableness.[34]

"Contrary to all expectation, the rally was a brilliant success." Starhemberg claimed that forty thousand men from all over Austria assembled on the grounds of Schönbrunn Palace for speeches and a march into the city. There were all the trappings of national homage to the aristocratic Heimwehr leader whose ancestor had defended Vienna in 1683 and of fealty to the Dollfuss government. To emphasize the patriotic character of the occasion, Dollfuss appeared in public for the first time in his bemedaled uniform of a lieutenant in the old imperial army (which also made him look better beside Starhemberg), with the addition of the Heimwehr cap with the rooster feather. A field mass was celebrated. Then Fey led three loud "Heils!" for Starhemberg, the man who would free them, and he also called on Dollfuss, whom Starhemberg called the savior of Austria, to remain firm. After repeating his pledge of loyalty to Starhemberg, Dollfuss shouted, "Austria over all, if

The principal participants at the Heimwehr's "Austrian" rally at Schönbrunn on 14 May 1933: Major Fey, Chancellor Dollfuss (wearing his imperial uniform), Prince Starhemberg. (Bildarchiv der österreichischen Nationalbibliothek.)

it only will," which was to become a slogan for his Fatherland Front. Charmatz describes the occasion as a victory celebration for the Heimwehr.[35]

The opposition unsurprisingly tried to disrupt, belittle, and ridicule the rally. During the procession into the city many Nazis interspersed rooster calls with taunts that Starhemberg's "five-schilling boys" were the protectors of Jews. The *Neue Freie Presse* reported that the police arrested 409 Nazis and 58 socialists. The *Panther*, now a Nazi publication, asserted that only twenty-five thousand "stage extras" of all political colors, given a free excursion to the capital, participated in the "black" Heimwehr rally, and that only the ten thousand who wore old uniforms could be considered tried and true followers.[36] The German minister in Vienna reported in the same vein that all participants received free transportation, food, and two schillings pocket money; he saw the rally as an artificial production which found no popular echo.[37] While the Nazis belittled, the socialists ridiculed. On the day of the rally the *Arbeiter-Zeitung* ran a cartoon of two men—who greatly resembled Starhemberg and Alberti—standing at a latrine wall: said one, "Now I dunno, ha' we freed the Turks or did the Turks free us from Marxism?" To which the other replied, "Dunno that either, but anyhow the Starhemberg was there!" In reporting a "pitiable" meeting the next day, the socialist paper observed that Army Minister Vaugoin, who was by a recent promotion entitled to wear a general's uniform, appeared in civilian dress, since otherwise Lieutenant Dollfuss would have had to salute his minister, and "that would not do."

The detractors certainly exaggerated. But the important thing about the rally was more its impact on Dollfuss than the genuineness of the popular enthusiasm for the government. Dollfuss obviously relished the accolades of the large numbers of armed men and must have fancied himself as appearing quite dashing in his imperial uniform. After the rally he became determined to create his own semifascist party, a broad Fatherland Front, that would encompass all "loyal" political and paramilitary groups in the country and become the only legal vehicle of political activity. Through such an emulation of his powerful neighbors, Dollfuss hoped to gain control both of the Heimwehr and of the moderate elements in his own party, who had recently—contrary to usual practice—denied the chancellor the chairmanship in favor of Vaugoin. It was to be a more difficult task than he foresaw, for many in the CSP as well as in the Heimwehr insisted on retaining their own identity. Dollfuss proclaimed the creation of the Fatherland Front on May 20, but for most of 1933 it was more a thing of talk than of fact.[38]

The Nazi response to Dollfuss's effort to evoke patriotic fervor for
Austria as a second German state different in tradition and mission
from the Reich left the chancellor increasingly dependent on the Heimwehr and its Italian connection, with which he was not particularly
happy. To counter the Heimwehr demonstration on May 14, the Nazis
imported from Germany both the Reich and the Bavarian ministers of
justice. The latter was persona non grata to the Austrian government
because of an earlier radio address in which he had taken it to task for
oppressing Nazi comrades and fellow Germans in Austria. When they
arrived in Vienna on May 13, the Bavarian, Hans Frank, was informed
by a police official that his presence was not desired but that every
precaution would be taken to insure his personal safety. That night
Frank addressed a huge gathering on the "liberation of Vienna from
the Turks," obviously intending to convey the meaning of Nazi liberation from Dollfuss. The next day he proceeded to the Nazi stronghold
of Graz, where he told his audiences that they would soon be united
with Germany and that as reprisal for his rude treatment, no German
would come to Austria during the summer. On the fifteenth the Austrian government requested that the German government order Frank
to return home, but Hitler refused to intervene. Before Frank could
deliver a speech later that day in Salzburg, Austrian authorities expelled him.[39]

Despite this abrupt exercise of sovereignty, which the Nazis naturally found an intolerable insult, Dollfuss continued to hope that his adversaries, would come to reason, as he saw it. In the days following
Frank's visit he tried once again to reach an accord with the Austrian
Nazis. With Rintelen acting as intermediary, Dollfuss authorized Schuschnigg and Buresch to negotiate with Habicht and Proksch, and it is
almost certain that he met Habicht personally, but whether before or
after the Frank episode is not clear. But these efforts collapsed under
Habicht's intransigent demand for three or four seats in the cabinet
(Dollfuss offered two, excluding the security ministry), the ejection of
the Heimwehr from the governing alliance, and new elections.[40] Rintelen soon resigned his cabinet post under pressure because of his opposition to the government's anti-Nazi measures, and in August Dollfuss
sent him as Austrian minister to Rome in a vain attempt to get him
away from domestic intrigues.

Soon after these negotiations with the Nazis broke down came
the most severe economic measures Hitler took against Austria: the
"thousand-mark barrier." Announced on May 27 to take effect on June
1, this was a visa fee imposed on German citizens traveling as tourists

Heimwehr and government leaders assemble on Vienna's Schwarzenbergplatz to review the *Aufmarsch* on 14 May 1933: Field Marshal Ludwig Hülgerth (wearing soft hat), Heimwehr military leader; Dr. Kurt Schuschnigg (wearing overcoat), minister of justice and education and leader of the Sturmscharen; Dr. Richard Steidle, Heimwehr leader and director of security in the Tyrol; Dr. Engelbert Dollfuss, chancellor; Carl Vaugoin (wearing civilian clothes), minister of the army and chairman of the Christian Social Party; Odo Neustädter-Stürmer, state secretary in the ministry of social administration; Major Emil Fey, Viennese Heimwehr leader and minister of public security. (Bildarchiv der österreichischen Nationalbibliothek).

to Austria and was clearly intended—despite official explanations that it was to protect Germans against Austria's anti-Nazi regulations—to bring about the economic collapse of the country. It was combined with a boycott of certain Austrian exports that virtually severed all economic ties between Germany and Austria, as a result of which Hitler seemed fully to expect the fall of the Dollfuss government before the end of the summer.

Nazis in Austria accompanied Germany's economic boycott with a vicious campaign of terrorism, to which the government responded with police-state methods. At most of the country's universities and in many of its cities, brawls between government supporters and Nazis became daily occurrences, as did the widespread explosions of bombs and the like. Furthermore, Hitler insisted that Habicht be appointed press attaché to the German legation in Vienna, but the Austrian government refused thus to give diplomatic immunity to the agitator. In fact, it was making plans to expel him as part of its general response to the Nazi agitation. It had already dissolved Nazi student organizations, closed party buildings, and prohibited circulation of Hitler's *Völkischer Beobachter* (Munich). On June 11 Nazis attempted to assassinate Steidle in front of his Innsbruck home as a reprisal for the measures he directed against them in the Tyrol. Steidle escaped with a severe arm wound and greater fervor. With Dollfuss in London for the World Economic Conference, Fey was largely in control of the government's response. He had Habicht arrested and issued an edict that made the provincial security directors immediately subordinate to the federal minister, not to the governors.[41] Two days later he deported Habicht to Germany, an action to which Hitler responded by arresting and then withdrawing diplomatic recognition from the press attaché at the Austrian legation in Berlin.[42] Terroristic activity became especially atrocious during the next week. Its climax came near Krems on June 19, when Nazis ambushed a column of young men who were training for auxiliary police duty, killing one and injuring several. Fey immediately persuaded the cabinet to dissolve the NSDAP in Austria, and without consulting his colleagues he also decreed the dissolution of the pro-Nazi Styrian Heimatschutz the next day. Starhemberg issued a proclamation in which he welcomed the government's action in dissolving these inimical groups.[43]

All this turmoil did have some beneficial effects from the standpoint of the Austrian government. The country won considerable sympathy abroad for its brave defiance of its bullying neighbor. Dollfuss was warmly received at the World Economic Conference in London and

Funeral procession in Vienna on 23 June 1933, for Heimwehr member (Alois Süssenbock) killed by Nazis. At the head of the Heimwehr contingent march Fritz Lahr, Emil Fey, and Ernst Rüdiger Starhemberg. (Bildarchiv der österreichischen Nationalbibliothek.)

scored a diplomatic triumph in his presentation of Austria's plight and with his pleas for foreign tourists and other economic aid. He craftily transferred the press attaché expelled from Berlin to the London legation, producing first-hand evidence for the western diplomats. Finally Dollfuss was able to secure part of the loan promised in the Lausanne Agreement signed the year before. This assistance, which would have been of great help to Austria much earlier, did relieve some of the country's financial burden at a crucial time. Moreover, the publicity given Austria and Dollfuss in June brought tourists from other western European countries, thus replacing some of the income lost through the German boycott. When Italy began to absorb large quantities of Austrian exports, it became clear that Hitler would not be able to bring Austria to her knees through economic warfare.[44]

After a brief period of adjustment, the Nazis resumed their offensive in early July. From headquarters in Munich Habicht directed underground activity in Austria, although destructive activity did not occur as frequently as before the party's dissolution. Habicht was joined in Bavaria by a growing number of political refugees, who were grouped into "labor camps" and given military training. These men became known as the Austrian Legion, and the government in Vienna protested that Habicht planned to use them in an attack against it. During July Habicht also began other forms of propagandistic activity. On the fifth he commenced a series of regular radio broadcasts in which he incited the Austrians against their government. This form of agitation was supplemented by a series of airplane flights from Germany in which leaflets with seditious contents were showered on Austrian cities. Austrian protests availed nothing. But in the face of diplomatic representations from abroad, awkward though they were, the German government did promise in mid-August to try to restrain these activities. There followed some respite from the broadcasts and flights, but Nazi agitation by no means ceased and the Austrian Legion remained stationed near the border.[45]

In this tense atmosphere Fey continued to find fuel for his ambitions. During July and August he became a dominant figure in the news and appeared to be the coming strong man. In his capacities both as a federal minister and as a principal Heimwehr leader, he often appeared with either Dollfuss or Schuschnigg before Fatherland Front rallies, where he directed attacks with equal venom against the socialists and the Nazis, who during these months came to regard Fey as their most dangerous and determined opponent.[46] Early in July Fey won another struggle in the cabinet, largely against the objections of Vaugoin and Winkler, by finally securing approval for the creation of a second voluntary auxiliary force to be drawn from the ranks of the progovernment paramilitary groups and to be called the Schutzkorps. This new defense corps, as an auxiliary to the federal police and gendarmery, was to be subordinated to Fey's ministry. Threatened with the prospect that Fey would completely upset the balance that Dollfuss had maintained in the cabinet, Vaugoin worked frantically to inculcate an "Austrian" consciousness in the army and to purge it of Nazi sympathizers in order to make it a more reliable instrument.[47]

Fey's fame received a boost in the middle of July, when a Nazi conspirator allegedly boasted too freely about a plot against him to one of the Mädel in a Viennese bar. Thereafter, Fey began hinting at plans for additional repressive measures against opponents of the government. On August 17 he told an audience in Linz that the Austrian government had not played its last card; Austrians, being much more conciliatory than Germans, did not "yet" have concentration camps. If anyone thought life would be better in the Third Reich or in Moscow, he could leave. The implication was clear. On the sixteenth the cabinet accepted Fey's recommendation to deprive Austrians of their citizenship if they supported activities in foreign countries that were inimical to the government. A few days later Langoth told an acquaintance that a "serious" person who had recently heard Fey speak, commented, "Either this man is convinced that he can and will seize power day after tomorrow, or he is a fool."[48]

By midsummer a three-way struggle for power between Dollfuss, Fey, and Starhemberg had clearly developed. Fey must have been pleased when relations between Dollfuss and Starhemberg became strained, especially over the issue of Heimwehr participation in the Fatherland Front. Evidently fearing that he would lose direct command over his followers to Dollfuss and a camouflaged CSP, Starhemberg asserted that he was responsible for the Fatherland Front idea in the first place and warned that it must not be misused for party purposes.[49] Nevertheless, seasoned observers like Winkler felt sure that in a showdown Dollfuss would side with Starhemberg against Fey.[50] In fact, Dollfuss probably hoped to play Starhemberg off against Fey, and the Nazis off against the Italians. Such hopes would be in keeping with his request that Starhemberg, who thought that as a private citizen he "could risk an attack [against Hitler] which went beyond the limits of diplomatic usage," moderate his rhetoric for a while.[51] For one reason or another, Starhemberg yielded to the request, and during most of August quietly "convalesced" (whether from an operation, as claimed, or from political wounds is not clear), part of the time on the Lido.[52]

The fact that Mussolini also played the two Heimwehr leaders off against each other—and against Dollfuss—complicated their rivalry considerably and thwarted Dollfuss's plans. In a sense Dollfuss was waging a struggle on three, not two, fronts, for he found the constant pressure from Mussolini to make Austria "fascist" unwelcome. That he resisted and retained some freedom of action as long as he did is rather remarkable, since Mussolini did his best to see to it—not without success—that Austria had no other place to turn. The harsh antisocialist policies which the Heimwehr and Mussolini forced upon Dollfuss placed new strains on Austria's relations with the western powers, who in any case seemed inclined to leave Italy with the burden of protecting Austria's independence. Nevertheless, during the summer Dollfuss did attempt to draw the western governments into the protection of Austria in order to avoid complete dependence on Mussolini and sub-servience to his tutelage.

It was to counter these efforts as well as to block any chance that Dollfuss might alter his policies toward the Social Democrats that Mus-solini had the Austrian chancellor come to Riccione. Dollfuss felt con-strained to agree by and large to pursue the program that his host laid before him, labeled by the *Duce* himself a putsch, and to announce his intentions in a major speech early in September. Dollfuss would make Austria a corporative state and transform all parties into a fascist front under the motto of the independence and renewal of Austria. Musso-lini thought that Dollfuss should have a new "corporate" constitution ready by the end of September, but the chancellor would not yet com-mit himself to a timetable in that matter. Mussolini further urged Doll-fuss to take Starhemberg and Steidle into his cabinet at once in place of the Landbund, a suggestion that Dollfuss seemed to receive coolly.[53]

Nevertheless, Dollfuss may have seriously considered restructuring his cabinet in a way that would give him some freedom of movement while at the same time following Mussolini's suggestion. There is in-triguing, albeit indirect, evidence that he might have tried to strike a deal with Starhemberg, whom he met in Venice on August 21. From "most-reliable sources" the German consul in Linz heard that Dollfuss discussed with Starhemberg a startling realignment of the cabinet, one that would greatly increase the Heimwehr representation but at the same time replace the Landbund ministers with Nazis (who would thus counterbalance the Heimwehr's influence).[54] But if there was any truth at all to what the consul heard, it was probably a garbled version. It is more likely that Starhemberg demanded three posts for the Heimwehr than that Dollfuss offered them, and that Dollfuss in turn wanted to discuss it only if some counterbalance could be achieved. No agree-ment was reached, and Starhemberg soon took the matter up again with Mussolini.

Starhemberg's trip to Rome later in August was advertised as if it were his first. For his effusive praise of the "incomparable leader of Italian fascism" he was rewarded with the honorary dagger of the "Be-nito Mussolini Militia," which he subsequently wore at nearly all public appearances, and the insignia of the Roman Legion. More important, he was able to see the *Duce* about critical developments in Austrian politics. The two men agreed that Starhemberg should take a hard line concerning both the makeup of the cabinet and the relations of the Heimwehr with the Fatherland Front. When Starhemberg returned from Italy, he assured his demonstrative Heimwehr welcoming committee that Italy would support their fight to make Austria a totalitarian fascist state. Just as ominous was the telegram he sent to Mussolini, from whose inspiration he found the "hot wish" to try to erect quickly and completely in an independent Austria the wonderful system he had seen in Italy. Mussolini followed this up with another long letter to Dollfuss in which he reiterated the advice he gave at Riccione and, in a clear warning, supported Starhemberg's reserve about entering the Fatherland Front, in order to maintain greater freedom of action and greater drawing power for the dissident youth who were demanding the renewal of Austria. In other words, Dollfuss should hurry up and lose his freedom of action. But the chancellor, asking Mussolini not to push him too much from behind, continued to seek other combinations in his losing effort to avoid doing just that.[55]

The German Catholic Congress held in Vienna from September 8 to 13 as a commemoration of deliverance from the Turks provided the backdrop for dramatic developments in Austrian politics. The diary kept by Richard Schmitz, a strongly clerical Viennese politician whom Dollfuss wanted to appoint minister of social administration, reveals the divisions and tensions within the cabinet and recounts some of the backstage maneuvering among the contenders for power. Especially serious were the antipathy between the Heimwehr and the Landbund and the personal rivalry between Fey and Vaugoin (who had recently announced that the army would enlist a short-term military assistance corps of eight to ten thousand men recruited from all parts of the population, not just members of paramilitary organizations).[56] Dollfuss had doubts about Fey, but at the same time he was determined to get rid of Vaugoin, who as chairman of the CSP was an obstacle to his Fatherland Front. At the same time, since he was unable to divide the Heimwehr, the chancellor wanted to retain the Landbund as a counterweight to the demands made by Starhemberg, who caused him considerable anxiety during the congress. Dollfuss complained, even to the Italian minister, that Starhemberg's enthusiasm for fascism would delay the reforms that he planned to make, and Schmitz intimated that he was greatly disappointed not to be able to announce that both the Heimwehr and the Landbund's new National Estates Front[57] had joined his Fatherland Front. Throughout the congress Starhemberg's behavior provoked questioning comments. According to Schmitz Starhemberg invited himself to ride at the head of the festive procession with Dollfuss and Fey, although he was not in the government or the Fatherland Front. Afterward a visiting Frenchman wrote Schmitz about his im-

During the commemoration of the lifting of the Turkish siege of Vienna in 1683, Prince Starhemberg, standing before the monument to his ancestor who defended Vienna in that memorable year, calls on Chancellor Dollfuss, standing somberly at the left, to free Vienna from the "bolsheviks" in city hall, in front of which they have gathered on 12 September 1933. Starhemberg wears the fascist dagger Mussolini had given him. To Dollfuss' left stands Major Fey. The seated woman at the right is Starhemberg's mother. Princess Fanny. (Bildarchiv der österreichischen Nationalbiblio-

pression that Starhemberg was not capable of mastering his undisciplined reflexes and should be carefully watched.[58]

The highlight of the congress was Dollfuss's speech before the first general convocation of the Fatherland Front at the race track in the Prater on September 11. "Parliamentarism with its political parties belongs to the past. The death knell of liberal capitalism has sounded, and with it also that of materialistic Marxism and its war of classes. Our aim henceforth is to build up the German state of Austria, Christian and social, on the basis of a corporative system and under the leadership of a government which shall be authoritative but not arbitrary." The speech has become famous as Dollfuss's commitment to the creation of the type of state envisaged in Pius XI's encyclical *Quadragesimo Anno* (1931).[59] More accurately it could be said that the speech represented a combination of personal political philosophy and the pressure that Mussolini and the Heimwehr had been bringing on him to destroy the Social Democrats and create a fascist system.

Clearly, however, Dollfuss had not adequately demonstrated his commitment to the Heimwehr's goals. The next day it was Starhemberg's turn to speak when Austria's notables gathered around the statue of his illustrious ancestor that stands in front of Vienna's city hall. Early in the ceremony Dollfuss and Fey equated the prince of 1933 with the hero of 1683. Starhemberg began his reply with polite bows to his comrades, thanked Dollfuss for entering Austrian history at the right time, and pledged his loyalty to him. Then, gesturing toward the neo-Gothic Rathaus, he concluded with an ominous and concrete request, which was broadcast on the state's radio system: "This demonstration of Catholic Vienna makes the presence of bolshevism in the city hall unbearable; 1933 as 1683 should be a year of liberation for Vienna, from another, perhaps greater danger. Mr. Chancellor, let us do it; let us throw them out and not be too long about it! The people expect it; fulfill that expectation. For that we are ready to risk not only words, but, if must be, also our lives. Austria lives, and in it Chancellor Dollfuss should be the leader!" Winkler reported that this call to civil war angered Dollfuss greatly.[60]

Immediately after the congress, the cabinet crisis became acute. According to Winkler, Dollfuss tried desperately to retain the Landbund as a counter to Fey and Starhemberg but proved too weak to do so. On September 15 Dollfuss and he agreed that the cabinet would resign within the coming week; Dollfuss would form a new one that excluded both the Landbund and the Heimwehr, and then the National Estates Front would associate itself with the Fatherland Front. But on Septem-

ber 17 the feud between the Heimwehr and the Landbund emerged
fully into the open. Starhemberg, appearing with Steidle among six
thousand Heimwehr men at Kufstein, called on Dollfuss to purge from
the ranks of his collaborators those who were not willing to work hon-
estly in the reconstruction. In Graz, before about seventeen thousand
adherents of the National Estates Front, Winkler joined Starhemberg
in demanding that Dollfuss choose between them. Maintaining that it
was necessary to work against extremes from either the Right or the
Left, he asserted that his group would not bow to Starhemberg's demands that the Heimwehr control the state and its leadership. The next
day the Heimwehr leaders released a communique reaffirming their
commitment to fascist ideas and announcing that Starhemberg would
see to it that Dollfuss countered Winkler's words with deeds and would
report on the result of his talks with the chancellor by September 27.[61]

The Heimwehr apparently put the gun to Dollfuss's head. His concession, by no means insignificant, was the exclusion of all "party" leaders—notably Vaugoin and Winkler—from the cabinet, the sine qua non
for further Heimwehr collaboration. But the Heimwehr was unable to
sweep into control of the cabinet; in fact, it seemed to take a step backward. Dollfuss thwarted its drive by taking a leaf from Mussolini's
notebook. He finally agreed to unite the army and the police under one
person as an indication that he was moving in the dictatorial direction
demanded by the Heimwehr. But he would be that person. Thus, he
not only refused to appoint Starhemberg and Steidle and/or Alberti to
the cabinet, but he also removed Fey from the security department and
made him vice-chancellor without portfolio. When Dollfuss told Winkler on September 20 that he would have to renege on their understanding of the fifteenth, the Landbund leader suspected that the chancellor
was trying to sidestep the rivalry between Fey and Vaugoin as much as
to set aside the parties. Winkler claimed that he got Dollfuss to sign an
aide-memoire promising not to let Fey even temporarily direct the ministries of security or the army and to oppose totalitarian aspirations,
especially by the Heimwehr.[62]

Dollfuss reorganized his cabinet on September 21. The chancellor
concentrated in his own hands the vital portfolios of public security,
national defense (the renamed army ministry), and foreign affairs, as
well as that of agriculture and forestry. By thus overburdening himself
he was able to avoid giving either rival faction an important post, and,
more importantly, to blunt Fey's drive to gain control of the army. He
gave the working responsibility in several of his ministries to state secretaries. The most important appointment was that of seventy-four-year-

old Prince Schönburg-Hartenstein as state secretary in the defense ministry. A former member of the defunct House of Lords, a retired lieutenant general of the imperial army, and since late April a nominal member of Fey's Heimatschutz, Schönburg was a man whose first loyalty would be to the chancellor (perhaps second only to Otto) and who would strive to keep political agitation out of the army. However, the new state secretary for security, Carl Karwinsky, was viewed as a puppet of Fey's. Winkler's National Estates Front was represented by a state secretary in the justice ministry and by a high official in the chancellery. Neustädter-Stürmer remained at his old post, and Schmitz joined the cabinet as minister of social administration. To emphasize the idea that this was a cabinet of personalities, not of parties, all members who held seats in parliament were required to resign them, certainly a meaningless gesture.[63]

The relations between the Heimwehr and the Fatherland Front remained undetermined. While Dollfuss was forming his new government, Starhemberg temporarily forbade the Heimwehr to participate in Front demonstrations, complaining that the Front was still being misused for party purposes. Obviously, however, the exclusion of Vaugoin, Winkler and Schumy from the cabinet met one of the conditions for Heimwehr cooperation with the Front. Starhemberg told a correspondent from Budapest that the fascist idea had conquered, and that the Heimwehr stood behind Dollfuss, the dictator of Austria. On the twenty-third he released a statement to his followers in which he pledged the Heimwehr's "united" loyalty if Dollfuss continued to move toward the same goals. One of the unfulfilled demands was the dissolution of the CSP, in accord with Dollfuss's plans to end the party state. To set the proper example, Starhemberg magnanimously dissolved the "superfluous" parliamentary Heimatblock. He then announced that Dollfuss and he would soon work out the exact details of Heimwehr participation in the Fatherland Front, which it would join as a corporate body.[64]

At a festive convocation of the Vienna Heimatschutz on the evening of September 27 Fey assured the crowd, which had just heard the "Major-Fey March," that he was still there. The country did not need the remark to be aware that Fey was still very much there, somewhat disgruntled, and determined to retain as much personal power as possible. He, too, had talked with the Budapest reporter, and did "not deny that I am an advocate of politics of the strong hand." And on the twenty-fourth Fey had told a "heroes' memorial" near Melk that by agreement with Dollfuss—he may have been referring to the appointment of Karwinsky—he would continue to devote his full attention to the affairs of the security service: "In order to document this clearly, let it be said that yesterday I signed a new emergency decree, whereby one must not wait until after the accomplished deeds to bring persons behind lock and key, but even before that, when it can be assumed that the activities of these persons are not above suspicion." Fey thus had no intention of backing out of the three-way rivalry for power and very obviously continued to wield influence over the auxiliary forces.[65] Moreover, from some source he procured money to keep alive the Heimwehr's evening paper after Starhemberg had had to give up the effort to publish three daily papers.[66]

Each of the three rivals sought to secure his power by enlisting the support of the illegal yet dynamic Nazi underground. During the last months of 1933 each entered into clandestine negotiations with various Nazi representatives. Culminating in early January, these intrigues form an important, but confusing and complex, episode. The course of the various conversations with Nazis by the Austrian triumvirate is too intricate to follow in complete detail, especially since each tried to go through several channels and to keep his rivals unaware of his contacts, usually unsuccessfully.

From the available sources[67] it appears that Fey made the first serious moves. During the summer he had several talks with a German aristocrat vacationing in Carinthia, who late in September told officials in Berlin that Fey wanted him to sound out the possibilities of compromise between the two countries which would safeguard Austria's independence. The German had the impression that Fey felt himself strong enough, even after the cabinet change, to alter his government's policies if he found the necessary support in Germany.[68] But Fey soon understood that to get anywhere he would have to work through party channels and not through unofficial diplomatic couriers. Thus in late August and in September he extended several feelers to Habicht and his Viennese subordinates, *Gauleiter* Alfred Frauenfeld and Franz Schattenfroh, who was a member of the Bundesrat. Habicht craftily insisted that Fey's various emissaries produce written authorizations, which Fey for a time prudently withheld.[69]

Habicht preferred to deal directly with Dollfuss. Hoping to take advantage of the chancellor's predicament in the cabinet crisis building up during the Catholic Congress, he fueled putsch rumors and then proposed negotiation. On the day before Dollfuss's speech at the race track in the Prater, Habicht outlined, albeit disdainfully, the terms for a settlement between the "victorious" Nazis and the Austrian government. The Austrian Nazis' rights as a political party should be fully restored; all repressive measures against them should be withdrawn; the Nazis should receive representation in the cabinet in proportion to their strength, which should be determined by immediate elections. Asserting that this program would not be tantamount to *Anschluss,* Habicht concluded that a Nazi government in Austria, "supported by the confidence of the entire people," was a better guarantee of European peace than "the present Dollfuss government, hourly threatened with downfall."[70] In his speech the following day Dollfuss assumed an amicable attitude towards Germany: Austria would stretch out her hand in friendship to Germany at any time, on condition only that Germany was ready to take it on reasonable terms.

The next moves were not so promising. At a reception at Schönbrunn Palace, the German minister and Dollfuss broke their long silence. Rieth assured the chancellor that he would do all he could to facilitate an understanding. Dollfuss, replying that he would welcome any steps that would bring the conflict to an end, then stated what he saw as the prerequisites for good relations: Germany must cease all unfriendly acts against Austria and recognize its independence and right to self-determination, including the right to prohibit a political party that received its directions from abroad. Evidently Hitler and Habicht had not expected such a resolute reply, for there was no official follow-up to the exchange, and in Geneva later in the month Dollfuss was unable to get together with the German foreign minister. However, Habicht, that "indefatigable aspirant to Austrian leadership," as the American ambassador in Berlin characterized him, did not give up and kept himself available for negotiations. He had a busy autumn.[71]

Throughout October Fey and Dollfuss waged a clandestine contest for nationalist support. Each hoped to present the other with a fait accompli, yet apparently neither tried completely to eliminate the other. Fey finally provided Count Alberti with a written authorization to represent him in negotiations with the Nazis, and on October 13 Alberti met Frauenfeld and Schattenfroh in Hungary. Fey suggested a merger of the Heimwehr and the Nazis as an "Austrian Fascist Front" under a "neutral" person, if not Dollfuss, then perhaps General Bardolff or Governor Rintelen. If Habicht approved, then the two men should meet personally to agree on details. Although Habicht may have been briefly interested, he later told his men that they should drag out these talks but that he had no intentions of tying himself to the Heimwehr. He noted that from about the middle of October renewed differences between Fey and Starhemberg, who also sent representatives to see him in Czechoslovakia, began to complicate the many-sided negotiations.[72]

Meanwhile, in two long conversations Langoth and Foppa found the chancellor apparently eager for a settlement with his nationalist opposition, who represented a clamorous—no one knew exactly how numerous—part of his country's population. However, he wanted to come to an agreement with government circles in Berlin, not with Habicht in Munich. In discussing conditions on October 13, he seemed to want to keep Fey in the cabinet, but he could see why Starhemberg was not acceptable to the Nazis. On the twentieth Habicht told his emissaries that Dollfuss could retain Fey if he wished but that the Heimwehr as such must be excluded from any cabinet which the nationalists joined and that neither Starhemberg nor Steidle was acceptable. Hoping to talk personally with Dollfuss, Habicht promised a two-week truce after discussions began. But Dollfuss, rejecting Habicht's bases for negotiation, which included control of half the cabinet posts, stalled for time. Trying to use other channels, Dollfuss sent representatives to Germany at the end of October and again at the end of November, only to learn that he would have to deal with Habicht. But the chancellor still held back, in part to deal with other problems. When informed by Habicht's Austrian intermediaries about Fey's contacts with the Nazis, Dollfuss responded that he tolerated them as a defense against eventual Heimwehr criticism of his own efforts.[73]

During the last two months of 1933 jockeying for predominance in the Fatherland Front intensified the conflict between the Heimwehr and the CSP and further confused the relations among the uneasy triumvirate of Dollfuss, Starhemberg, and Fey. Hoping to get some cooperation from Starhemberg, the chancellor appointed him deputy leader of the Front in mid-October. This arrangement remained very tenuous, however, as followers of each man began to claim ascendancy for their leader over the other, and as Starhemberg insistently demanded that the government get on with the business of creating a fascist state.[74] Moderate members of the CSP, unhappy in any case with the Fatherland Front, protested against Heimwehr aspirations to dominate what was to be the only legal vehicle of political activity. With relations thus strained between Dollfuss and Starhemberg, the chancellor once again conducted negotiations with the Landbund about reentering the cabinet and countenanced new efforts by Fey and other Heimwehr leaders to oust Starhemberg. But Starhemberg learned about the anti-Fey agreement reached by Dollfuss and Winkler in September and used it against Dollfuss, proclaiming publicly that he was sure Dollfuss would never have made such a deal.[75] Meanwhile, in an attempt partially to meet another of Starhemberg's demands, Dollfuss named Steidle the head of the new bureau for patriotic propaganda (Heimatdienst), a federal post if not a powerful ministry.[76]

By December relations among the triumvirs and the Nazis became utterly bewildering. Early in the month Schattenfroh reported to Habicht that representatives of the "four" Heimwehr groups—Starhemberg, Steidle, Fey, and Alberti, each angry at Dollfuss for depriving him of influence—took turns in contacting him, each trying to cut out the others, but none in a position to take a decisive step. But on the twelfth Rieth observed that "the Italians and the Heimwehr have again gained the upper hand," as a result of the failure of Dollfuss's negotiations with Habicht's representatives and of his attempts to play off the Landbund against the Heimwehr.[77] Rieth's judgment was vindicated by the exchanges between Dollfuss and the leading Heimwehr personalities a couple of days later. Meeting in a surprising atmosphere of accommodation, they agreed with Starhemberg's demand that Austrian fascism be put through against all resistance. Equally unexpected was the *Kampfgemeinschaft* (fighting alliance) signed on the sixteenth by Starhemberg and Fey for the Heimwehr and Schuschnigg and Kimmel for the Sturmscharen, which only the previous day had proclaimed itself subordinate to Dollfuss.[78]

Thus hard-pressed at home, Dollfuss also felt renewed pressure from Germany, a combination of circumstances that prompted him again to extend feelers toward Habicht. Describing the situation as "highly fluid and subject to rapid shifts," Rieth interpreted these exploratory moves as the result of the recent visit to Berlin by Fulvio Suvich, Italy's undersecretary for foreign affairs: Dollfuss feared that an agreement between Germany and Italy would leave him isolated. There may have been other reasons. Rieth also reported that Dollfuss's old rival, Rintelen, who made frequent visits home from his post in Rome, was beginning to conspire with the Nazis. And on December 15 the German minister of the interior, Wilhelm Frick, told the Austrian minister that complete freedom of action for the Nazis—including elections—was essential for an understanding; rather threateningly, it seemed, Frick advised a conference with Habicht.[79] Whatever his reasons, Dollfuss had evidently decided to make a supreme effort to reach a compromise with the Nazis in order to reduce his dependence on both the Heimwehr and Italy. On December 29 the Austrian minister in Berlin hinted to an official in the German foreign office that Dollfuss would like to come to an understanding with the German government before Suvich's imminent visit to Vienna, and on 1 January 1934, he told Foreign Minister Neurath that Dollfuss wanted to talk with Habicht with Hitler's knowledge and consent. Within the next few days Hitler approved plans for Habicht to fly to Vienna on 8 January 1934, for a clandestine conference with Dollfuss at the secluded home of Minister Buresch near the airport on the east side of the Danube.[80]

The conversation never took place. Early on the morning of January 8, Austria's minister informed the German foreign office that Dollfuss had decided not to receive Habicht. The official explanation for the abrupt withdrawal of the invitation was a series of terroristic incidents which occurred throughout Austria during the first week of the new year. In reality, after a stormy conference at his apartment late the evening of the seventh, Dollfuss felt compelled by the Heimwehr's objections to cancel his plans. It is not known whether he voluntarily informed his allies at the last moment of plans he thought it too late to change, or whether the Heimwehr leaders learned of them from other sources; also unclear are the exact roles played by Starhemberg and Fey and the influence of the Italian representatives in Vienna.[81] In a later telephone conversation with Berlin on the morning of the eighth, Rieth hinted that Dollfuss acted under pressure from the Heimwehr and the Italians, but that he still desired a meeting and was merely postponing it until after the forthcoming visit of Suvich. If so, it was a permanent postponement.[82]

With the Heimwehr forcing itself more noticeably into the position of arbiter, fateful decisions followed swiftly. On January 8 the cabinet decided to adopt a more unyielding attitude toward both the Social Democrats and the Nazis, proclaimed indefinite martial law, and announced that it would seize the assets of suspected enemies. On the same day the volunteer Schutzkorps was fully mobilized in Vienna. Starhemberg issued a proclamation calling for a fascist Austria and announcing the Heimwehr's determination to bring the Nazi terror to an end and to continue the fight against the Social Democrats. There followed a series of conferences between the Heimwehr leaders and Dollfuss, and on January 11 Fey again assumed ministerial responsibility for internal security and thus regained independent control of the country's police and gendarmery. He immediately ordered officials under him to use every means at their disposal in combating all enemies of the state.[83]

Nationalists such as Winkler and Langoth called January 8 a black day in Austria's history. The former felt that Fey was beginning "an era which was to become fateful for the country and for the Austrian people." This raises again the question of whether Fey did not, after all, play the leading role on the seventh. If not, did Starhemberg sponsor Fey's increase in power after the eighth, or was Fey independently strong enough to make a power grab himself after Starhemberg had clipped Dollfuss's wings? Such questions remain unanswered. But certain it is that the rivalry between Starhemberg and Fey—not only for governmental power but also for Mussolini's favors—soon intensified.[84]

An epilogue to Habicht's abortive flight showed that the Heimwehr leaders were far from united. On the night of January 11/12, Viennese police raided the home of *Gauleiter* Frauenfeld, where they discovered him, his Nazi colleague Schattenfroh, and Prince Waldeck-Pyrmont, a counselor of legation in the German foreign office and a member of Hitler's entourage, conferring with Count Alberti. The Austrians present were arrested, and Waldeck, sent by Habicht on an "exploratory mission," was quietly returned to Germany.[85] Hoping to keep the affair hushed, Starhemberg secured the release of Alberti, who agreed to resign as Heimwehr leader of Lower Austria, and named Kubacsek of Gloggnitz in his place. However, Alberti's stubborn insistence that he had acted with Starhemberg's knowledge and consent soon made the affair national news. Within a few days Starhemberg, feigning shock at the revelation that Kubacsek, too, was trying "to take the Heimwehr to the Nazis," assumed the provincial leadership himself—though he soon delegated it to Baron Eduard Baar von Baarenfels—and prohibited all negotiations with other political groups without his written consent.[86] When Alberti tried again publicly to defend his "personal honor" against what he deemed to have been Starhemberg's duplicity,[87] he was expelled from the Heimwehr and then arrested for treasonous activities.

As much uncertainty about the respective roles of Starhemberg and Fey surrounds this affair as it does that of January 7/8. Probably Starhemberg, after having upset Dollfuss's plans, tried to use the contacts with the Nazis for himself and was a party to the encounter between Alberti and the Nazi leaders. How the police found out about it is not known; but, in his report from Vienna on January 12, the German counselor of legation observed that the raid on Frauenfeld's apartment was led by Deputy Police President Skubl, who was considered Fey's trusted lieutenant. It would seem a tight case had not Alberti, during the autumn negotiations with Habicht and his men, functioned as Fey's representative, at one time allegedly carrying a written authorization from Fey.[88]

Such internecine disputes notwithstanding, the events between January 7 and 11 marked a turning point in Heimwehr fortunes under Dollfuss. They inaugurated a new phase in the struggle of the regime against both the Nazis and the Social Democrats, and they became major factors in determining the course of events which resulted in the smashing of socialist power by the Austrian government in mid-February and in leading to the abortive Nazi putsch in July. Fey was again in the ascendant in Austria's internal affairs. He, more than Star-hemberg, was in a position in which he could set the pace for the suppression of the socialists and for the creation of authoritarian control throughout Austria. For the next few months, the Heimwehr, now no longer a popular movement but a minority group which found itself fortuitously in a position of power, played the most decisive role in its history. Between 8 January and 1 May 1934, the Heimwehr came as close as it ever would to a realization of its goals.

9
Apparent Victory
Mid-January to 1 May 1934

Early in 1934 the Heimwehr reached its second peak of power. In January and February it seemed to set the pace for events and to fight all who opposed its "fascist" goals. It was no longer the *Volksbewegung* that it appeared to be in 1929, but now, whatever the number of its followers, it possessed what it had not enjoyed then—governmental power. More important, it had largely become Mussolini's voice in Austrian affairs, and together they pushed toward the elimination of all the old parliamentary parties and usages and the creation of an authoritarian dictatorship. Emil Fey, the ruthless leader of the Viennese Heimwehr, again controlled the nation's police and gendarmery, plus perhaps ten thousand semiofficial volunteer auxiliary police. Prince Starhemberg was also a force to be reckoned with. He was the leader of the national Heimwehr organization, weakened though it was from defections; he usually enjoyed close ties with Mussolini; and he also had an official place, at least nominally, as the deputy leader of Chancellor Dollfuss's Fatherland Front. The Heimwehr would have wielded greater influence than it did had Starhemberg and Fey not been personal rivals.

But when it came to dealing with their enemies on the Left they generally spoke with one voice. The Heimwehr never wavered in its goal of ending all political influence by any who called themselves democratic socialists. Starhemberg constantly demanded that the Reds in Vienna's city hall be "chased to the devil," but it was Fey who demonstrated the greatest antipathy toward the working class, perhaps because he more than his aristocratic rival feared the loss of status. Throughout the previous autumn he asserted that he wanted to see unemployment halved by the end of 1934—but not for those he called traitors and demagogues. Repeatedly he promised to do what he could toward eliminating "elements inimical to the state" from public and private enterprises. In the cabinet he pushed a measure that would give contracts only to firms that obligated themselves to employ exclusively members of associations that were "true" to the fatherland.

Equally characteristic, Fey saw to it that elements of the Heimwehr—for the most part those enrolled in the Schutzkorps—were constantly in appearance throughout Vienna.[1]

Dollfuss fully intended to remove the Social Democrats from their positions of power, but wanting to keep himself the arbiter among all political forces in the country, he hoped he could peacefully divide the socialists and get the moderate wing to join the Fatherland Front as an anti-Nazi balance against the Heimwehr. For the most part, socialist leaders, in a good appeasement fashion virtually forced upon them by western attitudes, showed that they would accept considerable abuse from Dollfuss rather than face a worse fate under more implacable foes. Many hoped that Dollfuss would ultimately have to turn to them for support against the Nazis. There were numerous gestures at accommodation late in 1933 and early in 1934, but extremists on both sides prevented agreement. Checked by Mussolini and the Heimwehr, as well as by his own sentiments, Dollfuss always found reasons to look upon serious offers of compromise as either inadequate or too late.[2]

The socialists' alienation grew, leading to despair in some quarters and to talk of defiance in others. Frantically the leaders tried to sustain the morale of their followers, only to be harassed in the most peaceable of their undertakings. At the same time the underground Schutzbund attempted to maintain its armaments—much new material came via Czechoslovakia—and its preparedness to oppose the counterrevolution by force, as promised in the Linz program of 1926 and, under certain conditions, in a party statement in October 1933. Even though the party leadership displayed little desire or willingness to use force at a time when armed conflict might result in victory for the Nazis, an air of dreadful expectancy seemed to pervade the working classes.[3]

The three-day visit of Italian Under-Secretary for Foreign Affairs Fulvio Suvich added greatly to the pressure on Dollfuss to speed the destruction of Social Democracy and to draw back from his approaches to France and England. From the time of his arrival on January 18, he demonstratively supported the Heimwehr in general and Fey in particular, whom he seemed to treat as Austria's coming strong man. He awarded Fey a high Italian order and publicly expressed Mussolini's greetings. Rumors circulated that the Italians might be viewing Fey as possibly a more reliable chancellor than Dollfuss, who on the day of Suvich's arrival had appealed for cooperation from the "honorable" workers' leaders. All this was primarily intended to deliver a message to Dollfuss. To make sure that he got it, Suvich sent him a reminder shortly after returning to Rome. In accord with Mussolini, who agreed

that there was still hope that the Dollfuss government would be able
to dominate the situation, Suvich wrote Dollfuss that the Heimwehr
was "indispensable in order to give the impression of a popular reaction
against the Nazis" as well as "to keep the army and the police loyal to
the government, since they otherwise would feel themselves isolated
from the general public." But for Dollfuss to retain his active and
youthful supporters he would have to move with "greater decisiveness
and precision" in the work of renovation, which would entail a "few
sharply outlined principles": "The fight against Marxism, the reform of
the constitution in an antiparliamentary and corporative sense, the
elimination of parties and the strengthening of the Fatherland Front;
finally, that the moment for carrying out this more decisive work can
no longer be postponed."[4]

Fey speedily moved to realize such a program. He was probably behind the confiscation of *Arbeiter-Zeitung* editorials intended as positive
replies to Dollfuss's appeal to moderate socialists. No doubt he was
pleased when indications that the radical socialists were preparing resistance provided an excuse for "defensive" measures.[5] On January 27
the Schutzkorps, Fey's personal although semiofficial army, engaged
in military maneuvers in a suburb of Vienna. The next day Fey announced that a bonus would be paid on February 1 to all executive
troops, including the Schutzkorps, as compensation for their strenuous
duty in maintaining order against disturbances from both left and
right.[6] Members of the Viennese Heimwehr were encouraged to set
aside occupational concerns "at this decisive hour" and to place themselves at the disposal of the state. The Heimwehr of Vienna's Mar-
gareten District circulated a statement to its members asserting that
"the federal government is now determined, under all circumstances
to bring about a decision"; the men were reminded that "it is naturally
a duty to follow the call, or rather command, of our leaders to honor
our oath as volunteer fighters for homeland and people, for a free,
Christian, German Austria." Schutzkorps volunteers were to assemble
on January 29.[7]

In all of these warnings and preparations there were overtones of the
"two-front struggle" against both socialists and Nazis. Continued Nazi
terrorism both before and after the Habicht episode kept everyone
tense and resulted almost automatically in measures directed against
the Nazis, although in many cases Fey used them against the socialists
with greater diligence. Starhemberg in particular castigated the Nazis;
perhaps he was trying to counter the impression left by the Alberti
embarrassment, but in any event he called on Hitler to recognize in

writing the independence of Austria and agree that the Heimwehr alone should represent fascism there. Still speaking in an anti-Nazi context, he admonished his followers to use active antiterror under the law of self-defense; he would intercede for them.[8] People began to wonder what the first anniversary of Hitler's accession might bring. It may be that the Heimwehr leaders fully expected to have to fight both socialists and Nazis, but their intentions are not entirely clear. The forceful, impatient action that the Heimwehr took against most provincial governments in late January and early February failed to provide a clear-cut answer to the question.[9]

The alleged spark for the provincial uprisings was the murder of a customs official in the Tyrol, presumably by Nazis, on January 29, and a broadcast from Germany warning Nazis in the Tyrol to remain off the streets on January 30, the first anniversary of Hitler's accession. Asserting that these events indicated that a Nazi putsch was about to take place, the provincial Heimatwehr was mobilized on the morning of the thirtieth, and throughout the day nearly eight thousand armed men streamed into Innsbruck, determined, it was said, to put an end to the Nazi terror in cooperation with Security Director Anton Mörl.[10] Mörl, however, claiming that he warned State Secretary Karwinsky—a subordinate of Fey's—earlier that something was afoot, interpreted events somewhat differently. From various sources he heard that during a maneuver of the Innsbruck army garrison the Heimatwehr would take steps to "make order" in the Tyrol and that it intended to "roll up Austria from the west" and to seize power. He concluded that the broadcast from Munich meant that the Nazis knew what was to happen and were merely warning their followers and that the Heimatwehr then used the broadcast for its own purposes. Mörl, who observed that the Innsbruck garrison was indeed on maneuvers on January 30, had other reasons for believing that from the outset this was more than a simple demonstration against Nazi terror. He learned at 3:00 A.M. on January 31 that the Heimatwehr intended to occupy the government buildings in Innsbruck during the morning. Acting promptly, he saw to it that the Heimatwehr men found each building defended by machine guns manned by the army's crack Alpenjäger. When Karwinsky called from Vienna later in the day, Mörl said that he had the situation in hand.[11]

Foiled in the attempt to occupy official buildings, the Heimatwehr leaders continued the battle on the political level by presenting a long list of peremptory demands to the provincial governor. First of all they wanted a special committee attached to the governor's office, whether for other than advisory purposes was not clear; its five members were to be two representatives of the Heimatwehr, the chairmen of the Bauernbund and the Young Peasants' League, and one representative of the Sturmscharen. The Heimatwehr further demanded that a commissioner be sent to all communities threatened with disorders; that every district administrator (Bezirkshauptmann) be assigned a Heimatwehr liaison; that a thorough purge of anti-government elements in the courts and bureaucracy be undertaken; that all inimical organizations be disbanded; and that the Nazis be forced to pay for all damages resulting from their terror campaign, including the costs of mobilizing the Heimatwehr. Governor Stumpf reportedly promised fulfillment of the demands, beginning immediately. From Vienna Fey informed the Heimatwehr leaders that Dollfuss would support their action and continue the "cleansing" of Austria.[12]

On the same day Dollfuss supported Fey's statement in a proclamation to the Austrian people. The chancellor recognized that the "self-help" and "self-defense" action of the Heimatwehr was the result of Nazi terror, which "had exhausted the patience of the patriotic and indigenous population." Therefore, as of January 30 all the Tyrolean paramilitary organizations had been drafted into Schutzkorps service, and the security director, acting on orders from the federal chancellery, had begun a purge in all of the Tyrol. Fey had instructions to take any and all measures to bring their enemies to reason. Dollfuss further announced that the new federal commissioner for personnel affairs would go to work immediately in the Tyrol. Promising that he and his colleagues wanted to create bread and work for all Austrians, Dollfuss called upon "all the population of good will" to support these measures. Whoever resisted their efforts was an enemy of the people and the fatherland, and must be totally opposed.[13]

Many questions remain about the Heimwehr's action in Tyrol and soon after in most other provinces, almost all of which still functioned democratically. Was the first action part of a general plan or a spontaneous response to a local situation? Was it, as General Muff, the German military attaché, concluded, launched by subordinate leaders without the knowledge of Fey and Starhemberg? Were the coups instigated by Mussolini, or were they intended to demonstrate the Heimwehr's worthiness to him?[14] These provincial coups may have been directed chiefly against either the Nazis, who posed a threat to Heimwehr strength and to domestic peace, or the socialists, especially in those provinces where the SDP participated in coalition governments. Or they could have been directed at all other political factions, including some nominal allies. On balance, the most probable explanation would combine all these possibilities. That is, the Heimwehr began a preconceived if not wholly planned process of "rolling up Austria from the west." In the Tyrol Nazi activities provided a pretext, but Christian Social opponents of Heimwehr dominance would also be caught in the coup, as they would in other provinces, such as Lower Austria, where the socialists would be the chief threat. The Heimwehr would set the intended example as it moved, province by province, toward Vienna. Whether or not there was civil war would depend on the response of the socialists. But from the beginning the Heimwehr met greatest resistance, even in the Tyrol, from the moderate and strongly clerical CSP, which rigorously opposed its brand of totalitarianism. Alerted by events in the Tyrol, moderate leaders in other provinces could prepare defensive measures. In a sense, the Heimwehr came to need a civil war against the socialists in order to cover its differences with the CSP and to "unite" all the "loyal" forces in the face of a "bolshevik threat."

A critical confrontation within the "bourgeois" camp occurred in Vienna on February 2. On that day Governor Reither led over a hundred thousand peasants from Lower Austria into the capital for a massive demonstration in behalf of "strength with moderation." What was Reither's purpose? The socialists seemed to fear that it was part of the Heimwehr program and, fearing that Fey was about to invade city hall, they successfully sought French intervention with Dollfuss. It seems more likely, however, as the keen German observer Muff reported, that the hastily assembled throng was intended to block rather than to support plans that the Heimwehr might have had for action in Vienna on the second. Indeed, the peasants' only demands were for internal order and forceful government action against the Nazi terrorists, and they cheered Reither's call for cooperation with the workers. If Friedrich Funder's corroborating implication is correct, the presence of the peasants did provide Dollfuss with the support he needed to order Fey not to occupy the Rathaus on that day. And according to the French minister in Vienna, Gabriel Puaux, Dollfuss promised the French government—which fell four days later—not to move against the SDP, its control of city hall, or its labor unions. Funder thought Fey surprised at Dollfuss's command, Puaux thought him furious; in any event he promised that "today" nothing would happen. It was an ominous note.[15]

Checked but not reversed, Heimwehr leaders persisted with slightly veiled threats of force to push for whatever negotiated concessions they could obtain. They began to argue that they merely wanted to see created as soon as possible, especially on the provincial level, the authoritarian regime promised by Dollfuss in September. Since selfish party interests and the socialists were obviously sabotaging Dollfuss's plans, it was necessary for the Heimwehr to come to his support. On February 1 the *Innsbrucker Nachrichten* backed the demands for authoritarian rule in the Tyrol: the Heimatwehr leaders could no longer shoulder the whole weight of defense against the Nazis; there must be fundamental reform in public life. From Vienna the *Reichspost* saw the Heimatwehr working for "renewal" as well as for defense. On the third, with eight hundred men still "occupying" Innsbruck, the Heimwehr leaders increased their demands: the provincial government should dissolve the SDP and the other parties should dissolve themselves. (The *Reichspost* saw this only as a suggestion, not as an ultimatum.) They also wanted their proposed committee to replace the provincial council and not to be responsible to the legislature. In reply Governor Stumpf said merely that he was ready to comply with the Heimatwehr demands insofar as he had the constitutional authority to do so, and the Christian Social leaders began to express opposition to any illegal changes in the existing structure.[16]

On February 4 Starhemberg joined Steidle, who had come from Vienna on the second, in lobbying for the Heimatwehr demands. Averring that the action was in support of Dollfuss's program, he proclaimed that the ultimate enemy was Marxism, for only when they had defeated the socialists could they fight the Nazis effectively. After lengthy negotiations, during which Starhemberg was frequently in contact with Vienna, the governor appointed an advisory committee similar to that demanded by the Heimatwehr, but its exact functions were left undefined. The Heimatwehr leaders immediately asserted that this development should serve as an example for the other provinces, since all elected governments, especially coalitions, should disappear. But while leaving a decision on this to the chancellor, they called more units to Innsbruck. On the fifth Dollfuss invited Stumpf and members of the Tyrolean council to come to Vienna on the ninth, after his return from a trip to Budapest. He also decided to allow Heimatwehr men to act as liaisons to the district commissioners. The next day the fence-straddling *Reichspost* gave a "correct" account of events in the Tyrol: the new committee would serve as an advisory group through which the governor could maintain contact with the patriotic population; more extensive changes would require approval by the diet.[17]

By the end of the first week in February, Heimwehr leaders in other provinces, either following orders or simply drawing their own conclusions, began to issue demands to their governments. In Upper Austria on February 6 several Heimwehr leaders called on Governor Schlegel and State Secretary Gleissner, the head of the provincial Fatherland Front. With several hundred armed men converging on Linz, Heinz Wenninger told the governor that certain changes, similar to those demanded in the Tyrol, had to be made if the Heimwehr were not to lose its followers to the Nazis, especially in Revertera's Mühl-viertel. Wenninger especially wanted a Heimwehr man appointed as provincial director of security, and provincial commissioners sent to govern the cities of Linz and Steyr, both socialist strongholds. Gleissner thought most of the demands justified, and Schlegel said he was ready to discuss those points that could be effected without breaking the constitution. Wenninger told the governor that in times of crisis one must sometimes overcome such inhibitions. It was the Heimwehr, not the Social Democrats, who restrained the Nazis, so why did the social-ists still enjoy such good positions in Upper Austria? Disregarding the governor's reference to the outcome of the elections of 1931, Wenninger added that the Marxists were the Heimwehr's hereditary foe, even if the Nazis were the more immediate danger. Schlegel promised to con-sider the matter carefully and to talk with the chancellor. Count Re-vertera urged him not to delay too long. On the eighth the socialists presented a protest against the Heimwehr demands to Schlegel, who said he would examine their position also and would report on both to the chancellor.[18]

On February 7 the "movement for renewal" spread to Styria. Berger-Waldenegg and other leaders of the "Austrian" Heimatschutz called on Governor Dienstleder with written demands similar to those in the Tyrol and Upper Austria. By now the confrontations had assumed a standard format. Dienstleder acknowledged the demands and promised to reply to them as soon as he could talk with the chancellor. He added that the federal government would have to decide some points, the Styrian diet others. On the same day all the so-called patriotic groups of the Burgenland, led by the provincial leader of the Fatherland Front, presented to Governor Walheim a list of demands including one for the dissolution of cultural and sports associations that harbored the state's enemies. The governor gave the usual reply. The Heimwehr of Salz-burg acted on the eighth. But the executive committee of the Carin-thian Heimatschutz adopted a somewhat different tactic. Since they saw no use in making demands of their governor, who represented the Landbund, they decided to send a deputation to Dollfuss with a resolu-tion in which they declared their support for enactment of the chan-cellor's program of September 11; they planned to remain in session until a decision was made. On the ninth the Vorarlberg Heimatdienst, led by Dr. Wilhelm Mohr and Toni Ulmer, presented Governor Ender with the standard demands, which Ender received without committing himself.[19]

The presentation of most of these demands occurred just before Dollfuss departed for Budapest on the seventh, and a resolution of the crisis had to await his return. Given the apparent opposition by the provincial governments and the old nonsocialist parties, there were grounds to assume that the Heimwehr would be contained. The Landbund and other moderate nationalists were prepared to make common cause with such men as Reither, the peasant spokesman and governor of Lower Austria, and Leopold Kunschak, the Catholic labor leader in Vienna, in support of Dollfuss, but not in support of policies dictated by the Heimwehr and Mussolini. These opponents also tried to gain support from moderate socialist leaders, who especially in Lower Austria responded affirmatively. The moderates on all sides shuddered at the imminence of civil war—as symbolized by Kunschak's famous appeal in the Viennese diet on February 9 for reconciliation "before folk and country stand at the side of graves and weep."[20]

But anyone who thought the Heimwehr completely checked by such opponents misread the situation. By now Dollfuss did not really welcome their intervention. When he returned from Budapest on the ninth, he entered a furious round of deliberations. What would the Heimwehr do—what would Mussolini do—if he altered his course? Would it, backed by Mussolini, simply oust him in favor of Fey? Would its following go over to the Nazis if he took a step "backward" toward democratic compromises? The Heimwehr could do more harm to him—and, it seemed, to Austria—than could the despairing politicians. Besides, he could not really control or count on the decentralized CSP as it had previously functioned. While wishing that he, rather than Fey or Starhemberg, were setting the pace, Dollfuss was committed to the "renovation" of Austria in an authoritarian sense, especially where political parties were concerned. At some time between the late summer of 1933 and mid-February 1934 he had become a dictator in outlook, an uneasy and humane one, perhaps, but a dictator all the same.[21] Furthermore, he was supported in his policy by the corporatist element in the CSP. He hoped to weather this storm and emerge clearly in control. Then he would be happy to have the help of the politicians, and of "patriotic" workers' representatives, in balancing the Heimwehr, but only within the framework of his Fatherland Front, only on his terms. Meanwhile, he prepared to back the Heimwehr's demands in the provinces and to remove the Social Democrats from Vienna's city hall, which final step carried with it the threat of socialist "revolution." At least the socialists had said time and again, and some of them seemed to mean, that an attack against the Rathaus would be the signal for armed resistance to the counterrevolution.

To make sure that Dollfuss stuck to his guns Fey, who had fewer scruples about civil war than the chancellor, kept up the pressure. On the day that Dollfuss departed for Budapest, Fey issued several orders concerning the volunteer Schutzkorps. He activated large groups throughout the country, created mobile radio detachments, and gave special powers to units in towns where there was previously no security office directly under his ministry, especially those controlled by Social Democrats. He also ordered strict discipline in the country's concentration camps. On the eighth Fey, who himself showed signs of severe strain, had many of the leaders of the underground socialist Schutzbund arrested, while intensifying the searches for weapons. The discovery of some weapons "proved" that the socialists planned to revolt. On the day after Dollfuss returned from Budapest, Fey's ministry relieved Mayor Seitz of authority in the realm of public security and appointed Police President Eugen Seydel as director of security in Vienna. Such steps were obviously designed to weaken and confuse the socialists. If they were reduced to the point where they thought it useless to resist, well and good; but if they chose to fight, so much the better, for soldier Fey could play the hero with little risk of losing.[22]

On the evening of February 11 Fey made his notorious speech in Lang-Enzersdorf at the conclusion of the day's Heimwehr maneuvers. His assertion that "tomorrow we shall go to work, and we shall make a thorough job of it" has often been interpreted as an announcement of the civil war that broke out the next morning.[23] But in all fairness it must be noted that the rest of the sentence invites another interpretation. Fey went on to say they would "go to work . . . for our fatherland, which belongs only to us Austrians alone, which we will let no one take from us, and for which we will fight as those heroes, whom we greet with the greeting: Heil Austria!" That could have been directed as much, if not more, toward the Nazis as toward the socialists.[24] Undoubtedly Fey was moving toward a decisive encounter with the socialists, but whether or not he would, or did, announce on the eleventh plans for major battle on the twelfth depends on whether or not he was aware of intercepted messages indicating that the Schutzbund leader in Linz would undertake, against orders from party headquarters in Vienna, armed resistance should be police attempt to search for weapons. Defenders of Dollfuss contend that the government had not made plans for military action on the twelfth.[25] One young participant in these events recalled, however, that on February 11 his Heimwehr group in Vienna was warned that the socialists were planning "something" for the next day.[26]

Whatever Fey meant with regard to the Nazis and the socialists, his speech had much broader implications than just a warning to and about them. A key passage is very revealing: "I can assure you . . . the discussions of yesterday and the day before have given us the certainty that . . . Dollfuss is ours." The discussion of the previous day concerned primarily the future form of provincial government and the relations between the central and provincial governments. The Heimwehr demands largely undermined the concept of provincial autonomy, including some of the oldest traditional rights of the diets. Dollfuss planned to meet again with representatives of several provincial governments and of the "patriotic" groups on February 12. Not surprisingly, most provincial leaders wanted Dollfuss to take a more moderate course than that demanded by the Heimwehr. Even before the meeting, however, Governor Reither of Lower Austria complained to his socialist lieutenant governor that Dollfuss seemed determined to follow the extreme course; according to Helmer Dollfuss threatened Reither with arrest if he proceeded with the meeting of the Lower Austrian diet scheduled for the fourteenth and if he continued to oppose the planned new order in the state.[27] Fey was probably telling his men that after the twelfth they could begin governing the provinces.

The civil war that raged in many parts of Austria, especially in Vienna, from February 12 to 15 is one of the most extensively treated episodes in the history of the First Republic. Certainly those who wanted such a blood-letting were few indeed. But given the constellation of past events, personalities, and outside pressures, there hovers over the conflict an aura of inevitability. It must be admitted that the sustained drive toward war came from the nonsocialist camp and especially from the Heimwehr, and that the final provocation was directed by Fey. But for years the socialists' "dialectical" language and political practices had led the possessing, proud, and pious classes to view them as implacable foes with whom there must be a struggle to the finish. The fact that the principal socialist leaders had shown themselves averse to a resort to arms—regardless of whether from principle or from fear of failure—either was not appreciated or was taken as an invitation to the final reckoning. Unquestionably the socialist leaders were spared a momentous decision when the subordinate in Linz ordered his men to resist the police; there is no way of knowing what they would have done when the government moved against the Rathaus in Vienna. Once the socialists began armed resistance, Dollfuss had little choice but to suppress it. He was deeply saddened by the violence and surely wished that it had not occurred, but, as extremely difficult as was his position and as impressive as was his political tenacity, he, too, committed many of the blunders that produced the "inevitable" conflict.

It is generally thought that the fighting during these days showed that the army and the permanent executive forces remained the backbone of the state's military power. The Heimwehr and other small paramilitary organizations enrolled in the Schutzkorps did not, however, shrink from their "duty," and made considerable contributions to the effort. Particularly in Vienna they took part in some of the heaviest fighting. Of the 115 fatalities suffered by government forces, 40 were members of paramilitary auxiliary groups. The table below indicates the number of men from different "patriotic" paramilitary formations mobilized by province in the Schutzkorps as of February 15, according to data transmitted to the German Foreign Ministry.[28]

	Heimatschutz	Sturmscharen	FHB	Turnerbund	Totals
Vienna	5,755	1,200	630	410	7,995
Lower Austria	9,990	460	180	300	10,930
Styria	4,670	1,219	883	346	7,118
Upper Austria	4,426	96	120	203	4,845
Carinthia	1,643	560	—	—	2,203
Tyrol	4,390	1,176	510	504	6,580
Burgenland	508	150	14	20	692
Salzburg	1,309	113	—	22	1,444
Vorarlberg	554	—	—	—	554
Totals	33,245	4,974	2,337	1,805	42,361
Fatalities[29]	31	4	5	—	40

The government's defense followed the lines of a plan drawn up for such a contingency after the events of July 1927. Although all operations were carried out under the nominal direction of Fey as minister of public security, the army and permanent police retained separate command of their units, while the auxiliary Schutzkorps and other mobilized paramilitary units stood directly under the orders of Fey. By and large the three-cornered arrangement worked harmoniously, but the army managed to see to it that its officers in any given area had sufficient rank to take command of most operations, as did the police in most of the cleanup and holding operations in which it was engaged with the Schutzkorps. In the capital the auxiliary forces and the police each provided about six thousand men, the army only four thousand, for a total of sixteen thousand against an estimated ten thousand socialist combatants. Another ten thousand socialists scattered throughout the rest of the country were even more sadly outnumbered by progovernment forces.[30] Fey, in his official capacity, helped direct the defense of Vienna, which meant chiefly driving the resisting socialists from their fortresslike tenements, often with greater firepower than was necessary. He appeared on most of the "fronts" and, after artillery had softened the enemy, personally led several charges; such "heroism" was to be the basis of his exaggerated claims that he had saved the country from Marxism. For his part, Starhemberg, who on Fey's request mobilized the entire Heimwehr on the twelfth, directed the "reduction" of Steyr, a large industrial city in Upper Austria.[31]

The government took full advantage of the opportunity to suppress the major opposition party. On the twelfth it pronounced the dissolution of the SDP, and stubborn Mayor Seitz, passively defending his office, was carried from city hall and placed under arrest, an event cheered by the *Reichspost* as the fall of the red bastille. The next day the socialist trade unions were disbanded, as were party-sponsored sports and cultural clubs.[32] During the course of the fighting both Otto Bauer and Julius Deutsch managed to slip across the Czechoslovakian frontier, thus sparing the government the agony of deciding what to do with them. By the fifteenth most resistance had been broken and the war was over. There was never a mass uprising; a general strike failed miserably at the outset; and the resisters never really had a chance, a fact which, after a few anxious hours, the authorities realized. Under these circumstances the government may have used excessive force, especially in the use of artillery against the workers' tenements, thereby causing considerable casualties to women and children. Unnecessary, too, were the punitive summary executions of socialist combatants under the cloak of martial law, which Dollfuss personally halted, if somewhat belatedly, under the pressure of western opinion. The chasm formed by the graves of the fallen of February 1934 and the subsequent discrimination against workers and their families left a legacy so bitter that it kept the tragedy alive even in the revival of the republic after World War II. It took the catastrophe of the world war, Nazi persecution of both sides, and the threat of Russian domination partially to reconcile the former enemies.

The end of the SDP made much easier the reorganization—supposedly without breaking the constitution—of the provincial governments, which had been interrupted by the civil war. The most significant change took place in Vienna. As long planned, Dollfuss appointed Richard Schmitz the new federal commissioner of the capital. Schmitz's cabinet post was assumed by the Heimwehr's Odo Neustädter-Stürmer, formerly the state secretary of social administration. Within the next three weeks all the provincial diets either granted greatly increased power to the governors or voted themselves entirely out of existence. In every case the Heimwehr won "official" participation in the government, with its men becoming governors, lieutenant governors, counselors, or directors of security, not to mention numerous lesser functionaries such as mayors and district administrators.[33] For example, in Carinthia Governor Kernmaier of the Landbund was judged disqualified because his election had depended on Social Democratic votes; on March 7 the truncated diet elected General Hülgerth as governor. But the Landbund remained strong enough in Carinthia to elect Schumy first president of the diet and to send one of three delegates to the Bundesrat, along with representatives of the CSP and the Heimatschutz.[34] In Lower Austria Governor Reither enjoyed too much popularity with the Catholic peasantry to be removed. There the rump legislature elected acting Heimwehr leader, Baar von Baarenfels, as lieutenant governor.

The change of governors in Upper Austria was the result of one of the cheapest acts of Starhemberg's public career. The Heimwehr had long disliked Governor Schlegel because he refused to give priority to its wishes or to discriminate against the Social Democrats. Before the smoke of battle had cleared, Starhemberg used the tragedy to bring about Schlegel's fall. At the burial of one of the Heimwehr casualties on the fifteenth, he laid the entire responsibility for the "sad events" in the province on Schlegel's softness toward the socialists. The prince swore to his followers that they had not fought in order that such corruption could continue at their expense. The next day he sent Schlegel a telegram demanding that he neither attend nor speak at the memorial services for the government's fallen in Upper Austria. On the seventeenth Schlegel resigned, allegedly at Dollfuss's request, and a Heimwehr leader, Mayrhofer, became acting governor. On the twenty-seventh the diet gave extensive legislative powers to the provincial government, to be composed of a governor, at least two counselors elected by the diet and three appointed by the governor. At the wish of Dollfuss, the diet elected his friend and colleague, Heinrich Gleissner, the new governor. On March 5 Count Revertera became the director of security for Upper Austria. Franz Langoth led the opposition of four Pan-German and Landbund deputies to these changes and to the selection of Heimwehr leaders Mayrhofer and Wenninger as counselors, but they did vote for Gleissner, who after World War II served many years as freely elected governor.[35]

In the Tyrol, where it all started, and in Vorarlberg the Heimatwehr did not get its way quickly or completely. The various factions could not agree on the new arrangements, and the Tyrolean diet postponed its consideration of them. Finally, on February 27 it voted legislative power to the governor and lieutenant governor and then dissolved itself, a move to which the CSP agreed only on Dollfuss's assurance that after a short transition period Tyrol would elect a legislature on a corporative basis. The governor was to name a council composed of two representatives of the Heimatwehr, two from the CSP, and one from the Bauernbund. But that did not end the political strife. In mid-March Governor Stumpf appointed three active provincial counselors, including the merchant, Dr. Ernst Fischer, who was both acting leader of the Heimatwehr and the provincial leader of the Fatherland Front, and Professor Hans Gamper, an academician who represented the Christian labor unions and who was so disliked by the Heimatwehr that he was physically accosted by three of its members in the Landhaus.[36] An exchange between Gamper and Steidle at the last meeting of the Tyrolean diet indicated the dissension within the new "cabinet": Gamper warned that the time would come when they would exhume democracy with bloody fingernails, to which Steidle replied caustically, "This comedy I must indeed see." Steidle and Fischer announced that they would not cooperate with a government that included Professor Gamper, and they did not attend the first meeting of the new council on March 26. It was left to Dollfuss to settle the differences, and the feud smoldered for several weeks.[37] In Vorarlberg Governor Ender saw to it that a man of his own choosing, Toni Ulmer, headed both the Heimwehr and the Fatherland Front. Moreover, the diet limited the requisite grant of special powers to the governor while overwhelmingly confirming Ender in the office.[38]

Even the partial success of its provincial coups greatly enhanced the Heimwehr's influence at all levels of government. The destruction of the socialists may have ended its perennial rallying cry, but now there was a new state to create and places in it to fill. There were also other enemies of the homeland to oppose. Thus, patronage power and the Nazi threat kept the Heimwehr a vigorous contender for political power. In the weeks after the civil war the Heimwehr, followed by the smaller paramilitary groups, staged an expansion drive in order to obtain greater bargaining power vis-à-vis the Fatherland Front, or rather vis-à-vis the Catholic party in securing place and influence in the Front. For example, in Vienna Mayor Schmitz and Deputy Mayor Lahr, one of Fey's friends, soon came to unpleasant disagreements over the dispensation of patronage.

The removal of the common enemy left the way open, then, for the rivalry within the ruling coalition to become more intense than ever. Dollfuss was by no means master of the situation. His old party was badly divided; the moderate nationalists denounced his dictatorial regime; the sullen workers seemed to be a potential recruiting ground for the Nazis, who had stood aside during the recent conflict hoping that the government would mortally weaken itself through its repressive policies. Worse, even the army seemed susceptible to Nazi blandishments. In fact, to close observers it appeared likely that in the euphoria following its brief moment of glory the Heimwehr would attempt to seize power exclusively for itself,[39] or rather that Fey was preparing to make himself the dictator of Austria.

After the civil war Fey aspired to be Austria's man on horseback. (In fact, he frequently appeared astride a white mount, as at the head of the funeral procession for the goverment's fallen, when he reminded Puaux of Dürer's "Knight, Death, and the Devil.")[40] The vice-chancellor and minister of public security thought his hour had come and sought to make the most of it. In a radio address on the evening of the thirteenth, before the fighting ended, Fey gave an intimation of the way he intended to use events when he thanked those who "with me" so bravely defended home and fatherland. Several publicists directed a propaganda campaign calculated to make the major appear the indispensable savior of the country. On the sixteenth the creation of a Fey-fund, to be raised by popular subscription, for the families of the casualties of the government's regular and volunteer forces was announced. His "order of the day," similar in tone to his radio address on the thirteenth, promised that the government would meet the basic needs of these families. Also in a well-publicized ceremony on the sixteenth President Miklas decorated Fey and thanked him personally for his services, a recognition that apparently caused resentment among many army officers. In a press conference on the eighteenth, Fey still found it beyond him to use conciliatory language toward the socialists. On following days Fey decorated the wounded of the regular and volunteer forces, claimed that he had many loyal reserves, and declared that "the leadership of the country today is in the hands of the Heimatschutz." In early March he garnered another plum when the cabinet agreed to pay a small bonus to the unemployed members of the Schutzkorps who had served in February. There was no doubt that with many Heimwehr men Fey was the most popular leader.[41]

Fey's brazen power play gave Dollfuss one opening he needed, for it also threatened Starhemberg's position in the Heimwehr. Although Dollfuss was unable to find a political counterweight to the Heimwehr at the moment, it became possible for him to play upon the widening rift between Fey and Starhemberg, which was not long concealed by the mutual homage they paid each other at the Heimwehr victory celebration in front of the Rathaus on February 18. Had the two been able to work in concert at this point, they might indeed have been able to seize power—if not to hold it. But, in view of their differences in personality and past quarrels, it proved impossible for each to tolerate the ambitions of the other. Already late in February and early in March Dollfuss and Starhemberg groped toward the creation of an alliance directed against Fey. Starhemberg later claimed that at the end of the fighting Dollfuss asked him to help "manage Fey, who was overdoing everything and had developed such a megalomania that there was no talking to him."[42]

Although the alliance with Dollfuss did not come about as smoothly and soon as Starhemberg implied, a semiofficial press conference held by Starhemberg on February 27 gave public evidence that it was in the making. The high point of the conference, which was moderated by Eduard Ludwig, a chancellery official, and attended by several English and American reporters, was Starhemberg's declaration of loyalty to Dollfuss, in whom he said the Heimwehr had "complete confidence." He went on to speak of, and to, the defeated Schutzbund in phraseology for which Fey had shown little aptitude. While charging the other side with the worst brutalities in the civil war, Starhemberg explicitly complimented the bravery of the rank and file of his Schutzbund opponents and said, not for the first time, that the Heimwehr wanted to show the workers the errors of Marxism and to provide them with bread and work, not to treat them as enemies.[43]

Then on March 6 Dollfuss and Starhemberg clearly teamed up against Fey at a crucial gathering of Heimwehr and Front leaders at the chancellor's apartment. Earlier that day Fey, obviously replying to Starhemberg's news conference, had addressed the workers via radio and had tried to appear less truculent: "My struggle was never directed at you, but at your leaders and their false doctrines."[44] But when Dollfuss, emphasizing the dangers from Germany and the coolness of the western governments, called for a "genuine truce" with the workers and full integration of the Heimwehr into the Front, he met Fey's adamant opposition. A participant in the conference, K. M. Stepan, later reported that Fey and Neustädter-Stürmer replied to Dollfuss's appeal with a long tirade against the "gentlemen of the Fatherland Front" who had divided the spoils of victory between them while the Heimwehr was still fighting; in view of this "planned campaign to suppress" the Heimwehr, there could be no thought of paramilitary integration. Then, according to Stepan, Starhemberg, "who had been sipping his wine till then in complete silence and apparent boredom," came to Dollfuss's rescue at the decisive moment with a declaration to the effect that "the *Heimwehr* is part of the Fatherland Front. Stories that we want to rule the country by ourselves are just nonsense, a nonsense believed in by a few misguided careerists and then spread by stupid or wilful rumour-mongers. In my view, all the fighting forces should be unified and an agreement should be drawn up to this effect."[45]

While Starhemberg supported Dollfuss against Fey, it is improbable that he spoke so bluntly or that he meant what he said literally. He was by no means ready to subordinate himself unquestioningly to Dollfuss. Another six weeks of intrigue followed before Dollfuss could place any faith in Starhemberg's collaboration—and that not before the chancellor got important assistance from Mussolini.

For the moment it was the federal army's resentment of the acclaim given to, or appropriated by, Fey and his Schutzkorps that proved most useful to Dollfuss. Indeed, Prince Schönburg-Hartenstein, who had a strong dislike for Fey, pushed harder than even Dollfuss desired, in view of the army's potential pro-Nazism, for elevation to full ministerial rank. Officials in the defense ministry resented especially the removal at Fey's behest of the head of the weapons office, a Vaugoin appointee who had opposed the distribution of weapons and ammunition to the Schutzkorps, and they feared a general purge. Moreover, the army felt that its own military assistance corps, which was created in the fall of 1933 to provide sufficient short-term recruits (about eight thousand) to bring the army up to its treaty level of thirty thousand men, received poorer treatment and fewer favors than did the Schutzkorps. The latter was a loose organization of fluctuating size composed of volunteers from the paramilitary societies who served for various and unspecified periods; it amounted to a public works project devoted to military activities under the control of the minister of public security (i.e. Fey). The men received from two and a half to three schillings a day, with some of their pay being accounted for by the corresponding reduction in the dole, but their mobilization did represent a serious drain on the treasury. For a while after the civil war, the Schutzkorps was expanded, both to meet Fey's demands and to discourage any putsch attempt by the Nazis. But the army opposed this expansion, which hurt its efforts to bring its own auxiliary corps up to full complement, because the Schutzkorps enjoyed higher pay, looser discipline, and potentially longer service, in addition to the coveted employment certificates (giving them first consideration for jobs) when they were discharged, an advantage which was not given retiring army or auxiliary personnel. To counter Heimwehr pressure Dollfuss readily agreed to the added expense necessary to increase the size of the regular long-term army by about two thousand men and to a program of rearmament, which was to be kept secret. Finally, on the eve of his departure for an important trip to Rome in mid-March, Dollfuss surrendered his defense portfolio to Schönburg, who feared that Fey as vice-chancellor might otherwise have tried to exercise command over him as a mere state secretary in Dollfuss's absence.[46]

The primary reason for Dollfuss's journey to Rome was to conclude negotiations for a consultative treaty between Italy, Austria, and Hungary. Dollfuss was reluctant to enter such a pact, because it would commit him to keep his partners informed about all his diplomatic undertakings. Furthermore, England and France had expressed their disapproval of such a step, but the western governments were not willing to back their desire for an Austria independent of Germany and friendly toward them and the Little Entente with sufficient economic support. Mussolini on the other hand would take increasing amounts of Austrian exports and provide subsidies for rearmament, and Dollfuss was left with little choice. That the treaty was not more binding in the economic sphere than it was was due to the fact that Hungary was already being courted by Germany, which it did not wish to offend by granting exclusive privileges to Italy. Despite the long pre-Hitlerian collaboration between Italy and Hungary, the latter could in the long run expect more help from Nazi Germany for treaty revision than from Italy. For that reason Hungary, which hoped desperately to see the Austro-German dispute settled, insisted that the Rome Protocols of March 17 leave open the way for other states to become party to the consultative pact. Thus, the treaty by no means formed an anti-German front, even if it did take for granted Austrian independence. Less economically dependent than Austria, Hungary retained considerable freedom of movement, but the pact, which was viewed with suspicion by the Little Entente and the western powers, made Austria little more than a satellite of Italy.[47]

By his capitulation in the matter of the Rome Protocols, Dollfuss did win from Mussolini renewed support in his domestic struggles. Apparently the *Duce* gave up any thought of sponsoring a Fey dictatorship. In addition to preferential treatment for imports from Austria, he promised to help build up the Austrian army, and several diplomatic observers thought it probable that he agreed to regulate the flow of subsidies to the Heimwehr as a means of keeping it in line. Thus strengthened, Dollfuss could return and face a showdown with Fey.[48]

While Dollfuss was in Rome, Fey, with undampened ardor, continued his campaign to win public acclaim and greater power. Through the papers he again thanked the populace for the thousands of letters assuring him of grateful loyalty. Reports of more serious action spread by word of mouth: on March 17 Anton Mörl heard that the Heimwehr had overthrown Dollfuss. The rumor was false, but the uncertainty was great. On March 22 Vienna celebrated Fey's birthday with a torchlight parade through the Inner City by the official forces under him and by his Heimwehr followers, ten thousand altogether. There were more encomiums to his leadership.[49] The *Neue Freie Presse* of the following days was filled with reports of speeches by Fey, articles praising him, and reports of organizations which put themselves "under" him. But to close observers it was becoming evident that Fey had passed the peak of his power. Not willing, or unable to attempt a coup d'etat, he could also no longer expect advancement as a result of his February exploits. Early in March apparently both Italians and Germans had considered him Austria's coming strong man, but a month later the German Foreign Ministry was waiting until the struggle for position in Austria was clearly resolved.[50]

After Dollfuss returned from Rome indications of the changing balance in the Austrian government came surprisingly soon. One clear sign was the decision to reduce greatly the size of the Schutzkorps. Fey's price for the release of his followers from the defense corps was additional governmental efforts to provide for them in other ways. He had already won from the government regulations requiring employers in all kinds of enterprises to hire discharged Schutzkorps men at the ratio of one for every twenty-five employees. Now he and Neustädter-Stürmer, minister of social affairs, persuaded the cabinet to order the federal railway system to hire twenty-two hundred Schutzkorps men, whose services were not needed. Other places were created by an intensification of efforts to dismiss from public, and as much as possible from private, service those workers who had been "convicted" of infractions of some of the many antisocialist regulations. On the day after Fey's birthday celebration, Miklas, Dollfuss, and Fey participated in a ceremony to mark the beginning of the Schutzkorps demobilization. Two days later there was a big army parade in which the short-term auxiliary corps was featured.[51]

The big question of the struggle was whether or not Dollfuss and Starhemberg could reach a lasting agreement. Starhemberg was torn between his desire to keep the Heimwehr a distinct entity within the Fatherland Front and his antipathy toward Fey. Dollfuss offered Starhemberg a cabinet post, but in exchange wanted all the paramilitary organizations combined in one Wehrfront (defense front)—in which the Heimatschutz, as it was increasingly called, would be paramount—to operate within the framework of his Fatherland Front, which would be the sole political channel of the renewal movement. Despite his pronouncement on March 6, Starhemberg proved extremely recalcitrant, claiming that he had not "the least desire for a portfolio" which would cost him his "freedom of speech and action." On March 22 the attentive Mörl heard that Starhemberg and Dollfuss had fallen out with each other. A few days later the Heimwehr made the disturbing announcement of plans to create a civilian organization of its own, which would somehow "cooperate" with the Front. Starhemberg thus equivocated and prevented the promulgation of the new constitution on Easter (April 1).[52]

The whole matter was once again complicated by another round of talks with Nazis that pitted Starhemberg and Fey against each other. Starhemberg may have entered them because he thought Mussolini still favored Fey, or because he knew that Fey was negotiating with Otto Wächter, Habicht's new deputy in Vienna, to whom he promised to release several Nazis from detention. Starhemberg contended that the SA rivals of Habicht approached him out of fear that Fey was about to make a deal at their expense, and that Dollfuss "bade me pursue the connection with due discretion." In any event, on March 26 and 27 two of Starhemberg's emissaries, who made contradictory statements about his knowledge of what they were doing, presented similar astoundingly naive proposals in his behalf at the German legation in Vienna. Starhemberg would like to be royal regent in Austria until Anschluss was possible and to have German subsidies totaling forty thousand marks a month to replace the one hundred thousand schillings received from Italy and the Dollfuss government.[53] Nothing came of these contacts,

but Starhemberg maintained them throughout April even while he began undertaking other commitments to Dollfuss and Mussolini.

At this time Mussolini once again played a decisive role in Heimwehr-
government relations. The *Duce* apparently acted on the assumption
that Dollfuss, now a pact partner, would be a surer guarantee against
Anschluss than the Heimwehr. In mid-April he called Starhemberg to
Rome. Just before the visit there appeared an official announcement of
an "agreement in principle" between Dollfuss and Starhemberg, and
the *Reichspost* reported that Dollfuss intended to "call Starhemberg
into the government." The next day the *Presse* added that the agreement called for the various military formations, while temporarily retaining autonomy, to coalesce in a Wehrfront under Starhemberg's
command. But the paper stated that the situation would be known
exactly only after Starhemberg's visit to Italy.[54] Starhemberg's memoirs
contain nothing about this meeting with Mussolini. Some observers
thought that the *Duce* personally still favored Fey, but that both Suvich
and the Vatican preferred to aid Starhemberg as more tractable from
their standpoint than the "Brandenburger with Freemason tendencies,"
as Fey's detractors called him. Dollfuss clearly preferred Starhemberg,
perhaps, as the German minister put it, because he felt that it would be
easier to get rid of the prince, "who never had his own ideas," than
Fey, who was violent and stubborn. In any event, Starhemberg evidently returned from his trip on April 21 with Mussolini's financial
backing and instructions to cooperate with Dollfuss.[55]

Events very quickly reached a climax, as Starhemberg and Dollfuss
formed a partnership to keep Fey in check. It was announced on April
26 that Starhemberg would replace Fey as vice-chancellor and that Fey
would retain the security portfolio. As Dollfuss's deputy in the leadership of the Fatherland Front, Starhemberg would also command the
Wehrfront, which as the military branch of the country's only legal
political vehicle, would coordinate all the loyal paramilitary societies.
The new position at least gave Starhemberg the appearance if not the
substance of greater authority. The pact was sealed at a large Heimwehr rally in Vienna's Konzerthaus on the evening of the twenty-sixth,
at which Starhemberg promised that as long as Dollfuss was the chancellor and he was the leader of the Heimwehr no one would be able to
come between them. Taking another oblique swipe at Fey, Starhemberg also asserted that Heimwehr "totality" did not mean that its adherents should occupy every post but that its principles should become
the leading ideas of the state.[56] However, if the duumvirs tried, as
seems likely, to remove Fey from the cabinet, they were unsuccessful.

Still strongly supported by his Viennese Heimwehr legions, the major refused to accept the Austrian consulate at Budapest even if it were accompanied by promotion to the rank of general.[57]

On April 30 a rump session of the Nationalrat, "legal" now that the Social Democratic mandates were invalidated, approved 471 decrees that the government had issued since 7 March 1933. This included one dated 24 April 1934—the country's new authoritarian and corporative constitution—and also the new concordat with the Vatican. The Nationalrat then voted itself out of existence. The parliamentary farce was put on to make the new constitution more acceptable in the eyes of Britain and France, but the fact that it was approved in the form of a decree already issued conformed to Heimwehr wishes that it be promulgated in an authoritarian manner.[58] Supplemented by "transition" laws, this "May Constitution" became effective the next day, although most provisions were not put into effect for several months and some not ever. Also on May 1 the cabinet was reconstructed along the lines of the agreement between Dollfuss and Starhemberg, with the latter becoming vice-chancellor and deputy leader of the Fatherland Front. Fey remained minister of security and Neustädter-Stürmer minister of social administration.

With the proclamation of the new authoritarian constitution the Heimwehr came as near as it ever would to the attainment of its goals. Most of its Korneuburg program had been realized: Marxian socialists had been driven from public life; the democratic republic with its "western" parliament had formally given way to an avowedly authoritarian "federal state"; there were apparently no political parties; and there was, or supposedly soon would be, a "corporative" system. The elusive goal that yet remained, and that was never to be attained, was complete Heimwehr domination of a "fascist" state.

The Heimwehr's real moment of glory, the height of its negative accomplishments, came during the three days in mid-February. Its archenemy, weakened by a long process of attrition and doomed by international developments, had been vanquished in the long-predicted "rebellion" for which the Heimwehr and its sponsors at home and abroad were largely responsible. The elimination of the Social Democrats from political life paved the way for a new era in which the Heimwehr, at least as long as it was backed by Mussolini, had "earned" its share of patronage and power. At a time when votes no longer counted, when the size of the army was still restricted, and when paramilitary groups could intervene decisively in domestic politics, Dollfuss could not govern without the Heimwehr, which represented the largest "popular" armed force supporting the government. On the other hand, the Heimwehr, given the limitations of its size and of Mussolini's support, had to accept a subordinate position, one that it, of course, expected to be permanent and increasingly powerful.

10
Gradual Eclipse
1 May 1934 to 10 October 1936

From Dollfuss to Dualism

For this story, developments during the short authoritarian period—what Schuschnigg called the "third" Austria—are in a sense anticlimactic. The Heimwehr seemed to have attained a permanent and powerful position in the new dictatorship that it had helped bring about. But there proved to be no more worlds for it to conquer. Having achieved its earlier purposes in the spring of 1934, its existence became much more artificial and its realizeable objectives much more limited after May 1. For two years it served, largely with Mussolini's support, as a counterweight to the Nazis in Austria and as a check on any inclination its governmental partners had toward compromise with Hitler. This purpose it fulfilled, not without some wavering, as long as Mussolini was determined to prevent German domination of Austria. It was also the paramilitary-political support on which the dominant clerical-conservatives felt they had to rely until they were permitted to conscript a citizen army. The Heimwehr still aspired to its own brand of totalitarian rule but, for several reasons, had to accept junior partnership in the new dictatorship. Paradoxically, it actually hindered the creation of a totalitarian political system. That is, in demanding its brand of fascism and competing with the heirs of the old Christian Social party for place and influence within the Fatherland Front, it was one of the forces that kept the Front from attaining the "totality" that was envisioned for it. Thus, for a while the Heimwehr commanded considerable separate influence, but it was never powerful or daring enough fully to triumph.

Authoritarian Austria was brought into existence largely by the currents dominant in Europe's "fascist era." Yet, just as it was necessary to find a special label to identify the "Austro-Marxists," so the regime in existence from early 1934 to early 1938 must be specially characterized as "clerical-fascist." Significantly, it remained and became more traditionally conservative, clerical if one will, than fascist or, for that

matter, corporative. Its governors shared with the regime in Italy and
Germany a virulent anti-Marxism and renunciation of liberal democracy, and they tried to emulate some of the practices of their larger
neighbors (the creation of a single mass party, public demonstrations,
control of labor, Austrian "nationalism," etc.). But, at least in theory,
they tried to link the state with God, not with people or party or
person.[1] The ideal—regardless of the extent to which practice diverged
from it—differed greatly from the egotistical militarism and racist
doctrines of fascism and national socialism. Furthermore, Austria's conservative rulers showed little inclination to "revolutionize" the bourgeoisie or completely to vulgarize political life (though in practice
venality flourished). Partly because their own authoritarianism was at-
tractive to classes accustomed to such a rule,[2] and partly because those
who professed themselves more radically secular and fascist were divided, Austria's conservatives never had to surrender control of affairs
completely to an indigenous fascist group. They established a procapi-
talist, proclerical dictatorship that was without enthusiastic popular
following and that rested ultimately on military force. Their major objectives were to keep the working classes out of political life and to
keep Austria independent of Germany. To these ends they set about
to build a system that would preserve social and religious traditions
against the "revolution of nihilism" threatened by the Nazis, or indeed
by their partners the Heimwehr.

A look at the constitution of the new regime will illustrate some of
the theory and provide a basis for discerning divergence from it in
practice.[3] It provided for one legislative council, the Bundestag (Federal Diet), which was to be composed of fifty-nine delegates from four
advisory chambers. Of these, only the Bundeswirtschaftsrat (Federal
Economic Council) and the Bundeskulturrat (Federal Cultural Council) were corporative; and together they sent only one more representative to the Bundestag than did the two noncorporative bodies, the
Länderrat (Council of the Provinces) and the Staatsrat (State Council),
the latter a group of forty to fifty notables appointed for ten years by
the federal president on the advice of the chancellor. When these consultative chambers were created in the fall of 1934, the new Stände had
not yet been created; all the members were named by authorities who
were either appointed by or responsible to the federal cabinet instead
of being freely selected by local constituencies or by the members of
occupational groups. The functions of the advisory bodies were strictly
consultative. The cabinet could solicit advice from them on economic,
cultural, or federal problems if it chose and could consult the Staatsrat,

a clearly authoritarian chamber, on any matter, but it was not bound to do so. On all procedural issues the councils were subject to executive regulations. The Bundestag had no power to vote the executive out of office and was not given authority to initiate bills. It could only reject or accept without change policies submitted to it by the executive.

The immense powers of the executive were divided between the head of state (the president) and the head of government (the chancellor). The president was elected for a seven-year term by all the mayors in Austria, an arrangement which gave control of that office permanently to the Catholic-controlled villages. His actions, except in dismissing and appointing a chancellor, had to be approved by the chancellor, who had legal preeminence within the cabinet and was the virtual ruler as long as he enjoyed the confidence of the president. In addition to its nearly complete control over federal legislation, the cabinet could remove the authoritarian governors of the provinces at will, and the chancellor had an absolute veto over all provincial legislation. As if it needed them, the executive also had far-reaching emergency powers, albeit with the legal fiction that their exercise was controlled by the Bundestag and federal court. Furthermore, especially through the political monopoly at least nominally enjoyed by the Fatherland Front, the government, or its factions, controlled all patronage and could exert decisive influence on the operation of the corporations, only two of which (agriculture-forestry and civil service) were ever thoroughly organized.

Thus, the authoritarian aspects of the new regime proved much more prominent than either its federal or its corporative features.[4] Most political power was in the hands of the strongly clerical wing of the old CSP, which was in the process of reforming itself as the dominant faction in the Fatherland Front, under the mantle of which all the old nonsocialist parties except for the dedicated Nazis continued to compete. There were among these centralizing clericals some genuine advocates of an anticapitalist, organic corporatism free of class conflict, but most of them favored authoritarian corporatism primarily as a means of suppressing political groups that challenged the influence of the Church and the earnings of the industrialists.

Fortunately, the competition among these various elements in the Fatherland Front, and perhaps even echoes of Austria's liberal-democratic traditions, necessitated compromises that kept the regime from becoming completely totalitarian. Indeed, some observers think that a kind of corporative democracy could have unfolded even under such an authoritarian regime if circumstances had been more favorable, and others suggest that the *Ständestaat* contributed important examples which were incorporated into Austria's system of "parity" after World War II.[5] On the other hand, it can be argued that under more favorable conditions such a regime would never have been created.

As it was, without widespread popular support and under constant pressure from Germany, the regime never attempted to institute self-determination of functional corporations; in fact, given its statist and capitalistic inclinations, it probably never would have done so. In industry and commerce there was no meaningful effort to bring employer and employee together. Instead, a single state-supervised, but not obligatory, Gewerkschaftbund (trade union confederation) was established. Although boycotted at first by most socialist workers, it did not surrender its members' interests entirely to the employers and eventually attracted a large proportion of the laborers, including those carrying on underground Nazi or revolutionary socialist activities. The labor front was led by Josef Staud, formerly the head of the Catholic labor unions and still a spokesman of the Freiheitsbund, the workers' group led by Leopold Kunschak that continued to oppose the Heimwehr claims to totality in paramilitary affairs. Thus, in labor matters, also, the Heimwehr found itself outranked by its Catholic and not altogether undemocratic rivals.

In fact, for the rest of its existence the Heimwehr was primarily engaged in a losing battle with Austria's Catholic conservatives. With its affirmation of the secular and militarist state, it reflected, far more than did its proclerical colleagues, the fascist context of the times and gave to the authoritarian regime most of its fascist character. It had three major factors in its favor: the vogue of vulgarized and militarized politics that marked the fascist era; its connection with Mussolini, which cost it some support from anti-Italians but which guaranteed it an influential voice in political affairs; and its patronage power. But its appeal was sharply limited by the fact that the leading components of southern European fascist ideology, corporatism and nationalism, were preempted, the one by its conservative partners and the other by its Nazi rivals.

Other factors also made it highly unlikely that the Heimwehr would ever be able to achieve totality in the fashion of Mussolini's Fascists or Hitler's National Socialists. Both its leadership and its constituency of about forty-five thousand (not counting youth groups)[6] were seriously divided. Fey led the Viennese déclassés, as Sauer calls the petite bourgeois "losers" in the age of industrialism,[7] but he was so limited by his own hierarchical, disciplined, and militaristic outlook that he could never personify their bitter sense of anomie, failure, and frustration, nor even grasp the revolutionary egalitarianism at the base of fascism's appeal to the mob. Fey enjoyed the acclaim of the crowd, but he could get it only from those whom he put on the state's payroll as auxiliary policemen or in jobs from which political enemies could be driven. Starhemberg wielded more authority in the country districts, where Heimwehr support came largely from the anticlerical peasantry (a minority of that class) and the village artisanry, socioeconomic groups that nowhere formed the mainstay of truly fascist movements. For all their anticlericalism, Starhemberg's followers lacked the dynamism associated with the bourgeois and the intellectual adherents of Nazism, a characteristic reflected in the fact that, after the defection of Pfrimer and the eclipse of Steidle, nearly all Starhemberg's principal subordinates were former aristocrats. In neither segment of the Heimwehr did there emerge a leader with truly mass appeal. In short, while some Heimwehr leaders and adherents were patriotic Austrian as opposed to pro-German fascists, the organization after 1933 represented essentially a group of men who seemed to feel that because they bore arms in a patriotic political cause they were entitled to run the state in a dictatorial fashion. It was primarily the fact that anti-Nazis were in control of the government and could provide jobs, or at least a few schillings for marching, that most of the rank and file still adhered to the Heimwehr rather than to the Nazis. Of course, the longer they opposed the Nazis the more it seemed necessary to continue to oppose them.

With his decision to support Dollfuss, Starhemberg made a fateful step. It was a decision based largely on the inability to come to terms with the Nazis at any price short of total surrender. Not only did he renew his commitment to Austrian independence and thus enmity toward Hitler, but he also placed the Heimwehr at the service more of traditional authoritarianism than of the fascism that he continued to proclaim. Thus, by supporting Dollfuss to the extent that he did, Starhemberg strengthened the Austrian government against the Nazis. And at the cost of the loss of some "freedom of action"—either to try to govern alone or to join the Nazis—Starhemberg also assured for himself and his followers a voice in government policies and considerable, indeed potentially disruptive, influence in the Fatherland Front. His entry into the government as the leader of a paramilitary political group not yet integrated into the Front laid the foundation for the "dualism" that emerged in Austria after Dollfuss's death.

In the two months before that event the partisan struggle for dominance within the cabinet and the Fatherland Front continued much as before the introduction of the new constitution. As a backdrop the Nazis renewed their terroristic violence and demoralizing propaganda, which featured efforts to sow distrust—not without success—among Dollfuss, the Italians, and the Heimwehr rivals. Dollfuss began to plan a major move to broaden the base of his government by including the moderate Nazis led by Anton Reinthaller and "pronounced nationalists," as cautious Nazi sympathizers called themselves. It seems likely that Dollfuss expected to get Mussolini's backing for significant new departures after their meeting scheduled in late July. Starhemberg claimed that Dollfuss assured him that after that "all these questions would be settled" in an acceptable manner. But probably aware of Fey's contacts with the Habicht clique, Dollfuss decided early in the month to reduce Fey's powers. Starhemberg's position regarding the situation is not clear. He claimed to have taken a strong anti-Nazi and anti-Fey line, especially after Gömbös warned him early in June that Fey was connected with plans for an imminent Nazi putsch. (Anton Mörl recorded in his diary on May 31, without noting sources of information, that "the struggle between Starhemberg and Fey begins.") From German observers, however, came reports that Starhemberg and Fey collaborated against Dollfuss over an unspecified issue in mid-June and that Starhemberg joined Neustädter-Stürmer in opposing Dollfuss's proposal to dismiss Fey altogether. In any event the relationship between Dollfuss and his new vice-chancellor was not as smooth as Starhemberg implied. Continuing differences between them over the integration of the Heimwehr into the Fatherland Front were reflected in tension which connected both with further reconstruction of the provincial governments, especially in Styria, and with military matters.[8]

In view of these currents and in preparation for his meeting with Mussolini, Dollfuss carried out an important reorganization of his cabinet on July 10 and 11. He once again concentrated in his hands control of all the armed forces, official and semiofficial. Schönburg-Hartenstein left the cabinet and Fey remained—seething—with only the nebulous title and responsibilities of "general state commissioner for defense against treasonous activities in the private economy." Dollfuss appointed state secretaries to function under him in the ministries of national defense and of security: General Wilhelm Zehner and Carl Karwinsky, who, however, did have close ties with Fey. The Heimwehr acquired another post when Egon Berger-Waldenegg became minister of justice in place of Schuschnigg, who remained minister of education (and who Starhemberg understood was to play a major role in the Fatherland Front). To some extent, the Heimwehr gain was balanced by bringing into the government Stefan Tauschitz, a moderate Landbund adherent and former minister to Berlin, as secretary of state in the foreign office, and by sending the bothersome Steidle to Trieste as consul general. By these changes Dollfuss hoped to be in a strong enough position to move in any direction after his talks with Mussolini; he also sought to reconcile in his own person the conflict between the army and the Heimwehr.[9]

As already mentioned, the fanatical Nazis under Habicht had resumed their violent opposition after May 1. In their propaganda and personal contacts they tried to convince everyone that the Italians, impatient with Dollfuss's inability to pacify the Nazis, might back a "neutral" personality who could make peace at home and ease relations with Germany, that the Italians still favored Fey within the Heimwehr, and that the Heimwehr bitterly opposed clerical tendencies of the new regime.[10] Such confusion also influenced Hitler, whose wishes in any event weakened his judgment in the matter. He returned from his first and rather inconclusive meeting with Mussolini at Venice in mid-June erroneously convinced that the latter would not seriously oppose a change in the Austrian leadership.[11] Nazi terror began to assume frightening proportions, and late in June Habicht and his Austrian collaborators decided to attempt an armed putsch. The elimination of the SA leadership in Germany on June 30 disrupted the SA in Austria, with whom Dollfuss had been in contact throughout June, and worked to Habicht's advantage since his clique had long been feuding with the SA. After that the conspirators had a freer hand to proceed with their plans. Moreover, the government's decree requiring the death penalty for the use or possession of explosives hardened the conspirators' determination to remove Dollfuss.[12]

The Nazi putsch and the uprising that followed in several provinces form another well-described episode in the tragic history of the First Republic. The conspirators hoped that a three-pronged stroke would succeed so quickly that a popular rebellion would be unnecessary unless the Heimwehr tried to be heroic. The heart of the scheme was to be the capture of the entire cabinet during a meeting in the chancellery and the simultaneous kidnapping of President Miklas, then vacationing in Carinthia, who would be forced to dismiss Dollfuss and appoint Anton Rintelen as head of a new government and thus of the armed forces. Rintelen, minister to Rome, was already in Vienna awaiting the "invitation" to form a cabinet. Small groups were then to seize the state's radio station and broadcast the "news" that Dollfuss had resigned and that Rintelen had assumed the chancellorship. The participants, members of a Viennese SS unit composed primarily of former army personnel dismissed because of their pro-Nazi activities, were to wear army uniforms to make the action appear to be a military coup.

But the plans went awry at the outset. The rebels' first misfortune occurred before they even got started. The coup was originally planned for the twenty-fourth, but at the last moment Dollfuss postponed the cabinet meeting until the next day. During the delay a couple of conscience-stricken accessories betrayed the plans to lower police officials. For a while the report was treated as just another rumor, and there are indications that some of the police officials who heard it may have been sympathetic to the plot. Word of it did reach Fey mid-morning on July 25, but he kept the news to himself for nearly two hours, though he did set some of his Heimwehr troops in motion. All in all, then, adequate precautions to guard the chancellery were not undertaken until it was too late. Alert officials did intercept the conspirators who were on their way to kidnap the president, however, thus largely foiling the plot even before the further tragedy unfolded in the capital.

In effect the abortive putsch was a one-day affair. Early on the afternoon of July 25 SS men wearing army uniforms briefly gained control of both the chancellery and the radio studio from which they made the planned broadcast. Their only success, however, was the assassination of Dollfuss, whom one of the intruders shot in the neck as he was apparently trying to escape into a secret passage; the mortally wounded chancellor died within three hours without benefit of either physician or priest. But except for Fey, Dollfuss was the only minister still in the chancellery, for upon Fey's last-minute warning that "something was afoot," he had broken off the cabinet meeting and instructed his colleagues to return to their respective offices in other buildings. They soon began to gather in the well-protected defense ministry, where they were informed via telephone by President Miklas, safe in Carinthia, that he would not recognize any commitments made by any of the captives and that in the absence of Vice-Chancellor Starhemberg, who was vacationing in Venice, he wanted Schuschnigg to take charge of the government during the emergency. The ministers then ordered army and Heimwehr units to surround the chancellery and to recapture the radio facilities, and they had Rintelen, who was in a downtown hotel, placed under arrest, during which procedure he inflicted a critical wound on himself. Isolated and desperate, the rebels in the chancellery warned that an assault on the building would be answered with reprisals against the captive clerks. Next, through the mediation of Fey, they attempted first to gain the recognition of Rintelen as chancellor and then to negotiate favorable surrender terms. Late in the afternoon, at least two hours after Dollfuss had died, the Nazis were promised safe passage to the German border on the understanding, the government officials contended, that there had been no loss of life. The rebels claimed—and the account by Foder, who was on the Ballhausplatz that afternoon, corroborates their claim—that there was no such condition and that the government later fabricated it as an excuse to arrest and punish them. By early evening the chancellery was again in the hands of the government and Vienna was quiet.[13]

The opaque role played by Emil Fey on July 25 has ever since stirred speculation that he became either early or late a party to the conspiracy. Almost assuredly he seriously compromised himself on all sides, but he probably intended far more to advance himself than to serve the Nazis. In all likelihood had he acted on what he knew, he could have prevented the seizure of the chancellery. One of the conspirators, not wanting to compromise himself with the police and knowing that Fey and his adjutant, Major Wrabel, had recently been in touch with Nazi circles, informed Wrabel on the morning of the twenty-fifth of the blow planned against the cabinet. Wrabel told Fey, who, after his recent demotion, was no longer responsible for internal security. Instead of immediately informing Dollfuss or Karwinsky, Fey ordered several units of his Viennese Heimatschutz to assemble in the Prater, where the men were issued weapons and ammunition. Undoubtedly he hoped that he would be able to save the day and prove himself indispensable. Only after the cabinet had already assembled did he take Dollfuss aside to tell him something that will forever remain a secret. After Dollfuss was wounded, the captive Fey continued to play his ambiguous role. Whether under threat to his person, as he later claimed, or voluntarily, as evidence suggests might have been the case, he acted as middleman between the conspirators and the dying chancellor, who Fey said willingly agreed to see Rintelen succeed him to bring peace to the land. From a balcony Fey negotiated on that basis with government officials outside the chancellery. He was thus in a very compromised position when it became clear that Schuschnigg was in control of the situation and that the rebels would have to surrender. Fey continued his role as middleman in trying to arrange terms for surrender, with results that have already been seen. For some time afterwards Fey was a chastened person. But the government chose, for several reasons, not to take action against him, and when Starhemberg later accused him of treason, an officer's inquest cleared him of any willful wrongdoing. In the long run, however, he was not cured of his vainglory and desire for power.

In Venice, Starhemberg was kept informed of events by the Italian government. As soon as he heard about the crisis, he ordered all Heimwehr units placed on military alert for action anywhere in the country. It is not clear whether he was already in communication with the rest of the cabinet, but it seems likely that, not knowing fully the situation and fearing a nationwide rebellion, he wanted thus to commit himself and the government to forceful resistance, for which he had Mussolini's prompting and backing. Because of a severe storm over the mountains, Starhemberg was unable to fly to Vienna until early on the morning of the twenty-sixth, when he temporarily became chief of the cabinet.[14]

The government's immediate task was to crush armed rebellion, for Nazis in several of the mountain provinces took up arms. Most notably in Styria, Carinthia, and parts of Upper Austria, bloody battles were fought into the fourth day. Once again the army bore the brunt of the fighting—Starhemberg's claims to the contrary notwithstanding—but it did so with much less enthusiasm than it had shown against the socialists in February. The Heimwehr also took an active part in the fighting, also with less enthusiasm than in February but with grim determination against men who wanted to take their place in governing the country. Casualties were high on all sides, but large numbers of Nazis managed to make their way into Yugoslavia and safety (Starhemberg claimed because the army failed to move energetically enough to cut them off). Had the Austrian government not been able to master the situation, troops from several neighboring countries might well have made its territory a battleground.[15]

By the end of July the crisis had passed. For the immediate future the Nazi threat was over and the country's independence assured. Mussolini's show of military force at the Austrian border was not necessary to seal Austria's Italian connection for another year and a half, but this dramatic demonstration of Germany's diplomatic isolation helped persuade the *Führer* to leave the shattered Nazi ranks in Austria to their own devices for a while. As the Austrians began to make arrangements for the post-Dollfuss era, they now had a martyr around whom a cult of anti-German patriotism could be built. But Dollfuss the improviser and opportunist contributed more to the independence of the country alive than dead, and in the long run his death was a grievous loss to the cause.

The major question facing the country in the aftermath of the Nazi uprising was the role of the Heimwehr, or Heimatschutz, as Starhemberg's organization was now officially named.[16] By its support of the regime against the Nazis it had clearly earned a major share of power, even more than it had by its action against the socialists in February. For several reasons Starhemberg was in a position to expect the chancellorship, and some of his more ardent followers urged him to claim it. But apparently he did not demand the office, although he might have been disappointed not to get it. Given President Miklas's strong disapproval of the Heimwehr's anticlericalism, not to mention his own aversion to desks and files, it was probably sensible of Starhemberg not to press the matter too far. According to Schuschnigg, whom Miklas preferred as chancellor, the question of the chancellorship was never put to Starhemberg, who willingly accepted his suggestion for a compromise solution. Schuschnigg proposed a formal division of power between the two men in which he would become chancellor and deputy leader of the Fatherland Front and in which Starhemberg would become vice-chancellor and leader of the Front, which was the only legal political "party." In addition, Schuschnigg would control the army and Starhemberg the police and gendarmery. Such an arrangement seemed to make it possible for each man to check any move that the other might attempt against him.[17]

Dualism was a risky device from the chancellor's standpoint. In the first place, it made it virtually impossible to broaden the government's base of support, which was so narrow that contemporary observers doubted that the new arrangement would last through 1934.[18] It also seemed to require a measure of collaboration between Schuschnigg and Starhemberg that was hardly to be expected. The two men always spoke and later wrote correctly about each other, and there did seem to be a certain mutual respect between them, but they were entirely different in temperament and outlook, and their relationship was never as spontaneous and open as that between Dollfuss and Starhemberg had been. Starhemberg had more armed partisans behind him than did Schuschnigg, and at the time there always seemed to exist the possibility that the former might attempt to seize power exclusively for himself. Meanwhile, by his control of the Fatherland Front Starhemberg could conceivably so strengthen himself that he would someday become the de facto ruler of the country. On the other hand, Schuschnigg had several factors in his favor: he governed at the will of the president, not of the Fatherland Front; he could rely on the army against the Heimwehr; and he could assume that the Heimwehr would never be numerically dominant in the Fatherland Front, in which he enjoyed the loyalty of the most capable politicians. Whether or not such was part of his calculations, Schuschnigg could count also on the fact that Starhemberg was hardly a monomaniacal politician, that the prince in fact had a thorough dislike of application to administrative affairs and went through periods of disinterest and laziness. Finally, as secure as was the Heimwehr's participation for the moment, the rationale for its existence gradually diminished. Time and circumstance proved to be on the side of the clerical partners in the new dualism.

Schuschnigg differed greatly from Dollfuss. He was less a man of the common people, stiffer in his relations with his colleagues, and less flexible in his political conceptions. The son of an imperial officer who earned the right to use the "von" in his name, Kurt Schuschnigg was born in 1897 in the garrison town of Riva on Lake Garda near the Italian border. He received most of his education at an isolated and strictly disciplined Jesuit school in Vorarlberg, where as an apt pupil he was a favorite of his instructors. Like Dollfuss and Fey, he too served on the Italian front during the war as an artillerist, but unlike the other two future leaders he spent several months following the war as an Italian prisoner. After his return he took a degree in law at the University of Innsbruck and established a law practice there for several years before his election in 1927 to the Nationalrat, where he became a protégé of Seipel. Described by the *Times* correspondent in the spring of 1936 as "austere, diligent, sober, entirely untheatrical, infused by an almost religious faith in his mission of statesmanship," Schuschnigg zealously sought to maintain the independence of an authoritarian Austria in close alliance with the Church—a mission which at that time would have been served better by a leader with popular appeal than by a reserved autocrat. By birth, education, and experience, Schuschnigg was inclined to a kind of mystical Pan-Germanism, one that harked back to the Holy Roman Empire and thus saw Austrian Catholicism as more representative of the German spirit than Nazism, but one that grieved spiritually, probably more than had Dollfuss, over the division between the two Germanic peoples. As long as it seemed necessary, he would lean on Italy for support and concede some authority to Starhemberg. But Schuschnigg always hoped for a reconciliation with Germany that would safeguard Austria's independence and for domestic developments that would permit him to escape from Starhemberg's "fraternal embrace," which could easily be seen as a "mutual stranglehold."[19]

From Dualism to Dissolution

The Schuschnigg-Starhemberg cabinet took office in a tense atmosphere on 30 July 1934. A strong guard protected the chancellery during the final deliberations, more against the prospect of demonstrations by Fey's followers than against the Nazi danger. Dualism was formally inaugurated, and the new cabinet seemed evenly balanced between traditional and Heimwehr forces, although for reasons already noted the former had a slight edge. Until Mussolini changed his policies toward Austria at the beginning of 1936, this balance within the Austrian cabinet remained roughly the same. No major reconstruction of the cabinet took place before October 1935, and that, just at the beginning of Mussolini's Abyssinian campaign, seemed to represent a slight strengthening of Starhemberg's position. All the while, however, within the limited scope available, the various factions in Austria jockeyed for power. Besides the ever troublesome German question, the following may be viewed as the principal issues between the Heimwehr and the proclericals in the continuing conflict: control of the Fatherland Front and the type of "totality" that it would impose, the size and makeup of the army, and, from time to time, the question of the restoration of a monarchy.

The major problem facing the new government was its relations with Germany and the nationalists in Austria. As has been indicated, Hitler responded to the Nazi putsch with exaggerated propriety. He closed the border both to the Austrian Legion in Bavaria and to the rebels in Austria; he recalled Minister Rieth, who allowed himself to become compromised with the putschists; and he left the radical Nazis without sufficient backing to continue their terroristic methods. Then, in another stroke of political genius, he dispatched Franz von Papen as his personal emissary extraordinary, officially for the purpose of restoring normal relations between the two governments. Papen, for a few months in 1932 the chancellor of Germany, was an urbane, smooth talking aristocrat who emphasized his allegiance to the Catholic faith. Although Hitler would not for the time being formally acknowledge Austria's right to independence and indeed maintained the visa fee against Germans traveling to Austria, Papen was able after a few months of cold treatment to weasel into most leading circles in Austria's social and political life and guilefully to contribute to the jealousies and suspicions which existed among them.

During the following two years the Heimwehr's chief role was to oppose nationalist aims. The *Heimatschützer* hammered away with an
anti-Nazi theme, and Starhemberg later remembered that "the period
between [Papen's] arrival and the disbandment of the Heimatschutz
was one long duel for Austria between Papen and myself, and it ended
in victory for Papen."[20] As long as he had the backing of Italian Minister Preziosi and Press Attaché Morreale, Starhemberg could block any
effort of Schuschnigg to draw moderate Nazis and non-Nazi nationalists
into his entourage, as when late in October 1934 he rudely broke up a
meeting between Schuschnigg and several men of the "nationalist opposition."[21] When in April 1935 the French and British governments
joined Mussolini in a renewal of their commitment to Austria's independence, they further strengthened the anti-German forces in Austria,
who were able to retain the upper hand through 1935 despite the diligent efforts of Papen to get Schuschnigg to sign a treaty of friendship.[22]

Where the relations with the nationalists were not a factor, however,
the Heimwehr could not dominate. The appointment of the advisory
councils called for by the new constitution provided another occasion
for competition between the government partners. Although Starhemberg demanded a majority in the Staatsrat for the Heimwehr as the
major armed popular force behind the government, Schuschnigg drew
up a list that was dominated by old Christian Socials and other non-
Heimwehr notables. The smaller paramilitary groups backed the chancellor. The extent to which the Heimwehr was in the minority became
evident when of the fifty appointees only fourteen could be considered
Heimwehr men. Christian Socials likewise dominated the two "corporative" chambers (the Länderrat was appointed later). A Heimwehr
adherent, Railways Director Werner Nouakh, did, however, become
the first president of the Staatsrat and thus automatically of the Bundestag. But within three weeks Nouakh was removed from his legislative
positions at the behest of the cardinal of Vienna because of his divorce
and remarriage by civil proceeding. This exercise of Church authority
angered the Heimwehr, but the fact that Nouakh was succeeded by
another active Heimwehr member, Count Rudolf Hoyos, helped in
some measure to smooth their ruffled feathers.[23]

At the end of 1934—and for thirty months thereafter—Starhemberg's
own marital difficulties affected the relationship between the chancellor
and him. The prince wanted his marriage annulled on the grounds that
his wife could not bear him children. Schuschnigg intervened in his
behalf with the pope, who apparently agreed at the time to an eventual
annulment (which, however, did not occur until March 1937). The

American minister believed that as a result of Schuschnigg's intercession Starhemberg began to tone down the demands he had raised earlier in the fall for the Heimwehr to have sole control of youth organizations and to agree publicly that the Church should have some role in the indoctrination of the nation's youth. But from time to time this issue continued to divide Starhemberg and the clericals, and the delay in the annulment may have been seen by both Schuschnigg and the Church as a means of holding Starhemberg in line.[21]

The point most frequently at issue between Starhemberg and Schuschnigg was the creation and control of the single Front militia. Starhemberg wanted to command a militia that would be largely an enlargement of the Heimwehr. Such a merger was opposed by the other two significant paramilitary groups: the Sturmscharen, who in any event owed their allegiance first to Schuschnigg; and the Freiheitsbund, the workers' organization that took on special importance as an opponent to Starhemberg's legions. Repeated pronouncements that all these groups would be absorbed into a united fascist militia under Starhemberg never affected their separate existence. Starhemberg's plans also met strong opposition from the army, which did not want to see an enlarged politicized rival under the control of a nonarmy man. Even in local situations the army occasionally refused to cooperate with the Heimwehr.[25] Schuschnigg backed his military leaders, of course, and once again took up the proposal for a larger conscript army with the Germain powers, which would only grant permission to continue for another year the eight thousand man military assistance corps that would keep the army's strength at thirty thousand. The result during the fall of 1934 was a standoff, with Starhemberg maintaining the old Schutzkorps, revived in July and expanded to about eleven thousand men, as an official auxiliary of his security ministry.[26]

The issue was revived in the wake of Hitler's announcement in March 1935 that Germany was rearming. Political adversaries of Starhemberg, with Reither and Kunschak as the established "democratic" politicians in the forefront of those who opposed the Italian connection, began to call for the dissolution of all paramilitary groups and the introduction of universal service. Starhemberg and the Heimwehr opposed the creation of a large conscript army of short-term recruits. They may have feared that it would destroy the basis of their political strength, as indeed it would have, but they argued that the government needed politically committed armed forces behind it. There occurred several bitter exchanges between Heimwehr spokesmen on one side and those for the Freiheitsbund and Sturmscharen, who favored conscription, on the other. In a few instances rival partisans disrupted opponents' meetings and provoked violent encounters. General Wolf-gang Muff, the German military attaché, heard from sources in the defense ministry that at a military parade on April 7 Schuschnigg had intended to announce universal service but was prevented from doing so by Heimwehr pressure, which was so great that some military offi-cials feared that the Heimwehr might try to occupy army barracks during the parade. According to Muff Schuschnigg also complained that Mussolini wanted to limit the expansion of the federal army to no more than fifty to sixty thousand men plus an improvement of arma-ments, thus leaving, in the face of German developments, a role for the paramilitary organizations.[27]

At the same time Starhemberg seemed to be preparing to convert the Heimwehr into a part of the regular army, but in such a way that the members would keep their identity and places intact. Such was the impression gained by Lieutenant Colonel M. C. Shallenberger, the American military attaché, when by personal invitation of some friends on the Heimwehr staff he attended, as the only foreign observer, large-scale maneuvers conducted by the Heimwehr in late March. Shallen-berger was impressed by the military character of the exercises and by the Heimwehr's armament and general equipment, which was prac-tically the same as that in the federal army. Transport appeared to be even more motorized than that of the army, because the Heimwehr impressed private vehicles of members and sympathizers. Several air-planes—privately registered—also took part under the personal com-mand of Starhemberg. The Heimwehr undertook such maneuvers on their own without the cooperation of the army and almost without its knowledge. Shallenberger did not state how many men were involved but suggested that at least three brigades from Vienna and five from Lower Austria participated. He reported that the general organization of the Heimwehr had taken on a military character with a highly cen-tralized control. The former loose formation in the provinces had been tightened so that all units belonged to regiments and were organized into brigades composed of three regiments, as was the case with the federal army. The officers also wore new insignias of rank that were similar to those in the army. The attaché saw no rank higher than major general, and remarked that Fey and Starhemberg still wore their old uniforms with no distinctive insignias.[28]

The dispute over the militia, which persisted throughout the spring of 1935, became the focus for Starhemberg's demand that "his" Fatherland Front exercise political totality in line with Heimwehr ideals. The Heimwehr was greatly disturbed by an impressive demonstration of the Freiheitsbund early in May, and thereafter launched a bitter propaganda campaign against these "Catholic Reds." Indeed, the Freiheitsbund, which Shallenberger thought numbered about twenty-five thousand, had begun to attract former socialists, generally middle-aged men who had never entirely left the Church, as well as those who were inclined toward anti-Semitism but who also felt themselves democrats opposed to the fascism proclaimed by the Heimwehr as "the universal doctrine of the twentieth century." The Sturmscharen, somewhat larger than the Freiheitsbund, also came under Heimwehr criticism as a haven for the men who joined a paramilitary organization simply in order to provide for themselves under a new dispensation of which they really did not approve. In hopes of improving the Heimwehr's membership, which stood at about one hundred thousand or somewhat more, relative to its rivals,[29] Starhemberg ordered that all members of those groups associated with the Fatherland Front who joined after January 1934 should be purged unless they had proven themselves in the fighting of that year. But this directive left considerable discretion in the hands of the commanders and was not widely heeded. The Freiheitsbund and the Sturmscharen made clear their support of Schuschnigg, who agreed in principle to the amalgamation of the armed societies into a militia but contended that its command should lie with the defense ministry in order to avoid a relapse into party factions and rivalries.[30] Thus the stalemate remained.

At the height of the struggle for the control of the planned militia, rumors spread that Starhemberg intended to use the occasion of a paramilitary parade on 2 June 1935 to proclaim himself regent of Austria. In reports to Hitler on May 10 and May 17, Papen dramatized his fears that a Starhemberg regency or a "total Heimwehr dictatorship . . . would mean the complete strangulation of all pro-German tendencies, the consequent purging of the government machine and, above all, an attempt to detach the army from German influence." Papen's exaggeration reflected both his efforts to sow dissension in Austria and to persuade Hitler to make a public statement that might open the way for an agreement between Schuschnigg and the moderate nationalist opposition.[31] Papen did not manufacture his report out of thin air. Monarchists had become extremely active and much more hopeful than their popular support warranted. They were encouraged by the fact that Schuschnigg was personally in favor of a restoration, although the chancellor never let his emotions blind him to the fact that a return of the Habsburgs might be viewed as a casus belli by both Czechoslovakia and Yugoslavia. On the other hand, a Starhemberg regency, to which Schuschnigg was opposed, might be acceptable to the Little Entente and would presumably strengthen the anti-German forces in Austria. It is almost impossible to say what Starhemberg's intentions in the matter were. Undoubtedly there were moments when he wanted to secure the dominant role in Austrian politics. Since he could hardly have been elected president under the electoral system prescribed by the constitution, he must at times have considered seriously the idea of a regency as a legitimate road to power. It would also be a means of preventing a return of the Habsburgs, with whom he was not on the best of terms and by whom his own ambitions would be checked. But publicly Starhemberg never presented himself as a candidate for presidency, throne, or regency. While he did acknowledge that the only legitimate claimant to the throne was Otto, he kept his distance from the monarchists through most of 1935. And at the rally on June 2 he once again pledged his loyalty and support to Schuschnigg.[32]

As the American minister reported a few days later, Starhemberg may well have felt that things were developing in his favor "in a natural way."[33] The new chief-of-staff of the federal army, Major General Alfred Jansa, who had a camouflaged title, won Schuschnigg's approval—over the objection of State Secretary Zehner—for the use of the paramilitary organizations in the defense buildup along the German border. It was a means for Schuschnigg to appease Starhemberg without really increasing his power or settling the issue of the ultimate control of the paramilitary formations. The arrangement whereby the army was enrolled in the Fatherland Front (despite all the earlier efforts to remove it from politics) was probably intended also to lull Starhemberg, the leader of the Front, into a false sense of security. The compromise plan stipulated that the soldiers' oath of loyalty could in no way be construed to bring them into conflict with the federal president. Since Schuschnigg remained defense minister, the addition of the army was actually a dilution of Starhemberg's forces in the Front. But Schuschnigg thereby restored a temporary peace among himself, the army, and the Heimwehr.[34]

In other matters, however, Heimwehr agitation became more menacing. In Vienna Fey and his followers, who may well have pushed their leader, used their hostility to the Freiheitsbund as a means of attacking archclerical Mayor Schmitz, whose control of city administration they bitterly resented. Fey almost certainly entertained notions of gaining control of Vienna, much as Starhemberg sometimes thought he might like to rule Austria, and he agitated within the cabinet for greater responsibilities.[35] Following a ceremony late in June 1935, at which banners of the Freiheitsbund were dedicated in the square facing the Rathaus, Heimwehr demonstrators expressed anger that their colors were not, as usual, displayed on city hall. Schmitz had tried to remain neutral by not flying the colors of either group, but Fey's followers protested what they interpreted as a slight to them by pointing machine guns at the Rathaus and by blowing the horns of their trucks in chorus for about ten minutes. A few of the men forced their way into the building by a side door that had been left unlocked and draped the green-white Heimwehr flag from a balcony. Finally Fey appeared and calmed the demonstrators by promising that he would investigate the absence of their flag and that he would see to it that order was created in the Rathaus.[36]

To some extent such incidents, about which the Austrian public learned very little through the newspapers, reflected internal tension within the Heimwehr as well as its opposition to other political groups. Within certain circles of the Heimwehr there was dislike of Starhemberg's dependence on Italy and impatience at his inability to gain the upper hand over the Catholic element in the Fatherland Front. During September and October these conflicts again came to the surface. Papen, who was surely doing all he could to stir such dissension, claimed that in mid-September a large group of Heimwehr leaders agreed to try to force Starhemberg to resign. Steidle, on leave from his post in Trieste, appeared to be leading the opposition, the timing of which Papen attributed to some alleged strains in the relations between Starhemberg and Mussolini. This time the agitation against Starhemberg was not limited to the Viennese followers of Fey, who was not much admired outside the capital. As often in the past, there were signs of disaffection in Steidle's Tyrol, perhaps furthered by the infiltration of Nazi elements into the Heimatwehr there.[37]

For the moment Starhemberg was saved by the international storm that, after a long buildup, broke in October 1935. The outbreak of war in east Africa placed the Austrian government, divided as it was, in a serious dilemma. Austria's close ties with Italy and the strength of the Heimwehr made it almost impossible for the government not to support Mussolini at the League of Nations, and the pressure from Rome for such support was disagreeably strong. On the other hand, Austria still needed economic favors from London and Paris, and Finance Minister Buresch and National Bank President Kienböck, supported by President Miklas and Chancellor Schuschnigg, wanted to tone down any statement in support of Mussolini in order not to offend the western powers, especially since it was already feared that Mussolini's adventure would in the long run weaken his ability to defend Austria against Germany. But Foreign Minister Berger-Waldenegg, a Heimwehr enthusiast, had the Austrian delegate at the League of Nations dissociate his country from the League's actions against Italy in a way that irritated the British government. According to Messersmith, Schuschnigg began to plan a thorough overhaul of the government in order to weaken Starhemberg and relieve the Italian pressure. But when word of it leaked out, Starhemberg decided forcefully to strengthen his position within both the cabinet and the Heimwehr.[38]

The flash of self-promotion undertaken by Fey on October 16, the third anniversary of his participation in the government, reinforced Starhemberg's determination. That evening Fey feted himself with a large torchlight parade. At the rally he bitterly accused unnamed people of working against him "in the dark with lies and calumny," and his dependable friend, Vice-Mayor Lahr, proclaimed that any enemy of Fey's was an enemy of the state and added that "obstacles are there to be overcome." Whether Fey was primarily assailing his clerical opponents in Vienna, or attacking Starhemberg, who he probably knew was planning to replace him, and whom he accused of consorting with the "Blacks," is not certain. In any event, he was clearly making a bid for greater power for himself within the government as a counterweight to Starhemberg—one with pro-German leanings.[39]

Thus challenged, Starhemberg moved quickly to head off any possible alliance between Fey and either Schuschnigg or the Nazis. Diplomatic observers called the swift reconstruction of the cabinet that removed Fey and several others a "cold putsch" by Starhemberg and a pro-Italian thrust. Muff called it a "Christian Social putsch" of Starhemberg against the dissident elements in the Heimwehr instead of one against the government and reported that Morreale and Mandl had been urging Starhemberg to draw closer to the Christian Socials. The event was given special drama by the deployment of police and Heimwehr forces in Vienna. According to Papen Fey learned before the cabinet meeting of the proposal to drop him and immediately ordered his Heimwehr adherents in Vienna to occupy public buildings. To parry this move, federal police under Starhemberg's orders "reinforced" this occupation. While the cabinet meeting was in session some four thousand Heimwehr men from adjacent Lower Austria who were loyal to Starhemberg converged on Vienna where they remained throughout the evening as a further warning to Fey.[40] After a long session Fey agreed to his dismissal and called on his men to maintain discipline.

Also dismissed were Neustädter-Stürmer, the Heimwehr minister of social administration who was close to Fey and unpopular with labor; Buresch, minister of finance who opposed Starhemberg's Italian policies and could not seem to find enough money for the Heimwehr; Reither, minister of agriculture who, as a popular peasant leader in Lower Austria, had long been critical of Starhemberg's fascism; Karwinsky, state secretary in the justice ministry who had become unpopular with the workers; and Hammerstein-Equord, state secretary under Fey in the interior ministry. Buresch remained in the cabinet without a portfolio.

The new appointees represented a compromise between Schuschnigg and Starhemberg, who even at this moment of his supreme effort was not able to gain an impregnable position. Baar von Baarenfels, the Heimwehr governor of Lower Austria and heretofore a loyal lieutenant of Starhemberg, succeeded Fey as minister of interior, and Starhemberg's close friend and able financial counselor, Dr. Ludwig Draxler, became the minister of finance. The responsibility of office in rapidly changing conditions sobered both these men, and they proved a disappointment to Starhemberg. Three of the new cabinet members were clearly Schuschnigg's men: Dr. Josef Dobretsberger, minister of social administration; Ludwig Strobl, agriculture and forestry; and Dr. Robert Winterstein, justice. Berger-Waldenegg, whose position would be most precarious in the event of a setback to the Italian policy, remained foreign minister.

Starhemberg wrung one further concession from Schuschnigg. The new cabinet immediately approved the unification of the paramilitary organizations. All the groups would theoretically lose their political character and become known as the *Freiwillige Miliz–Oesterreichischer Heimatschutz*. In a broadcast late the evening of the seventeenth Starhemberg stated that the new militia would cooperate closely with the army but would be under his command and not that of the defense ministry. Again, however, Starhemberg won more in form than in substance, for he was unable to turn the smaller formations into instruments of his will. The militia proved to be only a paper step on the road to universal service.[41]

While things seemed to be moving in his favor, Starhemberg pushed his advantage over Fey to an apparently final decision. His surface success was certainly not unconnected with Fey's vulnerable financial situation, for with his political eclipse Fey's creditors began to demand payment of his sizeable debts. Early in November he had to suspend publication of his daily newspaper when he lost the financial backing for it. A few days later it was announced that Fey would resign as

Heimwehr leader of Vienna and would become director of the Danube Steamship Travel Company at a considerably higher salary than he received as a minister. Before the public Fey seemed to accept this change in his status with good grace, but he was not happy at losing his Heimwehr command, and on the day after he surrendered control he issued a pointed statement about Starhemberg's taking over the leadership from a freely elected leader. With his accession in Vienna, Starhemberg became formal leader of the Heimwehr in all the provinces except in Styria, where it was led by his good friend Berger-Waldenegg.[42]

For several reasons these gains that seemed to have brought Starhemberg another step closer to total power were Pyrrhic victories. For one thing, the cabinet changes meant a narrowing of the government's base, since Reither's departure increased the opposition of both the Freiheitsbund and of much of the peasantry. Furthermore, the dismissal of Fey, while probably welcome throughout much of the country, left the Heimwehr as divided as ever. In a more fundamental sense, Starhemberg reached the peak of his power just as the bases for it began to give way. His position was posited almost entirely on the Italian connection, and Mussolini's African war proved to be its undoing. The war was very unpopular in Austria, and Starhemberg's effusive support of it was widely resented. He banked too much on a swift victory that did not come about. The change in Italo-Austrian relations was quickly felt, not least, apparently, in Heimwehr coffers. As Italy began to be of less help to Austria economically, Vienna had to seek aid elsewhere, and it became clear that Mussolini might foster an Austro-German settlement, opposition to which Starhemberg seemed the embodiment.

There naturally followed an intense debate among Austria's ruling circles about the direction in which they should turn. A number of men, including Revertera, a Heimwehr leader and security director of Upper Austria, thought a reconciliation with Germany would be the best course to follow. Others, predominant for the moment, hoped to improve ties with the Little Entente as well as with the western powers. Within the Heimwehr apparently Berger-Waldenegg, foreign minister and proponent of the Italian alliance, and Draxler, finance minister, were also drawn in this direction. Starhemberg, too, saw the problem, but he had become such a symbol of the Italian connection, both in the west and in Austria, that a major policy change could be made only at his expense. The only thing that prevented an immediate turnabout was the unwillingness of the western powers, who chided Austria for its support of Mussolini, to assume the responsibility for its defense against Germany. Thus, although Starhemberg's position was undermined from several directions, he could hold his place until Mussolini decided to sacrifice him. He could even protect the foreign minister's post in the cabinet by posing conditions for his dismissal that Schuschnigg could not accept: the defense ministry for Starhemberg.[43]

As Starhemberg became aware of the tenuousness of the Italian support, he became more temperamental and inconsistent. He hoped that Italy would conquer quickly and return to the watch on the Brenner. He knew what was at stake and was told by Preziosi, with whom he had collaborated for many years, that he was following the Abyssinian campaigns more closely than an Italian.[44] Caught in the agony of suspense, he seemed to be unsure of what to do. While flirting again with the monarchists, he lamely tried to appeal to the workers with the much-heralded promise that Austria should become "the most social state (der sozialste Staat)." He intensified his demands for the "totality" of his Fatherland Front, and asserted that those who did not affirm Austria and adhere to the Front must be considered enemies of the state who did not deserve full rights of citizenship. He appeared to lash out at opponents simply to demonstrate that he was still a power to be reckoned with, as when he forced into retirement the head of the intelligence section of the defense ministry on the charge of being anti-Heimwehr.[45] While such actions were calls for opposition to Anschluss, Starhemberg nevertheless cautiously established indirect contacts with Papen, probably without knowing definitely that Mussolini was about to initiate the diplomatic steps that would soon give Schuschnigg a relatively free hand vis-à-vis the Heimwehr.[46] Starhemberg's dilemma was not eased by his trip to London and Paris in February 1936 to attend the funeral of George V. In the western capitals he had impressed upon him the extent of Mussolini's isolation and of the Little Entente's opposition to a Habsburg restoration. On his return he assured Messersmith that Austria must draw closer to the Little Entente.[47] But he was still not convinced that it could or that he wanted it to do so.

Starhemberg's approach to Papen was probably much more sincere.[48] He realized that close ties with the Little Entente were impossible unless Austria withdrew completely from the Rome protocols with Italy and Hungary, which it could not do without a guarantee of support from France and Britain. Moreover, Starhemberg's personal inclinations clearly lay with fascist authoritarianism; it was more the politics of circumstance and of personal ambition than anything else which had driven him into the anti-German camp and kept him there, during which time, it is true, he had come to value Austria's independence.

With the prop of his power crumbling, he was now seeking a way to save both himself and Austria. Prompted by Papen, Starhemberg advocated the formation of an ideological bloc that would include Germany, Italy, Austria, and Hungary. He hoped that he could win Mussolini's support for a "fascist international" in which all the participants would honor the others' integrity, and in which he rather than Schuschnigg would be the most suitable ruler in Austria. For his part, Papen was probably open for any development: either that Mussolini would back Starhemberg in such a project or that his contacts with Starhemberg would spur the Christian Socials to come to the kind of bilateral agreement with Germany that Papen had long tried to bring about.

Without Mussolini's backing, Starhemberg held a very weak hand, and the *Duce* very swiftly dealt himself out as the prince's partner. This was clearly the price that Hitler demanded for a settlement of their conflict over Austria. The *Führer* responded somewhat cautiously to Mussolini's first overture, and he instructed Papen to be cautious in his approaches to Starhemberg. He wanted to see if Mussolini would produce a change in Austrian policy, which would really be evident only if he withdrew his support of the Heimwehr as an anti-German instrument.[49] Hitler's remilitarization of the Rhineland on March 7 gave Mussolini reason to pause briefly in his approach to Germany.[50] But Mussolini was increasingly paying more attention to a different group of advisers who reinforced his pro-German inclination. Under-Secretary Suvich, who opposed a German course, began to lose favor, as did Preziosi and Morreale in Vienna, both of whom had been close to Starhemberg; Francesco Salata, the head of the Italian cultural institute in Vienna and Mussolini's liaison with Schuschnigg, began to come to the fore.[51] By the time that the signatories of the Rome protocols met late in March, Mussolini had decided to come to terms with Germany and to back Schuschnigg as the leader who could best ease him out of his Austrian entanglement. Both Gömbös and Mussolini urged Schuschnigg to pursue a German rather than a Czech connection. Schuschnigg, who had already renewed contact with Papen about a treaty of friendship, moved with great rapidity.[52]

A week after his return from Rome Schuschnigg demonstrated clearly the changing relations of power within the Austrian government and inaugurated six weeks of intense political agitation. On April 1 the Bundestag sanctioned a law making all Austrian men between the ages of eighteen and forty-two liable for public service with or without arms (which provision made it possible for the government to screen the political reliability of draftees into the army). This introduction of uni-

versal compulsory service destroyed the rationale for the paramilitary
formations and was a direct blow at those whose political power was
based on them. Immediately there were renewed calls for the dissolution of the paramilitary bands. At the same time Papen placed funds at
the disposal of the Freiheitsbund, which intensified its anti-Heimwehr
activity, in hopes of driving the paramilitary question to a denouement.[53]

Put on the defensive, Starhemberg became frantic. He unsuccessfully
demanded the defense ministry and argued, not without some cogency,
that a conscript army would be able neither to defend the country
against a German invasion nor to provide the government with political
support.[54] Still hoping to win out with his plan for a fascist alliance, for
which he apparently had some encouragement from Gömbös, he sent
Franz Hueber to see Göring about a meeting in Hungary.[55] At home he
broke a long public silence with a vigorous speech before a Heimwehr
audience at Horn, Lower Austria, on April 26. He asserted that the
Heimwehr would be disarmed only over his dead body and, bitterly
attacking the "liberals" in and out of the cabinet as well as the leaders
of the Freiheitsbund, he assured Schuschnigg that the Heimwehr would
support him in "rooting out weeds" in the patriotic brotherhood. Starhemberg's intensified demand for totality within the Fatherland Front
caught Schuschnigg in growing pressure from anti-Heimwehr officials
in the Front, with Colonel Walter Adam, its general secretary, threatening to resign. The conflict reached a high point during a Freiheitsbund
parade on May 10, which brought into the open the fact that Fey was
again emerging as a spokesman for the Viennese Heimwehr. An angry
chancellor, whose attendance Fey had tried to discourage, responded
to Heimwehr disruptions by marching for a while with Staud, the FHB
leader, and his ally Strobl, the minister of agriculture. Several Heimwehr men were arrested, but Starhemberg ordered their release soon
thereafter.[56]

Starhemberg pushed the crisis to its climax a few days later. Apparently Schuschnigg, not wanting to give the great powers the impression
that Austria was unstable at a time of international uncertainty, was
willing to let things ride for a while and to make a truce with the Heimwehr short of granting Starhemberg's demand for the defense ministry.[57] But for the Heimwehr the matter was urgent. A large debt
payment was due by May 18, and state funds were no longer available;[58] this need for money made it imperative that Starhemberg try to
force a decision in his favor. With the *Heimatschützer* boasting that
Italy's victory in Africa demonstrated the correctness of the Heimwehr's

"foreign policy," Starhemberg published on the thirteenth a telegram in which he congratulated Mussolini on the capture of Addis Ababa "with my whole heart in the name of those who fight for Fascism in Austria and in my own name on the famous and magnificent victory of the Italian Fascist armies over barbarism; on the victory of the Fascist spirit over democratic dishonesty and hypocrisy; on the victory of Fascist sacrifice and disciplined courage over democratic falsehood."[59] This desperate appeal was a serious mistake. It was too late to regain Mussolini's support, and, although Starhemberg's jibes at democracy were directed mainly at his domestic opponents, the western powers vigorously protested what they took to be gratuitous insults. Schuschnigg, who had previously been unable to replace Berger as foreign minister because of Starhemberg's opposition, now asked both of them to resign in a general reorganization of the cabinet. Starhemberg put up a show of resistance (feigning surprise at western response to his telegram and at Schuschnigg's coup) but finally agreed to go if Dobretsberger and Strobl went as well. Schuschnigg restructured the cabinet early on May 14 and disbanded the skeletal Schutzkorps, down to about 340 men of all ranks, on May 17.

By combining the leadership of the Fatherland Front with the chancellorship, Schuschnigg put an end to the dualistic arrangement. He also retained responsibility for foreign affairs, which he soon delegated to a pro-German friend from his school days, Guido Schmidt. According to Guido Zernatto, who became a state secretary in the chancellery and a few days later the general secretary of the Fatherland Front, Schuschnigg tried to form a cabinet without any Heimwehr participation but could not come to terms with the nationalists. The Heimwehr thus remained strongly represented in the new cabinet. Baar von Baarenfels, who had succeeded Fey in October 1935, now assumed in addition the portfolios surrendered by Starhemberg and became the top-ranking Heimwehr spokesman in the government. Baar also took over from Starhemberg the leadership of the militia, which was renamed the *Frontmiliz*, and, according to Baar himself, was to be fully depoliticized or rather fully aligned with the Fatherland Front. Draxler, who was sympathetic to the enlargement of the army, remained as finance minister. Three of the cabinet members had looser ties with the Heimwehr but were not closely connected with Starhemberg, who now held only two public positions: federal sports leader and chairman of the mothers' aid section of the Fatherland Front—which latter appointment may be regarded, in view of Starhemberg's reputation as a man about town, as an expression of Schuschnigg's cutting wit. Perhaps the appointments did, however, just barely accord with Mussolini's request that Schuschnigg treat Starhemberg "in view of my personal friendship with [him] . . . politically speaking . . . decently."[60]

Starhemberg's last plaintive appeal to Mussolini, who had not answered his telegram, proved unavailing. In his capacity as sports leader he went to Rome, in accord with earlier plans, to award a trophy at a soccer game between Austrian and Italian teams. He left Vienna and arrived in Rome asserting that he would continue the fight when he returned. But Mussolini, observing that both the army and the police would oppose a putsch, advised him to exercise restraint and to hold himself in reserve in case Schuschnigg should fail. This may not have been altogether meant as merely a gentle put-down, for German observers in Rome at the time and Papen later in the summer suspected that Mussolini did not intend to drop Starhemberg completely and might even have wanted to see him replace Miklas.[61] But in the short run Schuschnigg did not fail, and the outbreak of civil war in Spain soon brought Hitler and Mussolini closer, weakening further Mussolini's will to keep a strong voice in Austrian affairs. The *Duce* never again had occasion to employ the Heimwehr leader; this was their last meeting. Apparently Mussolini also eased Starhemberg's fall by providing enough financial assistance to meet the Heimwehr's most pressing debts. That his help was not sufficient to maintain Heimwehr wages was a great relief to Schuschnigg.[62]

From that point on it was merely a matter of time until the Heimwehr lost all significance as a political force. Perhaps the long-range implication of Starhemberg's fall is best illustrated by the fact that Jewish circles in Vienna were despondent about it.[63] Starhemberg fell, not because he espoused fascism, but because he was the symbol of resistance to the Nazis. When Mussolini urged the dominant partners in the Austrian dictatorship to come to terms with Germany, he sealed the doom of the Heimwehr and ultimately of Austria itself. Starhemberg knew it, and, although he vainly tried then and later to make himself acceptable to the Germans, he was undoubtedly chagrined at the prospect of *Anschluss*.

Starhemberg initially responded to his demotion with a brave show of belligerence and business, in which he still fiercely championed the Heimwehr and the Austrian cause. The *Heimatschützer* cheered Starhemberg's being free once again to devote all his time to the movement. The paper, ridiculous in its simple efforts to fool the faithful, claimed that Starhemberg had become the world's most interesting personality, whose every word was attended—whether for a reading of central Europe's political barometer or only for comic relief it did not say. It began to make much of the "old Dollfuss goals" and threw boldly back to critics like Kunschak the boast, "We were fascists, we are fascists, we will remain fascists."[64]

But all the effort to give the situation the most favorable interpretation could not conceal the Heimwehr's distress. For instance, no matter what was said publicly, the removal of headquarters from Vienna to Linz—Starhemberg's first and last stronghold, where he hoped to find greater economy and loyalty—clearly meant retreat and retrenchment. For a while Starhemberg seemed to hope that Fey and he might reconcile their differences in order to give the Heimwehr more weight, but their bitter rivalry proved unbridgeable. Moreover, numbers of Starhemberg's formerly trusted colleagues, including Baar and Draxler, soon began to move away from him as his star sank; diplomats took special note of Baar's defection, which some thought Schuschnigg purchased by arranging settlement of extensive debts. And Berger-Waldenegg, the former foreign minister and faithful ally, was "exiled" as Austrian minister to Italy.[65]

Feeling his isolation, Starhemberg, always the playboy more than the politician, became increasingly indolent. Behind the scenes he flirted with monarchists and had some contact with nationalists but withdrew steadily from political affairs. When he moved his headquarters late in May, he named one of his oldest and truest colleagues, Heinz Wenninger, who was also governor of Upper Austria, as codeputy leader (with Baar) and as staff commander in Linz. Thereafter his position weakened rapidly. Early in July Starhemberg told Papen that "he intended to spend the summer in rest and travel and that he would not again occupy himself intensively with the affairs of the Heimwehr until the autumn." At the end of the month he did order all active Heimwehr formations to complete their vacations and be ready for duty by September 1, but for all practical purposes he abdicated in favor of Wenninger, who assumed de facto leadership. Starhemberg himself later called his withdrawal a grave mistake, for while he sulked Schuschnigg and the Sturmscharen, Kunschak and the Christian workers, and Reither and the peasants were working behind the scenes to consolidate their forces.[66]

Starhemberg's vacationing was disrupted by unhappy news and events. The severest blow was the announcement of the Austro-German treaty of friendship on 11 July 1936. With Schuschnigg coming to terms with Hitler and still in favor with Mussolini, there was less likelihood than ever that either camp would have a place for him or for the Heimwehr, most of whose members would take their cue from the government's rapprochement with the nationalists. Starhemberg was furious, taking his wrath especially out on Vice-Chancellor Baar for giving up so easily and sending to Mussolini the message, *"Finis Austriae."* Two weeks later he was humiliated when Nazi youth, emboldened by the treaty, directed a rowdy demonstration against him when he was speaking at a ceremony marking the passage of the Olympic flame through Vienna on its way to Berlin. Finally, he was saddened when his Italian collaborators of many years, Minister Preziosi and Press Attaché Morreale, were recalled.[67] Their recall indicated clearly how superfluous the Heimwehr had become. In truth, there was little basis from which Starhemberg could fight back, even had he been disposed to do so.

The country witnessed the Heimwehr's death agony in the early autumn. But it proved to be largely an unsavory internecine quarrel that presented no threat to the government. In fact, Schuschnigg cleverly used the revitalized rivalry between Starhemberg and Fey, who was backed by Steidle, Lahr, and Neustädter-Stürmer, to induce a crisis in miniature that he could then use as an excuse to dissolve the Heimwehr and the other paramilitary bands that remained in existence only as counters to it. Late in August there were public rumblings of opposition to Starhemberg by those in the Heimwehr who wanted action instead of his do-nothing policy, and in mid-September Fey, who "resumed" the leadership in Vienna, and Starhemberg alternately excommunicated each other from the movement. The imbroglio so agitated Starhemberg that eventually he seemed eager to be free of the whole Heimwehr involvement. Briefly, however, he emerged from his apparent lassitude and fought back at Fey and, when he decided that he had been tricked by the chancellor, at Schuschnigg also. In the latter regard, he charged that Schuschnigg urged him to stand fast against Fey's challenge but then suddenly backed Fey on the grounds that Starhemberg had been too severe with him.[68]

Much has been made of the emotional farewell that Starhemberg made to his faithful lieutenants—in "the best speech of my career"—at Wiener Neustadt on October 4. With Morreale, who was about to leave Austria, present in his fascist uniform, Starhemberg made incriminating insinuations about Fey's role in July 1934, excoriated Schuschnigg for his "treachery" at some length, and then closed with the dramatic words, *"Auf Wiedersehen,* and—if it must be—in Wöllersdorf!" (Austria's best-known detention camp). The speech seemed to be a pledge to continue to pursue in some way the anticlerical, anti-German policy of the Heimwehr of the mid-1930s. But Starhemberg had always engaged in exaggerated rhetoric in public and in unbacked bluster in private. It was enough that he leave the stage with a flourish. He knew that events had now cast him aside, and in some ways he must have been relieved to be well out of it. The American minister may have been reporting only gossip, but in many ways it rings true: when urged by colleagues to adopt a vigorous program, Starhemberg was said to have replied that there was no program to adopt and that he did not intend to go to Wöllersdorf.[69]

In fact, Starhemberg again acted, perhaps deliberately, to hasten rather than to impede the inevitable. Clearly faced with a campaign to divide the Heimwehr by elevating Fey, who was elected leader in the Tyrol and Carinthia as well as in Vienna, Starhemberg evidently preferred its dissolution to Fey's succeeding him. By making a boldly offensive demand he precipitated the denouement. It may be, as Goldinger states, that Schuschnigg sought to ease the impending blow of dissolution and to retain the loyalty of much of the Heimwehr membership by bringing Starhemberg back into the government (and thus continuing to play Heimwehr leaders off against each other). But if so, Starhemberg's demands were greater than Schuschnigg was prepared to meet, although it is likely that Starhemberg deliberately made them unacceptable. On October 9 he demanded that Schuschnigg come out against Fey and that he appoint another Heimwehr representative, presumably himself, to the cabinet (according to Papen he wanted the leadership of the Frontmiliz); otherwise, he would have to ask Baar and Draxler to resign. Schuschnigg called a meeting of the cabinet, which lasted into the morning hours of the tenth. With Draxler trying to mediate, the chancellor, pushed by the nationalists who joined the cabinet in July, decided to dissolve all the paramilitary bands. Baar, Draxler, and Perntner, who represented the Sturmscharen, resigned during the voting, but were invited to rejoin the cabinet as "loyal citizens." The decree of dissolution was announced on the tenth; at the same time the Frontmiliz was placed under the control of the defense ministry rather than under the vice-chancellor (Baar). Before leaving for Budapest to attend the funeral of Gömbös, Schuschnigg reinforced the guards at public buildings.[70]

The caution was not needed. Hard core followers in both wings of the Heimwehr expressed anger, but neither of the leading rivals was willing to resort to force. By and large the public was unmoved by the dissolution of an organization that only three years before had set the pace for major political changes and that had had a major voice in ruling the country for nearly two years. Advised by Mussolini to remain

calm, Starhemberg issued a public statement—as so often before at vari-
ance with earlier bombast—to maintain discipline. He also announced
that he had explicitly requested that Draxler remain in the cabinet (he
pointedly ignored Baar) and that Heimwehr members in public employment be allowed to retain their positions.[71] It was nearly over.

Three weeks later Schuschnigg dropped the former Heimwehr ministers from the cabinet. As a final gesture he did invite the governor of
Carinthia and Heimwehr patriarch, Field Marshal Hülgerth, to become vice-chancellor and leader of the Frontmiliz, which soon became
an adjunct of the army. Schuschnigg always made it a point to speak
in glowing terms of admiration and gratitude for the service which the
Heimwehr had earlier rendered the country, and by and large his hopes
that it would now quietly fade away were fulfilled. There was some
effort to form "*alt*-Heimatschutz" clubs of former members who wanted
to keep alive the Heimwehr's "cultural" goals—that is, to oppose clericalism and to propagate fascism.[72] But in the ensuing months less and
less was heard from the Heimwehr.

Thus, only two years after it had achieved apparent victory and a
share of the new dictatorship, the Heimwehr had played out its role in
Austrian politics and formally ceased to exist. A shifting combination of
reactionary, paramilitary organizations based in the Austrian provinces,
the Heimwehr was a phenomenon that appeared solely in the interwar
years. Like most such fascist groups that proliferated throughout Europe at this time, it was a reaction to the aftermath of the world war
—political revolution, social upheaval, and economic chaos. But the
Heimwehr, like Austria itself, had difficulty in finding an identity and
in producing a capable leader. With leaders and followers always beset
by torn loyalties and divided purposes, the Heimwehr was unable to
sustain the momentum of a mass movement or to rule alone. In the
Nazis it had more dynamic rivals; through the Christian Social conservatives it saw its "positive" corporative program preempted. It helped
align Austria with the Italo-Hungarian orbit more as a result of political
convenience than of conviction. Yet with all its internal dissension and
numerical weakness, the Heimwehr—with foreign support—did contribute significantly to the realization of its most generally held goal:
the destruction of Austria's socialist party and of its democratic institutions. While the Heimwehr became for a while a symbol of Austria's
independence, its accomplishments probably hastened the end of Austria and thus of peace in Europe.

Biographical Appendix

Leading participants in the Heimwehr met a variety of fates after the dissolution of the organization late in 1936. The following biographical sketches are intended briefly to complete their story. There is no attempt to tell the whole story of their lives, though occasionally reference will be made to the background of some of them. Pertinent information about their careers between 1918 and 1936 can be found by using the index. Needless to say, the list is highly selective.

BAAR VON BAARENFELS, Baron Eduard: b. 3 Nov. 1885 in Laibach; d. 14 March 1967 in Saalfelden. Vice-chancellor at the time of dissolution, Baar remained in that office for about three weeks, and was then sent as the Austrian minister to Budapest until the *Anschluss*. He suffered considerably during the Nazi occupation, and spent a number of months in concentration camps. He spent most of his postwar life on his estate in Lower Austria.

BERGER-WALDENEGG, Baron Egon (technically Egon Berger, Freiherr von Waldenegg): b. 14 Feb. 1880 in Vienna; d. 12 Sept. 1960 in Styria. Berger-Waldenegg remained Austria's minister in Rome until March 1938. During the entire Nazi period he remained in Italy in the employment of an Italian insurance firm. He founded an Austrian Society (Büro) after the withdrawal of German troops from Rome. In 1948 he returned to Styria, where he spent most of his remaining years on his estate.

FEY, Major Emil: b. 23 March 1886 in Vienna; d. 16 March 1938. Fey remained active in veterans' affairs and business ventures after the dissolution of the Heimwehr. He enjoyed the satisfaction of having a military "honor" inquiry clear him of the accusations of treason in July 1934 that Starhemberg made. Nevertheless, his role at the time of the Nazi putsch has never been made clear. And he felt so compromised vis-à-vis the Nazis that he, his wife, and his son all committed suicide —perhaps under duress—shortly after the fall of Austria.

HEINRICH, Prof. Dr. Walter: b. 11 July 1902 in Haida, Bohemia. Out of favor with the Nazis, Heinrich took employment with Austrian business. In 1945 he returned to his professorship, which he had held from 1933 to 1938, at the Institute for World Commerce (Hochschule für Welthandel) in Vienna.

HUEBER, Dr. Franz: b. 6 Jan. 1894 in Grünburg bei Steyr. Hueber, the brother-in-law of Göring, was made the minister of justice upon the resignation of Schuschnigg and acted in that capacity until the formal *Anschluss* two months later. In law and business throughout the war, he was also a member of Hitler's Reichstag. Detained for a while by the Allies after the war, he resumed law practice in Mattsee, Salzburg.

HÜLGERTH, Field Marshal Ludwig: b. 26 Jan. 1875 in Vienna; d. 13 Aug. 1939 in Carinthia. Hülgerth served Schuschnigg as vice-chancellor from 3 Nov. 1936—after the dissolution—until 11 March 1938; he also acted as commandant of the Frontmiliz, the paramilitary side of the Fatherland Front.

NEUSTÄDTER-STÜRMER, Odo (originally named Gozzani): b. 3 Nov. 1885 in Laibach; d. 19 March 1938 in Hinterbrühl. A career civil servant who had found favor with the Heimwehr because of his enthusiasm for corporatism, Neustädter-Stürmer was in and out of the cabinet frequently during the 1930s, including a stint after the dissolution of the Heimwehr (from 6 Nov. 1936 to 20 March 1937 as minister for security and preparation for the new corporative order). During the last months of his life he tried unsuccessfully to mend fences with the Nazis. He, like Fey, felt himself so threatened by the Nazi occupation that he committed suicide.

PABST, Major [Capt.] Waldemar: b. 24 Dec. 1880 in Berlin; d. 20 May 1970 in Düsseldorf. After his expulsion from Austria in June 1930 Pabst worked for a number of years with the German steel concern of Rheinmetall as a political adviser, Austrian specialist, and lobbyist; much of the time in the 1930s he also served as a liaison between Hitler and the Heimwehr (see text). Fearing the consequences of Hitler's conduct of the war he emigrated to Switzerland, where he remained resident until 1955, when, still connected with the steel industry, he returned to Düsseldorf. In 1962 the German government formally cleared him of legal responsibility for the deaths of Rosa Luxemburg and Karl Liebknecht in January 1919.

PFRIMER, Dr. Walter: b. 22 Dec. 1881 in Marburg/Drava; d. 1968 in Judenburg. Forced out of active paramilitary activity by the dissolution of his pro-Nazi Heimwehr in June 1933, Pfrimer practiced law in Judenburg. After *Anschluss* he became a member of the German Reichstag. In 1945 he destroyed all his papers shortly before being arrested and detained for nearly two years by the British. After his release he lived in semiretirement, but continued active in the law whenever his failing health permitted.

RAAB, Diplom Ingenieur Julius: b. 29 Nov. 1891 in St. Pölten; d. 5 Jan. 1964 in Vienna. Never a committed Heimwehr man in any fascist sense, Raab withdrew from Heimwehr activities as Starhemberg came to the fore. He served prominently in the corporative Bundeswirtsschaftsrat from 1934 to 1938 and briefly as minister of commerce and transportation in the weeks before *Anschluss*. During the war he worked with a road construction firm and read extensively, especially in history. After the war he was a cofounder of the People's Party, the revived form of the CSP. He served as federal chancellor from 1953 to 1961.

RAUTER, Hans: b. 4 Feb. 1895 in Klagenfurt; d. 1949 in the Netherlands. Pfrimer's deputy until the abortive putsch in Sept. 1931, Rauter was one of several Styrian Heimwehr leaders to work his way into the Nazi camp. He became an SS officer and the general commissar for security in the occupied Netherlands, where he was hanged as a war criminal by the victorious Allies.

STARHEMBERG, Prince Ernst Rüdiger: b. 10 May 1899 in Eferding, U.A.; d. 15 March 1956 in Schruns, Vbg. After his political eclipse Starhemberg won the annulment of his first marriage and then married Nora Gregor, an actress at the Burgtheater who bore him his son and heir, Heinrich. There is evidence that during the final Heimwehr crisis in the fall of 1936 Starhemberg harbored hopes that he could still make a deal with the Nazis, hopes that died hard and that were revived when Franz Hueber visited him in St. Moritz early in March 1938. But events moved too fast, and in view of Hitler's treatment of those who had taken up the cudgels against him Starhemberg was very fortunate to be outside the country when it was occupied by the Germans. While Starhemberg never came to terms with democracy, it should be noted that early in the war, after his efforts to found an Austrian Legion foundered over partisan disputes, he served for several months as a flyer with De Gaulle's Free French forces, based in Brazzaville. He left the service in Dec. 1941 because of a combination of malaria and irritation over being kept out of combat, and in June 1942 settled in Argentina, where he remained until he moved to Chile in 1950. During the early 1950s his lawyers successfully contested the confiscation of his estates in Austria. Late in 1954 Starhemberg went to Spain, and early in 1955 he returned to Austria, at first visiting his sister in Carinthia. But his health was failing, and he died at a health resort in Vorarlberg from an attack brought on by his outraged reaction to the efforts of a communist journalist to take his picture.

STEIDLE, Dr. Richard: b. 1881 near Meran, South Tyrol; d. 30 Aug. 1940 at Buchenwald. Finishing his service to Austria as consul general in Trieste, Steidle was arrested soon after the *Anschluss*. He was killed by guards, allegedly while trying to escape; indeed, his death may have been a form of suicide.

WENNINGER, Heinrich (Heinz): b. 7 July 1887 in Wels, U.A.; d. 5 Oct. 1950 in Linz. Starhemberg's last faithful coleader, Wenninger was sent to Dachau in March 1938. He was released after about a year but, forbidden to return to Austria, he worked in Munich throughout the war. After the war he returned to his home and became connected with the manufacture of construction materials.

Notes

INTRODUCTION

1. Ernst Nolte, *Three Faces of Fascism: Action Française, Italian Fascism, National Socialism*, trans. by Leila Vennewitz (New York: Holt, Rinehart and Winston, 1965), pp. 3–16. The original title is *Der Faschismus in seiner Epoche* (Munich: R. Piper & Co., 1963).

2. The following works are among the most notable: Gilbert Allardyce (ed.), *The Place of Fascism in European History* (Englewood Cliffs, N.J.: Prentice-Hall, 1971); F. L. Carsten, *The Rise of Fascism* (Berkeley: Univ. of California Press, 1967); Nathanael Greene (ed.), *Fascism: An Anthology* (New York: Crowell, 1968); H. R. Kedward, *Fascism in Western Europe 1900–45* (Glasgow: Blackie, 1969); Walter Laqueur and George L. Mosse (eds.), *International Fascism 1920–1945* (New York: Harper & Row, 1966); John Weiss, *The Fascist Tradition: Radical Right-Wing Extremism in Modern Europe* (New York: Harper & Row, 1967); Eugen Weber, *Varieties of Fascism* (Princeton, N.J.: Van Nostrand, 1964); S. J. Woolf (ed.), *European Fascism* (New York: Vintage, 1969 [c. 1968]); S. J. Woolf (ed.), *The Nature of Fascism* (New York: Vintage, 1969 [c. 1968]); Otto-Ernst Schüddekopf, *Fascism* ("Revolutions of Our Times Series"; New York: Praeger, 1973). See also Seymour Martin Lipset, *Political Man: the Social Bases for Politics* (Garden City, N.Y.: Doubleday, 1960), pp. 131–176 (Chap. 5: "Fascism—Left, Right, and Center").

3. See especially Charles A. Gulick, *Austria from Hapsburg to Hitler* (2 vols.; Berkeley: Univ. of California Press, 1948), which is strongly prosocialist.

4. A partial exception is the recent book by F. L. Carsten, *Fascist Movements in Austria: From Schönerer to Hitler* (London and Beverly Hills: Sage Publications, 1977), which appeared while this work was in press; it combines treatment of the Heimwehr with that of the Nazis and other right-wing groups. For examples of good summary or peripheral treatments, see Ludwig Jedlicka, "The Austrian Heimwehr," in Laqueur and Mosse (eds.), *International Fascism*, pp. 127–144; Fritz Fellner, "The Background of Austrian Fascism," in Peter F. Sugar (ed.), *Native Fascism in the Successor States, 1918–1945* (Santa Barbara, Calif.: ABC-Clio, 1971), pp. 15–23; K. R. Stadler, "Austria," in Woolf (ed.), *European Fascism*, pp. 88–110; Andrew Whiteside, "Austria," in Hans Rogger and Eugen Weber (eds.), *The Euro-*

pean Right: A Historical Profile (Berkeley: Univ. of California Press, 1966), pp. 308–363.

5. See his "Italien, Ungarn und die österreichische Heimwehrbewegung 1928–1931," *Oesterreich in Geschichte und Literatur*, 9/1 (Jan. 1965): 1–13; "Die 'Weisse Allianz': Bayrisch-österreichisch-ungarische Projekte gegen die Regierung Renner im Jahre 1920," *Oesterreichische Osthefte*, 7/5 (Sept. 1965): 355–358; and *Abenddämmerung einer Demokratie: Mussolini, Gömbös und die Heimwehr* (Vienna: Europa Verlag, 1966).

6. The names of the provincial organizations varied. The terms *Heimatdienst* (Home Service), *Selbstschutzverband* (Self-Defense League), *Heimwehr* or *Heimatwehr* (Home Guard) and *Heimatschutzverband* (Home Defense League) were all used. When referring to specific provincial organizations, I will generally use the appropriate German names, as nearly according to contemporary usage as possible. When referring to the movement in general or to Heimwehr confederations, I will use the name *Heimwehr* (even in instances where they had other titles, such as the Selbstschutzverbände); however, when speaking of several provincial units as autonomous groups I will use the plural term *Heimwehren*. Unfortunately, I have found it impossible to be consistent in every case. The Social Democratic paramilitary organization will be referred to as the Schutzbund.

7. A.F.K. Organski, "Fascism and Modernization," in S. J. Woolf (ed.), *The Nature of Fascism*, pp. 28–31; and Weiss, the *Fascist Tradition*, pp. 4–7. See also Miklós Lackó, "Ostmitteleuropäische Faschismus," *Vierteljahrshefte für Zeitgeschichte*, 21/1 (Jan. 1973): 39–51.

8. See Grete Klingenstein, "Bemerkungen zum Problem des Faschismus in Oesterreich," *Oesterreich in Geschichte und Literatur*, 14/1 (Jan. 1970): 1–13.

9. Arno J. Mayer, *Dynamics of Counterrevolution in Europe, 1870–1956* (New York: Harper & Row, 1971).

10. Wolfgang Sauer, "National Socialism: Totalitarianism or Fascism?" *American Historical Review*, 73/2 (Dec. 1967): 411.

CHAPTER 1

1. Adam Wandruszka, "Oesterreichs politische Struktur. Die Entwicklung der Parteien und politischen Bewegungen," in Heinrich Benedikt (ed.), *Geschichte der Republik Oesterreich* (Munich: R. Oldenbourg, 1954), pp. 289–485.

2. Klemens von Klemperer, *Ignaz Seipel: Christian Statesman in a Time of Crisis* (Princeton, N.J.: Princeton University Press, 1972), pp. 274–292.

3. See Hellmut Andics, *Der Staat den Keiner Wollte: Oesterreich 1918–1938* (Vienna: Herder, 1962).

4. See Ludwig Jedlicka, *Ein Heer im Schatten der Parteien: Die militärpolitische Lage Oesterreichs, 1918–1938* (Graz, Cologne: Hermann Böhlaus Nachf., 1955).

CHAPTER 2

1. Karl Gutkas, *Geschichte des Landes Niederösterreich* (3 vols.; [Vienna] Kulturreferat des Amtes der niederösterr. Landesregierung, 1957–1962), III: 175–176; and Otto Bauer, *Die österreichische Revolution* (Vienna: Volksbuchhandlung, 1923), p. 97.

2. F. O. Lindley [British High Commissioner in Austria] to Lord Curzon (confidential), Vienna, 11 Jan. 1921, enclosing a report by Col. de Ligny [French member of the Inter-Allied Military Commission] on the various armed formations in Austria, Public Record Office (London), Foreign Office, Series 404/3, pp. 10–16. The 404 series of the foreign office documents are "confidential prints" of selected diplomatic correspondence concerning central Europe. Hereafter citations from British diplomatic papers will be PRO (London), F.O.; and those from the unprinted 371 series will include archive reference no./document no.

3. See incensed account of soldiers' homecoming in Emil Fey, *Schwertbrüder des Deutschen Ordens* (Vienna: Julius Lichtner, 1937), pp. 218–220.

4. Such an incident is described by Ernst Rüdiger Starhemberg, *Between Hitler and Mussolini* (New York: Harper Brothers, 1942), pp. 5–6; see also his *Memoiren* (Vienna: Amalthea, 1971), p. 40.

5. Erwin Steinböck, *Die Volkswehr in Kärnten unter Berücksichtigung des Einsatzes der Freiwilligenverbände* (Vienna, Graz: Stiasny, 1963), pp. 8–9, 52.

6. Wandruszka, "Oesterreichs pol. Struktur," pp. 360–361.

7. Rudolf Kanzler, *Bayerns Kampf gegen den Bolschewismus: Geschichte der bayrischen Einwohnerwehren* (Munich: Parcus, 1931), p. 205. His authorization is printed in Hans Beyer, *Von der Novemberrevolution zur Räterepublik in München* ([East] Berlin: Ritten & Loenig, 1957), p. 166.

8. Kerekes, "Italien . . . und . . . Heimwehrbewegung," pp. 2–3, and "'Weisse Allianz'," pp. 355–358.

9. *Heimatschutz in Oesterreich*, published by propaganda office (Vienna, 1934), p. 239 [hereafter cited as *HS in Oesterr.*]; Kanzler, *Bayerns Kampf*, pp. 86–92, 246; report by Col. de Ligny, in Lindley to Curzon (confidential), Vienna, 11 Jan. 1921, PRO (London), F.O. 404/3, p. 13.

10. Interview with Dr. Walter Pfrimer, Judenburg, Styria, 23 June 1963; Jakob Ahrer, *Erlebte Zeitgeschichte* (Vienna, Leipzig: Winkler, 1930), pp. 70–72; Anton Rintelen, *Erinnerungen an Oesterreichs Weg. Versailles-Berchtesgaden-Grossdeutschland* (2nd ed.; Munich: R. Bruckman, 1941), pp. 59–60, 126ff.; Kanzler, *Bayerns Kampf*, pp. 94–96; [Sepp Kogelnik (ed.)] *Oesterreichisches Heimatschutz-Jahrbuch 1933* (Graz: Landesleitung des Heimatschutzverbandes Steiermark, 1934), pp. 55–56 [hereafter cited as *Oesterr. HS Jahrbuch*]; Franz Winkler, *Die Diktatur in Oesterreich* (Zurich: Orell Füssli, 1935), p. 24; German consul [Müller] to foreign ministry, Graz, 4 Feb. 1921, Politisches Archiv des Deutschen Auswärtigen Amtes (Bonn), Abteilung II, Politik 2 Nummer 3 (*Heimwehrorganisation*

in Oesterreich), vol. 1 (1920–1926). Hereafter references to material from this archive are cited PADAA (Bonn), II, with *foreign ministry* shortened to F.M. and the words *Abteilung, Politik,* and *Nummer* omitted (thus, II: 2/3); titles and dates of the volumes are given only the first time each is cited.

11. *Hiltl Gedenkblatt* (Vienna, 1930), pp. 9, 74–80; *HS in Oesterr.*, p. 7; Ingeborg Messerer, "Die Frontkämpfervereinigung Deutsch-Oesterreichs: Ein Beitrag zur Geschichte der Wehrverbände in der Republik Oesterreich" (Ph.D. diss., Univ. of Vienna, 1963), pp. 4–7, 49; Ludwig Jedlicka, "Austrian HW," p. 131; report by Col. de Ligny, in Lindley to Curzon (confidential), Vienna, 11 Jan. 1921, PRO (London), F.O. 404/3, pp. 15–16.

12. Kanzler, *Bayerns Kampf*, pp. 101–102; Kerekes, "Italien . . . und . . . Heimwehrbewegung," p. 3; German legation to F.M., Vienna, 16 Sept. 1920, PADAA (Bonn), II: 2/3, vol. 1. The legation's report was based on information provided by an "apparently well informed" Austrian officer and on Col. de Ligny's report on armed formations in Austria.

13. Kanzler, *Bayerns Kampf*, p. 104; notes on comments by Dr. Escherich to representatives of the Austrian self-defense leagues, Munich, 25 July 1920, PADAA (Bonn), II: 2/3, vol. 1; *Neue Freie Presse* [*NFP*], 1 Aug. 1920.

14. Kerekes, "Italien . . . und . . . Heimwehrbewegung," p. 2, and "'Weisse Allianz'," pp. 360–362.

15. A notable example occurred at the time of the Kapp putsch in Germany, when a rightist delegation vainly attempted to enlist the aid of the German minister in Austria for a coup d'état. See from the F.O. 371 series in PRO (London) the following dispatches: Lindley to Curzon, Vienna, 19 March 1920, 3536/187077; Lindley to Curzon (confidential), Vienna, 6 June 1920, enclosing reports by Col. F. W. Gossett, chief of the British delegation to the Inter-Allied Military Control Commission, Vienna, 29 May 1920, and by Lt. Col. T. M. Cunninghame, British military attaché, Vienna, 4 June 1920, 3538/C20303; and Lindley to Curzon (confidential), Vienna, 10 July 1920, 4648/C1429.

16. A copy of Steidle's report is in German consulate to F.M., Innsbruck, 21 Sept. 1920, PADAA (Bonn), II: 2/3, vol. 1.

17. Rosenberg to F.M. (telegram), Vienna, 11 Nov. 1920, PADAA (Bonn), II: 2/3, vol. 1; Lindley to Curzon, Vienna, 29 Nov. 1920, with copy of report by Gossett, Vienna, Nov. 19, PRO (London), F.O. 371: 4641/C12430; Lindley to F.O. (telegram), Vienna, 30 Nov. 1920, ibid., 4641/C12686; Lindley to Curzon, Vienna, 2 Dec. 1920, with copy of report by Gossett, Vienna, Nov. 30, ibid., 4641/C13025; Inter-Allied Control Commission in Austria, Liquidation Office, to the federal chancellor and minister for foreign affairs (trans. into German), Vienna, 29 June 1921, recounting orders and inquiries dating from 15 Dec. 1920, Allgemeines Verwaltungsarchiv des österreichischen Staatsarchivs (Vienna) [hereafter cited as AVA (Vienna)], Bundesministerium für Inneres und Unterricht, 164760/1921.

18. Ibid. (The note also recounted the government's earlier replies.)

19. Decree of section 7 of the federal ministry of interior to all provincial governments, Vienna, 8 July 1921, AVA (Vienna), Bundesministerium für Inneres und Unterricht, 164760/1921, which final version took a much softer line towards the paramilitary groups than the ministry's preliminary draft; "urgent" memorandum within federal ministry of interior, undated [ca. mid-June 1922], 35792/1922, in folder 63880/1922, 21 Nov. 1922, AVA (Vienna), Bundesministerium für Inneres und Unterricht.

20. For the attitude of provincial officials towards prosecuting men accused of stealing weapons, see, among others, superior state's attorney's office in Innsbruck [Pansky] to federal ministry of justice, 6 June 1921 [copy], and federal ministry of justice to federal ministry of interior, Vienna, 5 July 1921, both in AVA (Vienna), Bundesministerium für Inneres und Unterricht, 15930/21 and 167983/21. For an example of complaints about the socialists' display of arms, see Gov. Josef Schraffl (signed by his deputy, Schumacher) to the federal ministry of interior, Innsbruck, 2 Dec. 1920, AVA (Vienna), Bundesministerium für Inneres und Unterricht, 2708/21.

21. German legation [Von Schoen] to F.M., Vienna, 23 Jan. 1921, PADAA (Bonn), II: 2/3, vol. 1.

22. Theo Russell to Curzon (confidential), Bern, 4 Mar. 1921, with copy of memorandum by Lt. Col. C.C.F. Oppenheim, PRO (London), F.O. 371: 5770/C4855. It should be noted in passing that a year earlier Seipel had made a similar request of the Hungarian minister in Vienna.

23. Katalin Gulya, "Die Westungarische Frage nach dem Ersten Weltkrieg. Das Burgenland und die Politik der ungarischen Regierungen 1918–1921," *Oesterreichische Osthefte*, 8/2 (March 1966): 97 & 100, n. 26; Kerekes, "Italien . . . und . . . Heimwehrbewegung," p. 3. See also Gulick, *Austria*, 1:128–129.

24. On 21 Feb. 1922, the new German consul in Innsbruck, Kuenzer, wrote the foreign ministry that according to a "reliable source" the Heimatwehr's Bavarian subsidy had been cut off (PADAA [Bonn], II: 2/3, vol. 1). But there is some question about the point of origin of such subsidies. A year earlier Steidle told the German consul that he received no financial aid from Bavaria (Külmer to F.M., Innsbruck, 26 Jan. 1921, PADAA [Bonn], II: 2/3, vol. 1); and Ludgar Rape asserts in his informative dissertation that Kanzler provided direct subsidies for organizational and propaganda purposes only to groups in Salzburg and Styria, that other provinces got help only in the form of salaries of the Orka staff; see Rape, "Die österreichische Heimwehr und ihre Beziehungen zur bayrischen Rechten zwischen 1920 und 1923" (Ph.D. diss., University of Vienna, 1968), pp. 247–249.

25. Kanzler, *Bayerns Kampf*, pp. 105–106, 248; also several German diplomatic reports in PADAA (Bonn), II: 2/3, vol. 1.

26. Much of the next five paragraphs is based on Ludgar Rape's dissertation (cited in n. 24), especially pp. iii–iv, 259, 404–556. His work deals largely with the extremely complicated struggle among the various paramili-

tary organizations in Bavaria for control of the Austrian Heimwehren, and is based primarily on documents from the Orka records for 1920–1921, housed in the PADAA (Bonn); from the record of the Bund Bayern und das Reich in the Kriegsarchiv in Munich; and in the Col. Max Bauer Nachlass in the Deutsches Bundesarchiv in Koblenz.

27. For Steidle's proposed budget, see Steidle to Seipel, Innsbruck, 10 July 1922, Archiv der Bundes-Polizeidirektion, Vienna [hereafter cited as ABP (Vienna)], Schober Archiv, Fasc. HW. Steidle requested only 20 million crowns for Vienna and Lower Austria. However, Rape reports that 30 million crowns were allotted to these two provinces; his source is a report by Capt. von Oberwurzer, Vienna, 15 July 1922, in the Bauer Nachlass ("Oesterr. HW," p. 448).

28. German consulate (Gebsattel) to F.M., Innsbruck, 20 Oct. 1921, PADAA (Bonn), II: 2/3, vol. 1.

29. "Lebenserinnerungen des Fürsten Ernst Rüdiger Starhemberg von ihm selbst verfasst in Winter 1938–39 in Saint Gervais in Frankreich" (typescript in the Archiv des österreichischen Instituts für Zeitgeschichte [OeIZ] [Vienna]), pp. 34–35. See also Starhemberg, Memoiren, p. 42.

30. There is some confusion about Pabst's rank. In Austria he was always known as "Herr Major," and Harold J. Gordon, Jr., reports that in July 1919 Pabst was eased out of the army "with a terminal promotion to . . . major" (The Reichswehr and the German Republic, 1919–1926 [Princeton, N.J.: Princeton University Press, 1957], pp. 97–98). However, Gustav Noske contended that he did not promote Pabst before retiring him from active duty (Von Kiel bis Kapp. Zur Geschichte der deutschen Revolution [Berlin: Verlag für Politik und Wirtschaft, 1920], p. 200). When in 1929 the German government cut off Pabst's pension on the ground that he was no longer a citizen—a ruling that Pabst successfully contested—he was still officially referred to as a captain. See relevant documents from late 1929 and early 1930 in PADAA (Bonn), II: 2/3, vol. 3 (20 Sept. 1929–1 Dec. 1931).

31. Interview with Waldemar Pabst at Düsseldorf, 7 Dec. 1963; interview with Peter Revertera at Helfenberg, U.A., 22 and 23 July 1963; Wilhelm Hoegner, Die Verratene Republik. Geschichte der deutschen Gegenrevolution (Munich: Isar, 1958), p. 105; Hans W. Gatzke, Stresemann and the Rearmament of Germany (Baltimore: Johns Hopkins Univ. Press, 1954), pp. 51–52; Winkler, Diktatur, p. 25; "Waldemar Pabst," Der Spiegel, 16/16 (18 April 1962): 39; Starhemberg, Between Hitler and Mussolini, pp. 7–12, and Memoiren, pp. 41–47; Austria, Stenographische Protokolle über die Sitzungen des Nationalrates, 3. Gesetzgebungsperiode, vol. 3 (26 Nov. 1929): 2989 [hereafter cited as NR Protokolle]; NFP, 15 June 1930, A.M., p. 8; Die Stunde, 2 and 15 Oct. 1931, n.p.

32. Report of Major Kundt to the war ministry, Vienna, 15 Dec. 1922, PADAA (Bonn), IIb, Politik 13 (Militärpolitische Berichten des Majors Kundt, Wien), vol. 1 (May 1920–Dec. 1927).

33. See NR Protokolle, 1/4 (14 Nov. 1922): 4687–4688, 4705–4720; also

Gulick, *Austria*, 1:130–131. The HW side of the story was quite different: interview with Pfrimer; and Rintelen, *Erinnerungen*, pp. 135–136.

34. *Die Fascistengefahr* (Vienna: Volksbuchhandlung, 1923), pp. 22, 36; *Wer rüstet zum Bürgerkrieg?* (Vienna: Volksbuchhandlung, 1923), *passim.* See also Gulick, *Austria*, 2:787.

35. Julius Deutsch, *Antifaschismus! Proletarische Wehrhaftigkeit im Kampfe gegen den Faschismus* (Vienna: Volksbuchhandlung, 1926), *passim;* Gulick, *Austria*, 1:132–133; interview with Dr. Julius Deutsch at Bad Hall, U.A., 23 July 1963; report by Col. de Ligny, included in Lindley to Curzon (confidential), Vienna, 11 Jan. 1921, PRO (London), F.O. 404/3, pp. 11–16.

36. See Gulick, *Austria*, 1:683–686; Friedrich Thalmann, "Die Wirtschaft in Oesterreich," in H. Benedikt (ed.), *Geschichte*, pp. 490–496; and K. W. Rothschild, *Austria's Economic Development between the Two Wars* (London: Frederick Muller, 1947), pp. 36–49.

37. Walter Goldinger, "Der geschichtliche Ablauf der Ereignisse in Oesterreich von 1918 bis 1945," in H. Benedikt (ed.), *Geschichte*, p. 137.

38. *Tiroler Heimatwehr-Blätter*, 11 Dec. 1924, p. 3; interview with Pabst. There was a slight stir when early in 1922 the socialists published a secret letter in which Steidle urged mayors throughout the Tyrol to use almost any means to prevent the socialists from organizing the postal workers. See no. 313, *Anhang zu den stenographischen Protokollen des Nationalrates*, 1/1 (20 March 1922): 625–626; also report from the superior state's attorney's office to federal ministry of justice, Innsbruck, 29 April 1922, AVA (Vienna), Bundesministerium für Justiz, 55306/22 in folder 51200/1923. This last document was placed before Seipel.

39. G-2 report, Vienna, 5 June 1925, U.S. National Archives (Washington), Records of the War Department, general and special staff, military intelligence division, record group no. 165 (military attaché reports): doc. no. 2657–FF–122/2. Hereafter citations from this collection will be USNA (Washington), War Dept., MID, RG–165.

40. A. H. Washburn, the U.S. minister to Austria from 1922 to 1930, was told "in strictest secrecy" about Rintelen's maneuvers to gain Mussolini's support by Camillo Castiglioni, an Italian war profiteer and entrepreneur living in Vienna, who claimed to be a middleman. Washburn found "much in this story to credit." See Washburn to secretary of state (confidential), Vienna, 31 Aug. 1927, USNA (Washington), Records of the Department of State, no. 863.00/176 (hereafter citations from this decimal file [Political Affairs, Austria] will be USNA [Washington], State Dept.). For other evidence of Rintelen's machinations in the first part of 1927 see D. Nemes, " 'Die österreichische Aktion' der Bethlen-Regierung," *Acta Historica* [Academiae Scientarum Hungaricae], 11/1–4 (1965): 191–192.

41. Kanzler, *Bayerns Kampf*, pp. 100–101; *HS in Oesterr.*, pp. 69–74; Erwin Rieger, *Fürstin Fanny Starhemberg* (Vienna: Im Montsalvat [1935]), pp. 180–181; interview with Revertera. See also Jedlicka, "Austrian HW," p. 130.

42. G–2 report, Vienna, 5 June 1925, USNA (Washington), War Dept., MID, RG–165: 2657–FF–122/1 and 2.

43. Ibid. About the agreement concerning the Burgenland see Heinrich Schneidmadl, "Der Weg zur Katastrophe. Ein Beitrag zur Geschichte des 12. Februar 1934" (Vienna, 1959) (typescript in the Stadtarchiv of St. Pölten), p. 1; and also Goldinger, "Der gesch. Ablauf," p. 152.

44. Guido Zernatto, Die Wahrheit über Oesterreich (New York, Toronto: Longmans, Green, 1938), pp. 71–73.

45. [Baron Artur Karg-Bebenburg] Die Gefahr im Staate (Vienna: Selbst-schutzverbandes NOe, 1926), pp. 1–16.

46. Report of Major W. W. Hicks, Vienna, 12 June 1928, USNA (Washington), War Dept., MID, RG–165: 2540–150/1. Hicks thought the total membership in mid-1928 to be about 150,000.

47. My own reasoned estimate. However, some contemptuous contemporaries guessed the Heimwehr's following to be much lower, perhaps only 18,000 early in 1927. See "Die österreichische Putschisten: erste wahrheits-gemässe Geschichte der Heimwehrbewegung" (manuscript no. 2252 in the Archive of the Austrian Resistance [Vienna]), p. 29, cited in Reinhart D. Kondert, "The Rise and Early History of the Austrian Heimwehr" (Ph.D. diss., Rice Univ., 1972), p. 51.

48. Lord Chilston to Sir Austin Chamberlain, Vienna, 14 and 20 July 1926, PRO (London): F.O. 371: 11212/C8052 and C8347; and Saller to Zech (private), Innsbruck, 12 Aug. 1926, PADAA (Bonn), II: 2/3, vol. 1.

49. See Gulick, Austria, 2: 1049, 1389–1390; and Julius Deutsch, Ein Weiter Weg. Lebenserinnerungen (Vienna: Amalthea, 1960), pp. 163–164, who regretted the use of such provocative phrases.

50. Saller to F.M., Innsbruck, 27 Oct. and 19 Nov. 1926, PADAA (Bonn), II: 2/3, vol. 1; Die alpenländische Heimatwehr [Alp. HtW], (Innsbruck), Nov. 1926, p. 1; Oesterr. HS Jahrbuch, p. 61.

51. Oesterr. HS Jahrbuch, p. 35.

52. In a series of letters to Count Zech at the Austrian desk in the second department of the German foreign ministry, Consul Saller gave a running account of affairs within the Heimwehr based on information he had received through "reliable" informants in Innsbruck. See Saller to Zech (very confidential), 8, 13, 19, 31 Jan. and 3 and 4 Feb. 1927, PADAA (Bonn), II: 5 Oe A (Geheime Akten betreffend Heimwehr Organisationen in Oester-reich), Jan. 1927–Feb. 1933. The information in the four paragraphs following comes chiefly from this correspondence. Other sources will be distinguished when necessary.

53. In addition to the letters cited above, see from the same file (PADAA [Bonn], II: Pol. 5 Oe A) Haniel to F.M. (confidential), Munich, 26 Jan. and 3 Feb. 1927; Wallraf to F.M. (confidential), Munich, Jan. 28; foreign ministry memoranda by Zech, Berlin, Jan. 22 and Feb. 3; and Zech to Saller (private), Berlin, Jan. 19 and Jan. 28. See also Lerchenfeld to F.M., Vienna, Feb. 22, PADAA (Bonn), II: 2/3, vol. 2 (1 Jan. 1927–19 Sept. 1929).

54. Lerchenfeld to F.M., Vienna, 22 Feb. 1927, PADAA (Bonn), II: 2/3, vol. 2.

55. Zech to Saller, Berlin, 26 Feb. 1927, PADAA (Bonn), II: 2/3, vol. 2.

56. Lerchenfeld to F.M., Vienna, 22 Feb. 1927, PADAA (Bonn), II: 2/3, vol. 2.

57. *Heimatschutz-Zeitung* [*HS-Ztg*], 14 Apr. 1927, p. 1, and April 21, pp. 2–3.

58. Saller to F.M., Innsbruck, 27 Apr. 1927, PADAA (Bonn), II: 2/3, vol. 2. However, Saller also observed that this increased activity coincided with Pabst's return from a long vacation in northern Italy.

59. *HS-Ztg*, 26 May 1927, p. 2; June 9, p. 2; and June 16, p. 1.

60. Steidle's speech as published in ibid., 14 July 1927, pp. 1–6.

61. Saller to F.M., Innsbruck, 23 July 1927, PADAA (Bonn), II: 2/3, vol. 2. See also *NR Protokolle*, 3/1 (27 July 1927): 223–229, 236–238.

62. Interview with Pfrimer; Rintelen, *Erinnerungen*, pp. 137–138; *Reichspost* [*RP*] (Vienna), 21 July 1927, p. 3; *NR Protokolle*, 3/1 (27 July 1927): 213–223; *Arbeiter-Zeitung* [*A-Z*] (Vienna), 6 Sept. 1928, p. 2 (testimony of two socialists present at the meetings with Pfrimer in Graz on 17 July 1927); *NFP*, 21 June 1929, A.M., p. 6 (account by Franz Winkler); 19 Nov. 1929, A.M., p. 4; *HS in Oesterr.*, pp. 122–123; and Gulick, *Austria*, 1:749.

63. See n. 40 above. Castiglione told the American minister that Rintelen had taunted him by insisting that if his "proposal of two years ago had been adopted the 15th of July would never have happened."

64. Interview with Pfrimer. For a similar point of view from a more sophisticated observer, see Eduard Ludwig, *Oesterreichs Sendung im Donauraum: Die letzten Dezennien österreichischer Innen- und Aussenpolitik* (Vienna: Oesterr. Staatsdruckerei, 1954), p. 61.

65. Interview with Revertera; *RP*, 23 July 1927, p. 2, and July 31, p. 9; *HS-Ztg*, July 21, p. 4; *HS in Oesterr.*, p. 75; and Franz Langoth, *Kampf um Oesterreich. Erinnerungen eines Politikers* (Wels, U.A.: "Welsermühl," 1951), pp. 31–33.

66. Pertinax [Otto Leichter], *Oesterreich 1934* (Zurich: Europa, 1935), pp. 153–154; *A-Z*, 16 Oct. 1927, pp. 5–6; Karl Heinz, "Nach dem 15. Juli," *Der Kampf* (Sozialdemokratische Monatsschrift), 20 (Sept. 1927): 404; and Deutsch, *Weiter Weg*, p. 172.

67. Saller to F.M., Innsbruck, 23 July 1927, PADAA (Bonn), II: 2/3, vol. 2; *NFP*, July 23, A.M., p. 5; *HS-Ztg*, July 28, p. 1. Seipel's diary records three visits by Steidle in mid-1927: June 28, July 26, Aug. 2; see Von Klemperer, *Ignaz Seipel*, p. 266, n. 143.

CHAPTER 3

1. *Der österreichische Volkswirt* [*Oesterr. VW*], 12 Nov. 1927, p. 170.

2. Lerchenfeld to F.M., Vienna, 3 Jan. 1928, PADAA (Bonn), II: 2/3, vol. 2.

3. Franz Klein, "Nach sechs Monaten," *Oesterr. VW*, 14 Jan. 1928, pp. 1253–54.

4. *NFP*, 17 Oct. 1927, P.M., p. 3; Kerekes, *Abenddämmerung*, p. 26, citing a report to the Hungarian government.

5. It should be noted, however, that Army Minister Vaugoin had so manipulated the system of representation that the Christian Socials in fact controlled the soldiers' councils (see Jedlicka, *Heer*, p. 76).

6. The socialists claimed that 21,857 persons left the Church in the second half of 1927 (compared with 7,227 in 1926); see *Jahrbuch der österreichischen Arbeiterbewegung, 1927* (Vienna: Volksbuchhandlung, 1928), p. 18.

7. Translation from Gulick, *Austria*, 1:765.

8. *A-Z*, 16 June 1929, pp. 1–2. See also Kondert, "The Rise and Early History of the HW," pp. 99–101.

9. Friedrich Funder, *Als Oesterreich den Sturm bestand* (Vienna, Munich: Herold, 1957), p. 22; August M. Knoll, *Von Seipel zu Dollfuss* (Vienna: Manz'sche, 1934), p. 10; Leopold Kunschak, *Oesterreich, 1918–1934* (Vienna: Typogr. Anstalt, 1934), p. 93; Lerchenfeld to F.M., Vienna, 25 Oct. 1927, PADAA (Bonn), II: 2/3, vol. 2. See also Kurt Schuschnigg, *Dreimal Oesterreich* (Vienna: Jakob Hegner, 1937), p. 147; Ludwig, *Oesterreichs Sendung*, p. 63; and Gulick, *Austria*, 2:777–779, 783–786.

10. *Oesterr. VW*, 12 Nov. 1927, p. 170, which also noted that Seipel had recently backed away somewhat from the HW in a parliamentary budget committee. Pertinax claimed to know that Seipel's diary entry for 30 Oct. 1927, showed that "at the moment" he was concerned about his line of policy regarding the HW (*Oesterreich 1934*, p. 58).

11. Fritz Hoenig [a HW *Kreisleiter* in U.A.] to Steidle [copy], Perg [Schober's home], 15 Feb. 1928, and Steidle to Schober, Innsbruck, 28 Feb. 1928, ABP (Vienna), Schober Archiv, Fasc. HW.

12. Steidle to Schober, Innsbruck, 30 May 1928, ibid., in which Steidle sought clarification of remarks concerning Schober's attitude made by Salzburg's Gov. Rehrl to the province's deputy HW leader Franz Hueber.

13. *NFP*, 5 Nov. 1927, A.M., p. 6; telegrams, Neurath to Schubert (very confidential), Rome, 20, 26, and 29 Oct. 1927, and telegrams, Lerchenfeld to F.M., Vienna, Nov. 4 and 7, PADAA (Bonn), Büro Staatssekretär, SO (*Akten betreffend deutsch-österreichische und deutsch-italienische Beziehungen*), vol. 7 (July 1927–Feb. 1928); Washburn to sec. of state, Vienna, Nov. 15, USNA (Washington), State Dept. 863.00/628.

14. Concerning Pfrimer see O. Haberleitner, "Rechtsanwalt Dr. Walter Pfrimer," *Freie Monatsschrift die Aula*, 11 (Dec. 1960): 41; also Pfrimer interview. Concerning the HW merger in Styria see *HS-Ztg*, 10 Nov. 1927, and Bruce F. Pauley, *Hahnenschwanz und Hakenkreuz: Steirischer Heimatschutz und österreichischer Nationalsozialismus 1918–1934* (Vienna: Europa, 1972), pp. 51–52.

15. *NFP*, 19 Sept. 1927, P.M., p. 3; *RP*, Sept. 19, p. 3; *A-Z*, Sept. 19, p. 2.

16. *NFP*, 28 Nov. 1927, P.M., p. 4; *A-Z*, Nov. 28, p. 2; Dec. 5, p. 2; *HS-Ztg*, Dec. 22, p. 8. For more on Wallisch see *NFP*, 23 July 1927, A.M., pp. 1–2; *NR Protokolle*, 3/1 (27 July 1927): 213–219.

17. Pabst interview.

18. Rothschild, *Austria's Economic Development*, pp. 81–82. A contemporary analyst contended that it was this discontented labor element instead of the conservative peasantry that gave the HW its "fascist" character (Aurel Kolnai, "Gegenrevolution," *Kölner Vierteljahrshefte für Soziologie*, 10 [1931–1932]: 189). See also Kondert, "The Rise and Early History," p. 89.

19. Lerchenfeld to F.M., Vienna, 14 June 1928, Deutsches Bundesarchiv [DBA] (Koblenz), R43I/110; Gulick, *Austria*, 2:780, 812.

20. *HS in Oesterr.*, pp. 299–306; *Oesterr. VW*, 14 Jan. 1928, p. 418; Kunschak, *Oesterreich*, pp. 94–95; Fritz Klenner, *Die österreichischen Gewerkschaften: Vergangenheit und Gegenwartsprobleme* (2 vols.; Vienna: Oesterr. Gewerkschaftsbund, 1951–1953), 2:986–988; C. A. Macartney, "The Armed Formations in Austria," *Journal of the Royal Institute of International Affairs*, 8 (Nov. 1929): 623.

21. The information in this and the next three paragraphs is drawn largely from Hicks's report, Vienna, 12 June 1928, USNA (Washington), War Dept., MID, RG–165: 2540–150/1.

22. Kerekes, *Abenddämmerung*, pp. 14–15 [my translation; compare with that in Jedlicka, "Austrian HW," p. 136].

23. Kerekes, *Abenddämmerung*, pp. 9–11. The information in the next four paragraphs comes also from this book, pp. 12–25, 36, 191–192.

24. Lerchenfeld to F.M., Vienna, 20 Sept. 1928, PADAA (Bonn), II: 2/3, vol. 2.

25. *HS-Ztg*, 5 July 1928, p. 1.

26. *NFP*, 6 Aug. 1928, P.M., p. 3; Aug. 11, A.M., p. 5; Sept. 12, A.M., p. 4; Sept. 13, A.M., p. 5; Sept. 14, A.M., p. 4; Sept. 15, P.M., p. 2; Sept. 18, A.M., p. 2.

27. Kerekes, *Abenddämmerung*, p. 25.

28. Gulick, *Austria*, 1:492–494, who follows the socialist lead; see Friedrich Austerlitz, "Seipels siebenter Oktober," *Der Kampf*, 21 (Nov. 1928): 533ff. See also Von Klemperer, *Ignaz Seipel*, pp. 279–281.

29. Kerekes, *Abenddämmerung*, p. 24; *NFP*, 26 Sept. 1928, P.M., p. 2; Oct. 2, A.M., p. 4; Oct. 3, A.M., pp. 2–3; Oct. 4, A.M., p. 1; *A-Z*, Oct. 2, p. 2; Gulick, *Austria*, 2:794–803; *NR Protokolle*, 3/2 (Oct. 3): 1601, 1610–28, 1632, 1641–42; *Oesterr. VW*, 13 Oct. 1928, p. 37.

30. Lerchenfeld to F.M., Vienna, 8 Oct. 1928, PADAA (Bonn), II: 2/3, vol. 2; *NFP*, Oct. 8, P.M., pp. 1–2; Sir Eric Phipps to Lord Cushendun (confidential), Vienna, Oct. 10, PRO (London), F.O. 371: 12851/C7733.

31. Ferdinand Maximilian Freiherr von Pantz, "Offener Brief an Herrn Bundesrat Dr. Richard Steidle," *Unsere Zukunft*, 25 Oct. 1928, pp. 5–6.

32. Pabst boasted thus in *NFP*, 1 Oct. 1930, P.M., p. 5.

33. Lerchenfeld to F.M., Vienna, 8 Oct. 1928, PADAA (Bonn), II: 2/3,

vol. 2; also Phipps to Cushendun (confidential), Vienna, Oct. 10, PRO (London), F.O. 371: 12851/C7733. See Gulick, *Austria,* 2:803, for a chronological catalog of conditions conceived by Seipel as prerequisites to disarmament, as compiled by *Oesterr. VW,* Nov. 3, p. 110; *HS-Ztg,* Oct. 20, pp. 1–2.

34. Ignaz Seipel, *Der Kampf um die österreichische Verfassung* (Vienna, Leipzig: Wilhelm Braumüller, 1930), pp. 130–135; *NFP,* 19 Dec. 1928, A.M., p. 4; Gulick, *Austria,* 2:805–808, also p. 811 for a long quotation from Seipel's speech; *Oesterr. VW,* 23 Feb. 1929, p. 529.

35. Its coordinating committee was composed of Hofrat Eduard Pichl, chairman; Bundesrat Franz Hemala; Gen. Heinrich Lustig-Prean; Gen. Edmund Kasamas; and Maj. Emil Fey. See *HS-Ztg,* 15 Dec. 1928, p. 7; Dec. 29, p. 9; 19 Jan. 1929, p. 7; Karl Wache, *Deutscher Geist in Oesterreich* (Dornbirn: C. Burton, 1933), pp. 242–243; and several memoranda and letters from Nov. and Dec. 1928 in the Nachlass Pichl (Kartons 69 and 70), housed in the AVA (Vienna).

CHAPTER 4

1. *A-Z,* 17 Feb. 1929, p. 1; *NFP,* Feb. 18, P.M., p. 1; Feb. 25, P.M., pp. 1–2; *RP,* Feb. 25, p. 1; *HS-Ztg,* March 2, pp. 1–2, for the quotation that follows in the text; Washburn to sec. of state, Vienna, Feb. 26, who thought the HW speeches "if anything, less moderate than the Socialists' appeals," USNA (Washington), State Dept., 863.00/650.

2. Kerekes, *Abenddämmerung,* pp. 32–35. The British chargé d'affaires noted that the Stahlhelm, seeking "to secure the collaboration" of the HW, had been repulsed first by Steidle and then reluctantly by Pfrimer at Seipel's behest; see J. H. Le Rougetel to A. Henderson (confidential), Vienna, July 4 and 18, 1929, PRO (London), F.O. 371: 13563/5095 and 5549.

3. *NFP,* 4 Feb. 1929, P.M., p. 4; *HS-Ztg,* Feb. 9, pp. 1–2; Josef Püchler, "Memoiren," typescript in OeIZ (Vienna); also "report(s) on the fracas [*Ausschreitungen*] in Gloggnitz on Feb. 3," AVA (Vienna), Bundeskanzleramt, Abt. 8, 98.108–8/29.

4. *HS-Ztg,* 30 March 1929, p. 2. See the recital of incidents in the inaugural issue of *Die Heimat,* 15 May 1929, p. 5.

5. Kerekes, *Abenddämmerung,* p. 34.

6. Wandruszka, "Oesterreichs pol. Struktur," pp. 362–363. But see Von Klemperer, *Ignaz Seipel,* p. 283, for suggestion that Seipel yielded to the HW in raising the demand for constitutional reform early in 1929, not viceversa.

7. For fuller treatments of Spann's thought and the political activities of the *Spannkreis,* see Alfred Diamant, *Austrian Catholics and the First Austrian Republic: Democracy, Capitalism, and the Social Order, 1918–1934* (Princeton, N.J.: Princeton University Press, 1960), pp. 229–240; Herman Lebovics, *Social Conservatism and the Middle Classes in Germany, 1914–1933* (Princeton, N.J.: Princeton University Press, 1969), pp. 109–138; Wil-

liam M. Johnston, *The Austrian Mind: An Intellectual and Social History, 1848–1938* (Berkeley: Univ. of California Press, 1972), pp. 311–315; John J. Haag, "Othmar Spann and the Politics of 'Totality': Corporatism in Theory and Practice," (Ph.D. diss., Rice Univ., 1969).

8. Von Klemperer, *Ignaz Seipel,* pp. 363–365; Hans Riehl, writing in *Festschrift Walter Heinrich* (Graz: Akademische Druck- und Verlagsanstalt, 1963), p. 4; *Die Heimwehr,* 21 June 1929, p. 1; Schweiger, "Geschichte der n–ö HW," pp. 216–217, who assumes that Pfrimer first established ties with the *Spannkreis* and implies that Riehl and Heinrich were active in the HW by 1928; Haag, "Othmar Spann," p. 110, n. 102; *HS in Oesterr.,* p. 181; Pabst interview; interview with Walter Heinrich, Vienna, 19 Nov. 1963.

9. Othmar Spann, *Die Irrungen des Marxismus* (Vienna, Graz, Klagenfurt: Steirischer Heimatschutzverband, 1929), *passim.*

10. Joseph Eberle, "Zum Rücktritt Seipels," *Schönere Zukunft,* April 14, pp. 583–584. See *NFP,* April 4, A.M., p. 3, for Seipel's announcement that he did not want his person to hinder the search for solutions to the pressing problems facing the nation. For various explanations of the resignation, see Gulick, *Austria,* 2:815–816; Ludwig, *Oesterreichs Sendung,* pp. 65–66; Funder, *Als Oesterreich,* p. 24; Von Klemperer, *Ignaz Seipel,* pp. 344–347.

11. E. Phipps to F.O. (telegram), Vienna, 12 April 1929, PRO (London), F.O. 371: 13563/C2611; Hoffmann to Bülow (private), Vienna, Aug. 23, PADAA (Bonn), II: 5 Oe A (*Geheim*); *NFP,* April 9, A.M., p. 1; *HS-Ztg,* April 13, p. 1.

12. *NFP,* 5 April 1929, A.M., p. 3; April 9, A.M. and P.M., pp. 1–5 and 2; April 15, P.M., p. 3; May 4, P.M., pp. 2–3.

13. *NR Protokolle,* 3/2 (7 May 1929): 2563–75; Spectator Noricus, "Bemerkungen zur Regierungskrise," *Volkswohl,* 20/6 (June 1929): 202; *Times* (London), May 6; Gulick, *Austria,* 2:822–825, for cabinet crisis, and 1:490–503 for discussion of bills.

14. Ernst von Streeruwitz, *Springflut über Oesterreich* (Vienna, Leipzig: Bernina, 1937), pp. 395–398; Kerekes, *Abenddämmerung,* p. 35; *NFP,* 16 May 1929, A.M., p. 5; Ludwig, *Oesterreichs Sendung,* p. 68; Pabst interview.

15. Kerekes, *Abenddämmerung,* pp. 38–39; also Le Rougetel to Henderson (confidential), Vienna, 8 Aug. 1929, PRO (London), F.O. 371: 13563/C6228.

16. Le Rougetel to Henderson (confidential), Vienna, 4 July 1929, PRO (London), F.O. 371: 13563/C5095; [Consul] Haas to F.M., Klagenfurt, 18 June 1929, commenting at length on the basic cleavages between the Styrian and Tyrolean centers of the HW, PADAA (Bonn), II: 2/3, vol. 2; also Streeruwitz, *Springflut,* p. 408.

17. *NFP,* 11 May 1929, P.M., p. 2; May 13, P.M., p. 1; May 14, A.M., p. 5; May 15, A.M., p. 4; several communications between the Austrian ministry of interior and both Stumpf and Rintelen, Vienna, May 10, Innsbruck, May 13, Graz, 28 May 1929, in AVA (Vienna), Bundeskanzleramt [BKA], Abteilungen 8 and 9, 122.337–8/1929.

18. For criticism of the Church's role, see Karl Heinrich, "Heimwehr und Kirche," *Neuland* [Blätter jungkatholischer Erneuerungsbewegung], 6 (June 1929): 135–137. In Jan. 1930 the episcopacy revised the regulations for flag dedications to stipulate that the Church could not bless the flags of political associations because of its suprapolitical position. See August M. Knoll (ed.), *Kardinal Fr. G. Piffl und der österreichische Episkopat zu sozialen und kulturellen Fragen, 1913–1932: Quellensammlung* (Vienna, Leipzig: Reinhold, 1932), p. 166. The injunction was applied to certain radically nationalistic units of the HW, but did not affect it as a whole.

19. *NFP*, 27 May 1929, P.M., p. 4; *RP*, May 28, p. 1, which did criticize this "lack of discipline"; also Gulick, *Austria*, 2:826–828.

20. Seipel, *Kampf*, pp. 177–188; Gulick, *Austria*, 2:830–834, for extensive quotation and comment; Haas to F.M., Klagenfurt, 18 June 1929, PADAA (Bonn), II: 2/3, vol. 2.

21. *NFP*, 19 July 1929, A.M., p. 8; *HS-Ztg*, Aug. 10, p. 2; *HS in Oesterr.*, pp. 82–83; also *A-Z*, June 24, p. 1, for prediction of it. Streeruwitz considered Starhemberg little more than a Nazi at the time; see Lerchenfeld to F.M., Vienna, 24 Sept. 1929, PADAA (Bonn), II: 2/3, vol. 2. Also Max Dachauer, *Das Ende Oesterreichs: Aus der k. u. k. Monarchie ins Dritte Reich* (Berlin: C. A. Weller, 1939), p. 146. Starhemberg's career is treated more fully in chap. 5.

22. Washburn to sec. of state, Vienna, 12 Aug. 1929, USNA (Washington), State Dept., 863.00/665; Le Rougetel to Henderson (confidential), Vienna, Aug. 8, commenting on the HW's "remarkable progress . . . even in Socialist Vienna," PRO (London), F.O. 371: 13563/C6228.

23. *NFP*, 25 July 1929, P.M., p. 2. See issues of *A-Z* between June 16 and July 9; Gulick, *Austria*, 2:828–829, 836.

24. Kerekes, *Abenddämmerung*, pp. 41–42, 52.

25. *NFP*, 19 Aug. 1929, P.M., pp. 1–4; *HS-Ztg*, Aug. 24, pp. 1–2; Gulick, *Austria*, 2:836–838, uses the *NFP* as a major source but ignores its report that each side had a machine gun; instead, he cites Wallisch's wife's accusation that the HW fired one from the church tower (Paula Wallisch, *Ein Held Stirbt: Koloman Wallisch* [(Graz) Im Verlag der Sozialistischen Partei, 1946 (Prague, 1935)], pp. 192–196).

26. Ministerialratsprotokol [MRP], no. 579, 22 Aug. 1929, AVA (Vienna), BKA; report on the HW by the Police Administration [Schober], Vienna, 31 Aug. 1929, AVA (Vienna), BKA, Abt. 8–9, 161.124/1929.

27. Winkler claimed that on the 18th Pfrimer had most of the upper Styrian HS "on maneuvers" near Judenburg, ready for action (*Diktatur*, pp. 27–28). When I asked Pfrimer about this, he claimed a faulty memory about the whole affair. Rauter occasionally boasted that St. Lorenzen began a new stage in the development of the HW (anonymous police report on meeting of district leaders from Styria and Carinthia at Leoben, 11 Dec. 1929, ABP [Vienna], Schober Archiv, Fasc. HW).

28. See Hoffman to F.M., Vienna, 24 Aug. and 6 Sept. 1929, PADAA

(Bonn), II: 2/3, vol. 2; Lerchenfeld to F.M., Vienna, Sept. 23 [*sic.*—25], ibid., vol. 3; *A-Z*, Aug. 20, p. 1; *NFP*, Aug. 22, A.M., p. 3; 10 July 1931, A.M., p. 6.

29. Schweiger, "Geschichte der n–ö HW," pp. 120–121; *Oesterr. VW*, 31 Aug. 1929, pp. 1269–70; *HS-Ztg*, Sept. 28, p. 3.

30. *HS-Ztg*, 24 Aug. 1929, pp. 1–2; Sept. 14, p. 1; *NFP*, Aug. 24, P.M., p. 2; Aug. 26, P.M., p. 3, where Steidle denied being the spokesman.

31. *NFP*, 26 Aug. 1929, P.M., p. 3; Aug. 28, A.M., p. 6; Sept. 1, A.M., p. 8; Sept. 19, A.M., pp. 1–2, which reproached the HW for its "Last Warning"; *Alp. HtW*, Sept. 1929, p. 1; *Weg zu Oesterreichs Freiheit*, pp. 65, 58–59, 61–62, which Pabst told me was written by Anton Klotz, the editor of the *Tiroler Anzeiger*. See Gulick, *Austria*, 2:839–847.

32. Henderson to Streeruwitz [copy of personal letter], [Geneva] 14 Sept. 1929, referring to conversation earlier in the day, PRO (London), F.O. 371: 13564/C8109; Hoffman to Bülow (private), Vienna, 6 Sept. 1929, PADAA (Bonn), II: 5 Oe A (*Geheim*); also Lerchenfeld to F.M., Vienna, Sept. 24, PADAA (Bonn), II: 2/3, vol. 3.

33. Kerekes, *Abenddämmerung*, pp. 42–44.

34. Ibid., pp. 44–47, 52.

35. Memorandum by Brauer, Berlin, 19 Sept. 1929, PADAA (Bonn), II: 2/3, vol. 2; Lerchenfeld to F.M., Vienna, Sept. 23 [*sic*—25], ibid., vol. 3; Streeruwitz, *Springflut*, pp. 409, 419–420; Vinzenz Schumy, "Ungedruckte Aufzeichnungen," typescript in OeIZ (Vienna), pp. 30, 34; Spectator Noricus, "Von Seipel bis Schober," *Volkswohl*, 23 (April 1931): 249; Gulick, *Austria*, 2:879–880.

36. Schumy, "Ungedr. Aufzeichnungen," pp. 34, 77; *NFP*, 26 Sept. 1929, A.M., p. 4; P.M., p. 2; Sept. 27, A.M., pp. 3–4; Sept. 30, P.M., p. 2; Oct. 1, A.M., p. 6; *HS-Ztg*, Oct. 5, p. 3.

37. Kerekes, *Abenddämmerung*, pp. 51–52.

38. *NR Protokolle*, 3/3 (27 Sept. 1929); 2789–90, 2797; also Ludwig, *Oesterreichs Sendung*, p. 70.

39. Rudolf Sieghart, *Die letzten Jahrzehnte einer Grossmacht* (Berlin: Ullstein, 1932), p. 199.

40. See Gulick, *Austria*, 2:856–861, for account of bank crisis.

41. Kerekes, *Abenddämmerung*, pp. 53–55; Schumy, "Ungedr. Aufzeichnungen," p. 38.

42. *NFP*, 7 Oct. 1930, A.M., p. 3, which prefaced the document with this notice: "The draft was not that of the Heimwehr, but only the plans of its leadership, which came into existence more or less in a dictatorial way, without the authorization, without the knowledge . . . of the members." A typescript of most of the proposals can be found in the ABP (Vienna), Schober Archiv, Fasc. HW. See Kerekes, *Abenddämmerung*, pp. 58–60.

43. Ibid., pp. 52–53, also pp. 200–218, where is reproduced a detailed accounting by Steidle to Bethlen of AS 1,493,319.57 received from Italy in three installments and expended through Dec. 1930.

44. *The Times* (London), 5 Nov. 1929, p. 8; "Le Malaise Autrichienne," *Le Temps* (Paris), Nov. 6, p. 1.

45. Memorandum of conversation between Schober and Curtius in The Hague, 4 [5?] Jan. 1930, PADAA (Bonn), Büro Reichsminister [RM] 16 (*Akten betreffend Oesterreich*), vol. 3 (1 Aug. 1929–30 July 1930); Kerekes, *Abenddämmerung*, pp. 58, 61–62.

46. So Austrian Minister Frank told State Sec. Schubert on Nov. 18; see memorandum by S[chubert], Berlin, 19 Nov. 1929, PADAA (Bonn), Büro StSek SO, vol. 9 (Nov.–Dec. 1929).

47. Bülow to Lerchenfeld (confidential, exclusively for personal information), Berlin, 23 Nov. 1929, PADAA (Bonn), II: 5 Oe A (*Geheim*); Schumy, "Ungedr. Aufzeichnungen," p. 26; Schuschnigg, *Dreimal Oesterreich*, pp. 137–138; Kerekes, *Abenddämmerung*, p. 58.

48. See Kerekes, *Abenddämmerung*, pp. 62–63, for Vaugoin's reasons.

49. There are conflicting reports about the advice that Louis Rothschild gave the HW. Lerchenfeld reported that he allegedly warned that a putsch "over Schober's head" would endanger the schilling (to F.M., Vienna, 21 Nov. 1929, PADAA [Bonn], II: 2/3, vol. 3), but Kerekes cites evidence that on Nov. 18 Rothschild assured Steidle that if the HW seized power quickly and with little bloodshed the currency would remain stable (*Abenddämmerung*, pp. 49, 91). In Jan. 1931 Pabst repeated the claim (Kerekes, "Italien . . . und . . . Heimwehrbewegung," p. 11).

50. Lerchenfeld reported it to be his understanding that most domestic support for the HW went through the government (to F.M., Vienna, 27 Dec. 1929, PADAA [Bonn], II: 2/3, vol. 3), and according to Kerekes Schober told the HW leaders in Feb. 1930 that he would release AS 300,000 in subsidies withheld earlier (*Abenddämmerung*, pp. 62, 67). See also Winkler, *Diktatur*, p. 28.

51. Schumy, "Ungedr. Aufzeichnungen," p. 46, who also said that in the middle of November Schober told him that Pabst had to be evicted from Austria as soon as feasible. And Lerchenfeld reported that Schumy told him that Pabst's citizenship was being studied by the ministry of the interior (to Bülow [private], Vienna, 29 Nov. 1929, PADAA [Bonn], II: 5 Oe A [*Geheim*]). On Nov. 8 Pabst sent Schober a letter denying socialist charges that he was a frequent visitor to the Italian and Hungarian ministries (ABP [Vienna], Schober Archiv, Fasc. HW).

52. Memorandum, Vienna, 20 Nov. 1929, ABP (Vienna), Schober Archiv, Fasc. HW.

53. Except as noted, the account in the last two paragraphs was reconstructed from the following: Lerchenfeld to F.M., Vienna, 21 Nov. and 6 Dec. 1929, PADAA (Bonn), II: 2/3, vol. 3; Lerchenfeld to Bülow, Vienna, Nov. 29, PADAA (Bonn), II: 5 Oe A (*Geheim*); central office of the Reich bureau for intelligence [Strahl] to the state sec. in the chancellery [Pünder], Berlin, Nov. 28, DBA (Koblenz) R43I/110; Schumy, "Ungedr. Aufzeichnungen," pp. 43–48; and *NFP*, Nov. 19, A.M., p. 5. A year later the Land-

bund published details of alleged HW putsch plans from the fall of 1929 (*NFP*, 5 Nov. 1930, A.M., p. 5).

54. *Heimat*, 20 Nov. 1929, p. 1; Nov. 27, p. 1; Dec. 4, pp. 1–3.

55. Kerekes, *Abenddämmerung*, p. 64.

56. For a thorough discussion of Schober's original bill and the eventual compromise, see Gulick, *Austria*, 2:862–879; also Mary MacDonald, *The Republic of Austria, 1918–1934: A Study in the Failure of Democratic Government* (London, New York, Toronto: Oxford University Press, 1946), pp. 49–62. According to Schumy the HW leaders did not want the mere gesture toward corporatism included ("Ungedr. Aufzeichnungen," pp. 42–43).

57. Pabst interview. See police report (anonymous) of bitter exchanges among district HW leaders from Styria and Carinthia in Leoben on 11 Dec. 1929, in which Pfrimer accused Schober of betrayal and of not comprehending the HW's plans for a corporative constitution (in ABP [Vienna], Schober Archiv, Fasc. HW); also *NFP*, 30 Jan. 1931, A.M., p. 5; *Die Stunde*, 4 Oct. 1931.

58. So Pabst expressed himself a year later (see Kerekes, *Abenddämmerung*, p. 91; but on pp. 57 and 59 Kerekes cites evidence that both Mussolini and Grandi voiced impatience with the HW's inaction).

59. *HS-Ztg*, 14 Dec. 1929, pp. 1–2. See also Gulick, *Austria*, 2:881–884.

CHAPTER 5

1. Gulick, *Austria*, 2:882–884.

2. Notes on political discussions between Schober and Mussolini (secret), Rome, 4–7 Feb. 1930, Neues Politisches Archiv des österr. Staatsarchiv (Vienna) [hereafter cited as NPA (Vienna)], Karton 477, Foli 273–274. See also Kerekes, *Abenddämmerung*, pp. 66–67.

3. Memorandum of talk between Schober and Starhemberg, Vienna, 18 Dec. 1929, ABP (Vienna), Schober Archiv, Fasc. HW.

4. See *NFP* throughout late Dec. 1929 and early Jan. 1930; issues of *HS-Ztg* for Jan. 1930; Schumy, "Ungedr. Aufzeichnungen," pp. 26, 53; Le Rougetel to Henderson (confidential), Vienna, Jan. 9, PRO (London), F.O. 371: 14304/C322; confidential report on Austria from Abw[ehr] Abt[eilung] I.b., Feb. 10, DBA (Koblenz), R43I/111; Schober's remarks in MRP no. 606, 20 Dec. 1929, AVA (Vienna), BKA.

5. *NFP*, 10 Jan. 1930, P.M., p. 3; Jan. 15, P.M., p. 2; memorandum of conversation . . . with Pabst in Innsbruck, in Freiherr von d. Bussche to Köpke, Berlin, 13 Feb. 1930, PADAA (Bonn), II: 2/3, vol. 3; Saller to F.M., Innsbruck, Jan. 30, ibid.; Lerchenfeld to F.M., Jan. 15 PADAA (Bonn), Büro StSek SO, vol. 10 (Dec. 1929–May 1930); Kerekes, *Abenddämmerung*, p. 65. It was known that Schumy wanted to prove Pabst's naturalization invalid; see Le Rougetel to Henderson (confidential), Vienna, Jan. 9, PRO (London), F.O. 371: 14304/C322.

6. Lerchenfeld to F.M., Vienna, 27 Dec. 1929, PADAA (Bonn), II: 2/3,

vol. 3; Saller to F.M., Innsbruck, 9 and 30 Jan. 1930, ibid; report of central office of the Reich bureau for intelligence (Strahl) to the state sec. in the chancellery (Pünder), Berlin, Jan. 17, DBA (Koblenz), R43I/111. The U.S. military attaché, Col. J. A. Baer, who took a lively interest in political affairs, thought that Seipel, now a "radical reactionary," tried throughout Feb. 1930 to gain personal control of the HW (G–2 report, Vienna, April 15, USNA [Washington], War Dept., MID, RG–165: 2657–FF–131/3).

7. NFP, 22 Jan. 1930, A.M., p. 6; Jan. 29, A.M., p. 4; Heimat, Jan. 29, pp. 1–2; Oesterr. VW, Feb. 1, p. 473, which saw Seipel's support of Steidle and Pabst as a sign of his own weakness. Heinrich's lecture was published as Grundsätzliche Gedanken über Staat und Wirtschaft: Ein programmatischer Vortrag über die geistige Grundlage der Heimatwehrbewegung (Vienna: Bundesführung der österr. Selbstschutzverbände, 1930). Soon afterward Innsbruck's Vice-Mayor Schweinitzhaupt, a friend of Steidle's, published Vom Parteienstaat zum Heimatwehr-Ständestaat (Innsbruck: Deutsche Buchdruckerei [1930]).

8. Confidential report on Austria from Abw[ehr] Abt[eilung] I.b., 10 Feb. 1930, DBA (Koblenz), R43I/111. The author is not indicated; his information came from several HW leaders, two retired officers in circles close to Schober, a confidant of Seipel, an official in the army ministry, and Pabst. See NFP, Jan. 23, A.M., p. 4, for a description of the HW's new economic and corporative bureau; also a report on "the new tactics of the HW," Vienna, Jan. 25, ABP (Vienna), Schober Archiv, Fasc. HW.

9. Wache, Deutscher Geist, pp. 244–245, quoting Pichl's letter of resignation.

10. Alfred Proksch to Nazi headquarters in Munich, Linz, 22 Mar. 1930, DBA (Koblenz), R305I, Schumachersammlung. Proksch noted that from talks with Starhemberg, whom it was "valuable" to have around, the Austrian Nazis knew how things were in the HW.

11. See reports cited in n. 6 above.

12. Protocol of meeting of Gau leaders, Linz, 16 Mar. 1930, DBA (Koblenz), R305I, Schumachersammlung; Deutsch, Weiter Weg, p. 177.

13. See Gulick, Austria, 2:885–891, for an account of the passage and contents of this "law for the protection of freedom of work and assembly"; also Goldinger, "Der gesch. Ablauf," p. 171; HS-Ztg, 12 Apr. 1930, p. 1.

14. Lerchenfeld to F.M., Vienna, 2 Apr. 1930, PADAA (Bonn), II: 2/3, vol. 3; Hans Riehl writing in Festschrift Walter Heinrich, p. 4.

15. NFP, 31 Dec. 1929, A.M., p. 6; 2 Jan. 1930, P.M., p. 1. Jan. 23, A.M., p. 4; April 5, P.M., p. 5; April 8, A.M., p. 5; April 11, A.M., p. 5; A-Z, April 1, p. 2; April 11, p. 1; HS-Ztg, April 5, p. 3.

16. NFP, 12, 19, and 22 Jan. 1930, all A.M., pp. 8, 8, and 6; HS-Ztg, April 19, p. 3; Schweiger, "Gesch. der n–ö HW," pp. 150ff.

17. The socialists claimed that this military action was also intended to divert attention from the HW "fiasco" in which only 3,800 men appeared (Jahrbuch der öesterr. Arbeiterbewegung 1930, pp. 31–34). But see NFP,

May 5, P.M., pp. 1–5, estimating that at least 6,000 HW men were at St. Pölten, 16,000 at Laxenburg; and *Heimwehr* (Vienna), May 9, pp. 1–5, claiming that 9,600 HW men were at St. Pölten.

18. *HS-Ztg*, 3 May 1930, p. 1; English translation of Schober's letter, League of Nations, *Official Journal*, 11/5 (May 1930): 384; Kerekes, *Abenddämmerung*, pp. 65, 69–71, who notes that in May 1930 Pfrimer alone sought Hungarian aid.

19. *NFP*, 12 May 1930, P.M., p. 3; Lerchenfeld to F.M., Vienna, May 14, PADAA (Bonn), II: 2/3, vol. 3.

20. *NFP*, 19 May 1930, P.M., pp. 1–3; *HS-Ztg*, May 24, p. 2; *HS in Oesterr.*, p. 48; *Die Stunde*, 16 Oct. 1931, n.p. Winkler claimed that Steidle acted under pressure from the Styrians (*Diktatur*, p. 29). For Pfrimer's remarks at Korneuburg see his newspaper the *Panther*, May 24, pp. 1–2, which cheered this "falling of the dice" as a "complete victory for our policy in Lower Austria." Pfrimer would tell me little about events at Korneuburg, but did assert that he arrived late and was not present when Steidle read the oath.

21. *Die Stunde*, 16 Oct. 1931, n.p.; interviews with Pabst, Heinrich, who acknowledged responsibility for the basic outline of what he called a common effort but charged that last-minute changes were made in the statement without his knowledge, and Revertera, who suggested that Steidle was "probably more surprised than anyone else by his oath." See also Von Klemperer, *Ignaz Seipel*, p. 374.

22. *HS in Oesterr.*, pp. 47–48; *Alp. HtW*, May 1930, p. 2, which adds the "completely" after the fifth "We." Compare with the translation in Jedlicka, "Austrian HW," pp. 138–139. Both Kunschak (*Oesterreich*, pp. 118–119) and Winkler (*Diktatur*, p. 29) charged that Steidle's oath itself, not just his prefatory remarks, included an explicit avowal of fascism and open attacks on the Church and trade unions.

23. The *Tiroler Anzeiger*, 22 May 1930, claimed that Steidle's "fully improvised" speech was an effort to end the "inactivity" and the "so-called leadership crisis" resulting from his promise to Schober in the fall of 1929 not to undertake any major actions before 15 Apr. 1930 (cited in *NFP*, May 23, P.M., p. 2). Schober alluded to such a pledge in the cabinet meeting of May 20 (MRP no. 628, AVA [Vienna], BKA).

24. See Ludwig Jedlicka, "Zur Vorgeschichte des Korneuburger Eides," *Oesterr. in Gesch. und Lit.*, 7 (April 1963): 146–153.

25. MRP no. 628, 20 May 1930, AVA (Vienna) BKA.

26. *NFP*, 20 May 1930, P.M., p. 1; May 22, A.M., p. 3; *Heimat*, May 21, pp. 1–2, which printed a long list of requisites for HW agreement to disarmament, including among the usual antisocialist and antiunion diatribes demands for the expulsion of free-thinkers from the schools, the restoration of the honor of women as wives and mothers, and the elimination of jury trials.

27. MRP no. 629, 22 May 1930, AVA (Vienna) BKA; *NFP*, May 22, A.M.,

p. 1; P.M., p. 1; May 24, A.M., p. 2; *NR Protokolle*, 3/3 (May 23): 3711–14, 3725–26, 3729–31; Gulick, *Austria*, 2:895–896, for quotation regarding statesmen's "language"; Schumy, "Ungedr. Aufzeichnungen," p. 58.

28. *HS-Ztg*, 7 June 1930, p. 5; *NFP*, May 23, P.M., p. 2; May 26, P.M., p. 3. The government felt called upon to publish an official denial of Steidle's charges that Schober was protecting bolsheviks (*Wiener Zeitung*, May 28, pp. 1–2).

29. Huebmer, *Ender*, p. 126; *NFP*, 23 May 1930, A.M., p. 3; May 28, A.M., p. 5; June 4, A.M., pp. 5–6; June 5, A.M., pp. 4–5; P.M., p. 2; June 6, A.M., p. 3; June 14, A.M., p. 6; *Oesterr. VW*, June 7, 14, and 21, pp. 982, 1009, and 1038; Gulick, *Austria*, 2:896–898; Winkler, *Diktatur*, p. 30; *HS-Ztg*, June 7, pp. 4–5.

30. Lerchenfeld to F.M., Vienna, June 5, PADAA (Bonn), II: 5 Oe (*Akten betreffend Innere Politik, Parlaments- & Parteiwesen*), vol. 9 (16 Dec. 1929–16 Aug. 1930); *NFP*, June 6, P.M., p. 2; June 7, P.M., p. 2.

31. Confidential memorandum, Reinebeck to Köpke, Berlin, 4 June 1930, PADAA (Bonn), II: 2/3, vol. 3.

32. Kerekes, *Abenddämmerung*, pp. 74–76. At about this time Mussolini told Princess Fanny Starhemberg that he would like to meet her son; see memorandum, dated 10 June 1930, of talk between Princess Starhemberg and Schober, June 5, ABP (Vienna), Schober Archiv, Fasc. HW.

33. The question of Pabst's citizenship had been discussed by the Austrian and German governments since the fall of 1929, when Pabst appealed the termination of his officer's pension. In order to retain his pension, Pabst procured from the Tyrolean government a letter, dated 7 March 1930, stating that it considered him a German citizen; Pabst also possessed a valid certificate of domicile from Berlin. However, on March 22, Schober told Lerchenfeld that the chancellery had received an application from Pabst for Austrian citizenship, with the small Tyrolean village of Mieming ready to grant him the right of permanent domicile, which the socialists claimed it had given "W. Peters" in 1922 (see *NR Protokolle*, 3/3 [26 Nov. 1929]: 2989). Pabst was called "stateless" when deported. See several documents in PADAA (Bonn), II: 2/3, vol. 3.

34. *NFP*, 15 June 1930, A.M., pp. 1–2, 8; Lerchenfeld to F.M., Vienna, June 16, PADAA (Bonn), II: 2/3, vol. 3; Austria, *Stenographische Protokolle über die Sitzungen des Bundesrates* (hereafter *BR Protokolle*), 3 (June 17): 1652; Kerekes, *Abenddämmerung*, p. 75; Schumy, "Ungedr. Aufzeichnungen," pp. 46, 61–62, mentioning Pabst's ties with Eugenio Morreale, the Italian press attaché; *Neues Wiener Tagblatt*, 9 Oct. 1930, p. 4, for Landbund charges that Pabst schemed against the loan (see also *NFP*, Oct. 11, A.M., p. 6).

35. Jakoncig's plea was not given much publicity at the time. Otto Bauer reminded the country of it when Jakoncig entered Dollfuss's government (*NR Protokolle*, 4/2 [27 May 1932]: 2154–55). In a letter to me dated 8 Jan. 1964, Jakoncig stated, "The assertions of Dr. Otto Bauer are in no way

evidence, since to him any means were justified that would slander the Heimwehr leaders and the Heimwehr movement, which had ruined his communist plans."

36. Besides accounts of and reactions to the arrest in various newspapers, see Saller to Lerchenfeld, Innsbruck, June 20, PADAA (Bonn), II: 2/3, vol. 3.

37. *NFP*, 18 June 1930, A.M., p. 7; June 19, A.M., p. 7; *Panther*, June 21, pp. 1–2; *HS-Ztg*, June 28, p. 1, reinterpreting the oath; *Die Stunde*, 18 Oct. 1931, n.p., which mentions Spann's pleas; report on Austrian HW, German intelligence dept. to Ministerial Councillor Planck in the chancellery, Berlin, July 2, DBA (Koblenz), R43I/111; Saller to Lerchenfeld, Innsbruck, June 20, reporting that Heinrich, still a Czech citizen, had allegedly left Austria to avoid possible arrest because of his relations with Pabst (PADAA [Bonn], II: 2/3, vol. 3).

38. *NFP*, 18 June 1930, P.M., p. 5; June 19, A.M., p. 7; Rokitansky's *Unsere Zukunft*, June 25, pp. 3–6; July 25, pp. 5–6; *HS-Ztg*, July 12, p. 6; *Heimat*, Aug. 6, p. 3; *Panther*, Aug. 16, p. 1; report from Bundes-Polizei-direktion (Tandler) to several government offices, Vienna, Aug. 13, AVA (Vienna), BKA, Abt. 8, 185.975/30.

39. See the German intelligence report of 2 July 1930 (cited above), DBA (Koblenz), R43I/111.

40. Kerekes, *Abenddämmerung*, p. 76; Lerchenfeld to F.M., Vienna, 8 Aug. 1930, PADAA (Bonn), II: 5 Oe, vol. 9.

41. Starhemberg, "Lebenserinnerungen," pp. 3, 73–74, 95–97; his *Memoiren*, pp. 74–80; and his *Between Hitler and Mussolini*, pp. 20–30. Before visiting Bethlen and Mussolini, Starhemberg had a talk with Hitler, who he claimed was not interested in helping the HW and urged him to see Mussolini. Starhemberg says nothing about his ties with Schober.

42. Kerekes, *Abenddämmerung*, pp. 76–78; Lerchenfeld to F.M., Vienna, 8 Aug. 1930, PADAA (Bonn), II: 5 Oe, vol. 9; *NFP*, July 30, A.M., p. 5; July 31, A.M., pp. 1–2, 5; *Panther*, Aug. 2, p. 1; Phipps to Henderson (confidential), Vienna, Sept. 4, PRO (London), F.O. 371: 14307/C6867.

43. *NFP*, 6 Sept. 1930, A.M., p. 5, citing the *Vorarlberger Volksblatt; RP*, Sept. 5, p. 2; *Heimat*, Sept. 10, p. 1; *HS-Ztg*, Sept. 6, pp. 1, 7. Winkler wrote that at the time Starhemberg hated Steidle, promised Pfrimer his support at a secret meeting a few days before Sept. 2, but then turned against him also (*Diktatur*, pp. 28–31).

44. Starhemberg, *Memoiren*, pp. 41–66, and "Lebenserinnerungen," pp. 11–29.

45. Starhemberg, *Memoiren*, pp. 67–80, and "Lebenserinnerungen," pp. 5–9, 30–79 *passim*. Written in 1938–1939 largely as a call to arms against Hitler, these memoirs, later revised, were the basis of his English book, but the translation is not complete. Also *HS in Oesterr.*, pp. 84–91; Revertera interview; Rintelen, *Erinnerungen*, p. 134, who contended that Pfrimer took a personal hand in Starhemberg's becoming provincial leader. About this Pfrimer told me that some time after July 1927 Starhemberg asked him for

help in organizing the HW in U.A. and that "I helped," especially in "winning" the workers, an art Starhemberg never "mastered."

46. *Oesterr. VW*, 6 Sept. 1930, p. 1322; also *NFP*, Sept. 3, A.M., p. 2; P.M., pp. 1–2; Sept. 5, A.M., p. 2; *RP*, Sept. 6, p. 3.

47. Phipps to Henderson (confidential), Vienna, 4 Sept. 1930, PRO (London), F.O. 371: 14307/C6867; Lerchenfeld to F.M., Vienna, Sept. 11, PADAA (Bonn), II: 2/3, vol. 3; Lerchenfeld to F.M., Vienna, Sept. 22, PADAA (Bonn), II: 5 Oe, vol. 10 (13 Sept. 1930–8 May 1931). Through his personal secretary Raab told me that he was responsible for the election of Starhemberg but denied acting on behalf of Seipel (interviews with Dr. Robert Prantner, Vienna, 15 and 25 Nov. 1963). Already in the spring, however, the British minister could report on "noticeable friendship" developing between Starhemberg and Seipel (Phipps to Sargent, Vienna, April 30, PRO [London], F.O. 371: 14306/C3486).

48. *Starhemberg-Jäger*, 5 Sept. 1930, p. 1; *NFP*, Sept. 10, P.M., p. 3; Sept. 12, P.M., p. 1, which called Steidle's speech "almost mutinous"; *HS-Ztg*, Sept. 13, pp. 1–2, which said that it showed HW unity holding fast; Winkler, *Diktatur*, p. 31; Prantner (Raab) interview. For information on the women's (1929) and youth (1932) groups, see *HS-Jahrbuch*, pp. 135–147; and Pauley, "Hahnenschwanz," pp. 85–86.

49. Starhemberg, *Between Hitler and Mussolini*, pp. 30–33. Kerekes, "Akten," p. 359, observes that Starhemberg had close connections with Hungary's political leaders and that he sought their opinion in each of his enterprises, an observation verified by the report of the German representative in Budapest to the effect that "not merely personal ties exist between Gömbös and Starhemberg" (Schön to F.M., 11 Oct. 1930, PADAA [Bonn], II: 2/3, vol. 3).

50. Lerchenfeld to F.M., Vienna, 26 Sept. 1930, PADAA (Bonn), II: 5 Oe, vol. 10; Lerchenfeld to F.M., Vienna, Oct. 2, PADAA (Bonn), II: 2/3, vol. 3; Starhemberg, *Memoiren*, pp. 84–85; *RP*, Sept. 28, p. 1; Oct. 1, p. 1; *NFP*, Sept. 30, A.M., p. 3, reporting that on the 29th Starhemberg, Rauter, and Mayer conferred with Dr. Leopold Waber, the chairman of the Pan-German Party; *Starhemberg-Jäger*, 3 Feb. 1931, p. 2, where Starhemberg claimed that Fey, Steidle, and Raab forced him into the government. Pfrimer told me that he opposed HW entry into the cabinet, but went along with the majority of the provincial leaders; his *Panther*, however, asserted that Starhemberg acted on the insistence of the nationalist leaders in Styria, who would hold the ministers to their course (20 Oct. 1930, p. 1). See also Winkler, *Diktatur*, pp. 31–32; and *Die Stunde*, 22 Oct. 1931, n.p.

51. *NFP*, 18 Oct. 1930, A.M., p. 8; Oct. 25, A.M., p. 5. The committee was not formally abolished until 3 June 1932 (report by Baer, Vienna, 18 July 1932, USNA [Washington], War Dept., MID, RG–165: 2540–171); see Gulick, *Austria*, 2:909; also Jedlicka, *Heer*, pp. 80–81, n. 66.

52. MRP no. 653, 9 Oct. 1930, and no. 656, Oct. 29, AVA (Vienna), BKA.

53. Pfrimer interview. But both Raab and Hueber informed me that they knew of no such promises by Starhemberg.

54. *RP*, 2 Oct. 1930, p. 1. Rokitansky opined that Seipel approved a separate HW list in Carinthia and Styria with the hope that it could break the Landbund where the CSP could not (*Unsere Zukunft*, 5 Feb. 1931, pp. 4–6).

55. *A-Z*, 3 Oct. 1930, p. 1; *RP*, Oct. 4, p. 1; Oct. 5, p. 1; *NFP*, Oct. 3, P.M., p. 2; Oct. 5, A.M., p. 5.

56. Starhemberg, *Between Hitler and Mussolini*, pp. 35ff., 47–48, and *Memoiren*, pp. 85–96. Winkler, *Diktatur*, p. 32; Langoth, *Kampf*, p. 83; Hueber's letter to me; Kerekes, *Abenddämmerung*, pp. 84–86; *Die Stunde*, 24 Oct. 1931, n.p., concerning Apold's role. In Feb. 1938 Starhemberg contradicted his own contentions during contacts with a Nazi agent, who reported to his superiors that Starhemberg insisted that in 1930 he offered the HW to Hitler, who rejected his offer; see Jedlicka, "Ernst Rüdiger Fürst Starhemberg und die politische Entwicklung in Oesterreich in Frühjahr 1938," in *Oesterreich und Europa: Festgabe für Hugo Hantsch zum 70. Geburtstag* (Graz, Vienna: Styria, 1965), pp. 552–553, who cites U.S. State Dept., *Records of the German Foreign Office Received by the U.S. State Department*, Microcopy T–175, roll 58, folder 118, frames 2573403–407, letter and protocols of a conversation with Starhemberg by Hans Stuck, Davos, 13 Feb. 1938, in Keppler to RF-SS, Chief of German Police, 24 Feb. 1938.

57. *NFP*, 7 Oct. 1930, A.M., p. 3; Oct. 9, A.M., p. 5; *RP*, Oct. 9, pp. 4–5; *A-Z*, Oct. 11, p. 1.

58. Starhemberg, *Between Hitler and Mussolini*, p. 34, and *Memoiren*, pp. 99–100; Kerekes, *Abenddämmerung*, p. 86; *NFP*, 22 Oct. 1930, A.M., pp. 4–5; *RP*, Oct. 22, p. 1; memorandum of talk with Langoth, Oct. 23, Upper Austrian Landesarchiv, Linz, Landeshauptmann ex 1930, Zl. 184; G. B. Stockton to Sec. of State, Vienna, Nov. 4, citing Gunther, USNA (Washington), State Dept., 863.00/702.

59. Lerchenfeld to F.M., Vienna, 29 Oct. 1930, PADAA (Bonn), II: 2/3, vol. 3; Kerekes, *Abenddämmerung*, pp. 86–87; *Die Stunde*, 23 Oct. 1931, n.p.; *NFP*, 18 Sept. 1931, A.M., p. 3, for Vaugoin's testimony after the Styrian HS had indeed attempted a putsch eleven months later; and Ludwig, *Oesterreichs Sendung*, p. 81, arguing that Seipel used his influence to prevent a putsch in 1930.

60. *NFP*, 27 Oct. 1930, P.M., pp. 1–2; Oct. 28, A.M., pp. 1, 5; P.M., p. 1; Oct. 30, P.M., p. 1; *A-Z*, Oct. 28, p. 1; *Oesterr. VW*, 19 Sept. 1931, p. 1322, thus contending that Starhemberg felt himself betrayed by Pamer; *Die Stunde*, 23 Oct. 1931, n.p.; Franz Brandl, *Kaiser, Politiker, und Menschen: Erinnerungen eines Wiener Polizeipräsidenten* (Leipzig, Vienna: Johannes Günther Verlag, 1936), pp. 420–422; Pfrimer interview; Ludwig, *Oesterreichs Sendung*, p. 81.

61. See campaign proclamation of the Heimatblock (HB) in *HS-Ztg*, 21

Oct. 1930, p. 3; also Klaus Berchtold (comp.), *Oesterreichische Parteiprogramme, 1868–1966* (Munich: R. Oldenbourg, 1967), pp. 403–406.

62. *NFP*, 30 Oct. 1930, P.M., pp. 1–2; *RP*, Oct. 31, p. 1, which contended that Starhemberg "actually" said that the HW would hold on to the reins only as long as the will of the people supported it.

63. See *A-Z*, 4 Nov. 1930, p. 1; Nov. 5, pp. 1–2, 7; Nov. 8, pp. 1–2; *SD Jahrbuch, 1930*, pp. 69–73; Pertinax, *Oesterreich*, pp. 112–113. The HW accused Gov. Schlegel of U.A. of warning the socialists (*NFP*, 20 Nov. 1930, A.M., p. 4).

64. *NFP*, 5 Nov. 1930, A.M., pp. 5–6, reporting Styrian events; 24 Feb. 1931, P.M., p. 1, reporting Starhemberg's recollections voiced at a press conference.

65. *NFP*, 11 Nov. 1930, A.M., p. 3; *RP*, Nov. 10, p. 1. According to Austrian electoral law, a seat had to be won by a plurality in at least one electoral district in the country before remaining votes in other districts could be combined; thus, the HB won its "basic" seat in upper Styria, then two more from the voting region comprising Styria (12% of vote), Car. (8%), and Bgld. (4%); three from the region comprising U.A. (8%), Sbg. (6%), Tyrol, (9%), and Vbg. (no list); and two from L.A. (7%). See Walter B. Simon, "The Political Parties of Austria," (Ph.D. diss., Columbia University, 1957), p. 91. In provincial legislatures the HB won 6 seats of 48 in Styria and 3 of 36 in Carinthia.

66. *NFP*, 24 Feb. 1931, P.M., p. 1, for Starhemberg's claims; Kerekes, *Abenddämmerung*, pp. 91–92, citing Pabst to a Hungarian diplomat in Jan. 1931 about Starhemberg's continuing putsch hopes and Mussolini's advice.

67. *HS-Ztg*, 15 Nov. 1930, p. 1; *A-Z*, Nov. 11, p. 1.

68. *NFP*, 13 Nov. 1930, P.M., p. 4, as in Gulick, *Austria*, 2:916.

69. Saller to F.M., Innsbruck, 13 and 18 Nov. 1930, PADAA (Bonn), II: 2/3, vol. 3; *RP*, Nov. 17, p. 2, which, obviously embarrassed, quoted Starhemberg indirectly and qualified his inclusion of the Nazis with "in a certain sense"; *NFP*, Nov. 17, P.M., p. 2; Nov. 18, A.M., p. 4; P.M., pp. 1–2; *A-Z*, Nov. 21, p. 2; Kerekes, *Abenddämmerung*, p. 88.

70. *NFP*, 18 Nov. 1930, P.M., p. 2; Dec. 1, P.M., pp. 2–3; Dec. 2, A.M., p. 3; Dec. 3, A.M., pp. 4–5; *A-Z*, Nov 29, p. 1; *RP*, Nov. 30, p. 4; Dec. 2, p. 1, which called Schober's "forced exclusion" of the HB a misfortune; *SD Jahrbuch, 1930*, pp. 80–81; Gulick, *Austria*, 2:916–918; and Lerchenfeld to F.M., Vienna, Nov. 27, PADAA (Bonn), II: 2/3, vol. 3.

71. Gulick, *Austria*, 2:918–919, for the quotation.

72. Huebmer, *Ender*, p. 128; Gulick, *Austria*, 2:923–926; report by Baer, Vienna, 16 Feb. 1931, USNA (Washington), War Dept., MID, RG–165: 2657–FF–141/10; and Lerchenfeld to F.M., Vienna, 31 Dec. 1930, PADAA (Bonn), II: 2/3, vol. 3.

CHAPTER 6

1. Gulick, *Austria*, 2:924; Wandruszka, "Oesterreichs politische Struktur," pp. 366–367; *NFP*, 27 Nov. 1930, A.M., p. 4; Dec. 9, A.M., p. 6; Dec. 24, P.M., p. 3; Lerchenfeld to F.M., Vienna, Dec. 31, PADAA (Bonn), II: 2/3, vol. 3.

2. *NFP*, 29 Nov. 1930, A.M., p. 5. See also Ludwig, *Oesterreichs Sendung*, p. 34.

3. *NR Protokolle*, 4/1 (5 Dec. 1930): 26, 43–46; *NFP*, Dec. 5, P.M., p. 4; interview with G. Schmitz, who was a visitor in the gallery and recalled Starhemberg's antics. See the HB's long parliamentary program in Berchtold (comp.), *Oesterr. Parteiprogramme*, pp. 406–427.

4. See *SD Jahrbuch*, 1930, pp. 225ff.

5. Lerchenfeld to F.M., Vienna, 4 Feb. 1931, PADAA (Bonn), II: 2/3, vol. 3; report by Baer, Vienna, Feb. 16, USNA (Washington), War Dept., MID, RG–165: 2657–FF–141/10; and *A-Z*, Feb. 12, p. 3.

6. Much of the material in this and the next six paragraphs is based on numerous items in the *NFP* from mid-Nov. 1930 to mid-Feb. 1931; exceptions will be noted. For this paragraph see in addition Schuschnigg, *Dreimal Oesterreich*, pp. 152–154, and his "Protocol of answers to questionnaire submitted by Ludwig Jedlicka," Peertschach a.W., 13 July 1962, typescript in OeIZ (Vienna).

7. *RP*, Dec. 17, p. 4; Dec. 20, p. 3; *HS in Oesterr.*, p. 49; also *Niederösterr. Heimwehr* [*N–ö HW*], 20 Jan. 1930 [*sic*—1931], pp. 4, 6; 27 Jan. 1931, pp. 5–6.

8. *RP*, 16 Dec. 1930, p. 3. The Tyroleans accepted changes in the statutes proposed by Schweinitzhaupt's reform committee, but kept them secret.

9. *HS-Ztg*, Jan. 24, p. 2; *HW*, Feb. 4, p. 1; Raab's *N–ö HW* tried to belittle Neustädter-Stürmer by saying he was of Italian origin and once helped elect a socialist mayor of Braunau (March 3, p. 3).

10. *A-Z*, Feb. 12, p. 3; *Alp. HtW*, Feb. 1930 [*sic*—1931], p. 1.

11. Jakoncig, though he remembered that the encounter was in 1930 (letter, Innsbruck, 3 May 1963).

12. *A-Z*, 12 Feb. 1931, p. 3; *NFP*, Feb. 14, A.M., p. 5. Lustig-Prean had resigned as Hülgerth's military deputy at the time of the split (*NFP*, Jan. 31, A.M., p. 5). The U.S. military attaché reported that Rintelen was connected with the intervention of the industrialists (report by Baer, Vienna, Feb. 16, USNA [Washington], War Dept., MID, RG–165: 2657–FF–141/10).

13. *NFP*, 19 Feb. 1931, A.M., p. 5; P.M., p. 2; Feb. 20, A.M., p. 4; Feb. 21, A.M., p. 6; Feb 24, A.M., p. 5; Mar. 1, A.M., p. 8; Apr. 8, A.M., p. 4; *A-Z*, Feb. 19, p. 3; *Panther*, Apr. 4, p. 14. In mid-April Steidle took a long vacation in southern Italy, where he was joined by Pabst (*NFP*, Apr. 10, A.M., p. 6).

14. *HS-Ztg*, 7 Mar. 1931, p. 1; *Panther*, Mar. 14, p. 1; *NFP*, Mar. 10,

A.M., p. 6; *N–ö HW*, Mar. 17, p. 2; Winkler, *Diktatur*, pp. 34–35, who states that Starhemberg unsuccessfully sought financial aid in Germany.

15. *NFP*, 3 Mar. 1931, P.M., p. 2; Mar. 14, P.M., p. 2; Apr. 20, A.M., p. 2; May 19, P.M., p. 2; *RP*, Mar. 12, p. 4; *SD Jahrbuch, 1930*, pp. 88–89.

16. *NFP*, 25 Apr. 1931, P.M., p. 3; Apr. 26, A.M., p. 9; *RP*, Apr. 25, p. 4; Apr. 26, p. 7.

17. *NFP*, 2 May 1931, P.M., p. 1; May 3, A.M., p. 4; *RP*, May 3, p. 5; *HS-Ztg*, May 9, p. 3; *N–ö HW*, May 12, p. 3.

18. Rieth to F.M., Vienna, 31 May 1931, PADAA (Bonn), II: 2/3, vol. 3.

19. See Josef Hofmann, "Der Pfrimer-Putsch," Ph.D. diss., University of Vienna, 1962, pp. 42–43. I am heavily indebted to this work, which has since been published, and also to Dr. Hofmann for having discussed with me his findings.

20. *Panther*, 9 May 1931, pp. 1–2.

21. There were sixteen rallies in Styria and twelve in L.A. See *Panther*, 25 Apr. 1931, pp. 1–2; May 9, pp. 1–2; *NFP*, May 4, P.M., p. 4. *HS in Oesterr.*, pp. 49–50, later claimed that 35,000 men participated in L.A. alone, a figure probably exaggerated, since most L.A. peasants supported Raab's HW, not Alberti's HS.

22. Raimund Günther, *Diktatur oder Untergang: Neue Wege für Staat und Wirtschaft* (Vienna: Carl Konegen, 1930), pp. 7–9, 26–30, 48–49, 52, 142. Both *Panther* and *HS-Ztg* printed excerpts from the book in serial form. See also Hofmann, "Pfrimer-Putsch," pp. 48–50; and *HS-Ztg*, 6 June 1931 (Pfrimer's speech).

23. *Panther*, 28 Mar. 1931, p. 6.

24. Typescript in OeIZ (Vienna).

25. *HS-Ztg*, 16 May 1931, p. 1; May 23, pp. 1–3; *Panther*, June 20, p. 1; July 4, p. 9; July 11, p. 1; Hofmann, "Pfrimer-Putsch," p. 55: "Dr. Pfrimer imagined the seizure of power to be that simple."

26. Goldinger, "Der gesch. Ablauf," pp. 182–185; Gulick, *Austria*, 2:938–948.

27. Gulick, *Austria*, 2:948–951; Rothschild, *Austria's Economic Development*, pp. 51ff.

28. On May 19 the government, fearing violence during the tourist season, had prohibited all meetings and maneuvers by the paramilitary groups in the open air after May 31. The HW was angry especially with Interior Minister Winkler.

29. *Panther*, 27 June 1931, p. 6; Aug. 8, p. 3; *HS-Ztg*, June 27, pp. 1–2; July 4, p. 5; *Alp. HtW*, July 1931, p. 1; Hofmann, "Primer-Putsch," p. 57; Kerekes, *Abenddämmerung*, p. 95.

30. *Panther*, 13 June 1931, p. 3, which also reports that Starhemberg had rebuffed a Christian Social attempt to bribe him into leading a party guard in U.A.; June 20, p. 2; Aug. 22, p. 2; *HS-Ztg*, June 20, p. 2; July 18, p. 1; *NFP*, July 10, A.M., p. 6; July 29, A.M., pp. 5–6; *Alp. HtW*, Sept. 1931, p. 1;

Die Stunde, Oct. 28, 1931, n.p.; *HS in Oesterr.*, p. 278; Kunschak, *Oester-reich*, p. 128. For anti-Pfrimer presentations see *N–ö HW*, July 14, pp. 1–2, Aug. 24, p. 2.

31. Winkler, *Diktatur*, p. 35; Langoth, *Kampf*, p. 84; Hofmann, "Pfrimer-Putsch," pp. 58–59, citing letter to him from Revertera. Egon Berger-Waldenegg claimed that Rauter also favored a putsch ("Ungedruckte Erinnerungen," typescript in OeIZ [Vienna], p. 4). See also "Anklageschrift gegen Kammerhofer, Flechner, Hofer, Harter, Harant, Seitner, Riedlechner," St[yria] 6060–31/168, Graz, 21 Nov. 1931, typescript copy in OeIZ (Vienna), pp. 9, 11–12, 17–18 [hereafter cited as "Anklageschrift"]; *NR Proto-kolle*, 4/2 (1 Oct. 1931): 1223.

32. Winkler, *Diktatur*, p. 35; *Panther*, 8 Aug. 1931, pp. 1–2. The constitution stipulated that to be valid petitions must be in the form of a legislative bill and have 200,000 signatures; Pfrimer's did not comply with the first requirement.

33. Citations from "Anklageschrift" and *NR Protokolle* as in n. 31 above; Hofmann, "Pfrimer-Putsch," pp. 61–62; Starhemberg, *Between Hitler and Mussolini*, pp. 59–61, and *Memoiren*, pp. 105–106.

34. *Panther*, 12 Sept. 1931, p. 3; *HS-Ztg*, Sept. 12, p. 4.

35. Berger-Waldenegg, "Ungedr. Erinnerungen," p. 5; "Anklageschrift," pp. 10, 11–14, 18.

36. Hofmann, "Pfrimer-Putsch," pp. 67–70, citing primarily the "Anklage-schrift," pp. 16, 213; "Nachtrags-Anklageschrift gegen Dr. Walter Pfrimer," St[yria] 6060–31/217, Graz, 8 Dec. 1931, typescript copy in OeIZ (Vienna), pp. 4–5.

37. For photographic reproductions of the two placards see Gerd Rühle, *Das Grossdeutsche Reich, Dokumentarische Darstellung des Aufbaus der Nation: Die österreichischen Kampfjahre, 1918–1938* (Berlin: Hummelver-lag, 1940), p. 341; for a quotation of "Volk von Oesterreich" see Rintelen, *Erinnerungen*, pp. 145–146; *NFP*, 14 Sept. 1931, P.M., pp. 4–5. Later Pfrimer said that the "constitutional patent" stemmed from the autumn of 1929 and that the "proclamation to the people" was composed by several men in the summer of 1931. He contended that the placards were printed without his approval; that he did not know how they had been distributed (although his son was involved in the distribution); that they were supposed to have been posted only after the government had granted him full powers; and that he saw them in printed form only after his flight to Yugoslavia ("Nachtrags-Anklageschrift," pp. 5–6; *Panther*, Dec. 16, pp. 2, 4; Hofmann, "Pfrimer-Putsch," pp. 71–72). The placards were signed "Walther," although Pfrimer spelled his name "Walter," without the *h*. The alleged economic demands dealt primarily with easing tax burdens for those unable to pay, loosening credit, compulsory labor service for the unemployed, limitation of monthly earnings, tariff protection, and old wishes from the *Credit-Anstalt* petition (*Panther*, Dec. 16, pp. 2–3).

38. See Hofmann, "Pfrimer-Putsch," pp. 76, 80; Andics, *Staat den Keiner Wollte*, p. 357; Pauley, "Hahnenschwanz," p. 170; Kerekes, *Abenddämmerung*, p. 95.

39. Wallisch, *Held stirbt*, pp. 166–168; Deutsch, *Weiter Weg*, pp. 181–183; Stockton to sec. of state, Vienna, 15 Sept. 1931, USNA (Washington), State Dept., 863.00/719; *NR Protokolle*, 4/2 (Oct. 1): 1225; Berger-Waldenegg, "Ungedr. Erinnerungen," p. 8; Hofmann, "Pfrimer-Putsch," p. 111; *NFP*, Sept. 15, P.M., p. 3; Gulick, *Austria*, 2:951–956; "Anklageschrift," p. 41.

40. Hofmann, "Pfrimer-Putsch," pp. 108–111. For a while during mid-morning Pfrimer lay on a couch at his headquarters near Graz in a semi-stupor, and was transferred to a neighboring estate for quiet. There were reports at the time that he had suffered a mild heart attack. But Berger-Waldenegg reports that Pfrimer smelled "a yard away" of alcohol ("Ungedr. Erinnerungen," pp. 7–8), and Hofmann seems to accept the testimony of Frau Richter, the wife of the owner of the headquarters estate and a cousin of Starhemberg's, that Pfrimer had apparently been drugged.

41. *NFP*, Sept. 14, P.M., p. 2.

42. Rintelen, *Erinnerungen*, pp. 144–145; Hofmann, "Pfrimer-Putsch," pp. 74, 108; Berger-Waldenegg, "Ungedr. Erinnerungen," p. 4. There is conflicting opinion as to whether Pfrimer intended to elevate or arrest Rintelen, with Hofmann opting for the first and Berger-Waldenegg for the second.

43. Cited by *Oesterr. VW*, 26 Sept. 1931, p. 1345. See also *NR Protokolle*, 4/2 (Oct. 1): 1215; Gulick, *Austria*, 2:957–958.

44. Starhemberg, *Between Hitler and Mussolini*, pp. 61–65, and *Memoiren*, pp. 109–110; Berger-Waldenegg, "Ungedr. Erinnerungen," p. 10, and Revertera interview, both of whom defend Starhemberg; *RP*, 16 Sept. 1931, p. 3; *NFP*, Sept. 17, P.M., p. 2.

45. Memorandum by Curtius of talk with Buresch, Geneva, 16 Sept. 1931, PADAA (Bonn), II: 2/3, vol. 3.

46. Berger-Waldenegg, "Ungedr. Erinnerungen," pp. 7, 10–11; *HS-Ztg*, 19 Sept. 1931, p. 8; Rintelen, *Erinnerungen*, p. 146.

47. Hofmann, "Pfrimer-Putsch," pp. 143–147, XVI–XVII (letter from Revertera, 26 May 1962); Starhemberg, *Between Hitler and Mussolini*, pp. 61–62, and *Memoiren*, pp. 107–112; Kerekes, *Abenddämmerung*, pp. 95–96; *Die Stunde*, 28 Oct. 1931, n.p.

48. See A-Z on the days following the putsch; *Oesterr. VW*, 19 and 26 Sept. 1931, pp. 1321, 1345; *NR Protokolle*, 4/2 (Oct. 1): 1222–28, 1238–40; *Panther*, Oct. 24, p. 1. Rühle, *Das Grossdeutsche Reich*, pp. 146, 153; Dachauer, *Ende Oesterreichs*, pp. 148–149; and other Nazi authors agreed that the putsch strengthened their movement in Austria.

49. *NFP*, 14 Sept. 1931, P.M., p. 5. Ultimately 280 men were detained for questioning, and reports were compiled against approximately 3,500 others ("Anklageschrift," p. 41).

50. Memorandum by Curtius, quoting Buresch, Geneva, 16 Sept. 1931, PADAA (Bonn), II: 2/3, vol. 3; Clodius to F.M., reporting that officials in the interior ministry seemed convinced that Starhemberg knew and approved of Pfrimer's proclamation, Vienna, Sept. 14, ibid.; Clodius to F.M., Vienna, Oct. 15, ibid.; NFP, Sept. 18, A.M., p. 3, in which Winkler denied responsibility for the arrest; Sept. 19, P.M., p. 3; Berger-Waldenegg, "Ungedr. Erinnerungen," pp. 11ff., who was "embarrassed" not to be among the first arrested. Also MRP no. 728, Sept. 21, and no. 732, Sept. 26, AVA (Vienna), BKA.

51. Panther, 19 Sept. 1931, pp. 1–2; Sept. 26, p. 3; also HS-Ztg, Oct. 3, p. 3.

52. Panther, 19 Sept. 1931, pp. 1–2. On the 19th the Styrians elected Sepp Hainzl as new provincial leader, with Meyszner and Bachofen-Echt as his deputies, and Sepp Lengauer, Franz Harter, and Count Kunata Kottulinsky as members of an advisory council (Panther, Sept. 26, p. 1).

53. Alp. HtW, Sept. 1931, pp. 1–2.

54. NFP, 18 Sept. 1931, A.M., pp. 1, 3; Sept. 20, A.M., p. 9. Starhemberg claimed that he rejected advice to flee to Bavaria because he believed that his detention would be good propaganda, as apparently it was, and because he wanted to disappoint the Nazis (Between Hitler and Mussolini, pp. 65–67, and Memoiren, p. 111). Robert Ingrim thinks that Starhemberg had himself arrested to conceal his having left Pfrimer in the lurch (Der Griff nach Oesterreich [Zurich: Europa, 1938], p. 49).

55. Gulick, Austria, 2:960–964, who suggests that only after Buresch approached Starhemberg did the SDP bitterly interpellate the government about the Pfrimer putsch on Oct. 1; NR Protokolle, 4/2 (3 Oct. 1931): 1245–65; NFP, Oct. 2, P.M., p. 1; Oct. 3, A.M., pp. 2–3.

56. HS-Ztg, 17 Oct. 1931, p. 1; NR Protokolle, 4/2 (Oct. 27): 1367. See also Kerekes, Abenddämmerung, pp. 97–98, for report that Ambrozy cautioned Starhemberg not to excite further the peasantry.

57. Alp. HtW, Nov. 1931, pp. 4–6, quoting Steidle on Oct. 17; HS-Ztg, Oct. 31, p. 8; Kerekes, Abenddämmerung, p. 93.

58. Goldinger, "Der gesch. Ablauf," pp. 190–191; Andics, Staat den Keiner Wollte, pp. 370–371; Phipps to Reading (confidential), Vienna, 28 Oct. 1931, PRO (London), F.O. 371: 15156/C8165; Phipps to Simon (confidential), Vienna, Nov. 12, ibid., C8591.

59. Panther, 7 Nov. 1931, pp. 3–4; Nov. 14, p. 1; Pauley, "Hahnenschwanz," p. 189.

60. Starhemberg, Between Hitler and Mussolini, pp. 68–72, and Memoiren, pp. 113–115.

61. A-Z, 6 Nov. 1931, p. 2, which reported such a conference between Starhemberg, Seipel, and Mandl in Vienna on Nov. 4; Oesterr. VW, Nov. 7, p. 129, which detected Seipel's hand at work in the Tyrol. Winkler, Diktatur, pp. 37–38, stated that it was about this time that Starhemberg's HW became financially dependent on Mussolini.

62. Winkler, *Diktatur*, p. 38; Kerekes, *Abenddämmerung*, pp. 97–98.

63. *Panther*, 21 Nov. 1931, p. 4; Nov. 28, p. 3; Pauley, "Hahnen-schwanz," pp. 192–195.

64. Winkler, *Diktatur*, pp. 37–38; *NFP*, 23 Nov. 1931, P.M., p. 3; *HS-Ztg*, Nov. 28, pp. 3, 7; *Panther*, Dec. 5, p. 1.

65. *NFP*, 26 Nov. 1931, A.M., p. 5; Nov. 27, A.M., p. 3; Nov. 30, P.M., p. 4; *HS-Ztg*, Dec. 5, p. 2; Phipps to Simon (confidential), Vienna, Nov. 12, PRO (London), F.O. 371: 15156/C8591, who observed that Starhemberg was playing all sides.

66. *Panther*, 5 Dec. 1931, p. 1, and Rintelen, *Erinnerungen*, pp. 141–152, both quote the nine-point *Richtlinien*; Winkler, *Diktatur*, p. 38, who often repeats charges that Starhemberg went back on his "princely" word of honor.

67. Winkler, *Diktatur*, p. 38; *NFP*, 30 Nov. 1931, P.M., p. 4, which re-ported about Bund Oberland; Dec. 7, P.M., p. 4; *HS-Ztg*, Dec. 12, pp. 3–4; Pauley, "Hahnenschwanz," pp. 194–195; *Panther*, Dec. 12, p. 2.

68. *NFP*, 12 Dec. 1931, A.M., p. 6; Dec. 13, A.M., p. 8; [Stein] *N–ö HS*, p. 40. Raab's newspaper claimed that after Dec. 1930 the active membership in Alberti's HS fell from 55,000 to 14,000, of which ¾ were pro-Nazi (*N–ö HW*, Dec. 4, p. 2). *HS in Oesterr.*, p. 47, admits that L.A. troops loyal to Starhemberg fell to 10,000.

69. *NFP*, 15 Dec. 1931, A.M., p. 5; *HS-Ztg*, Dec. 19, p. 2; report by Baer, Vienna, 12 Feb. 1932, USNA (Washington), War Dept., MID, RG–165: 2657–FF–141/14, who reported that all three HW leaders recognized the political primacy of Seipel, who according to Goldinger had earlier sent Steidle to Paris to strengthen the legitimist wing of the CSP ("Der gesch. Ablauf," pp. 190–191).

70. Phipps to Sargent, Vienna, 2 Dec. 1931, PRO (London), F.O. 371: 15156/C9096.

71. Starhemberg, *Between Hitler and Mussolini*, p. 72; *HS-Ztg*, 19 Dec. 1931, p. 1; Hofmann, "Pfrimer-Putsch," p. 127, who believes that Pfrimer was ready to return earlier, but on the advice of Styrian leaders waited until things quieted down.

72. See accounts of trial in *NFP*, *RP*, and *A-Z*, 15–18 Dec. 1931; *Panther*, Dec. 16, p. 1; Dec. 18, p. 2; Berger-Waldenegg, "Ungedr. Erinnerungen," pp. 17–18, who commented on Rintelen's testimony; Hofmann, "Pfrimer-Putsch," pp. 131, 137–139; Rintelen, *Erinnerungen*, pp. 148–149. The social-ists claimed that the authorities instigated the Voitsberg incident to influence the jury at Graz (*NR Protokolle*, 4/2 [Dec. 18]: 1818–28); Gulick, *Austria*, 2:969–970.

73. *Panther*, 26 Dec. 1931, pp. 3, 6–7; Hofmann, "Pfrimer-Putsch," p. 148.

74. British Minister Phipps reported a formal and unusual inquiry by Italian Minister Auriti as to the attitudes of Britain and France toward a Seipel-Heimwehr government (to Simon [confidential], Vienna, 24 Dec. 1931, PRO [London], F.O. 371: 15156/C9745).

CHAPTER 7

1. *HS-Ztg*, 16 Jan. 1932, pp. 1–2.

2. MRP no. 772, 15 Feb. 1932, AVA (Vienna), BKA; *Oesterr. VW*, Jan. 23, pp. 399–400; *A-Z*, Jan. 14, p . 4; Jan. 17, pp. 1–2; *NFP*, Jan. 12, A.M., p. 5; *RP*, Jan. 14, p. 4.

3. *Neue Zürcher Zeitung*, cited in *A-Z*, 23 Jan. 1932, p. 2; Phipps to Simon, Vienna, Jan. 26 and Feb. 8, PRO (London), F.O. 371:15888/C886 and C1255.

4. *HS in Oesterr.*, p. 254.

5. *NFP*, 18 Jan. 1932, P.M., p. 4; *HS-Ztg*, Jan. 23, p. 3; *A-Z*, Jan. 16, p. 1, citing *Frankfurter-Zeitung* on Styrian attitudes.

6. *RP*, 13 Jan. 1932, p. 1; *A-Z*, Jan. 13, p. 1; Jan. 14, pp. 1–3; Jan. 19, p. 2; Jan. 24, p. 1; *SD Jahrbuch, 1932*, pp. 9–10; Gulick, *Austria*, 2:970; Brandl, *Kaiser, Politiker, und Menschen*, pp. 438–440. Regarding this event, it is interesting to note that Goldinger, in the revision of his history of the republic published in 1962, omits a comment he included in the earlier version to the effect that Police Pres. Brandl (appointed by Starhemberg in 1930) acted on his own to prevent Winkler, his political superior, from being able to reach a compromise with the SDP ("Der gesch. Ablauf," p. 186).

7. *NFP*, 22 Jan. 1932, P.M., pp 1–2.

8. *NFP*, 22 Jan. 1932, A.M., p. 5; Jan. 23, A.M., p. 5; *HS-Ztg*, Jan. 30, p. 3; see also *HS in Oesterr.*, pp. 15, 17, which states that the unification took place in Dec. 1931, and also that 1932 was devoted to a reorganization of the HW in Vienna.

9. Akt Emil Fey, Qualifikation-Faszikel 683, Kriegsarchiv (Vienna), cited in Josef Sitzwohl, "Emil Fey," unpublished seminar paper for Prof. Jedlicka, University of Vienna, summer semester 1963, pp. 3–6.

10. Fey, *Schwertbrüder*, pp. 218–220; Charmatz, *Vom Kaiserreich zur Republik*, pp. 187–188; Attilio Renato Bleibtrau, *Unser Fey, ein Bild des Helden* (Vienna, n.d.), p. 8.

11. *NFP*, 28 Jan. 1932, P.M., p. 2; Jan. 29, A.M., p. 3; Phipps to Simon, Vienna, Feb. 8, PRO (London), F.O. 371: 15888/C1255; Schuschnigg, *Dreimal Oesterreich*, pp. 176–178.

12. *NFP*, 19 Feb. 1932, A.M., p. 6; *Panther*, Mar. 5, p. 3; *HS in Oesterr.*, p. 254.

13. *NFP*, 9 Feb. 1932, A.M., p. 4; Mar. 2, A.M., p. 4; Mar. 9, A.M., p. 5; Mar. 10, A.M., p. 5; *RP*, Mar. 1, p. 1; Mar. 2, p. 3; Mar. 3, p. 2; Mar. 8, p. 3; *A-Z*, Mar. 2, p. 3; Mar. 31, p. 3.

14. *A-Z*, 19 Mar. 1932, p. 1; Mar. 30, p. 1; Mar. 31, p. 4; Apr. 12, p. 2; *NFP*, Mar. 8, A.M., p. 5; Mar. 30, A.M., pp. 1–2; Mar. 31, A.M., p. 3; Apr. 1, A.M., p. 4; Apr. 2, A.M., p. 5; Apr. 3, A.M., p. 10; *HS-Ztg*, Apr. 9, p. 5.

15. Habicht to Hitler's office in Munich, Linz, 18 Apr. 1932, DBA (Koblenz), R 305 I; Kerekes, *Abenddämmerung*, p. 100. Starhemberg wrote nothing about his talk with Hitler in Feb.

16. Kerekes, *Abenddämmerung*, pp. 100–101; Winkler, *Diktatur*, p. 38; *NR Protokolle*, 4/2 (31 May 1932): 2189, where Hueber told the socialists that the HW was glad to be able to welcome Pabst again as a fellow worker. But Pabst told me that he did not work with the HW after he moved to Germany, even though Hueber, Starhemberg (who would not heed advice), and Fey (for whom he expressed a certain admiration) asked him to take over again. Jakoncig informed me that at this time Pabst certainly functioned as the HW chief-of-staff (letter, 8 Jan. 1964); but Hueber recalled that Pabst's activities were limited to the Tyrol (letter, 3 Mar. 1964).

17. *NFP*, 25 Apr. 1932, P.M., p. 3–6; Gulick, *Austria*, 2:972–973; and Simon, "Political Parties," p. 331.

18. See Winkler, *Diktatur*, p. 38.

19. Kerekes, *Abenddämmerung*, pp. 105–106.

20. Starhemberg, *Between Hitler and Mussolini*, pp. 77–84, and *Memoiren*, pp. 118–124.

21. Starhemberg, *Between Hitler and Mussolini*, p. 85, and *Memoiren*, p. 125.

22. *NR Protokolle*, 4/2 (28 Apr. and 3 May 1932): 2047, 2053–56, 2061–62 and 2125; *NFP*, May 6, A.M., p. 2, which foretold a Dollfuss cabinet with the HB controlling the ministry of trade.

23. *NR Protokolle*, 4/2 (10 and 12 May 1932): 2128, 2132–45; *NFP*, May 10, A.M., p. 3; May 11, A.M., p. 3; P.M., p. 1; May 12, A.M., p. 5; May 20, A.M., p. 2; Ludwig, *Oesterreichs Sendung*, p. 102; Gulick, *Austria*, 2: 973–977.

24. *NFP*, 11 May 1932, A.M., p. 3.

25. See Starhemberg, *Between Hitler and Mussolini*, pp. 86–87, and *Memoiren*, pp. 125–127. With this explanation of his policy and relations with Dollfuss, Starhemberg's first wife concurred (interview with Countess Marilies Salm-Reifferscheidt, Vienna, 27 April 1963).

26. Cited in *A-Z*, 27 May 1932, p. 3.

27. The coalition controlled 83 votes (66 CSP, 9 Landbund, 8 HB), the opposition 82 (72 SDP, 10 Pan-German). The *NFP* viewed Dollfuss's cabinet coolly and called Jakoncig, a man with no experience in economic affairs or parliamentary life, its weak link (21 May 1932, A.M., pp. 1, 3).

28. See the chapter with that title in Heinrich Busshoff, *Das Dollfuss-Regime in Oesterreich. In geistesgeschichtlicher Perspektive unter besonderer Berücksichtigung der 'Schöneren Zukunft' und 'Reichspost'* (Berlin: Duncker U. Humbolt, 1968), pp. 16–52.

29. Besides memoirs and general works already cited, the comments on Dollfuss are based on J. D. Gregory, *Dollfuss and His Times* (London: Hutchinson, 1935), pp. 151–156; Louis Rambaud, *Le Grand petit Chancelier Dollfuss, 1892–1934* (Lyon, Paris: Emmanuel Vitte, 1948), pp. 159–187; Gordon Brook-Shepherd, *Dollfuss* (London: Macmillan, 1961), pp. 86–89; and Oesterr. Akademie der Wissenschaften, *Oesterreichisches Biographisches Lexikon, 1815–1950* (Graz: H. Böhlaus Nachf., 1954–), 1:192.

30. *A-Z*, 21 May 1932, p. 1; *NR Protokolle*, 4/2 (27 and 31 May): 2154–56 and 2190–94, 2204, for vituperative socialist criticism of Jakoncig. See also Deutsch, *Weiter Weg*, pp. 184–188.

31. For a concise appraisal of the arguments concerning the "impossibility" of political conciliation and the "inevitability" of Austria's demise, see Paul R. Sweet, "Democracy and Counterrevolution in Austria," *Journal of Modern History*, 22 (Mar. 1950): 57, n. 17.

32. *NFP*, 20 May 1932, A.M., p. 2; *Panther*, May 21, p. 1; Winkler, *Diktatur*, pp. 38–39; Berger-Waldenegg, "Ungedr. Erinnerungen," pp. 20–21.

33. *Zu uns!* early Apr. 1932, p. 2, which called for "Father Pfrimer" to take over the leadership, along with Heger in Vienna, of a Nazi-oriented HS; *HS-Ztg*, May 21, p. 3; Rintelen, *Erinnerungen*, p. 153; *A-Z*, May 26, p. 2, which quoted an exchange of brief telegrams between Pfrimer and Hitler; memorandum by Röhm, Frankfurt, May 21, DBA (Koblenz), *National-Sozialistische-Sammlung*, NS 26/Vorl. 640, which informed party notables that militarily Pfrimer's group would form the German *Jägerkorps*, with its commander appointed by Hitler at Pfrimer's suggestion and with Count Lamberg representing the Austrians on Röhm's staff, which would in turn have an attaché in Austria.

34. *Panther*, 21 May 1932, p. 1, June 4, p. 4. Pauley, "Hahnenschwanz," pp. 208–210, 214, for sketch of Kammerhofer and his impossible "tightrope walk," and for comments on the "Twelve Principles." These are quoted and interpreted also in *Oesterr. HS-Jahrbuch*, pp. 44–49, which interpretation is translated in Pauley, pp. 329–334.

35. Kerekes, *Abenddämmerung*, pp. 106–107; Starhemberg, *Between Hitler and Mussolini*, pp. 89–94, and *Memoiren*, pp. 129–131.

36. Kerekes, *Abenddämmerung*, pp. 108–109.

37. Von Klemperer, *Ignaz Seipel*, pp. 423–425.

38. Kerekes, *Abenddämmerung*, p. 111.

39. *NFP*, 29 July 1932, A.M., p. 1; July 30, A.M., pp. 1, 4, the editorial of which grudgingly acknowledged Starhemberg's achievement; P.M., p. 1; Aug. 2, A.M., p. 5. According to the hostile *Zu uns!* July 1932, pp. 3–4, Starhemberg threatened to use undated resignations he got from all the deputies except Lengauer in Dec. 1930.

40. *NR Protokolle*, 4/2 (2 Aug. 1932): 2481–84. One of the HB delegates, ill, had to be carried into the chamber (*NFP*, Aug. 3, A.M., p. 5); see also *A-Z*, July 29, p. 3; and Gulick, *Austria*, 2:980–985.

41. *A-Z*, 6 Aug. 1932, p. 4; *NFP*, Aug. 6, A.M., p. 2; Aug. 8, P.M., p. 2.

42. *NFP*, 16 Aug. 1932, P.M., p. 2; *NR Protokolle*, 4/2 (Aug. 17): 2524–28; *A-Z*, Aug. 18, p. 1; *RP*, Aug. 20, p. 5; and Gulick, *Austria*, 2:985–986.

43. *BR Protokolle*, 4 (19 Aug. 1932): 1905; *NR Protokolle*, 4/2 (Aug. 18 and 23): 2565–77, 2595–2603, 2615–18, for passage of measures creating a limited voluntary labor service and altering but not abolishing the law of entail, and 2639–40, for final passage of loan treaty. See also Gulick, *Austria*, 2:986–987.

44. *NFP*, 4 Sept. 1932, A.M., p. 7; also *A-Z*, Sept. 2, p. 2; Winkler, *Diktatur*, p. 39; Rokitansky in *Unsere Zukunft*, Oct. 25, p. 5.

45. *NFP*, 11 Sept. 1932, A.M., p. 8; also *A-Z*, Sept. 7 and 8, both p. 1.

46. *NFP*, 27 Sept 1932, A.M., p. 2; P.M., p. 1; Sept. 28, A.M., p. 4; Sept. 29, A.M., p. 3; Oct. 2, A.M., p. 8; *A-Z*, Sept. 14, p. 3; Sept. 27, p. 1.

47. In fact, Dollfuss had on Oct. 1 issued a decree based on the war economy enabling act of 1917. See Gulick, *Austria*, 2:997–998.

48. Memorandum by Bülow (secret), Berlin, 12 Oct. 1932, *RGFO*, T–120, 6079H/E450793–794; Neurath to chargé d'affaires in Vienna legation, Berlin, Oct. 14, *RGFO*, T–120, 6079H/E450800–803. See also Winkler, *Diktatur*, p. 22; Brook-Shepherd, *Dollfuss*, p. 96.

49. Langoth, *Kampf*, pp. 88–89.

50. *NFP*, 16 Oct. 1932, A.M., p. 10; *Oesterr. HS-Ztg*, Oct. 22, pp. 1–4.

51. *NFP*, 17 Oct. 1932, P.M., pp. 3–4; *RP*, Oct. 17, p. 4; Rieth to F.O., Vienna, Oct. 25, *RGFO*, T–120, 6079H/E450804–814.

52. See Gulick, *Austria*, 2:999; also *NFP*, 17 Oct. 1932, P.M., pp. 1–3.

53. Winkler claimed that Dollfuss also agreed to let him, as vice-chancellor, be the deputy security director, thus outranking Fey (*Diktatur*, p. 22).

54. *NFP*, 18 Oct. 1932, A.M., p. 2; *A-Z*, Oct. 18, pp. 1–2, and Oct. 19, p. 1, especially the editorials. Starhemberg later called his recommendation of Fey the "gravest mistake" of his political career, as if his decision alone settled the matter; he claimed that at the time he felt Fey preferable to another provincial leader, probably Hueber or Alberti, who wanted the post and who was in touch with the Nazis (*Between Hitler and Mussolini*, pp. 98–99, and *Memoiren*, pp. 134–135).

55. Rieth to F.O., Vienna, 25 Oct. 1932, *RGFO*, T–120, 6079H/E450804. Dollfuss had offered the socialists places in the cabinet again during the Lausanne debate (see Goldinger, "Der gesch. Ablauf," p. 195).

56. Gulick, *Austria*, 2:1003–06.

57. *NR Protokolle*, 4/3 (20 Oct. 1932): 2644, 2654–71; also Gulick, *Austria*, 2:1000–02.

58. *NR Protokolle*, 4/3 (21 Oct. 1932): 2676–77, 2696–97; *NFP*, Oct. 22, A.M., p. 4; Gedye, *Betrayal*, p. 54.

59. *NFP*, 21 Oct. 1932, P.M., p. 2; *NR Protokolle*, 4/3 (Nov. 24): 2779–85; (Nov. 29): 2788; (Nov. 30): 2808.

60. *A-Z*, 2 Dec. 1932, pp. 1–2; Dec. 7, p. 1; *SD Jahrbuch, 1932*, pp. 34–35.

61. *A-Z*, 24 Feb. 1933, p. 1; also *NR Protokolle*, 4/3 (Feb. 24): 3339–42.

62. See Gulick, *Austria*, 2:1008–13; Gedye, *Betrayal*, pp. 65–67; Goldinger, "Der gesch. Ablauf," p. 198.

63. Starhemberg, *Between Hitler and Mussolini*, p. 107, and *Memoiren*, p. 142; Kerekes, *Abenddämmerung*, pp. 125, 188; also Brook-Shepherd, *Dollfuss*, p. 97, who states without noting sources that the weapons were eventually used to reequip the Austrian army. On 10 Aug. 1933, Rieth reported from Vienna to the F.M. (strictly secret) that Mandl got Fey's as-

sistance in getting a shipment of weapons to Hungary past security officials in the Burgenland. (*RGFO*, T–120, 6057H/E446928–929).

CHAPTER 8

1. Konrad Heiden, *Adolf Hitler, Eine Biographie* (2 vols.; Zurich: 1937), 2:10. See also Gerhard L. Weinberg, *The Foreign Policy of Hitler's Germany: Diplomatic Revolution in Europe, 1933–1936* (Chicago: Univ. of Chicago Press, 1971), pp. 3, 18, 87–90.

2. Paul Seabury, *The Wilhelmstrasse: A Study of German Diplomats Under the Nazi Regime* (Berkeley: Univ. of California Press, 1954), p. 25; Gordon Craig, "The German Foreign Office from Neurath to Ribbentrop," in *The Diplomats, 1919–1939*, ed. by Gordon A. Craig and Felix Gilbert (Princeton, N.J.: Princeton University Press, 1953), pp. 418–419; but see Dieter Ross, *Hitler und Dollfuss: Die deutsche Oesterreich-Politik, 1933–1934* (Hamburg: Leibniz-Verlag, 1966), pp. 247ff.

3. Kerekes, *Abenddämmerung*, pp. 130–131, 135.

4. When in mid-Jan. 1933 the agency's HW specialist sought financial support from the F.M., he was told that assistance to the pro-*Anschluss* wing of the HW would be dangerous interference in Austrian affairs (memoranda by Hüffer [secret, for Köpke], Berlin, 21 Jan. and 17 Feb. 1933, PADAA (Bonn), 5 Oe A [*Geheim*]).

5. Kerekes, *Abenddämmerung*, p. 131; memorandum by Köpke, Berlin, 15 Mar. 1933, in U.S., Dept. of State, *Documents on German Foreign Policy, 1918–1945* [*DGFP*], series C: *The Third Reich: First Phase, 1933–1937* (5 vols.; Washington: Government Printing Office, 1957–66), 1:170, no. 89; memorandum by Köpke, Berlin, Mar. 23, *DGFP*, 1:207, no. 112; Neurath to Hassell [Rome], Berlin, Mar. 27, *DGFP*, 1:235, no. 128.

6. Rambaud, *Le Grand petit Chancelier*, p. 55.

7. *NR Protokolle*, 4/2 (21 May 1932): 2148; Erwin Wasserbäck to Theodor Hornbostel (secret), Paris, 22 Jan. 1934, cited in Lajos Kerekes, "Neuer Aktenfund zu den Beziehungen zwischen Hitler und Dollfuss im Jahre 1933," *Acta Historica*, 18/1–2 (1972): 152–154. See also Kurt Schuschnigg, *Im Kampf gegen Hitler: Die Ueberwindung der Anschlussidee* (Vienna, Munich, Zurich: Fritz Molden, 1969), p. 144.

8. Memorandum by Hüffer (secret), Berlin, 17 Feb. 1933, PADAA (Bonn), II: 5 Oe A (*Geheim*); memorandum by H[üffer], Berlin, 2 Mar. 1933, PADAA (Bonn), II: 5 Oe A (*Heimwehr-Organisation in Oesterreich*), vol. 1, recording Pabst's report that Habicht again refused to consider a truce.

9. Langoth alleges that Fey was in touch with Pabst (*Kampf*, p. 112); and Winkler states that Fey wanted to make Steidle a state secretary in the ministry of justice (*Diktatur*, p. 66).

10. *NFP*, 10 Mar. 1933, A.M., p. 5; *RP*, Mar. 12, p. 4; Berger-Waldenegg, "Ungedr. Erinnerungen," pp. 20–21, 321–322. See also series of regular re-

ports on HW activities in Styria in 1933 in AVA (Vienna), BKA, G.D.–1 and G.D.–2 (examples: Landesgendarmeriekommando für Steiermark to BKA, G.D.–1, Graz, May 16, no. 160.848/33; June 22, no. 177.530/33; Dec. 18, no. 253.618/33).

11. *NFP*, 21 Feb. 1933, A.M., p. 3; *Oesterr. HS-Ztg*, Feb. 25, pp. 1–2; Kerekes, *Abenddämmerung*, pp. 129–130.

12. *NR Protokolle*, 4/3 (4 Mar. 1933): 3388–93; Gulick, *Austria*, 2:1018–23.

13. Kerekes reveals that in the spring of 1933 Gömbös worked out for Dollfuss "a tactical plan for liquidating the organizations of the Left and for creating the institutions of a political system of the Right," what he called a "cold putsch" ("Akten," p. 359; *Abenddämmerung*, p. 135).

14. *NFP*, 8 Mar. 1933, A.M., pp. 3–4. For a discussion of the constitutionality of the emergency law and the decrees, see Gulick, *Austria*, 2:997–998, 1027–30; Anton Staudinger, "Die Mitwirkung der christlich-sozialen Partei an der Errichtung des autoritären Ständestaates," in *Oesterreich 1927 bis 1938: Protokoll des Symposiums in Wien 23. bis 28. Oktober 1972*, ed. by Ludwig Jedlicka and Rudolf Neck (Munich: R. Oldenbourg, 1973), pp. 68–70, 87–88, 130.

15. Gulick, *Austria*, 2:1033–37; Goldinger, "Der gesch. Ablauf," p. 201.

16. *NFP*, 16 Mar. 1933, A.M., p. 4.

17. *NFP*, 16 Mar. 1933, A.M., p. 6; P.M., p. 2; Mar. 17, A.M., p. 5; *A-Z*, Mar. 15, p. 5; Mar. 17, p. 3; *RP*, Mar. 16, p. 2; MRP no. 859, Mar. 17, AVA (Vienna), BKA; Goldinger, "Der gesch. Ablauf," pp. 201–202; Gedye, *Betrayal*, pp. 76–77; Stockton to sec. of state, Vienna, Mar. 22, USNA (Washington), State Dept., 863.00/771; also Kerekes, *Abenddämmerung*, p. 134.

18. *NFP*, 16 Mar. 1933, A.M., p. 5; P.M., p. 2; Mar. 17, A.M., p. 4. Anton Mörl, then security chief at Schwaz, noted in his diary on Mar. 16 that after the dissolution of the SB in Tyrol there was widespread anxiety in the Ziller Valley that the socialists would begin an arson campaign (*Erinnerungen aus bewegter Zeit Tirols, 1932–1945* [Innsbruck: Wagner, 1955], p. 11).

19. *Linzer Volksblatt*, 17 Mar. 1933, p. 1; Mar. 18, p. 1; *A-Z*, Mar. 17, p. 3; *NFP*, Mar. 21, A.M., p. 6.

20. Langoth, *Kampf*, pp. 94–96, 102–104.

21. So charged the Social Democrats in the Bundesrat (*BR Protokolle*, 4 [March 21, 1933]: 2059–60).

22. Steidle to Dollfuss (unsigned carbon copy sent to Rintelen), Innsbruck, 30 Mar. 1933, Styrian Landesarchiv (Graz), LH Korr[espondenz], P-H 42/1933.

23. *NFP*, 27 Mar. 1933, P.M., p. 3; Mar. 31, P.M., p. 1; Apr. 1, A.M., pp. 1, 4, which estimated the SB had 60,000 members, of whom 10,000 were in Vienna; P.M., p. 1.

24. Besides the minutes of cabinet debates themselves, see the treatment by Anton Staudinger, "Bemühungen Carl Vaugoins um Suprematie der

christlichsozialen Partei in Oesterreich (1930–1933)," (Ph.D. diss., Univ. of Vienna, 1969), pp. 163–184.

25. Jedlicka, *Heer*, pp. 96–97, 101–102, 106–108; MRP no. 866, 10 Apr. 1933, AVA (Vienna), BKA; *NFP*, Apr. 10, P.M., p. 1; Apr. 19, A.M., p. 4; *A-Z*, Apr. 2, p. 1; Apr. 10, p. 1; Apr. 13, pp. 1–2; Gulick, *Austria*, 2:1050.

26. The succession of auxiliary recruitments creates some confusion. In some provinces the HW was used as *Hilfspolizei* [Hipos] for some time before the recruitment of federal auxiliary forces began in the summer of 1933. Final permission for the army's short-term military assistance corps was not given by the Allies until late summer and enrollment did not begin until Nov. 1933.

27. Gulick, *Austria*, 2:1060–65.

28. *NFP*, 19 Apr. 1933, A.M., p. 3; *A-Z*, Apr. 23, p. 5; *Panther*, Apr. 29, p. 1; Pauley, "Hahnenschwanz," pp. 236, 239–243; *HS in Oesterr.*, pp. 129–130; Rintelen, *Erinnerungen*, pp. 153–155, reproducing the agreement verbatim; Rühle, *Das Grossdeutsche Reich*, pp. 170–171; report by Baer, Vienna, May 5, USNA (Washington), War Dept., MID, RG–165: 2657–FF–160/3.

29. The Nazis won 9 of the contested 20 seats (one-half the council), mostly at the expense of the Pan-Germans and to some extent at that of the SDP.

30. *NFP*, 4 May 1933, P.M., p. 1; May 5, A.M., pp. 1, 4. Later the ban on elections was extended to 31 Mar. 1934.

31. *A-Z*, 14 Apr. 1933, p. 1; Apr. 23, pp. 1–2, 5; *NFP*, Apr. 22, A.M., p. 5; Apr. 23, A.M., p. 6; Starhemberg, *Between Hitler and Mussolini*, p. 109, and *Memoiren*, pp. 149–150; Rokitansky, "Kampf um den nationalen Kurs in der Heimwehr," *Unsere Zukunft*, Apr. 25, pp. 2–3; reports by Lt. Col. F. N. MacFarlane, Vienna, Apr. 28 and 29, in Phipps to Sargent, Vienna, May 1, PRO (London), F.O. 371: 16637/C4140; Winkler, *Diktatur*, pp. 54–55; Langoth, *Kampf*, pp. 111–112.

32. *NFP*, 11 May 1933, A.M., pp. 1, 4. Only a week earlier Jakoncig had become the head of the HW's economic and corporative bureau (*NFP*, May 5, P.M., p. 3). Jakoncig contends that he gave notice in Mar. 1933 that he intended to withdraw from politics because he could no longer support the dictatorial policies of the CSP and that after he left the cabinet he severed all ties with the HW (letters to me, Innsbruck, 3 May 1963 and 8 Jan. 1964); see also *NFP*, May 11, P.M., p. 2.

33. Starhemberg, *Between Hitler and Mussolini*, pp. 102–110, and *Memoiren*, pp. 150–151. On 23 Dec. 1932, the British chargé d'affaires in Vienna reported that Italy had agreed to give the HW 2 million schillings in installments through Minister Auriti (Hadow to Sargent, PRO [London], F.O. 371: 15986/C10897). On Apr. 28 Mandl predicted that at least 35,000 HW members would take part in the convocation (see reports by MacFarlane cited in n. 31 above).

34. *RP*, 13 May 1933, p. 4; *NFP*, May 14, A.M., p. 8, about authorization.

35. Starhemberg, *Between Hitler and Mussolini*, p. 109, and *Memoiren*, pp. 151–152; *NFP*, 15 May 1933, P.M., pp. 2–4; *RP*, May 15, pp. 1–3; *Oesterr. HS-Ztg*, May 20, pp. 2–4; Charmatz, *Vom Kaiserreich*, p. 191.

36. *Panther*, 20 May 1933, pp. 3–4; Pauley, "Hahnenschwanz," pp. 242–243, reporting that 6,800 Styrians participated in the rally on May 14.

37. Rieth to F.M., Vienna, 19 May 1933, PADAA (Bonn), II: 5 Oe A (*HW-Org*), vol. 1.

38. Concerning the origins of the Fatherland Front, see Brook-Shepherd, *Dollfuss*, pp. 103–109; Schuschnigg, *Dreimal Oesterreich*, pp. 221–226; Zernatto, *Wahrheit*, pp. 79–98; Gulick, *Austria*, 2:1065–68; Langoth, *Kampf*, pp. 220–221; Irmgard Bärnthaler, *Die Vaterländische Front: Geschichte und Organisation* (Vienna, Frankfurt, Zurich: Europa, 1971).

39. For Frank's visit, see Austria, Bundeskommissariat für Heimatdienst, *Beiträge zur Vorgeschichte und Geschichte der Julirevolte: herausgegeben auf Grund Amtlicher Quellen* (Vienna, 1934), pp. 20–22 [hereafter cited as *Julirevolte*]; Gedye, *Betrayal*, pp. 70–71; and daily newspapers.

40. Most information about these negotiations comes from memoirists (Schuschnigg, Rintelen, Winkler, and Langoth), and all are vague about the timing. See also Gulick, *Austria*, 2:1082–84; Goldinger, "Der gesch. Ablauf," pp. 202–203; Ross, *Hitler und Dollfuss*, pp. 34–35, 265–266, n. 70, citing a news release on May 5 reporting that Habicht had seen Dollfuss personally (*Neuigkeitsweltblatt*); Rühle, *Das Grossdeutsche Reich*, p. 175, giving specific dates for talks between Habicht and Dollfuss in Rintelen's office: May 14 through May 21.

41. *Julirevolte*, pp. 5ff.; *NFP*, 11 June 1933, A.M., p. 8; June 14, A.M., p. 1; *RP*, June 12, p. 5; Langoth, *Kampf*, pp. 102–105, suggesting that Fey's desire to be rid of him was one reason for this edict.

42. *Julirevolte*, pp. 23–25.

43. *NFP*, 20 June 1933, P.M., pp. 1–2; June 21, A.M., p. 3, which announced the prohibition of the Styrian HS as of the 20th. The *Panther* appeared for the last time on July 22. See Winkler, *Diktatur*, p. 67; Gulick, *Austria*, 2:1086–87. Another result of the dissolution was the withdrawal of Franz Hueber from the HW. Starhemberg was elected to succeed Hueber as the leader of the Sbg. HW, but delegated the chores to Capt. Ernst Reichl (*NFP*, June 28, P.M., p. 1; *Oesterr. HS-Ztg*, July 8, p. 1).

44. *New York Times* [*NYT*], 13 June 1933, p. 6; June 14, p. 1; June 15, p. 9; June 16, p. 1; June 17, pp. 6, 12; *Times* (London), June 15, p. 15.

45. *Julirevolte*, pp. 29–39. The *Times*, Aug. 15, p. 9, reproducing part of a leaflet dropped over Austria; and Aug. 22, p. 10, providing translations. See also Gulick, *Austria*, 2:1099–1104.

46. At least so the German F.M. was led to understand by reports on the Austrian Nazis; see memorandum by H[üffer], Berlin, 12 Sept 1933, PADAA (Bonn), II: 11/3 Oe (*Akten betreffend Personalien österreichischer Staatsmänner*), vol. 2 (6 May 1931–26 Feb. 1936).

47. *NFP*, 1 July 1933, A.M., p. 6; July 2, A.M., p. 7; *RP*, July 1, p. 1;

Winkler, *Diktatur,* pp. 67–68; Gulick, *Austria,* 2:1113–14. In a top secret report on Aug. 16 the German military attaché, Gen. Muff, commented on Vaugoin's efforts to "cleanse" the army of its pro-Nazi members, who he thought at one time amounted to 20%, compared to the 40% to 60% claimed by Nazi politicians (*RGFO,* T–120, 5705H/E414170–184); see also Jedlicka, *Heer,* pp. 93–94.

48. *NFP,* 22 July 1933, A.M., pp. 1–2; July 23, A.M., pp. 5–6; July 24, P.M., p. 4; Aug. 16, A.M., p. 4; *RP,* Aug. 17, p. 1; Langoth, *Kampf,* p. 110.

49. See *Nachrichtenblatt des Bundesführers des österreichischen Heimatschutzes* (Vienna, 1933), pp. 10–12, quoting Starhemberg on June 24; also *Oesterr. HS-Ztg,* 15 July 1933, p. 1.

50. Langoth, *Kampf,* p. 108, reporting on conversation with Winkler.

51. Starhemberg, *Between Hitler and Mussolini,* p. 111, and *Memoiren,* p. 151. See also *NFP,* 26 Jan. 1933, P.M., pp. 3–4, and Rieth to F.M., Vienna, June 26, PADAA (Bonn), II: 5 Oe A (*HW-Org*), vol. 1, for reports on speech by Starhemberg.

52. See *RP,* 11 Aug. 1933, p. 4; Aug 12, p. 2; *NFP,* Aug. 11, P.M., p. 1, which papers also reported a foiled plot on Starhemberg's life.

53. See especially the letter from Mussolini to Dollfuss on July 1, that from Dollfuss to Mussolini on July 22; the note given to Dollfuss at Riccione and the brief memorandum Dollfuss made on the conference; and the report to Dollfuss on Richard Schüller's conversation with Mussolini on Sept. 15—all in *Geheimer Briefwechsel Mussolini-Dollfuss* (Vienna: Volksbuchhandlung, 1947), pp. 16–43 *passim* [translated by Paul R. Sweet, "Mussolini and Dollfuss," and appended to Braunthal, *Tragedy,* pp. 184–199]. See also Jürgen Gehl, *Austria, Germany and the Anschluss, 1931–1938* (London: Oxford Univ. Press, 1963), pp. 50–52, 64–70.

54. Langen [German consul] to F.M., Linz, 31 Aug. 1933, PADAA (Bonn), II: 5 Oe A (*HW-Org*), vol. 1. Langen was specific: the HW would receive the ministries of foreign affairs (Starhemberg), culture (Alberti), and justice (Steidle); and Fey would leave the cabinet.

55. Starhemberg, *Between Hitler and Mussolini,* pp. 113–114; *RP,* 31 Aug. 1933, p. 4; Sept. 1, p. 3; Sept. 2, p. 3; *NFP,* Sept. 7, A.M., p. 4; Sept. 8, A.M., p. 4; *A-Z,* Sept. 8, p. 1; Sept. 9, p. 2; letter, Mussolini to Dollfuss, Sept. 9, in *Geheimer Briefwechsel,* pp. 37–38.

56. *NFP,* 29 Aug. 1933, A.M., pp. 1, 4. See also Jedlicka, *Heer,* pp. 101–102, 110; Gulick, *Austria,* 2:1122–23, 1126–27. This new force was technically open to socialists; and Vaugoin demonstratively met with moderate socialist leaders in Salzburg in mid-Sept., a step that probably hastened his fall.

57. The National Estates Front [NEF] was the midsummer creation of Vice-Chan. Winkler (Landbund), who hoped thus to draw the illegal Nazis to his support.

58. See especially diary entries for Sept. 7 and 12 and translation into German from a letter from a distinguished foreigner [Pesez] for Chan. Dollfuss,

Vienna, 12 Sept. 1933, Staatsarchiv (Vienna), *Schmitz-Nachlass*, unnumbered carton (diary) and carton 14 (letter).

59. *RP*, 12 Sept. 1933, pp. 1–3. Schmitz took credit for the emphasis on the encyclical; see his diary entry for Sept. 12.

60. Quoted from *RP*, 13 Sept. 1933, p. 5; Winkler, *Diktatur*, p. 69. See also Baron [Pompeo] Aloisi, *Journal (25 Juillet 1932 to 14 Juin 1936)*, trans. from Italian into French by Maurice Vaussard (Paris: Librairie Plon [1957]), entry of Sept. 16, p. 145, recording a long conversation with Minister Preziosi, who wanted Mussolini to regulate the dispute between Dollfuss and Starhemberg, "which is certainly of capital importance."

61. *RP*, 18 Sept. 1933, pp. 1–3; Sept. 19, p. 4, which omitted some of Starhemberg's more belligerent statements, especially about Winkler; *A-Z*, Sept. 18, p. 1; Sept. 19, p. 1; *NFP*, Sept. 18, P.M., pp. 3–4; Sept. 19, A.M., p. 5; Winkler, *Diktatur*, pp. 70–74; Gulick, *Austria*, 2:1114–19.

62. Winkler, *Diktatur*, pp. 76–78; Langoth, *Kampf*, p. 116, stating that Bachinger told him the contents of an agreement between Dollfuss and Winkler signed on Sept. 23.

63. *NFP*, 21 Sept. 1933, P.M., pp. 1–2; *RP*, Sept. 22, p. 1; Gulick, *Austria*, 2:1122–25; report by Muff, Vienna, Nov. 2, RGFO, T–120, 5705H/E414215–222, saying that Schönburg had a strong dislike for Fey, if not always the political acumen to thwart him; Schmitz diary entry of Sept. 12 (as cited in n. 58 above), noting that Dollfuss said that Starhemberg approved of Schmitz's entry into the cabinet but still wanted Steidle given a post in the near future.

64. *A-Z*, 22 Sept. 1933, p. 2; *RP*, Sept. 22, p. 3; Sept. 23, p. 1; Sept. 28, p. 3; *NFP*, Sept. 22, A.M., p. 4; Sept. 28, A.M., p. 3.

65. This concentration camp decree "of the federal chancellor," who was in Geneva, was signed by Fey alone on Sept. 23 (*NFP*, 22 Sept. 1933, P.M., p. 2; Sept. 24, A.M., p. 7; *RP*, Sept. 25, p. 2).

66. Rieth thought that Mussolini had stopped HW subsidies just before Starhemberg's trip to Rome in Sept., as once previously when the government seemed to go too slowly in making Austria fascist (report to F.M., Vienna, 23 Oct. 1933, PADAA [Bonn], II: 5 Oe A [*HW-Org*], vol. 1). Interestingly Stürgkh told Col. MacFarlane that there appeared to be a "considerable gap between Italian promises and Italian cash" (report of Sept. 30 in Selby to Sargent, Vienna, Oct. 3, PRO [London], F.O. 371: 16638/C8788). Starhemberg's HW apparently did need money. On Nov. 7 a "sort of aide de camp of Starhemberg" requested in a letter to a banker friend in London a subsidy of "at least several hundred thousand schillings," perhaps from Jewish circles. The writer stated that neither Starhemberg nor Fey knew about his approach; "but the matter is of so great interest to the whole world that it can only be put off by a matter of weeks" (excerpts of letter from Rowe Dutton [treasury] to O'Malley [F.O.] [very confidential], London, Nov. 16, PRO [London], F.O. 371: 16639/C10097). Apparently the

HW also sought aid from Sir Oswald Mosley (memorandum by E. H. Carr, London, 3 Jan. 1934, PRO [London], F.O. 371: 18344/R375).

67. These negotiations are very well documented, if without adequate detail in some regards. The most immediate source is Langoth, *Kampf*, pp. 120–163, whose memoranda are verified and in some cases supplemented by several documents in the first and second volumes in series C of *DGFP*. See also Ross, *Hitler und Dollfuss*, pp. 90–125; and Gehl, *Austria and Anschluss*, pp. 69–77.

68. Memorandum by Bülow-Schwante, Berlin, 29 Sept. 1933, PADAA (Bonn), Büro RM 16 (*Akten betreffend Oesterreich*), vol. 12 (9 Aug.–30 Sept. 1933); memorandum by Heeren, Berlin, Sept. 30, ibid.; telegram, Erbach to F.M., Vienna, Oct. 3, ibid., vol. 13 (3 Oct. 1933–30 Apr. 1934).

69. Langoth, *Kampf*, pp. 120–122, recording a conversation with Habicht, 27 Sept. 1933. As emissaries Fey sent his deputy Fritz Lahr, a Bulgarian fascist leader, and a district HW leader in L.A.

70. *Völkischer Beobachter* (Munich), 11 Sept. 1933, p. 1; Dodd to sec. of state, Berlin, Sept. 13, U.S., Dept. of State, *Foreign Relations of the United States [FRUS]: Diplomatic Papers, 1933* (5 vols.; Washington: Government Printing Office, 1950), 1:444–445.

71. *Julirevolte*, p. 46; Dodd to sec. of state, Berlin, 30 Sept. 1933, *FRUS*, 1:446–447; memoranda of F.M. secretariat [Geneva], Sept. 26 and 28, *DGFP*, C, 1:840–841, no. 450. For evidence that Mussolini wanted to bring about an Austro-German rapprochement see Kerekes, "Akten," pp. 360–361; also Ross, *Hitler und Dollfuss*, pp. 92, 280–281, nn. 7–10.

72. Langoth, *Kampf*, pp. 134–135 (notes on conversation with Habicht, Munich, 20 Oct. 1933); memorandum by Hüffer (secret), Berlin, Oct. 13, *DGFP*, C, 1:919–920, no. 497.

73. Langoth, *Kampf*, pp. 126–130, 135–139, 140–151; memoranda by Hüffer (secret), Berlin, 21 and 30 Oct., 8 and 16 Nov. 1933, *DGFP*, C, 2: 33–34, 54–56, 87, 130–132, nos. 20, 35, 49, 71; memorandum by Bülow-Schwante, Berlin, Oct. 30, PADAA (Bonn), Büro RM 16, vol. 13; Winkler, *Diktatur*, p. 86; Schuschnigg, *Dreimal Oesterreich*, pp. 242–245; report by Hornbostel of talks in Berlin with Hess, Bormann, Kanzler and others, Nov. 30 and Dec. 1, in Kerekes, "Neuer Aktenfund," pp. 154–159.

74. *NFP*, 12 Oct. 1933, P.M., p. 1; *RP*, Oct. 13, p. 3; report by Lt. Col. Shallenberger, Vienna, Oct. 24, USNA (Washington), War Dept., MID, RG–165: 2657–FF–141/16; *Heimatschützer*, Nov. 18, p. 3, reporting Starhemberg's long speech at Graz on Nov. 11.

75. See Gulick, *Austria*, 2:1193–94, 1200ff. for extensive documentation; Selby to Simon (confidential), Vienna, 28 Nov. 1933, PRO (London), F.O. 371: 16639/C10547; *NFP*, Nov. 14, P.M., p. 3; Nov. 15, A.M., p. 4; Nov. 19, A.M., p. 6. See also Winkler, *Diktatur*, pp. 83–84; Deutsch, *Weiter Weg*, pp. 187–188; Langoth, *Kampf*, p. 150.

76. *NFP*, 4 Nov. 1933, A.M., pp. 1–2, 5. On Dec. 22 Steidle resigned as

security director of the Tyrol (*NFP*, Dec. 23, P.M., p. 3), and was succeeded
by Anton Mörl, who felt that his preferment was due to his anti-Nazi attitude, but noted that his relations with the HW were soon very tense (*Erinnerungen*, pp. 19–23).

77. Habicht to Hüffer, Munich, 6 Dec. 1933, in memorandum by Hüffer,
Berlin, Dec. 7, *DGFP*, C, 2:188, no. 106; Rieth to F.M. (telegram), Vienna,
Dec. 12, ibid., pp. 214–215, no. 124.

78. *NFP*, 16 Dec. 1933, P.M., p. 3; Dec. 17, A.M., p. 8; Dec. 18, Mon.,
p. 3, reporting Steidle's comments that he had seldom seen such unity among
his colleagues; *RP*, Dec. 17, pp. 3, 7. Dollfuss accepted the leadership of
the Sturmscharen on 10 Jan. 1934, but Schuschnigg remained acting leader
(*NFP*, Jan. 11, A.M., p. 4).

79. Rieth to Bülow, Vienna, 21 Dec. 1933, *DGFP*, C, 2:263–268, no. 143;
Julirevolte, p. 49. Informal reports also reached the British Foreign Office
about Rintelen's scheming; see memorandum by Carr, London, 3 Jan. 1934,
PRO (London), F.O. 371: 18344/R375.

80. Memorandum by Hüffer, Berlin, 30 Dec. 1933, *DGFP*, C, 2:289–291,
no. 156; memorandum by Neurath, Berlin, 1 Jan. 1934, ibid., p. 295, no.
160.

81. Starhemberg, *Between Hitler and Mussolini*, pp. 115–117, and *Me-
moiren*, pp. 154–157, claiming that he forced Dollfuss to back down. Eduard
Ludwig told me that the anti-Nazi Italian press attaché and liaison between
Mussolini and the HW, Eugenio Morreale, informed Starhemberg of Dollfuss's plans (interview, Vienna, 1 Aug. 1963); also Ludwig, *Oesterreichs
Sendung*, p. 126. Revertera told me that Morreale, Starhemberg, and Fey
cooperated, that they alerted the Viennese HW and were prepared to turn
Habicht back even against the will of Dollfuss (interview, Helfenberg, U.A.,
22–23 July 1963). The consensus of published accounts supports the view
that Starhemberg led the opposition and that Fey backed him: see especially
Winkler, *Diktatur*, p. 87; Ross, *Hitler und Dollfuss*, pp. 140–150; Gulick,
Austria, 2:1233–39; Ulrich Eichstädt, *Von Dollfuss zu Hitler: Geschichte des
Anschlusses Oesterreichs, 1933–1938* (Wiesbaden: F. Steiner, 1955), pp. 38–
39, 453/n. 106; Observator [Mikhailo Lozynskyi], *Die Tragödie Oesterreichs, mit 54 dokumentarischen Illustrationen* (Geneva, 1934), pp. 126–
128. Brook-Shepherd, *Dollfuss*, pp. 215–216, 287/n. 23, gives a careless and
confusing account: he wrote that the "*Heimwehr* Vice-Chancellor . . . argued
convincingly," but his context suggests he meant Starhemberg, not Vice-
Chan. Fey. However, both Jedlicka, *Heer*, p. 111, and Kerekes, *Abenddämmerung*, p. 174, suggest without citations that Fey was the chief HW actor.

82. Memorandum by Renthe-Fink, Berlin, 8 Jan. 1934, *DGFP*, C, 2:309–
311, no. 216. The official Austrian viewpoint is defined in *Julirevolte*, pp.
51–52. But Winkler, *Diktatur*, p. 87, contends that it was understood that a
"truce" would begin only after an agreement was reached. See also Langoth,
Kampf, pp. 73, 163.

83. *NFP*, 10 Jan. 1934, A.M., p. 4; Jan. 11, A.M., p. 4; Jan. 12, A.M., pp. 1, 4; *RP*, Jan. 9, p. 1; Jan. 13, p. 1; *A-Z*, Jan. 10, p. 2.

84. In a letter to me (Graz. 27 Sept. 1965), K. M. Stepan asserted that Starhemberg did push Fey's promotion, since Starhemberg himself had no desire for an office entailing responsibility and work, and that he and Fey really parted ways only after Feb. 1934. *RP* editor Funder thought Fey was given the office in the face of evidence of plans by radical socialists for a a showdown (*Als Oesterreich*, pp. 82–84).

85. Memorandum by Renthe-Fink, Berlin, 9 Jan. 1934, *DGFP*, C, 2: 312/n. 3, no. 167; Erbach to F.M., Vienna, Jan. 12, ibid., p. 347, no. 179; *Julirevolte*, p. 52.

86. *NFP*, 17 Jan. 1934, A.M., p. 4; Jan. 18, P.M., p. 3; *Heimatschützer*, Jan. 20, p. 1. Rühle, *Das Grossdeutsche Reich*, p. 348, reproducing a photocopy of a note allegedly in Alberti's handwriting dated Jan. 16, which Winkler, *Diktatur*, p. 140, also quotes. Berger-Waldenegg, "Ungedr. Erinnerungen," pp. 327–328, saying that at the turn of the year Starhemberg, with Dollfuss's consent, ordered Revertera and him to confer with Austrian Nazis, but that nothing came of the talks.

87. Appeal of Alberti to HS of L.A. (mimeographed typescript), 17 Jan. 1934, Styrian Landesarchiv, Graz, LH Korr[espondenz], P-H2/1934. Winkler, *Diktatur*, pp. 139–140, contending that Alberti's wife received a monthly subvention of AS 500 from the HW after Alberti's internment, proof that Starhemberg knew what her husband was doing. Moreover, one of Alberti's subordinates and close coworker, Hubert Sass, vigorously maintained that he clearly heard Starhemberg commission Alberti, who then resigned only because of loyalty to *Führerprinzip;* see report of telephone conversation with the *Bundeshauptmann* of Krems [Dr. Vogel], Jan. 17, in *Nachlass Sperl* [security director for L.A.], Karton 1, Folder Alberti, AVA (Vienna); also undated memorandum of report of socialist informant in the HW ("absolutely reliable"), in *Nachlass Helmer*, Karton 1, Folder HW, AVA (Vienna).

88. Erbach to F.M., Vienna, 12 Jan. 1934, *DGFP*, C, 2:347, no. 179. Goldinger, "Der gesch. Ablauf," p. 210, and Kerekes, *Abenddämmerung*, pp. 174–176, both contending that Fey broke up the Alberti-Starhemberg-Nazi collusion. Eichstädt, *Von Dollfuss*, p. 454/n. 109, doubting Starhemberg's involvement on the grounds that he could have protected the negotiators from the reach of Fey and Karwinsky. Ross, *Hitler und Dollfuss*, p. 154, assuming that Fey and Starhemberg acted together against a treasonous subordinate as a warning example.

CHAPTER 9

1. *Heimatschützer*, 4 Nov. 1933, p. 2; Nov. 11, p. 6; Gulick, *Austria*, 2: 1167, 1188; *A-Z*, Nov. 8, p. 1. See Spitzmüller, *Ursach*, pp. 383–384, for evidence of concern in managerial circles over Fey's demands. According

to the new U.S. military attaché, Lt. Col. M. C. Shallenberger, 1,000 HW-
Schutzkorps men were on permanent duty in Vienna, but 3,000 additional
members were in reserve; they received two schillings a day (ca. 25¢) plus
rations and other maintenance and felt that something was being planned
for them (reports of 24 Oct. and 20 Nov. 1933, USNA [Washington], War
Dept., MID, RG–165: 2657–FF–141/16 and 17).

2. Hugo Hantsch, "Engelbert Dollfuss (1892–1934)," in *Gestalter der Geschicke Oesterreichs,* ed. by Hantsch (Innsbruck, Vienna, Munich: Tyrolia,
1962), p. 621; Gulick, *Austria,* 2:1208ff.; Brook-Shepherd, *Dollfuss,* pp.
110ff.

3. Report on (socialists') Ordnerwehr by Lt. Col. F. N. MacFarlane, Vienna, 14 Aug. 1933, in War Office to Simon, London, Oct. 17, PRO (London),
F.O. 371: 16638/C9112.

4. *NFP,* 19 Jan. 1934, A.M., p. 4; memorandum by Hüffer, Berlin, Jan.
24, *DGFP,* C, 2:41, no. 213; Suvich to Dollfuss, Rome, Jan. 26, *Geheimer
Briefwechsel,* pp. 44–47, and Sweet, "Mussolini and Dollfuss," pp. 199–201;
see also Gehl, *Austria and Anschluss,* pp. 78–81.

5. Funder, *Als Oesterreich,* pp. 83–84; Gedye, *Betrayal,* pp. 89–90.

6. *NFP,* 28 Jan. 1934, A.M., p. 7.

7. Schneidmadl, "Weg zur Katastrophe," p. 80, who first quoted this
command before the diet of L.A. on 31 Jan. 1934; Gulick, *Austria,* 2:1251.

8. *NFP,* 29 Jan. 1934, Mon., p. 4; *Heimatschützer,* Feb. 3, pp. 1–2.

9. For brief discussions of the provincial coups, see Gulick, *Austria,* 2:
1251–60, and Goldinger, "Der gesch. Ablauf," p. 214.

10. *HS in Oesterr.,* pp. 258–259; *RP,* 31 Jan. 1934, p. 4; *NFP,* Jan. 31,
A.M., p. 5; Feb. 1, A.M., p. 4.

11. Mörl, *Erinnerungen,* pp. 24–25. For argument that the HW intended
to use the Tyrol as a starting and testing ground for seizing power throughout Austria, see Franz Grass (ed.), *Festschrift Landesrat Professor Dr. Hans
Gamper zur Vollendung seines 65. Lebensjahres* (Innsbruck: Wagner, 1956),
1:34–36.

12. *NFP,* 1 Feb. 1934, P.M., p. 1; *HS in Oesterr.,* p. 260. Mörl implied that
Stumpf did not accept the "revolutionary" HtW demands but scolded the
HtW leaders for the threat to "turn brown" if the demands were not met
(*Erinnerungen,* p. 27).

13. *NFP,* 1 Feb. 1934, A.M., p. 1; *HS in Oesterr.,* pp. 260–261.

14. Muff thought that the goal of the operation was to place Fey in control of the cabinet, with Dollfuss to be elevated to the presidency (report
[secret], Vienna, 9 Feb. 1934, RGFO, T-120, 5705H/E414268–272); Selby
thought that the HW wanted to prove to Mussolini its worthiness and/or to
block an appeal to the League of Nations (Selby to Simon, and Selby to F.O.
[telegram], Vienna, Feb. 5 and 7, PRO [London], F.O. 371: 18347/R867 &
18345/R785).

15. *NFP,* 2 Feb. 1934, P.M., pp. 1–2; Feb. 3, A.M., pp. 4–5; Muff's report as cited in n. 14 above; Funder, *Als Oesterreich,* pp. 129–131; Gabriel

Puaux, *Mort et Transfiguration de l'Autriche, 1933–1955* (Paris: Plon, 1966), p. 34. See also Gulick, *Austria*, 2:1247–48.

16. *NFP*, 2 Feb. 1934, A.M., p. 3; Feb. 3, P.M., p. 1; Feb. 4, A.M., p. 9; *RP*, Feb. 2, p. 3; Feb. 4, p. 4. HW "renewal" activities included a campaign of terrorism against Tyrolean Nazis. One Capt. Rudolf Penz, leader of a HtW "storm company" from Hötting, was considered a ringleader and a "favorite" of Steidle, whose son Othmar allegedly took part in the nightriding. See Observator, *Tragödie*, pp. 94–98, and Franz Pichlsberger, *Die Unentwegten: Aus Tirols Befreiungskampf von 1933–1938* (Innsbruck: Deutscher Alpenverlag, 1939), pp. 23–30. On Mar. 12 Saller sent to the German F.M. an extensive report of brutalities which he attributed to Penz's group, including detailed descriptions of nine cases (PADAA [Bonn], II: Po 5 Oe A [*HW-Org*], vol. 1).

17. *NFP*, 5 Feb. 1934, Mon., p. 1; Feb. 6, A.M., p. 3; *RP*, Feb. 5, pp. 1–3; Feb. 6, pp. 1–2; *Innsbrucker Nachrichten*, Feb. 5, p. 1; Mörl, *Erinnerungen*, p. 28, who noted that on Feb. 5 Innsbruck "boiled" when the additional men arrived, but that the 6th was quieter. Due to the death of a member of the Tyrolean council, the meeting with Dollfuss was rescheduled for Feb. 12 (*NFP*, Feb. 8, P.M., p. 3).

18. Memorandum of conversation of HS representatives with Gov. Schlegel, Linz, 6 Feb. 1934, Upper Austrian Landesarchiv (Linz), Zl. 13/1, Landeshauptmann ex 1934; *NFP*, Feb. 7, A.M., p. 4; P.M., p. 3; Feb. 9, A.M., p. 5.

19. *NFP*, 8 Feb. 1934, A.M., p. 5; Feb. 9, A.M., p. 5; Feb. 10, A.M., p. 4.

20. Report by Muff (secret), Vienna, 9 Feb. 1934, opining that the entire HW undertaking was a failure, *RGFO*, T–120, 5705H/E414268–272.

21. See R. John Rath, "Authoritarian Austria," in Sugar (ed.), *Native Fascism*, p. 31.

22. *NFP*, 7 Feb. 1934, P.M., p. 1; Feb. 8, A.M., p. 5; Feb. 11, A.M., p. 1; *A-Z*, Feb. 9, p. 1; report by MacFarlane, Vienna, Feb. 8, in Selby to Simon, Vienna, Feb. 9, to effect that Fey "looked thoroughly worn and haggard and just about at the end of his tether," PRO (London), F.O. 371:18349/R1236.

23. Especially Gulick, *Austria*, 2:1265; but see also Goldinger, "Der gesch. Ablauf," p. 215; Kerekes, *Abenddämmerung*, p. 179; and Starhemberg, *Between Hitler and Mussolini*, pp. 118ff., and *Memoiren*, pp. 160ff., who sees the speech itself as a provocation.

24. Funder, *Als Oesterreich*, pp. 139–143, critically comparing Gulick's abbreviated quotation with the official HW account that appeared in the *RP* on Feb. 12.

25. Funder, *Als Oesterreich*, pp. 143–144; Brook-Shepherd, *Dollfuss*, pp. 129–130.

26. Interview with Dr. Ernst Schmitz, Vienna, 24 May 1963.

27. *NFP*, 12 Feb. 1934, p. 1; Helmer, *50 Jahre*, p. 153.

28. Memorandum by Renthe-Fink, Berlin, 15 Feb. 1934, *RGFO*, T–120,

8645/E605383-385. Also listed were 657 other Schutzkorps men: 465 in a Christian HW under Schuschnigg in the Bgld.; Bauernwehr—32 in Styria and 6 in Car.; FKV—22 in the Tyrol and 2 in Styria. In addition, it was claimed that a large number of HS men served voluntarily without enrolling in the Schutzkorps: several thousand in the Tyrol; 1,200 in Vbg.; 2,000 in Vienna; and 5,000 to 6,000 in L.A. If these figures are reasonably accurate, there would have been about 45,000 HS men who could at least make a show of military activity. However, according to Renthe-Fink's information, only about 10,000 of these Schutzkorps members were effectively trained to fight alongside the approximately 40,000 members of the federal "executive," including the army, the military assistance corps, the police and gendarmery. See also reports by the U.S. military attaché, Lt. Col. Shallenberger, on Feb. 28 and Mar. 24, in which he reported on the membership of the HS and other paramilitary groups (from Vienna, USNA [Washington], War Dept., MID, RG–165: 2657–FF–141/20 and 21). On Mar. 24 he reported that Starhemberg claimed after an enlargement campaign to have 42,000 men under arms; Shallenberger would grant him that many on the rolls, but thought only about 30,000 by then militarily armed and organized, of whom 12,000 were in Vienna under Fey and 18,000 in the rest of Austria.

29. Police Pres. Seydel, "Treu—bis in den Tod!" *Oeffentliche Sicherheit* (Polizei Rundschau der österreichischen Bundes- und Gemeindepolizei sowie Gendarmerie), 14/3 (Mar. 1934): 1.

30. See Renthe-Fink's memorandum and Shallenberger's reports cited in n. 28 above.

31. For detailed description of military action throughout the country, see the daily newspapers, especially the *NFP*, for the days during and immediately after the fighting; also Gulick, *Austria*, 2:1278–92; report by Shallenberger, Vienna, 9 Mar. 1934, USNA (Washington), War Dept., MID, RG–165: 2657–FF–158/11; *Oeffentliche Sicherheit*, 14/3 (Mar. 1934), pp. 32–33; F. H. Fischer, *Gedenkschrift Wiener Heimatschutzregiment Nr. 4—19II34* (Vienna, 1934); Starhemberg, *Between Hitler and Mussolini*, pp. 124–129, and *Memoiren*, pp. 163–171; Jedlicka, *Heer*, p. 113; Gedye, *Betrayal*, p. 160.

32. *RP*, 14 Feb. 1934, p. 1. Starhemberg says he opposed the dissolution of the SDP, but that Fey as security minister forced it (*Between Hitler and Mussolini*, p. 130, and *Memoiren*, p. 170); Winkler agrees that Dollfuss was reluctant to dissolve the party on the 12th (*Diktatur*, pp. 101–102).

33. In this regard a memorandum in the Styrian Landesarchiv (Graz) is of interest. On 22 Feb. 1934, HS leader Berger-Waldenegg called Gov. Dienstleder with the request that the government postpone final decision about appointments of provincial commissioners to districts and towns until after his return from Vienna (LH Korr., P-H 2/1934). On Feb. 24 the *NFP*, A.M., p. 4, reported that Dienstleder had named Berger-Waldenegg and a representative of the Bauernbund as lieutenant governors and representatives of other "patriotic" groups as councillors. Berger-Waldenegg recalled that

Dollfuss and Starhemberg ordered him to enter the Styrian government ("Ungedr. Erinnerungen," pp. 330–331).

34. *NFP*, 6 Mar. 1934, A.M., p. 4; Mar. 8, A.M., p. 4.

35. *NFP*, 16 Feb. 1934, A.M., p. 6; Feb. 18, A.M., p. 10; Feb. 28, A.M., p. 2; Mar. 2, A.M., p. 4; Mar. 6, A.M., p. 4; *RP*, Feb. 18, pp. 9–10; Feb. 25, p. 5. See defense of Schlegel and criticism of Starhemberg in Spitzmüller, *Ursach*, pp. 389–390.

36. Mörl, *Erinnerungen*, pp. 31–32.

37. *NFP*, 28 Feb. 1934, A.M., p. 2; Mar. 16, A.M., p. 4; Mar. 21, A.M., p. 4; Mar. 22, A.M., p. 5; Mar. 28, A.M., p. 4. See *Gamper Festschrift*, pp. 35–36, for exchange in the diet.

38. *RP*, 22 Feb. 1934, p. 4; Huebmer, *Ender*, pp. 177–178; *Heimatschützer*, Feb. 24, p. 9; *NFP*, Mar. 3, P.M., p. 3; Mar. 6, P.M., p. 3.

39. Mörl noted in his diary on 23 Feb. 1934 the rumor that the HW was going to march on Vienna (*Erinnerungen*, p. 31).

40. Puaux, *Mort*, p. 39.

41. *NFP*, 14 Feb. 1934, A.M., p. 3; Feb. 17, A.M., pp. 2–3; Feb. 19, Mon. pp. 1–4; Feb. 20, A.M., p. 5; P.M., p. 3; Mar. 1, P.M., p. 3; Mar. 10, A.M., p. 2.

42. Starhemberg, *Between Hitler and Mussolini*, pp. 130–132, and *Memoiren*, pp. 170–172. See also Brook-Shepherd, *Dollfuss*, pp. 148–149, reporting that for a while Dollfuss kept Fey under constant surveillance; and Pertinax, *Oesterreich 1934*, pp. 155–156.

43. *NFP*, 28 Feb. 1934, A.M., pp. 3–4; *Heimatschützer*, Mar. 8, pp. 1–2; also Brook-Shepherd, *Dollfuss*, p. 151, for careless treatment.

44. *NFP*, 7 Mar. 1934, A.M., p. 4.

45. Brook-Shepherd, *Dollfuss*, pp. 151–152, who cites K. M. Stepan. See also Schuschnigg, *Im Kampf*, p. 155.

46. Jedlicka, *Heer*, p. 113, also n. 33; report by Muff (secret), Vienna, 2 Mar. 1934, *RGFO*, T–120, 5705H/E414301–307; Selby to Simon (telegram), Vienna, 16 Feb. 1934, United Kingdom, *Documents on British Foreign Policy [DBFP]*, ed. by E. L. Woodward and R. Butler, 2nd series, vol. 6 (*1933–1934*) (London: Her Majesty's Stationery Office, 1957), p. 424, no. 286. See also report by MacFarlane, Vienna, 30 Sept. 1933, in Selby to Sargent, Vienna, Oct. 3, PRO (London), F.O. 371: 16638/C8788.

47. Gehl, *Austria and Anschluss*, p. 86; Kerekes, "Akten," p. 361; Gulick, *Austria*, 2:1627.

48. Report by Muff (secret), Vienna, 22 Mar. 1934, *RGFO*, T–120, 5705H/E414282-285; Rieth to Köpke, Vienna, Mar. 27, *RGFO*, T–120, 8645/E605450–459. In his report of Mar. 2 (cited in n. 46 above) Muff had already noted that the Sturmscharen wore new Italian helmets and were receiving materiel from Hungary.

49. Mörl, *Erinnerungen*, p. 31; *NFP*, 16 Mar. 1934, A.M., p. 4; Mar. 23, A.M., p. 3.

50. Memorandum by Dr. Rudolf Weydenhammer about conversation with

Rintelen, Rome, 7 and 8 Mar. 1934, *DGFP*, C, 2:576, no. 308; Köpke to Rieth, Berlin, Mar. 15, *DGFP*, C, 2:615, no. 328; memorandum by Bülow (for Neurath), Berlin, Apr. 9, *DGFP*, C, 2:730, no. 389.

51. Reports by Muff, 22 Mar. 1934, and Rieth, Mar. 27, as cited in n. 48 above; report by Shallenberger, Vienna, Mar. 24, USNA (Washington), War Dept., MID, RG–165:2657–FF–141/21; *NFP*, Mar. 21, A.M., p. 4; Mar. 24, A.M., p. 4; Mar. 26, Mon., p. 3; Mar. 25, A.M., p. 8.

52. Starhemberg, *Between Hitler and Mussolini*, pp. 133–134, and *Memoiren*, p. 173; Mörl, *Erinnerungen*, p. 32; *NFP*, 27 Mar. 1934, A.M., p. 3; Mar. 29, A.M., p. 4; *RP*, Mar. 29, p. 2, which was terribly upset by the HW plan. See also Gulick, *Austria*, 2:1655–56.

53. Gehl, *Austria and Anschluss*, pp. 87–88; Ross, *Hitler und Dollfuss*, pp. 199–200, 308, n. 125; Starhemberg, *Between Hitler and Mussolini*, p. 133, and *Memoiren*, p. 172. Nothing more is known about Fey's contacts.

54. *RP*, 15 Apr. 1934, p. 1; *NFP*, Apr. 15, A.M., p. 1; Apr. 16, Mon., p. 1; see Eichstädt, *Von Dollfuss*, pp. 42–43.

55. Rieth to F.M., Vienna, 5 May 1934, PADAA (Bonn), II: Po 5 Oe A, vol. 1. Rieth also opined in this report that one of Starhemberg's conditions for entering the cabinet was that the last of his debts be paid, for after his return he was allegedly able to make a final payment of AS 500,000. See also Selby to Simon, Vienna, Apr. 27, *DBFP*, 2, 6:664–666, no. 411.

56. *NFP*, 26 Apr. 1934, A.M., p. 4; P.M., p. 1; Apr. 27, A.M., p. 4; P.M., p 2, which saw great political significance in the occasion; *Heimatschützer*, May 5, pp. 1–3. In view of Winkler's contention (*Diktatur*, p. 141) that in Munich the next day an emissary of Starhemberg cleared the way for an agreement with the SA to be concluded on May 3, Starhemberg's commitment to Dollfuss still might not have been unswerving. But he put off the meeting from hour to hour and finally cancelled it under pressure from Dollfuss.

57. In his "Protocol" Schuschnigg recalled that Fey always refused offers of a promotion because, he suspected, Fey wanted to remain *the* "Herr Major" (p. 4). See also Starhemberg, *Between Hitler and Mussolini*, pp. 133–134, and *Memoiren*, p. 173.

58. *NR Protokolle*, 4/3 (30 Apr. 1934): 3397–3466 [*sic*—3406]; *NR Beilagen*, 4/4, no. 503. See Goldinger, "Der gesch. Ablauf," p. 221; Gulick, *Austria*, 2:1404–23. More will be said about the constitution in the next chapter.

CHAPTER 10

1. The preamble states, "In the name of Almighty God from Whom all justice emanates, the Austrian people receives for its Christian, German, Federal State on a corporative foundation this Constitution" (quoted from Gulick, *Austria*, 2:1426–27). See Brook-Shepherd, *Dollfuss*, p. 156; Rath, "Authoritarian Austria," pp. 24–25.

2. Fellner, "Background," pp. 17–20.

3. For good discussions of the constitution, see Gulick, *Austria*, 2:1424–56; Diamant, *Austrian Catholics*, pp. 256–285; and Rath, "Authoritarian Austria," pp. 24–43.

4. Prof. Heinrich told me that the constitution of 1934 did not create the self-administered and mutually reconciling occupational estates that he had hoped for (interview, Vienna, 19 Nov. 1963).

5. See Goldinger, "Der gesch. Ablauf," p. 222; Günther Nenning, *Anschluss an die Zukunft: Oesterreichs unbewältigte Gegenwart und Vergangenheit* (Vienna: Europa, 1963), p. 53; Karl Gutkas, "Oesterreichs Aussen- und Innenpolitische Situation 1935–1937," in *Oesterreich, 1918–1938*, p. 139.

6. The figure comes from Starhemberg's interview with a Danish reporter in Nov. 1934 (German Minister Richthofen to F.M., Copenhagen, Nov. 30, PADAA [Bonn], II: Po 5 Oe A [*HW-Org*], vol. 1). By the summer of 1935, however, membership appeared to be considerably greater.

7. Sauer, "National Socialism," pp. 421–422.

8. Starhemberg, *Between Hitler and Mussolini*, pp. 141, 144–146, and *Memoiren*, pp. 178–183; Mörl, *Erinnerungen*, p. 33; report from Vienna [Wächter–?] in Habicht to Hüffer, Munich, 18 June 1934, *DGFP*, C, 3:44–45, no. 17; Rieth to Bülow (secret), Vienna, July 23, *DGFP*, C, 3:222–225, no. 112. See also Ross, *Hitler und Dollfuss*, pp. 234–235; Jedlicka, *Heer*, p. 115; Gulick, *Austria*, 2:1657.

9. Goldinger, "Der gesch. Ablauf," p. 225; Jedlicka, *Heer*, pp. 115, 117; Starhemberg, *Between Hitler and Mussolini*, p. 147, and *Memoiren*, pp. 183–184. Concerning plans to remove Steidle, see reports by Rieth to F.M., Vienna, May 5 (PADAA [Bonn], II: Po 5 Oe A [*HW-Org*], vol. 1) and May 15 (*RGFO*, T–120, 8647H/E605557–558); also Winkler, *Diktatur*, p. 66.

10. See Habicht's report of June 18 and Rieth's of July 23 cited above, n. 8.

11. See Ross, *Hitler und Dollfuss*, pp. 218–227.

12. Ibid., pp. 232–234. Also Gehl, *Austria and Anschluss*, p. 94, for information that Dollfuss established contact with Röhm during June. Starhemberg had been in touch with the SA throughout April.

13. The most recent treatment of these events is Walter B. Maass, *Assassination in Vienna* (New York: Charles Scribner's Sons, 1972). See also the official *Julirevolte*, pp. 61–121; Gedye, *Betrayal*, pp. 117–129; M. W. Fodor, *South of Hitler* (London: George Allen & Unwin, 1938), pp. 227–235; Brook-Shepherd, *Dollfuss*, pp. 231–284; Gulick, *Austria*, 2:1657–69; *NFP*, 26 July 1934, P.M., p. 2; Goldinger, "Der gesch. Ablauf," p. 228; Starhemberg, *Between Hitler and Mussolini*, pp. 163–164, and *Memoiren*, pp. 200–201; and Wladimir von Hartlieb, *Parole: Das Reich. Eine historische Darstellung der politischen Entwicklung in Oesterreich von März 1933 bis März 1938* (Vienna, Leipzig: A. Luser, 1939), pp. 226–227.

14. Starhemberg, *Between Hitler and Mussolini*, pp. 148–150, and *Mem-*

oiren, pp. 185–189. Also Elizabeth Wiskemann, *The Rome-Berlin Axis: A Study of the Relations between Hitler and Mussolini* (2nd ed.; London: Collins, 1966), pp. 56–57.

15. Jedlicka, *Heer,* pp. 117–118, who acknowledges that the army found the conflict painful; Starhemberg, *Between Hitler and Mussolini,* pp. 152–153, and *Memoiren,* pp. 189–190.

16. For the sake of easier reading I shall continue to use the name Heimwehr in most instances.

17. Schuschnigg, *Dreimal Oesterreich,* p. 263, and "Protocol," p. 6; Goldinger, *Geschichte,* pp. 208–209; Ludwig, *Oesterreichs Sendung,* pp. 176–177; memorandum by Wilhelm Miklas on events of 25 and 26 July 1934 (date not given), in L. Jedlicka (ed.), *Die Erhebung der österreichischen Nationalsozialisten im Juli 1934: Akten der Historischen Kommission des Reichsführers SS [1938]* (Vienna: Europa, 1965), pp. 208–209. Starhemberg wrote nothing about this; but his paper, *Der Heimatschützer,* reported that he proposed Schuschnigg's chancellorship (4 Aug. 1934, p. 1). There is some evidence that some Christian Socialists threatened Starhemberg with "revelations" about his private life (see Barbara Berger, "Ernst Rüdiger Fürst Starhemberg: Versuch einer Biographie," Ph.D. diss., Univ. of Vienna, 1967, p. 135); according to Christine Fessl, who cites an interview with Heinrich Drimmel, author of the introduction to Starhemberg's *Memoiren,* there were personal reasons for Starhemberg's not seeking the chancellorship ("Die innenpolitische Entwicklung in Oesterreich in den Jahren 1934–1938," Ph.D. diss., Univ. of Vienna, 1967, p. 96).

18. Selby to F.O. (telegram), Vienna, 3 Aug. 1934, and the lengthy minutes attached to it, PRO (London), F.O. 371: 18354/R4403 and R4405.

19. *Times* (London), 20 May 1936, p. 15; R. K. Sheridon, *Kurt von Schuschnigg: A Tribute* (London: English Universities Press, 1942), pp. 9–59; Ludwig, *Oesterreichs Sendung,* pp. 169–170.

20. Starhemberg, *Between Hitler and Mussolini,* pp. 184–185, and *Memoiren,* pp. 217–222.

21. Starhemberg, *Between Hitler and Mussolini,* pp. 172–178, and *Memoiren,* pp. 209–214; Selby to Simon (confidential), Vienna, 16 Oct. 1934, PRO (London), F.O. 371: 18358/R5758; *NYT,* Oct. 28, p. 12; Oct. 29, p. 6; Gulick, *Austria,* 2:1645–47; Gehl, *Austria and Anschluss,* pp. 106–108.

22. Gehl, *Austria and Anschluss,* pp. 109–110.

23. Ludwig, *Oesterreichs Sendung,* p. 179; Papen to Hitler (secret), Vienna, 3 Nov. 1934, *RGFO,* T–120, 6081H/E451141–147; report by Shallenberger, Vienna, Nov. 21, USNA (Washington), War Dept., MID, RG–165: 2657–FF–173/2.

24. G. S. Messersmith to William Phillips [undersec. of state] (personal and confidential), Vienna, 31 Dec. 1934, USNA (Washington), State Dept., 863.00/1172.

25. Selby to F.O. (telegram), Vienna, 3 Aug. 1934, PRO (London), F.O. 371: 18354/R4403.

26. Report by Muff (secret), Vienna, 30 Aug. 1934, *RGFO,* T–120, 6079H/E450938–944; report by Shallenberger, Vienna, Aug. 31, USNA (Washington), War Dept., MID, RG–165: 2540–188/1.

27. *Heimatschützer,* 6 and 13 Apr. 1935, pp. 1 and 1; reports by Muff (secret), Vienna, Apr. 4 and 10, *RGFO,* T–120, 5705H/E414533–538 and E414543–545; Selby to F.O. (telegrams), Vienna, Mar. 29 and Apr. 4, PRO (London), F.O. 371: 19481/R2204 and 19484/R2321.

28. Report by Shallenberger, Vienna, 28 Mar. 1935, USNA (Washington), War Dept., MID, RG–165:2540–200/1. Papen reported on May 10 that Mussolini had promised Starhemberg 6 million schillings for the purpose of making the HW into a militia on the Italian model (to Hitler [top secret], Vienna, *DGFP,* C, 4:147–148, no. 84).

29. It is difficult to ascertain the membership of the various paramilitary groups at this time. Estimates follow as reported by Muff ([secret], Vienna, 12 Apr. 1935, *RGFO,* T–120, 5705H/E414549–554) and by Shallenberger, who also indicated the number supposedly armed (Vienna, June 5, USNA [Washington], War Dept., MID, RG–165: 2657–FF–141/26).

	Muff	Shallenberger
Heimwehr	150,000	100,000/77,000 armed
Sturmscharen	46,000	32,000/25,000 "
Freiheitsbund	21,000	25,000/15,000 "
Christian Gymnasts	6,000	22,000/ 5,000 "
Totals	223,000	179,000/122,000 "

In addition, Shallenberger thought that there were about 20,000 armed men in the underground Schutzbund and about 5,000 armed Nazis. (His break-down of the HW's strength in thousands [members/armed] in each province follows: Vienna—20/16; L.A.—22/18; Styria—18/12; U.A.—10/8; Tyrol —15/10; Car.—6/5; Sbg.—5/5; Vbg.—3/2; Bgld.—1/1).

30. *Heimatschützer,* 11 May, 1 June, and 24 Aug. 1935, p. 1 in each case; *Times* (London), June 7 and 10, p. 15 and p. 9; also Goldinger, "Der gesch. Ablauf," pp. 239–240.

31. Papen to Hitler (top secret), Vienna, 10 May 1935, *DGFP,* C, 4: 147–148, no. 84; Papen to Hitler, Berlin, May 17, *DGFP,* C, 4: 169–171, no. 96. Papen commented on Starhemberg's ambitions as early as Feb. 15 (to Hitler [secret], Vienna, *RGFO,* T–120, 6081H/E451219–223). Schuschnigg recalled that in Aug. 1934 Mussolini hinted at a Starhemberg regency (*Austrian Requiem,* trans. by Franz von Hildebrand [New York: G. P. Putnam's Sons, 1946], p. 112); his date may have been wrong.

32. *NFP,* 3 June 1935, Mon., p. 8; *Times* (London), June 3, p. 13. Hellmut Andics states that Starhemberg and Otto met for the only time in Feb. 1933, when they sharply disagreed over policies regarding the socialists (*Der Fall Otto Habsburg: Ein Bericht* [Vienna, Munich: Fritz Molden, 1965], p. 75).

33. Messersmith to sec. of state (confidential), Vienna, 14 June 1935, USNA (Washington), State Dept., 863.00/1197.

34. Ibid.; *Times* (London), 27 May 1935, p. 13; Jedlicka, *Heer*, p. 132.

35. MRP no. 1002, 28 June 1935, AVA (Vienna), BKA.

36. *NYT*, 1 July 1935, pp. 1, 6.

37. Papen to Hitler, Berlin, 23 Sept. 1935, *RGFO*, T–120, K1100/K282731–732. Muff heard indirectly that Gov. Hülgerth of Carinthia, an old HW adherent, thought that Starhemberg had the solid support of only half the HW membership ([secret], Vienna, Oct. 4, *RGFO*, T–120, 5705H/E414605–608).

38. Messersmith to sec. of state, Vienna, 18 Oct. 1935, USNA (Washington), State Dept., 863.00/1223; Selby to Hoare, Vienna, Aug. 5, PRO (London), F.O. 371: 19482/R4915, already showing concern in Vienna about Italy's ability to continue economic aid.

39. *Times* (London), 18 and 29 Oct. 1935, p. 14 and p. 15. The American minister reported rumors that Fey had been dealing with Papen (Messersmith to sec. of state [confidential], Vienna, Oct. 30 and Nov. 8, USNA [Washington], State Dept., 863.00/1225—1 and 2). Note Goldinger, "Der gesch. Ablauf," p. 240, suggesting that Schuschnigg was suspicious, not receptive, of Fey's leanings toward the Nazis.

40. Report by Muff (secret), Vienna, 21 Oct. 1935, *RGFO*, T–120, 5705H/E414615–622. See also Papen to Hitler, Vienna, Oct. 18, *DGFP*, C, 4: 751–753, no. 363; W.H.B. Mack to Hoare (confidential), Vienna, Oct. 23, PRO (London), F.O. 371: 19482/R6484; Selby to Sargent, Vienna, Nov. 4, PRO (London), F.O. 371: 19482/R6824; Schuschnigg, *Im Kampf*, pp. 169–170.

41. Report by Shallenberger, Vienna, 23 Oct. 1935, USNA (Washington), War Dept., MID, RG–165: 2540–188–4; report by Muff (secret), Vienna, Oct. 21, *RGFO*, T–120, 5705H/E414615–622; Starhemberg, *Between Hitler and Mussolini*, p. 194, and *Memoiren*, pp. 227–228.

42. *Times* (London), 7 Nov. 1935, p. 14; Nov. 8, p. 13; Nov. 22, p. 13; Erbach to F.M., Vienna, Nov. 20, enclosing a clipping from the *Wiener Zeitung* (Nov. 20, p. 3), *RGFO*, T–120, K1100/K282744–746; Messersmith to sec. of state, Vienna, Nov. 22, USNA (Washington), State Dept., 863.00/1226. In May 1936 the U.S. legation reported that along with the leadership of the Viennese HW Starhemberg assumed a debt of AS 180,000 schillings (J. B. Young to sec. of state [confidential], Vienna, May 8, USNA [Washington], State Dept., 863.00/1276).

43. Papen to Hitler, Vienna, 26 Nov. 1935, *DGFP*, C, 4: 852–856, no. 428.

44. Starhemberg, *Between Hitler and Mussolini*, pp. 208–209, and *Memoiren*, pp. 242–243.

45. *Heimatschützer*, 30 Nov. 1935, p. 1; Dec. 14, p. 1; *Times* (London), Dec. 13, p. 13; report by Shallenberger, Vienna, Dec. 19, USNA (Washington), War Dept., MID, RG–165: 2657–FF–141/27.

46. Hassell to F.M. (telegram), Rome, 7 Jan. 1936, *DGFP*, C, 4: 974–977, no. 485, reporting Mussolini's proposal that Germany and Italy clear up all outstanding differences between them; Austria could become a satellite of Germany in foreign affairs as long as its formal independence was maintained.

47. Messersmith to undersec. of state (confidential), Vienna, 7 Feb. 1936, USNA (Washington), State Dept., 863.00/1249. Also Starhemberg, *Memoiren*, pp. 230–238.

48. As early as 13 June 1935, Papen informed Hitler of a two-hour talk with Starhemberg that was so revealing he would prefer to report orally (Vienna, *RGFO*, T–120, 6081H/E451287–289). See especially Papen's reports of contacts in the winter of 1935–1936, all from Vienna: Dec. 11, *RGFO*, T–120, 6081H/E451353–356; Jan. 10, *DGFP*, C, 4: 980–985, no. 488; and Feb. 12 (secret), *DGFP*, C, 4: 1126–28, no. 556. For Starhemberg's account see *Between Hitler and Mussolini*, pp. 217–220, and *Memoiren*, pp. 217, 247–250.

49. Memorandum by Hassell on talk with Hitler, Berlin, 20 Jan. 1936, *DGFP*, C, 4: 1013–16, no. 506.

50. Hassell to F.M. (telegram), Rome, 7 Mar. 1936, *DGFP*, C, 5: 36–38, no. 18, for report on Mussolini's agitation over both the reoccupation and Hitler's expression of willingness to return to the League of Nations.

51. See Zernatto, *Wahrheit*, pp. 153–156; Gehl, *Austria and Anschluss*, p. 125; and Wiskemann, *Rome-Berlin Axis*, p. 64.

52. Kerekes, "Akten," pp. 363, 369–370; Schuschnigg, *Im Kampf*, pp. 183–184; also note about dispatch (not printed) from Papen, Vienna, 22 Feb. 1936, *DGFP*, C, 4:1190, no. 586, n. 1.

53. About Papen's support of the FHB see his reports to Hitler of 20 Mar. 1936 (secret) and May 12 (confidential), both from Vienna, *DGFP*, C, 5:224–227 and 530–534, nos. 172 and 319. See also Gulick, *Austria*, 2: 1711–12.

54. *Times* (London), 12 May 1936, p. 15. Starhemberg does not report that he demanded a ministry; see *Between Hitler and Mussolini*, pp. 223–226, and *Memoiren*, pp. 253–255.

55. Memorandum by Renthe-Fink on talk with Hueber, Berlin, 6 May 1936 (Hueber stated that Hitler had given his approval for a meeting between Göring and Starhemberg), *DGFP*, C, 5:511, no. 311. Starhemberg makes it sound as if Göring sent Hueber to him; see *Between Hitler and Mussolini*, pp. 226–229, and *Memoiren*, pp. 250–252.

56. *Heimatschützer*, 2 May 1936, p. 1; Schuschnigg, *Im Kampf*, p. 178; *Times* (London), 11 May 1936, p. 11; *NYT*, May 11, p. 10; Papen to Hitler (confidential), Vienna, May 12, *DGFP*, C, 5:530–534, no. 319; Goldinger, "Der gesch. Ablauf," p. 241, suggesting that Fey and Starhemberg might have been collaborating at this point.

57. French Minister Gabriel Puaux reported on 25 Apr. 1936, that Schuschnigg said he would soon further consolidate his "alliance" with Star-

hemberg (to Flandin [very confidential telegram], Vienna, in France, Ministère des Affaires Étrangères, *Documents Diplomatiques Français*, 2nd series: *1936–1939*. [Paris: Impr. Nationale, 1964], 2:190–191, no. 117). See also Selby to Eden (confidential), Vienna, May 16, PRO (London), F.O. 371: 20361/R2907.

58. Young to sec. of state (confidential), Vienna, 8 May 1936, USNA (Washington), State Dept., 863.00/1276. On Mar. 3 Selby opined to Sargent that Italian subsidies had been discontinued about the middle of 1935 and that the HW was living "from hand to mouth" (PRO [London], F.O. 371: 20360/R1315).

59. Quoted in Gehl, *Austria and Anschluss*, p. 128; see also Gulick, *Austria*, 2:1712; and *Heimatschützer*, 9 May 1936, p. 1.

60. *Times* (London), 15 May 1936, p. 16; May 18, p. 14; Schuschnigg, *Austrian Requiem*, p. 121, and *Im Kampf*, pp. 176–177, 403–405 (for text of Mussolini's aide-memoire in support of Schuschnigg); Zernatto, *Wahrheit*, p. 158; Starhemberg, *Memoiren*, pp. 256–260; Young to sec. of state (strictly confidential), reporting on Starhemberg's conditions for resigning, Vienna, 22 May 1936, USNA (Washington), State Dept. 863.00/1285; Selby to Eden, Vienna, May 16 (confidential), 19, and 26 (with memorandum by Maj. K.V.B. Benfield [military attaché]), PRO (London), F.O. 371: 20361/R2907, R3074, and R3086.

61. On this point see Hassell to F. M. (confidential), Rome, 22 May 1936, *DGFP*, C, 5:574–575, no. 343; Papen to Hitler, Vienna, Aug. 21, *RGFO*, T–120, 2019H/443758–762.

62. Young's report of 22 May 1936, as cited in n. 60 above; Starhemberg, *Between Hitler and Mussolini*, pp. 230–234, and *Memoiren*, pp. 260–264; Gehl, *Austria and Anschluss*, p. 129; Sir E. Drummond to F.O. (telegram), Rome, May 18, PRO (London), F.O. 371: 20361/R2856, opining that Schuschnigg had become "persona gratissima" with Mussolini.

63. *Times* (London), 20 May 1936, p. 15.

64. *Heimatschützer*, 16 May 1936, p. 1.

65. *Times* (London), 20 May 1936, p. 16, which also reported that Count Berthold von Stürgkh succeeded Berger-Waldenegg as HW leader in Styria; confidential reports to sec. of state by Young, May 22 (saying "on some authority" that Schuschnigg had recently settled a number of Baar's private debts), by Young, May 29, and by Messersmith, June 19 (reporting indications that Baar was not as loyal to Starhemberg "as he might be")—all in USNA (Washington), State Dept., 863.00/1285, 1286, and 1292; Selby to Eden, Vienna, May 30, PRO (London), F.O. 371: 20361/R3355; *Heimatschützer*, May 30, p. 1; June 20, p. 1.

66. Papen to Hitler, Vienna, 3 July 1936, *DGFP*, C, 5:724–725, no. 426; Messersmith to sec. of state (confidential), Vienna, July 31, USNA (Washington), State Dept., 863.00/1298; Starhemberg, *Memoiren*, pp. 275–278. There are no figures available on the size of the HW at this time, though it was undoubtedly smaller than the estimate of 70,000 to 80,000 reported by

Selby on March 3 (to F.O., Vienna, PRO [London], F.O. 371: 20360/R1315).

67. Starhemberg, *Between Hitler and Mussolini*, pp. 235–248, and *Memoiren*, pp. 269–275.

68. Messersmith to sec. of state (confidential), Vienna, 24 Aug. 1936, USNA (Washington), State Dept., 863.00/1302; Selby to Eden, Vienna, Aug. 26, PRO (London), F.O. 371: 20361/R5237; report by Shallenberger, Vienna, Sept. 25 (reporting on dissatisfaction in and out of the HW with Starhemberg's life of "wine, women, and song"), USNA (Washington), War Dept., MID, RG–165: 2657–FF–141/29; Starhemberg, *Between Hitler and Mussolini*, pp. 250–255, and *Memoiren*, pp. 281–284. See *Times* (London), 15 Sept. 1936, p. 14; Sept. 16, p. 11; Oct. 3, p. 11. Among other things Starhemberg accused Fey of treason in July 1934 and said he had documents proving that Fey had connived with Wächter (report by Shallenberger, Vienna, Oct. 15, USNA [Washington], War Dept., MID, RG–165: 2657–FF–141/31); but Schuschnigg kept the charge out of the papers. See also police reports of Sept. 11 and Oct. 9 in AVA (Vienna), BKA, G.D. 356.212—St.B./1936.

69. Several typescript copies of Starhemberg's speech are in AVA (Vienna), BKA, G.D. 356.212—St.B./1936. See *Times* (London), 5 Oct. 1936, p. 11; *Heimatschützer,* Oct. 10, p. 1 (very short report); Starhemberg, *Between Hitler and Mussolini,* pp. 255–256, and *Memoiren,* p. 284; Messersmith to sec. of state (confidential), Vienna, Oct. 9, USNA (Washington), State Dept., 863.00/1308.

70. Goldinger, "Der gesch. Ablauf," p. 249; Paper to Hitler, Vienna, 12 Oct. 1936, *RGFO,* T–120, 2019H/443766–771; Messersmith to Sec. of State (confidential), Vienna, Oct. 9 and 12, USNA (Washington), State Dept., 863.00/1308 and 1310; report by Shallenberger, Vienna, Oct. 15, USNA (Washington, War Dept., MID, RG–165: 2657–FF–141/31; Papen to Hitler, Vienna, Oct. 12, *RGFO,* T–120, 2019H/443766–771; Selby to Eden, Vienna, Oct. 8, PRO (London), F.O. 371: 20362/R6122.

71. Copy of Starhemberg's statement in *Memoiren,* p. 285; Messersmith to sec. of state (strictly confidential), Vienna, 24 Oct. 1936 (referring to alleged telephone conversation between Mussolini and Starhemberg on Oct. 10), USNA (Washington), State Dept., 863.00/1312.

72. See last issue of *Heimatschützer,* 21 Nov. 1936, p. 1; Gulick, *Austria,* 2:1735–37; Selby to Eden, Vienna, 25 Jan. 1937, PRO (London), F.O. 371: 21118/R670.

Selected Bibliography

Part I: Primary Sources

A. UNPUBLISHED DOCUMENTS, MEMOIRS, PAPERS

AUSTRIA

Allgemeines Verwaltungsarchiv des österreichischen Staatsarchiv (Vienna): Bundeskanzleramt: Abteilung 8–9, 1929–1930; G.D. 1 & 2, 1933–1936; Ministerratsprotokolle, 1927–1936.

Bundesministerium für Inneres und Unterricht, Abteilung 7 (Inneres), 1921–1923.

Bundesministerium für Justiz, 1921–1924.

Nachlässe Helmer, Pichl, and Sperl.

Archiv des Bundes-Polizeidirektion (Vienna): Schoberarchiv, Fasc. Heimwehr.

Archiv des österreichischen Instituts für Zeitgeschichte (Vienna):

Anklageschrift gegen Kammerhofer, Flechner, Hofer, Harter, Harant, Seitner, und Riedlechner, Graz, 21 Nov. 1931 (copy of typescript), St[eiermark] 6060–31–168.

Berger-Waldenegg, Egon. "Ungedruckte Erinnerungen" (typescript).

Heimatschutzverband Steiermark. "Programm der Ständeorganisation Oesterreichs" [1931] (typescript).

Nachtrags-Anklageschrift gegen Pfrimer, Graz, 8 Dec. 1931 (copy of typescript), St[eiermark] 6060–31–217.

Püchler, Josef. "Memoiren" (typescript).

Schumy, Vinzenz. "Meine Lebenserinnerungen" (typescript).

⸻. "Ungedruckte Aufzeichnungen [1938, 1961]" (typescript).

Schuschnigg, Kurt. "Protocol of answers to questionnaire submitted by Ludwig Jedlicka, Peertschach a.W., 13 July 1962" [in German] (typescript).

Starhemberg, Ernst Rüdiger. "Lebenserinnerungen des Fürsten Ernst Rüdiger Starhemberg von ihm selbst verfasst im Winter 1938–1939 in Saint Gervais in Frankreich" (typescript).

Diözesanarchiv (Vienna): Nachlass [Kardinal Fr. G.] Piffl.

Dokumentationsarchiv der österreichischen Widerstandsbewegung (Vienna): Heimwehr correspondence, 1935 (Xerox copies).

"Richtlinien für die Heimwehrredner" (copy of typescript).

Neues Politisches Archiv des österreichischen Staatsarchivs (Vienna):
  Karton 20: Budapest, 1934; Karton 81: Rome, May–Dec. 1928; Karton
  82: Rome, 1930–June 1931; Karton 83, Rome, July 1931–1933; Karton
  84: Rome, 1934–June 1935; Fasz. 277: Liasse Oesterreich 2/3 (In-
  nere Lage, 1931–1933); Fasz. 477: Liasse Italien I/1 (Oesterreichisch-
  italienische Beziehungen, 1928–1930; Fasz. 481: Personalia Geheim.
Oberösterreichisches Landesarchiv (Linz): Landeshauptmann ex 1930, Zl
  184; ex 1934, Zl 13/1.
Staatsarchiv (Vienna): Nachlass [Richard] Schmitz.
Stadtarchiv St. Pölten: Schneidmadl, Heinrich. "Der Weg zur Katastrophe:
  Ein Beitrag zur Geschichte des 12. Februar 1934" [1959] (typescript).
Steiermärkisches Landesarchiv (Graz):
  Bh Bruck: B 8/1 1931, Zl 7053–Pr–1931.
  Landeshauptmann Korrespondenz: P–H, 42/1933; P–H, 2/1934.

GERMANY

Deutsches Bundesarchiv (Koblenz):
  R43I/109-111: *Akten der Reichskanzlei betreffend Oesterreich.*
  R 305 I: *Schumachersammlung.*
  NS 26: *National-Sozialistische Sammlung.*
Politisches Archiv des Deutschen Aussenamtes (Bonn):
  Abteilung II, Politik 2, Nummer 3: *Heimwehrorganisation in Oesterreich.*
  Band 1: 1920–1926; Band 2: 1 Jan. 1927–19 Sept. 1929; Band 3: 30
  Sept. 1929–1 Dec. 1931.
  Abteilung II, Politik 5 Oe A: *Heimwehr-Organisation in Oesterreich.* Band
  1: 26 Jan. 1932–30 Nov. 1935.
  Abteilung II, Politik 5 Oe A: *Geheime Akten betreffend Heimwehr-
  Organisationen in Oesterreich.* Jan. 1927–Feb. 1933.
  Abteilung II, Politik 5 Oe: *Akten betreffend Innere Politik, Parlaments-
  und Parteiwesen.* Band 9: 16 Dec. 1929–16 Aug. 1930; Band 10: 13
  Sept. 1930–8 May 1931.
  Abteilung II, Politik 6a: *Südtiroler Frage.* Band 15: 12 May–23 June 1926.
  Abteilung II, Politik 11, Nummer 3 Oe: *Akten betreffend Personalien ös-
  terreichischer Staatsmänner.* Band 2: 6 May 1931–26 Feb. 1936.
  Abteilung II, Politik 13 Oe: *Akten betreffend Militärangelegenheiten.*
  Band 2: Jan. 1928–7 April 1936.
  Abteilung IIb, Politik 13: *Militärpolitische Berichten des Majors Kundt,
  Wien.* Band 1: May 1920–Dec. 1927.
  Abteilung IIb, Politik, Nummer 3: *Politische Beziehungen zwischen Jugo-
  slawien und Oesterreich.* Band 1: May 1920–Dec. 1930.
  Büro Reichsminister, 16: *Akten betreffend Oesterreich.* Band 3: 1 Aug.
  1929–21 July 1930; Band 12: 9 Aug.–30 Sept. 1933; Band 13: 3 Oct.
  1933–30 April 1934.
  Büro Staatssekretär, SO: *Akten betreffend deutsch-österreichische und
  deutsch-italienische Beziehungen.* Band 6: Dec. 1926–July 1927; Band

7: July 1927–Feb. 1928; Band 9: Nov.–Dec. 1929; Band 10: Dec. 1929–May 1930.

Nachlass Stresemann. Band 54: 24 May–14 June 1927.

Records of the German Foreign Office Received by the U.S. State Department (Microcopy T–120, serial numbers and file titles):

2019H: Politik IV Oe 5: *Innere Politik, Parlaments- und Parteiwesen*. Band 1: 14 May–19 Oct. 1936.

5705H: Abteilung II, Oesterreich: *Geheimakten, Militär-Attaché Wien (auch Bern und Sofia)*. Band. 1: Jan. 1931–March 1934; Band 2: 2 April 1934–6 Aug. 1935; Band 3: 2 Sept. 1935–6 April 1936.

6057H: Abteilung II, Italien, Politik 3: *Geheimakten, Politische Beziehungen zwischen Italien und Ungarn*. 1927–1935.

6077H: Abteilung II, Politik 2 Oe: *Geheimakten, Politische Beziehungen zu Deutschland*. Band 2: 1928–1936.

6079H: Abteilung II, Politik 5 Oe: *Geheimakten, Innere Politik, Parlaments- und Parteiwesen*. Band 1: Oct. 1927–May 1936.

6081H: Abteilung II, Politik 5 Oe, Nummer 1A: *Geheimakten, Berichte von Papen an den Führer*. Band 1: Aug. 1934–April 1936.

8645H: Abteilung II, Politik 5 Oe: *Innere Politik, Parlaments- und Parteiwesen*. Bände 12–17: Feb. 1933–May 1936.

8647H: Abteilung II, Politik 5 Oe: *Innere Politik, Parlaments- und Parteiwesen, Tirol und Vorarlberg*.

K1100: Abteilung II, Politik 5 Oe A: *Heimwehr-Organisation in Oesterreich*. Band 1: 26 Jan. 1932–30 Nov. 1935.

UNITED KINGDOM

Public Record Office (London)

Foreign Office 371: Political, Central Europe (Austria-Hungary; Austria), 1919–1937.

Foreign Office 404/3–6: *Confidential Prints, Further Correspondence respecting Central Europe, 1921–1922*.

UNITED STATES

National Archives (Washington)

Records of the Department of State: Decimal File 863.00, Political Affairs, Austria, 1927–1936.

Records of the War Department: General and Special Staffs, Military Intelligence Division, Record Group 165 (Military Attaché Reports), 1925–1936.

B. INTERVIEWS AND LETTERS

Berger, Peter. Interview. Vienna, 18 April 1963.

Deutsch, Julius. Interview. Bad Hall, U.A., 23 July 1963.

Heinrich, Walter. Interview. Vienna, 19 November 1963.

Hueber, Franz. Letter. Salzburg, 3 March 1964.

Jakoncig, Guido. Interview. Innsbruck, 23 April 1963.

———. Letters. Innsbruck, 3 May 1963; 8 January 1964.

Ludwig, Eduard. Interview. Vienna, 1 August 1963.

Pabst, Waldemar. Interview. Düsseldorf, 7 December 1963.

Pfrimer, Walter. Interview. Judenburg, Styria, 23 June 1963.

Revertera, Peter. Interview. Helfenberg, U.A., 22–23 July 1963.

Salm-Reifferscheidt, Marilies. Interview. Vienna, 27 April 1963.

Schmitz, Ernst. Interview. Vienna, 24 May 1963.

Schmitz, Gertrude. Interview. Vienna, 27 March 1963.

Stepan, Karl M. Interview. Graz, 26 June 1963.

———. Letter. Graz, 27 September 1965.

C. PUBLISHED DOCUMENTS

Austria. *Der Hochverratsprozess gegen Dr. Guido Schmidt vor dem Wiener Volksgericht.* Vienna: Verlag der österreichischen Staatsdruckerei, 1947.

Austria, Bundeskommissariat für Heimatdienst. *Beiträge zur Vorgeschichte und Geschichte der Julirevolte.* Herausgegeben auf Grund amtlicher Quellen. Vienna, 1934.

Austria, Bundesrat. *Stenographische Protokolle über die Sitzungen des Bundesrates.* III. & IV. Teile. Vienna: Verlag der österreichischen Staatsdruckerei, 1927–1934.

Austria, Nationalrat. *Anhang zu den stenographischen Protokollen des Nationalrates.* I. Gesetzgebungsperiode, Band I. Vienna: Verlag der österreichischen Staatsdruckerei, 1924.

———. *Beilagen zu den stenographischen Protokollen des Nationalrates.* III. Gesetzgebungsperiode, Band IV (1929–1930); IV. Gesetzgebungsperiode, Band IV (1932–1934). Vienna: Verlag der österreichischen Staatsdruckerei, 1930; 1934.

———. *Stenographische Protokolle über die Sitzungen des Nationalrates.* I.–IV. Gesetzgebungsperioden (1920–1934). Vienna: Verlag der österreichischen Staatsdruckerei, 1923–1934.

Berchtold, Klaus (comp.). *Oesterreichische Parteiprogramme, 1868–1966.* Munich: R. Oldenbourg, 1967.

France, Ministère des Affaires Étrangères. *Documents Diplomatiques Français, 1932–1939.* 2nd series (1936–1939), tome ii (1 April –18 July 1936). Paris: Impr. Nationale, 1964.

Geheimer Briefwechsel Mussolini–Dollfuss. Vorwort von Vizekanzler Dr. Adolf Schärf; Erläuternder Text von Karl Hans Sailer. Vienna: Wiener Volksbuchhandlung, 1949.

Jedlicka, Ludwig (ed.). *Die Erhebung der österreichischen Nationalsozialisten im Juli 1934. Akten der Historischen Kommission des Reichsführers SS [1938].* Vienna, Frankfurt, Zurich: Europa Verlag, 1965.

Kerekes, Lajos (ed.). "Neuer Aktenfund zu den Beziehungen zwischen Hitler und Dollfuss im Jahre 1933," *Acta Historica* [Academiae Scientiarum Hungaricae], 18/1–2 (1972): 149–160.

Knoll, August M. (ed.). *Kardinal Fr. G. Piffl und der österreichische Episkopat zu sozialen und kulturellen Fragen, 1913–1932: Quellensammlung.* Vienna, Leipzig: Reinhold-Verlag, 1932.

League of Nations. *Official Journal.* 11/5 (May 1930).

Sweet, Paul R. (ed.). "Mussolini and Dollfuss: An Episode in Fascist Diplomacy," in Julius Braunthal, *The Tragedy of Austria.* London: Victor Gollancz, 1948. Pp. 160–213.

United Kingdom, Foreign Office. *Documents on British Foreign Policy.* Ed. by E. L. Woodward and R. Butler. 2nd series, vol. vi (1933–1934). London: Her Majesty's Stationery Office, 1957.

United States, Department of State. *Documents on German Foreign Policy, 1918–1945.* Series C: *The Third Reich: First Phase, 1933–1937.* 5 vols.; Washington: Government Printing Office, 1957–1966.

————. *Foreign Relations of the United States: Diplomatic Papers, 1933.* 5 vols.; Washington: Government Printing Office, 1950–1952.

D. PUBLISHED DIARIES, MEMOIRS, TREATISES

Ahrer, Jakob. *Erlebte Zeitgeschichte.* Vienna, Leipzig: Winkler, 1930.

Aloisi, Baron [Pompeo]. *Journal (25 Juillet 1932–14 Juin 1936).* Tr. from the Italian into French by Maurice Vausard. Paris: Libraire Plon [1957].

Bauer, Otto. *Die österreichische Revolution.* Vienna: Wiener Volksbuchhandlung, 1923.

Brandl, Franz. *Kaiser, Politiker, und Menschen: Erinnerungen eines Wiener Polizeipräsidenten.* Leipzig, Vienna: Johannes Günther Verlag, 1936.

Buttinger, Josef [Gustav Richter]. *In the Twilight of Socialism: A History of the Revolutionary Socialists of Austria.* Tr. from the German by E. B. Ashton. New York: Frederick A. Praeger, 1953.

Deutsch, Julius. *Ein Weiter Weg.* Zurich, Leipzig, Vienna: Amalthea, 1960.

Eisenmenger, Anna. *Blockade: The Diary of an Austrian Middle-Class Woman, 1914–1924.* London: Constable, 1932.

Fey, Emil. *Schwertbrüder des Deutschen Ordens: die Heroica der Hoch- und Deutschmeister.* Vienna: Julius Lichtner, 1937.

Funder, Friedrich. *Als Oesterreich den Sturm Bestand: aus der Ersten in die Zweite Republik.* Vienna, Munich: Herold, 1957.

Günther, Raimund. *Diktatur oder Untergang: neue Wege für Staat und Wirtschaft.* Vienna: Carl Konegen, 1930.

Helmer, Oskar. *50 Jahre Erlebte Geschichte.* Vienna: Wiener Volksbuchhandlung [1957].

Ignaz Seipel: Mensch, Christ, Priester in seinem Tagebuch. Bearbeitung und Einführung von Rudolf Blüml. Vienna: Hilfswerk für Schulsiedlungen, 1933.

Kanzler, Rudolf. *Bayerns Kampf gegen den Bolschewismus: Geschichte der bayrischen Einwohnerwehren.* Munich: Parcus, 1931.

Kunschak, Leopold. *Oesterreich, 1918–1934.* Vienna: Typographischer Anstalt, 1934.

Langoth, Franz. *Kampf um Oesterreich: Erinnerungen eines Politikers.* Wels: "Welsermühl," 1951.

Ludwig, Eduard. *Oesterreichs Sendung im Donauraum: die letzten Dezennien österreichische Innen- und Aussenpolitik.* Vienna: Verlag der österreichischen Staatsdruckerei, 1954.

Mörl, Anton. *Erinnerungen aus bewegter Zeit Tirols, 1932–1945.* Innsbruck: Universitätsverlag Wagner, 1955.

Noske, Gustav. *Von Kiel bis Kapp: zur Geschichte der deutschen Revolution.* Berlin: Verlag für Politik und Wirtschaft, 1920.

Pertinax [Otto Leichter]. *Oesterreich 1934.* Zurich: Europa-Verlag, 1935.

Pichlsberger, Franz. *Die Unentwegten: aus Tirols Befreiungskampf von 1933–1938.* Innsbruck: Deutscher Alpenverlag, 1939.

Puaux, Gabriel. *Mort et Transfiguration de l'Autriche, 1933–1955.* Paris: Plon, 1966.

Renner, Karl. *Oesterreich von der ersten zur zweiten Republik.* Vienna: Wiener Volksbuchhandlung, 1953.

Rintelen, Anton. *Erinnerungen an Oesterreichs Weg: Versailles, Berchtesgaden, Grossdeutschland.* 2nd ed.; Munich: F. Bruckmann, 1941.

Schuschnigg, Kurt. *Austrian Requiem.* Tr. from the German by Franz von Hildebrand. New York: G. P. Putnam's Sons, 1946.

———. *Dreimal Oesterreich.* Vienna: Thomas-Verlag Jakob Hegner, 1937.

———. *Im Kampf Gegen Hitler: die Ueberwindung der Anschlussidee.* Vienna, Munich, Zurich: Fritz Molden, 1969.

Seipel, Ignaz. *Der Kampf um die österreichische Verfassung.* Vienna, Leipzig: Wilhelm Braumüller, 1930.

Selby, Walford. *Diplomatic Twilight, 1930–1940.* London: John Murray, 1953.

Sieghart, Rudolf. *Die letzten Jahrzehnte einer Grossmacht: Menschen, Völker, Probleme des Habsburger-Reiches.* Berlin: Ullstein, 1932.

Spitzmüller, Alexander. *". . . und hat auch Ursach, es zu lieben."* Vienna, Munich, Stuttgart, Zurich: Wilhelm Frick, 1955.

Starhemberg, Prince Ernst Rüdiger. *Between Hitler and Mussolini.* New York, London: Harper & Brothers, 1942.

Starhemberg, Ernst Rüdiger. *Memoiren.* Vienna, Munich: Amalthea, 1971.

Streeruwitz, Ernst Streer. *Springflut über Oesterreich: Erinnerungen, Erlebnisse, und Gedanken aus bewegter Zeit, 1914–1929.* Vienna, Leipzig: Bernina, 1937.

Wallisch, Paula. *Ein Held Stirbt: Koloman Wallisch.* [Graz] Im Verlag der Sozialistischen Partei, 1946 [Prague, 1935].

Winkler, Franz. *Die Diktatur in Oesterreich.* Zurich: Orell Füssli, 1935.

Zernatto, Guido. *Die Wahrheit über Oesterreich.* New York, Toronto: Longmans, Green, & Co., 1938.

E. NEWSPAPERS AND JOURNALS OF OPINION

Die alpenländische Heimatwehr (Innsbruck), 1925–1933.
Arbeiter-Zeitung (Vienna), 1927–1934.
Der Hahnenschänzler (Klagenfurt, Graz, Vienna) 1929–1930.
Die Heimat! (Vienna), 1929–1930.
Der Heimatbote (Wiener Neustadt), 1931–1932.
Der Heimatschützer [offizielles Organ des österreichischen Heimatschutzes] (Vienna), 1933–1936.
Heimatschutz-Zeitung [offizielles Organ des Heimatschutzverbandes Kärnten] (Klagenfurt, Graz, Vienna), 1927–1932.
Die Heimwehr [offizielles Organ des Selbstschutzverbandes Niederösterreich und des Kriegsverbandes Niederösterreich] (Vienna), 1928–1931.
Innsbrucker Nachrichten, 1934.
Der Kampf [Sozialdemokratische Monatsschrift] (Vienna), 1927–1933.
Linzer Volksblatt, 1933.
Neue Freie Presse (Vienna), 1927–1936.
Neues Wiener Tagblatt, 1930.
New York Times, 1933–1936.
Niederösterreichische Heimwehr (St. Pölten, Vienna), 1931–1932.
Oesterreichische Heimatschutzzeitung [offizielles Organ des österreichischen Heimatschutzes] (Vienna), 1932–1933.
Der österreichischer Volkswirt (Vienna), 1927–1934.
Der Panther [steirische Heimatschutzzeitung, later österreichische Heimatschutzzeitung] (Graz), 1930–1933.
Reichspost (Vienna), 1927–1934.
Der Starhemberg-Jäger [Kampforgan der Heimatwehr Oberösterreichs und der heimattreuen Oesterreicher aller Bundesländer] (Linz), 1930–1931.
Die Stunde (Vienna), 1931.
The Times (London), 1933–1936.
Tiroler Anzeiger (Innsbruck), 1926, 1930.
Tiroler Heimatwehr-Blätter (Innsbruck), 1924.
Unsere Zukunft (Vienna), 1928–1933.
Völkischer Beobachter (Munich), 1933.
Wiener Neueste Nachrichten, 1930.
Wiener Zeitung, 1930.
Zu uns! [Nachrichtenblatt des Deutschen Heimatschutzverbandes Oesterreich] (Krems), 1932.

F. PARTISAN ARTICLES AND PAMPHLETS

Arthofer, Hans. *1918–1936: Vom Selbstschutz zu Frontmiliz.* Mit dokumentarischem Anhang [Vienna: Zoller, 1937].
Bleibtrau, Attilio Renato. *Unser Fey, ein Bild des Helden.* Vienna, n.d.

Deutsch, Julius. *Alexander Eifler, ein Soldat der Freiheit.* 2nd ed.; Vienna: Volksbuchhandlung [1947].

———. *Antifaschismus! Proletarische Wehrhaftigkeit im Kampfe gegen den Faschismus.* Vienna: Wiener Volksbuchhandlung, 1926.

———. *Die Fascistengefahr.* Vienna: Wiener Volksbuchhandlung, 1923.

———. *Wer rüstet zum Bürgerkrieg? Neue Beweise für die Rüstungen der Reaktion.* Vienna: Wiener Volksbuchhandlung, 1923.

Dobretsberger, J. *Vom Sinn und Werden des neuen Staates.* Graz, Vienna: Kommissionsverlag, 1934.

Eberle, Joseph. "Zum Rücktritt Seipels," *Schönere Zukunft,* 4/28 (14 April 1929): 583–584.

[Fischer, F. H.] *Gedenkschrift Wiener Heimatschutzregiment Nr. 4–19II34.* Vienna: Propagandastelle der Bundesführung des österreichischen Heimatschutzes, 1934.

15 Jahre Tiroler Heimatwehr. Vienna: Zoller, 1935.

Heinrich, Karl. "Heimwehr und Kirche," *Neuland* [Blätter jungkatholischer Erneuerungsbewegung], 6 (June 1929): 135–137.

Heinrich, Walter. *Heimwehrbewegung in Oesterreich: Ständestaat.* Vienna, 1930.

———. *Grundsätzliche Gedanken über Staat und Wirtschaft: ein programmatischer Vortrag über die geistige Grundlage der Heimatwehrbewegung.* Vienna: Bundesführung der österreichischen Selbstschutzverbände, 1930.

[Karg-Bebenburg, Artur] *Die Gefahr im Staate.* Vienna: Selbstschutzverband Niederösterreich, 1926.

Oesterreichischer Heimatschutz, Bundesführung. *Allgemeine Richtlinien.* Vienna, 1932.

———. *Mitteilungsblatt.* Vienna, 1932.

Oesterreichischer Heimatschutz, Bundeswehramt. *Ausbildungsbehelf für den österreichischen Heimatschutz.* Vienna, 1933.

[Philipp, Hans] *Giftgas über Oesterreich.* Vienna: Wiener Volksbuchhandlung [1932].

———. *Hahnenschwanz—Hakenkreuz und Kaiserkrone.* Vienna: Wiener Volksbuchhandlung [1932].

Richter, Hans. *Kapitalismus und Sozialismus: das Gemeinsame ihrer Grundhaltung und die wahre Lösung der sozialen Frage.* Vienna, Graz, Klagenfurt: Verlag des steirischen Heimatschutzverbandes, 1929.

Schwarzenberg, Heinrich. "Die Heimwehrbewegung in Oesterreich," *Abendland* [deutsche Monatshefte für europäische Kultur, Politik, und Wirtschaft], 5 (Oct. 1929): 15–19.

[Schweinitzhaupt, Fr.] *Vom Parteienstaat zum Heimatwehr-Ständestaat.* Innsbruck: Deutsche Buchdruckerei [1930].

Seydel, Eugen. "Treu——bis in den Tod!" *Oeffentliche Sicherheit* [Polizei Rundschau der österreichischen Bundes- und Gemeindepolizei sowie Gendarmerie], 14 (March 1934): 1.

Sozius [Eli Rubin]. *Heimwehr oder Bürgerkrieg: die Blutschild der roten Gewerkschaften.* [Vienna, 1928].

——. *Ignaz Seipel—der Herr über den Vulkan.* Vienna: Wiener Volksschriften, 1929.

Spann, Othmar. *Die Irrungen des Marxismus: eine Darstellung und Prüfung seiner Wirtschaftslehre.* Vienna, Graz, Klagenfurt: Verlag des steirischen Heimatschutzverbandes, 1929.

Spectator Noricus, "Bemerkungen zur Regierungskrise," *Volkswohl* [Wissenschaftliche Monatsschrift], 20 (June 1929): 201–204.

——. "Von Seipel bis Schober: ein Kapitel aus der jüngsten politischen Geschichte," *Volkswohl* [Wissenschaftliche Monatsschrift], 22 (Feb., March, April, 1931): 161–166, 201–209, 241–250.

Steidle, Richard. "Die österreichische Heimatwehrbewegung," *Schönere Zukunft,* 4 (22 Sept. 1929): 1073–74.

Steinbruck, O. "Oesterreichische Heimwehr und Kirche," *Abendland* [deutsche Monatshefte für europäische Kultur, Politik, und Wirtschaft], 5 (Dec. 1929): 86–89.

Der Weg zu Oesterreichs Freiheit. Von einem Freunde der Heimatwehr [Anton Klotz–?] Innsbruck: Albert Schober [1929].

Part II: Secondary Sources

A. BOOKS
(indicated when clearly partisan)

Allardyce, Gilbert (ed.). *The Place of Fascism in European History.* Englewood Cliffs, N.J.: Prentice-Hall, 1971.

Andics, Hellmut. *Der Fall Otto Habsburg: ein Bericht.* Vienna, Munich: Fritz Molden, 1965.

——. *50 Jahre unseres Lebens.* Vienna: Fritz Molden, 1968.

——. *Der Staat den Keiner Wollte: Oesterreich, 1918–1938.* Vienna: Herder, 1962.

Ausch, Karl. *Als die Banken fielen: zur Soziologie der politischen Korruption.* Vienna, Frankfurt, Zurich: Europa, 1968. (anti-HW)

Axhausen, Günther. *Organisation Escherisch: die Bewegung der nationaler Einheitsfront.* Leipzig, Berlin: Theodor Weicher, 1921. (pro-HW)

Bärnthaler, Irmgard. *Die Vaterländische Front: Geschichte und Organisation.* Vienna, Frankfurt, Zurich: Europa, 1971.

Ball, M. Margaret. *Post-War German-Austrian Relations: The "Anschluss" Movement, 1918–1936.* Palo Alto, Cal.: Stanford Univ. Press, 1937.

Barker, Elisabeth. *Austria, 1918–1972.* Coral Gables: Univ. of Miami Press, 1973.

Benedikt, Heinrich (ed.). *Geschichte der Republik Oesterreich.* Munich: R. Oldenbourg, 1954.

Berenger, Jean. *La République Autrichienne de 1919 à nos Jours.* Paris, Brussels, Montreal: Didier, 1971.

Beyer, Hans. *Von der Novemberrevolution zur Räterepublik in München.* [East] Berlin: Rütten & Loening, 1957.

Birk, Bernhard. *Dr. Ignaz Seipel: ein österreichisches und europäisches Schicksal.* Regensburg: G. J. Manz, 1932.

Borkenau, Franz. *Austria and After.* London: Faber & Faber, 1938. (anti-HW)

Braunthal, Julius. *The Tragedy of Austria.* London: Victor Gollancz, 1948. (anti-HW)

Brook-Shepherd, Gordon. *Dollfuss.* London: Macmillan, 1961. (pro-HW)

Busshoff, Heinrich. *Das Dollfuss-Regime in Oesterreich. In geistesgeschichtliche Perspektive unter besonderer Berücksichtigung der 'Schöneren Zukunft' und 'Reichspost.'* Berlin: Duncker und Humbolt, 1968.

Carsten, F. L. *Fascist Movements in Austria: From Schönerer to Hitler.* London and Beverly Hills: Sage Publications, 1977.

————. *The Rise of Fascism.* Berkeley, Los Angeles: Univ. of California Press, 1967.

Charmatz, Richard. *Vom Kaiserreich zur Republik: Oesterreichs Kampf um die Demokratie, 1747–1947.* Vienna: Jedermann, 1947.

Craig, Gordon A. and Felix Gilbert (eds.). *The Diplomats, 1919–1939.* Princeton: Univ. Press, 1953.

Dachauer, Max. *Das Ende Oesterreichs: aus der k.u.k. Monarchie ins Dritte Reich.* Berlin: C. A. Weller [1939]. (Nazi; anti-HW)

Diamant, Alfred. *Austrian Catholics and the First Republic: Democracy, Capitalism, and the Social Order, 1918–1934.* Princeton: Univ. Press, 1960.

Eichstädt, Ulrich. *Von Dollfuss zu Hitler: Geschichte des Anschlusses Oesterreichs, 1933–1938.* Wiesbaden: F. Steiner, 1955.

Festschrift Walter Heinrich: ein Beitrag zur Ganzheitsforschung. Graz: Akademische Druck- und Verlagsanstalt, 1963.

Fodor, M. W. *South of Hitler.* London: George Allen & Unwin, 1938.

Gatzke, Hans W. *Stresemann and the Rearmament of Germany.* New York: W. W. Norton, 1969 [c. 1954].

Gedye, G.E.R. *Betrayal in Central Europe: Austria and Czechoslovakia, the Fallen Bastions.* New York, London: Harper & Bros., 1939. (anti-HW)

Gehl, Jürgen. *Austria, Germany, and the Anschluss, 1931–1938.* London, New York, Toronto: Oxford Univ. Press, 1963.

Goldinger, Walter. *Geschichte der Republik Oesterreich.* Vienna: Verlag für Geschichte und Politik, 1962.

————. "Der geschichtliche Ablauf der Ereignisse in Oesterreich von 1918 bis 1945," in H. Benedikt (ed.), *Geschichte der Republik Oesterreich* (Munich: R. Oldenbourg, 1954), pp. 15–288.

Gordon, Harold J., Jr. *The Reichswehr and the German Republic, 1919–1926.* Princeton: Univ. Press, 1957.

Grass, Franz (ed.). *Festschrift Landesrat Professor Dr. Hans Gamper zur Vollendung seines 65. Lebensjahres.* 3 vols.; Innsbruck: Wagner, 1956.

Greene, Nathanael (ed.). *Fascism: An Anthology.* New York: Crowell, 1968.

Gregor, A. James. *Contemporary Radical Ideologies: Totalitarian Thought in the Twentieth Century.* New York: Random House, 1968.

————. *The Ideology of Fascism: The Rationale of Totalitarianism.* New York: Free Press, 1969.

Gregory, J. D. *Dollfuss and His Times.* London: Hutchinson, 1935. (pro-HW)

Gulick, Charles A. *Austria from Habsburg to Hitler.* 2 vols.; Berkeley, Los Angeles: Univ. of California Press, 1948. (anti-HW)

Gutkas, Karl. *Geschichte des Landes Niederösterreich.* 3 vols.; [Vienna] Kulturreferat des Amtes der niederösterreichischen Landesregierung, 1957–1962.

Hannak, Jacques. *Johannes Schober—Mittelweg in die Katastrophe: Porträt eines Repräsentanten der verlorenen Mitte.* Vienna, Frankfurt, Zurich: Europa, 1966.

Hantsch, Hugo (ed.). *Gestalter der Geschicke Oesterreichs.* Innsbruck, Vienna, Munich: Tyrolia, 1962.

Hartlieb, Wladimir. *Parole: das Reich: eine historische Darstellung der politischen Entwicklung in Oesterreich von März 1933 bis März 1938.* Vienna, Leipzig: A. Luser, 1939. (Nazi; anti-HW)

Hayes, Paul M. *Fascism.* London: George Allen & Unwin, 1973.

Heiden, Konrad. *Adolf Hitler: eine Biographie.* 2 vols.; Zurich: Europa, 1936–1937.

Hoegner, Wilhelm. *Die Verratene Republik: Geschichte der deutschen Gegenrevolution.* Munich: Isar, 1958.

Hofmann, Josef. *Der Pfrimer-Putsch: der steirische Heimwehrprozess des Jahres 1931.* Vienna: Stiasny [1965].

Hoor, Ernst. *Oesterreich 1918–1938: Staat ohne Nation, Republik ohne Republikaner.* Vienna, Munich: Oesterreichischer Bundesverlag für Unterricht, Wissenschaft und Kunst, 1966.

Huebmer, Hans. *Dr. Otto Ender.* Dornbirn: Vorarlberger Verlagsanstalt, 1957.

Ingrim, Robert. *Der Griff nach Oesterreich.* Zurich: Europa, 1938 (Catholic)

Jahrbuch der österreichischen Arbeiterbewegung, 1927–1932. Vienna: Wiener Volksbuchhandlung, 1928–1933. (anti-HW)

Jedlicka, Ludwig. *Ein Heer im Schatten der Parteien: die militärpolitische Lage Oesterreichs, 1918–1938.* Graz, Cologne: H. Böhlaus Nachf., 1955.

Jedlicka, Ludwig and Rudolf Neck (eds.). *Oesterreich 1927 bis 1938: Protokoll des Symposiums in Wien, 23. bis 28. Oktober 1972.* Munich: R. Oldenbourg, 1973.

Johnston, William A. *The Austrian Mind: An Intellectual and Social History, 1848–1938.* Berkeley, Los Angeles: Univ. of California Press, 1972.

Kedward, H. R. *Fascism in Western Europe, 1900–45.* Glasgow, London: Blackie, 1969.

Kerekes, Lajos. *Abenddämmerung einer Demokratie: Mussolini, Gömbös und die Heimwehr.* Vienna, Frankfurt, Zurich: Europa, 1966. (Marxist; anti-HW)

Kleinschmied, Oskar. *Schober.* Vienna: Manz, 1930.

Klenner, Fritz. *Die österreichischen Gewerkschaften: Vergangenheit und Gegenwartsprobleme.* 2 vols.; Vienna: Verlag des österreichischen Gewerkschaftsbundes, 1951–1953.

Klingenstein, Grete. *Die Anleihe von Lausanne. Ein Beitrag zur Geschichte der Ersten Republik in den Jahren 1931–1934.* Wien, Graz: Stiasny, 1965.

Knoll, August M. *Von Seipel zu Dollfuss: eine historisch-soziologische Studie.* Vienna: Manz'sche Verlags- und Universitätshandlung, 1934. (Catholic)

[Kolbabek, Anton (ed.)] *Oesterreichische Zeitgeschichte in Geschichtsunterricht: Bericht über die Expertentagung von 14.12–16.12. 1960 in Reichenau.* Vienna: Oesterreichischer Bundesverlag [1961].

Kreissler, Felix. *Von der Revolution zur Annexion: Oesterreich 1918 bis 1938.* Vienna, Frankfurt, Zurich: Europa, 1970. (Socialist; anti-HW)

Lebovics, Herman. *Social Conservatism and the Middle Classes in Germany, 1914–1933.* Princeton, N.J.: Princeton Univ. Press, 1969.

Ledeen, Michael Arthur. *Universal Fascism: The Theory and Practice of the Fascist International, 1928–1936.* New York: Howard Fertig, 1972.

Leichter, Otto. *Otto Bauer: Tragödie oder Triumph.* Vienna, Frankfurt, Zurich: Europa, 1970.

———. *Zwischen zwei Diktaturen: Oesterreichs Revolutionäre Sozialisten, 1934–1938.* Vienna, Frankfurt, Zurich: Europa, 1968.

Lorenz, Reinhold. *Der Staat wider Willen: Oesterreich 1918–1938.* Berlin: Junker und Dünnhaupt, 1941 [c. 1940]. (Nazi; anti-HW)

Maass, Walter B. *Assassination in Vienna.* New York: Charles Scribner's Sons, 1972.

MacDonald, Mary. *The Republic of Austria, 1918–1934: A Study in the Failure of Democratic Government.* London, New York, Toronto: Oxford Univ. Press, 1946.

Mayer, Arno J. *Dynamics of Counterrevolution in Europe, 1870–1956.* New York: Harper & Row, 1971.

Mikoletzky, Hanns Leo. *Oesterreichische Zeitgeschichte: vom Ende der Monarchie bis zum Abschluss des Staatsvertrages 1955.* Vienna, Munich: Oesterreichischer Bundesverlag, 1962.

Musulin, Stell. *Austria and the Austrians.* New York: Praeger, 1972.

Nenning, Günther. *Anschluss an die Zukunft: Oesterreichs unbewältigte Gegenwart und Vergangenheit.* Vienna, Cologne, Stuttgart, Zurich: Europa, 1963.

Newman, Karl J. *European Democracy Between the Wars.* Tr. from the German by Kenneth Morgan. London: George Allen & Unwin, 1970.

Nolte, Ernst. *Der Faschismus in seiner Epoche: die Action française, der italienische Faschismus, der Nationalsozialismus.* Munich: R. Piper, 1963.
———. *Die Krise des liberalen Systems und die faschistischen Bewegungen.* Munich: R. Piper, 1968.
———. *Three Faces of Fascism: Action Française, Italian Fascism, National Socialism.* Trans. from the German by Leila Vennewitz. New York, Chicago, San Francisco: Holt, Rinehart and Winston, 1965.
Observator [Mikhailo Lozynskyi]. *Die Tragödie Oesterreichs: mit 54 dokumentarischen Illustrationen.* Geneva, 1934. (Nazi; anti-HW)
Oesterreich, Brandherd Europas. Zurich: Genossenschaft Universumbücherei, 1934. (Marxist; anti-HW)
Oesterreich 1918–1938. Herausgegeben vom Institut für Oesterreichkunde. Vienna: Ferdinand Hirt, 1970.
Oesterreich und Europa: Festgabe für Hugo Hantsch zum 70. Geburtstag. Herausgegeben vom Institut für Geschichtsforschung. Graz, Vienna: Styria, 1965.
Oesterreichisches Biographisches Lexikon, 1815–1950. Herausgegeben von der österreichischen Akademie der Wissenschaften. Graz, Cologne: H. Böhlaus Nachf., 1954–1965 [*A—Knoll*]; also Böhlaus/Vienna, 1969–1972 [*Knolz—(Maier), Simon Martin*]; Vienna: Verlag der österr. Akademie der Wissenschaften, 1975– [*(Maier), Stefan—*].
Oesterreichischer Heimatschutz, Propagandastelle. *Heimatschutz in Oesterreich.* Vienna, 1934. (pro-HW)
Oesterreichisches Heimatschutz-Jahrbuch 1933. Herausgegeben von der Landesleitung des Heimatschutzverbandes Steiermark. Graz, 1932. (pro-HW)
Pauley, Bruce F. *Hahnenschwanz und Hakenkreuz: Steirischer Heimatschutz und österreichischer Nationalsozialismus 1918–1934.* Vienna, Munich, Zurich: Europa, 1972.
Rambaud, Louis. *Le Grand petit Chancelier Dollfuss, 1892–1934.* Paris: Emmanuel Vitte, 1948. (pro-HW)
Reichhold, Ludwig. *Scheidewege einer Republik: Oesterreich 1918–1968.* Vienna: Herder, 1968.
Reimann, Viktor. *Zu Gross für Oesterreich: Seipel und Bauer im Kampf um die Erste Republik.* Vienna, Frankfurt, Zurich: Fritz Molden, 1968.
Rieger, Erwin. *Fürstin Fanny Starhemberg: das Lebensbild einer österreichischen Frau.* Vienna: Im Montsalvat-Verlag [1935]. (pro-HW)
Rogger, Hans and Eugen Weber (eds.). *The European Right: A Historical Profile.* Berkeley, Los Angeles: Univ. of California Press, 1965.
Ross, Dieter. *Hitler und Dollfuss: die deutsche Oesterreich-Politik, 1933–1934.* Hamburg: Liebniz-Verlag, 1966.
Rothschild, Joseph. *East-Central Europe between the Two World Wars.* Seattle: Univ. of Washington Press, 1974.
Rothschild, K. W. *Austria's Economic Development Between the Two Wars.* London: Frederick Muller, 1947.

Rühle, Gerd. *Das Grossdeutsche Reich: dokumentarische Darstellung des Aufbaues der Nation: die österreichischen Kampfjahre, 1918–1938*. Berlin: Hummel, 1940.

Scheu, Friedrich. *Der Weg ins Ungewisse: Oesterreichs Schicksalskurve 1929–1938*. Vienna, Munich, Zurich: Fritz Molden, 1972.

Schneller, Martin. *Zwischen Romantik und Faschismus: der Beitrag Othmar Spanns zum Konservatismus in der Weimarer Republik*. Stuttgart: Ernst Kletl, 1970.

Schüddekopf, Otto-Ernst. *Fascism*. New York: Praeger, 1973.

Schwend, Karl. *Bayern zwischen Monarchie und Diktatur: Beiträge zur bayerischen Frage in der Zeit von 1918 bis 1933*. Munich: Richard Pflaum, 1954.

Seabury, Paul. *The Wilhelmstrasse: A Study of German Diplomats under the Nazi Regime*. Berkeley, Los Angeles: Univ. of California Press, 1954.

Shepherd, Gordon [Brook-]. *The Austrian Odyssey*. London: Macmillan, 1957. (pro-HW)

Sheridon, R. K. *Kurt von Schuschnigg: A Tribute*. London: The English Universities Press, 1942. (pro-HW)

Stadler, Karl R. *Austria*. New York: Praeger, 1971.

———. *The Birth of the Austrian Republic, 1918–1921*. Leyden: A. W. Sijthoff, 1966.

[Stein, Chlodwig] *Der niederösterreichische Heimatschutz: Geschichte des Heimatschutzverbandes Niederösterreich*. [Vienna] Niederösterreichische Landpresse [1937]. (pro-HW)

Steinböck, Erwin. *Die Volkswehr in Kärnten unter Berücksichtigung des Einsatzes der Freiwilligenverbände*. Vienna, Graz: Stiasny, 1963.

Stolz, Otto. *Geschichte des Landes Tirol*. Innsbruck, Vienna, Munich: Tyrolia, 1955.

Strong, David F. *Austria (October 1918–March 1919): Transition from Empire to Republic*. New York: Columbia Univ. Press, 1939.

Sugar, Peter (ed.). *Native Fascism in the Successor States, 1918–1945*. Santa Barbara: ABC-Clio, 1971.

Suval, Stanley. *The "Anschluss" Question in the Weimar Era: A Study of Nationalism in Germany and Austria, 1918–1932*. Baltimore: Johns Hopkins Univ. Press, 1974.

Thalmann, Friedrich. "Die Wirtschaft in Oesterreich," in H. Benedikt (ed.), *Geschichte der Republik Oesterreich* (Munich: R. Oldenbourg, 1954), pp. 487–572.

Thimme, Annalise. *Gustav Stresemann: eine politische Biographie zur Geschichte der Weimarer Republik*. Hannover, Frankfurt: Goedel, 1957.

Thormann, Werner. *Ignaz Seipel, der europäische Staatsmann*. Frankfurt: Carolus, 1932. (pro-HW)

Toynbee, Arnold J. (ed.). *Survey of International Affairs, 1932; 1933; 1934*. London, New York: Oxford Univ. Press, 1933; 1934; 1935.

Tremel, Ferdinand. *Wirtschafts- und Sozialgeschichte Oesterreichs.* Vienna: Franz Deuticke, 1969.

Von Klemperer, Klemens. *Ignaz Seipel: Christian Statesman in a Time of Crisis.* Princeton: Univ. Press, 1972.

Wache, Karl (ed.). *Deutscher Geist in Oesterreich.* Dornbirn: C. Burton, 1933. (Nazi; anti-HW)

Wandruszka, Adam. "Oesterreichs politische Struktur: die Entwicklung der Parteien und politischen Bewegungen," in H. Benedikt (ed.), *Geschichte der Republik Oesterreich* (Munich: R. Oldenbourg, 1954), pp. 289–485.

Weinberg, Gerhard L. *The Foreign Policy of Hitler's Germany: Diplomatic Revolution in Europe, 1933–1936.* Chicago: Univ. Press, 1971.

Weiss, John. *The Fascist Tradition.* New York, Evanston, London: Harper & Row, 1967.

Welchert, Hans-Heinrich. *Oesterreichs Weg ins Reich, 1917–1938.* Hamburg: Hanseatische Verlagsanstalt, 1938. (Nazi; anti-HW)

Wiskemann, Elizabeth. *The Rome-Berlin Axis: A Study of the Relations between Hitler and Mussolini.* Rev. ed.; London: Collins, 1966.

Woolf, S. J. (ed.). *European Fascism.* New York: Vintage, 1969.

——— (ed.). *The Nature of Fascism.* New York: Vintage, 1969.

B. SCHOLARLY ARTICLES

Botz, Gerhard. "Faschismus und Lohnabhängige in der Ersten Republik," *Oesterreich in Geschichte und Literatur,* 21 (March-April 1977): 102–128.

Diamant, Alfred. "The Group Basis of Austrian Politics," *Journal of Central European Affairs,* 18 (July 1959): 134–155.

Drimmel, Heinrich. "Das österreichische Staatsbewusstsein in der Zeit von 1918–1938," *Oesterreich in Geschichte und Literatur,* 9 (June 1965): 308–317.

Fellner, Fritz. "The Background of Austrian Fascism," in Peter F. Sugar (ed.), *Native Fascism* (Santa Barbara: ABC-Clio, 1971), pp. 15–23.

Gulya, Katalin. "Die Westungarische Frage nach dem Ersten Weltkrieg: das Burgenland und die Politik der ungarischen Regierungen 1918–1921," *Oesterreichische Osthefte,* 8 (March 1966): 89–100.

Haberleitner, O. "Rechtsanwalt Dr. Walter Pfrimer," *Freie Monatsschrift Die Aula* [Kultur, Wirtschaft, Politik], 11 (Dezember 1960), 41–42.

Jagschitz, Gerhard, "Bundeskanzler Dollfuss und der Juli 1934," in L. Jedlicka and R. Neck (eds.), *Oesterreich 1927 bis 1938* (Munich: R. Oldenbourg, 1973), pp. 150–160.

Jedlicka, Ludwig. "Die Aera Schuschnigg," in L. Jedlicka and R. Neck (eds.), *Oesterreich 1927 bis 1938* (Munich: R. Oldenbourg, 1973), pp. 195–207.

———. "The Austrian Heimwehr," in W. Laqueur and G. L. Mosse (eds.), *International Fascism, 1920–1945* (New York: Harper Torchbooks, 1966), pp. 127–144.

————. "Ernst Rüdiger Fürst Starhemberg und die politische Entwicklung in Oesterreich im Frühjahr 1938," in *Oesterreich und Europa: Festgabe für Hugo Hantsch* (Graz, Vienna, Cologne: Styria, 1965), pp. 547–564.

————. "Oesterreich und Italien 1922–1938," *Wissenschaft und Weltbild*, 26 (Jan.–March 1973): 45–61.

————. "Zur Vorgeschichte des Korneuburger Eides (18. Mai 1930)," *Oesterreich in Geschichte und Literatur*, 7 (April 1963): 146–153.

Kerekes, Lajos. "Akten des Ungarischen Ministeriums des Aeusseren zur Vorgeschichte der Annexion Oesterreichs," *Acta Historica Hungarica*, 7 (1960): 355–390.

————. "Akten zu den geheimen Verbindungen zwischen der Bethlen-Regierung und der österreichischen Heimwehrbewegung," *Acta Historica Hungarica*, 11 (1965): 299–339.

————. "Italien, Ungarn und die österreichische Heimwehrbewegung 1928–1931," *Oesterreich in Geschichte und Literatur*, 9 (Jan. 1965): 1–13.

————. "Die 'Weisse Allianz': Bayrisch-österreichisch-ungarische Projekte gegen die Regierung Renner im Jahre 1920," *Oesterreichische Osthefte*, 7 (Sept. 1965): 353–366.

Klein, Anton. "War die Erste Republik tatsächlich ein Staat wider Willen?" *Oesterreich in Geschichte und Literatur*, 11 (Nov. 1967): 457–471.

Klingenstein, Grete. "Bemerkungen zum Problem des Faschismus in Oesterreich," *Oesterreich in Geschichte und Literatur*, 14 (Jan. 1970): 1–13.

Kolnai, Aurel. "Gegenrevolution," *Kölner Vierteljahrshefte für Soziologie*, 10 (1931–1932): 170–199, 295–319.

Lackó, Miklós. "Ostmitteleuropäischer Faschismus," *Vierteljahrshefte für Zeitgeschichte*, 21 (Jan. 1973): 39–51.

Leser, Norbert. "Austro-Marxism: A Reappraisal," *Journal of Contemporary History*, 1/2 (1966): 117–134.

Macartney, C. A. "The Armed Formations in Austria," *Journal of the Royal Institute of International Affairs*, 8 (Nov. 1929): 617–632.

Nemes, D. "'Die österreichische Aktion' der Bethlen-Regierung," *Acta Historica Hungarica*, 11 (1965): 187–258.

Novotny, Alexander. "Die erste Krise der Republik Oesterreich (1927 bis 1933)," *Oesterreich in Geschichte und Literatur*, 13 (April 1969): 161–172.

Petersen, Jens. "Konflikt oder Koalition zwischen christlich Sozialen und Sozialdemokraten, 1933/34," *Oesterreich in Geschichte und Literatur*, 16 (Oct. 1972): 431–435.

Rath, R. John. "Authoritarian Austria," in Peter F. Sugar (ed.), *Native Fascism* (Santa Barbara: ABC-Clio, 1971), pp. 24–43.

Rennhofer, Friedrich. "Bundeskanzler Dr. Ignaz Seipel und die Zehnjahrfeier der Republik 1929," *Oesterreich in Geschichte und Literatur*, 12 (Nov. 1968): 491–494.

————. "Die Desintegration Oesterreichs, 1920–1927," *Oesterreich in Geschichte und Literatur*, 11 (April [March—*sic*] 1967): 177–187.

————. "Ignaz Seipel zu Gedanken," *Oesterreich in Geschichte und Literatur*, 10 (Nov. 1966): 469–472.

Sauer, Wolfgang. "National Socialism: Totalitarianism or Fascism?" *American Historical Review*, 73 (Dec. 1967): 404–424.

Schmidt-Wulffen, Wulf. "Das Burgenland und die Deutsche Politik, 1918–1921," *Oesterreichische Osthefte*, 11 (Sept. 1969): 270–287.

Schwarz, Robert. "The Austrian Party Press and the First Republic: A Study in Political Journalism," *Western Political Quarterly*, 12 (Dec. 1959): 1038–56.

Stadler, K. R. "Austria," in S. J. Woolf (ed.), *European Fascism* (New York: Vintage, 1969 [c. 1968]), pp. 88–110.

Staudinger, Anton. "Die Mitwirkung der christlich-sozialen Partei an der Errichtung des autoritären Ständestaates," in L. Jedlicka and R. Neck (eds.), *Oesterreich 1927 bis 1938* (Munich: R. Oldenbourg, 1973).

————. "Die 'Sozialdemokratische Grenzländerkonferenz' von 15. September 1933 in Salzburg: ein sozialdemokratisches Angebot militärischer Kooperation mit der Regierung Dollfuss gegen den Nationalsozialismus," in Elisabeth Kovacs (ed.), *Festschrift Franz Loidl zum 65. Geburtstag* (Vienna: Brüder Hollinek, 1971), 3:247–260.

Sweet, Paul R. "Democracy and Counterrevolution in Austria," *Journal of Modern History*, 22 (March 1950): 52–58.

Vierhaus, Rudolf. "Faschistisches Führertum: ein Beitrag zur Phänomenologie des europäischen Faschismus," *Historische Zeitschrift*, 198 (1964): 614–639.

Von Klemperer, Klemens. "Austria, 1918–1920: Revolution by Consensus," *Orbis*, 10 (Winter 1967): 1061–81.

————. Chancellor Seipel and the Crisis of Democracy in Austria," *Journal of Central European Affairs*, 22 (Jan. 1963): 468–478.

"Waldemar Pabst," *Der Spiegel*, 16 (18 April 1962): 38–44.

Weinzierl, Erika. "Aus den Notizen von Richard Schmitz zur österreichischen Innenpolitik im Frühjahr 1933," in Gerhard Botz, Hans Hautmann, and Helmut Konrad (eds.), *Geschichte und Gesellschaft: Festschrift für Karl R. Stadler zum 60. Geburtstag* (Vienna: Europa, 1974), pp. 113–141.

Whiteside, Andrew. "Austria," in H. Rogger and E. Weber (eds.), *The European Right: A Historical Profile* (Berkeley, Los Angeles: Univ. of California Press, 1966), pp. 308–363.

C. UNPUBLISHED MONOGRAPHS

Bärnthaler, Irmgard. "Geschichte und Organisation der Vaterländischen Front: ein Beitrag zum Verständnis totalitärer Organisationen," Ph.D. dissertation, Univ. of Vienna, 1964.

Berger, Barbara. "Ernst Rüdiger Fürst Starhemberg: Versuch einer Biographie," Ph.D. dissertation, Univ. of Vienna, 1967.

Botz, Gerhard. "Beiträge zur Geschichte der politischen Gewalttaten in

Oesterreich von 1918–1933," Ph.D. dissertation, Univ. of Vienna, 1966.
Edmondson, C. Earl. "The Heimwehr and Austrian Politics, 1918–1934," Ph.D. dissertation, Duke Univ., 1966.
Fessl, Christine. "Die innenpolitische Entwicklung in Oesterreich in den Jahren 1934–1938," Ph.D. dissertation, Univ. of Vienna, 1967.
Haag, John J. "Othmar Spann and the Politics of 'Totality': Corporatism in Theory and Practice," Ph.D. dissertation, Rice Univ., 1969.
Haas, Karl. "Studien zur Wehrpolitik der österreichischen Sozialdemokratie 1918–1926," Ph.D. dissertation, Univ. of Vienna, 1967.
Hofmann, Josef. "Der Pfrimer-Putsch," Ph.D. dissertation, Univ. of Vienna, 1962.
Kendrick, Clyde K. "Austria under the Chancellorship of Engelbert Dollfuss, 1932–1934," Ph.D. dissertation, Georgetown Univ., 1958.
Kondert, Reinhart Ditmar. "The Rise and Early History of the Austrian Heimwehr," Ph.D. dissertation, Rice Univ., 1972.
Krüger, Hans-Jürgen. "Faschismus oder Ständestaat: Oesterreich 1934–1938," Ph.D. dissertation, University of Kiel, 1970.
Messerer, Ingeborg. "Die Frontkämpfervereinigung Deutsch-Oesterreichs: ein Beitrag zur Geschichte der Wehrverbände in der Republik Oesterreich," Ph.D. dissertation, Univ. of Vienna, 1963.
Oswald, Franz. "Die Stellung von Major a.D. Emil Fey in der Politik der Ersten Republik und des Ständestaates," Ph.D. dissertation, Univ. of Vienna, 1964.
Pauley, Bruce F. "Hahnenschwanz und Swastika: The Styria Heimatschutz and Austrian National Socialism, 1918–1934," Ph.D. dissertation, Univ. of Rochester, 1966.
Rape Ludger. "Die österreichische Heimwehr und ihre Beziehungen zur bayrischen Rechten zwischen 1920 und 1923," Ph.D. dissertation, Univ. of Vienna, 1968.
Schweiger, Franz. "Geschichte der neiderösterreichischen Heimwehr von 1928 bis 1930 mit besonderer Berücksichtigung des sogenannten 'Korneuburger Eides' (18. Mai 1930)," Ph.D. dissertation, Univ. of Vienna, 1964.
Silberbauer, Gerhard. "Kirche und Sozialismus in Oesterreich 1918–1938: ein geschichtlicher Rückblick" (Endzeitlicher Glaube: Schriften für christliche Verwirklichung, herausgegeben von August Zechmeister), Vienna (typescript, 250 copies), 1961.
Simon, Walter B. "The Political Parties of Austria," Ph.D. dissertation, Columbia Univ., 1957.
Sitzwohl, Josef. "Emil Fey," seminar paper for Prof. Ludwig Jedlicka, Univ. of Vienna, summer 1963.
Staudinger, Anton. "Bemühungen Carl Vaugoins um Suprematie der christlichsozialen Partei in Oesterreich (1930–1933)," Ph.D. dissertation, Univ. of Vienna, 1969.
Suval, Stanley. "The Anschluss Problem in the Stresemann Era (1923–1929)," Ph.D. dissertation, Univ. of North Carolina at Chapel Hill, 1963.

Index

Ach, Dr. Hermann, 160, 166
Adam, Col. Walter, 257
Agrarian League. *See* Landbund
Ahrer, Dr. Jakob, 23, 27, 35
Alberti, Count Albert, 125, 140, 147, 166, 178, 186, 189, 200, 307 (n. 54); talks with Nazis, 203, 205, 207, 311 (nn. 87–88)
Allies, 9–11, 18, 25–27, 32, 91, 305 (n. 26). *See also* France, Great Britain
Alpenländische Heimatwehr, 36, 94, 104, 135
Alpine Montan Gesellschaft, 39, 55, 57, 124, 140
Ambrozy, Lajos, 134, 297 (n. 56)
Anschluss, 15; prohibited, 10–11, 16, 18, 164; sought, 16, 27, 175; opposed, 16, 62–63, 163, 230, 255, 259; HW and, 25, 29, 94, 140, 143, 145–46, 157, 164–65, 229; Dollfuss and, 177
Anti-Semitism, 8, 24, 52, 54–55, 94, 132, 145–47, 189, 249
Arbeiter-Zeitung, 50, 56–57, 77, 96, 111, 113, 138, 151–52, 155–56, 165, 173, 186, 189, 211
Arbesser, Baron, 82, 152
Assistenz-Korps, 184–85
Auinger, Johann, 122
Auriti, Giacinto, 106, 168, 197, 298 (n. 74), 305 (n. 33)
Austria: conditions in after war, 2, 7, 9–19; economic dependence of, 7, 15, 21, 27, 34, 66, 86–87, 149, 154–55, 251; elections in (1919) 10, (1920) 22, (1923) 35, (1927) 42–43, (1930) 113–17, (local, 1931) 129, (Vienna, 1932) 156–57, (Innsbruck, 1933) 186, 305 (nn. 29–30); army in, 16–17, 19–20, 33, 50, 60–61, 184–85, 194, 197, 200–201, 220–31 passim, 242–43, 247, 250, 257, 263, 278 (n. 5), 307 (n. 47), 318 (n. 15); internal disarmament in, 25–26, 33, 65, 67–68, 87, 96, 100–101, 103, 152, 155–56, 280 (n. 33),

287 (n. 26); and international loans for, 30, 81–83, 91, 96, 100, 104, 134, 155, 158, 163–66, 177, 193, 301 (n. 43); in mid-1920s, 34–35; cabinet crises in, 43, 74–75, 81–82, 111–12, 119–20, 133, 154–55, 158–59, 187, 199–201, 230–31, 238–39, 243, 245, 252–53, 258, 262–63, 300 (n. 27); 1929 const. crisis in, 80–89; impact of Depression in, 91, 111, 122, 130–31, 133–34, 183; 1934 civil wars in, 219–21, 239–42; 1934 changes in provinces,, 222–23; 1934 const. in, 231, 234–35, 246, 313 (n. 1), 317 (n. 4). *See also* Bundesrat, July 1927, Nationalrat

Baar von Baarenfels, Baron Eduard, 207, 222, 253, 258, 260–63, 265, 322 (n. 65)
Bachinger, Hans, 154–56, 160, 308 (n. 62)
Bauer, Col. Max, 28
Bauer, Dr. Otto, 12, 40, 50, 143, 170–71, 221, 288 (n. 35)
Bauernbund of L.A., 79, 96, 102, 125, 214
Bauernbund of Tyrol, 30, 119, 124, 213
Bavaria: bolshevism in, 18, 20–21; aid for HW from, 21–22, 25, 27–29
Berger-Waldenegg, Baron Egon, 265; HW leader in Styria, 135–36, 140, 178, 186, 216, 254, 314 (n. 33); memoirist, 138, 295 (n. 31), 296 (nn. 40, 42), 297 (n. 50), 311 (n. 86); min. of justice, 238; foreign min., 252–54, 258; min. to Italy, 260
Bethlen, Count István, 61–63, 70–71, 83, 88, 96–97, 106, 109, 113, 115
Brandl, Dr. Franz, 116, 167, 180, 299 (n. 6)
Bund Bayern und das Reich, 28
Bundesheer. *See* Austria, army in
Bundesrat, 89, 103, 124, 157, 160, 165, 179, 304 (n. 21)

230; clash with Dollfuss, 214, 217–
19, 224–28, 230, 238, 315 (n. 42);
speech of 11 Feb. 1934, 218–19; de-
moted, 238; Nazi putsch and, 240–
42; leaves cabinet, 252. *See also* Aus-
tria, civil wars in; HW, demands for
"renewal" in provinces, propaganda
by Fey; Schutzkorps
Fischer, Dr. Ernst, 223
Foppa, Hermann, 204
France, 64, 87, 106, 131, 163, 166, 173,
185, 246–47, 254–55, 258. *See also*
Allies
Frank, Dr. Hans, 190
Frauenfeld, Alfred, 202–3, 207
Freiheitsbund, 57, 134, 220, 236, 246–
57 passim, 260, 319 (n. 29)
*Freiwillige Miliz–Oesterreichischer
Heimatschutz,* 253
Frontmiliz, 258, 262–63
Front Veterans' Association, 24, 34, 37–
38, 40, 42, 128, 134
Funder, Dr. Friedrich, 52, 214

Gamper, Prof. Hans, 223
Gedye, G. E. R., 171
Geneva Protocol, 16, 30, 164
German-Austrian Heimatschutz: in L.A.,
147, 162; in Styria, 178, 185–86, 192
Germany, 10, 16, 22, 31–32, 34, 41, 71,
130–31, 133, 167, 227; anti-Austrian
policy, 175–77, 184, 190, 192, 194,
205, 212, 236; rapprochement with
Austria, 239, 245, 252, 254, 256, 260,
321 (n. 46). *See also* Bavaria, Hitler,
Stahlhelm
Gleissner, Dr. Heinrich, 216, 222–23
Gömbös, Julius, 110, 113, 115, 163,
173–74, 238, 256–57, 262, 290 (n.
49), 304 (n. 13)
Göring, Hermann, 114, 186, 257, 321
(n. 55)
Goldinger, Prof. Walter, 180, 262, 299
(n. 6), 321 (n. 56)
Grandi, Dino, 63, 103, 285 (n. 58)
Great Britain, 64, 81, 87, 100, 173,
246–47, 252, 254–55, 258. *See also*
Allies
Günther, Raimund, 131–32, 135
Gulick, Prof. Charles A., 65, 69, 122,
143, 170

Habicht, Theodor, 144–45, 147, 149,
156, 176, 178, 190, 192–94, 202–6,
229, 239, 306 (n. 40), 310 (n. 81)

Habsburg, Emperor Charles von. *See*
Charles, Emperor/King von Habsburg
Habsburg, Otto von, 201, 250, 319 (n.
32)
Hainzl, Sepp, 105, 122, 125, 159, 162,
164–65, 171–72, 297 (n. 53)
Hauser, Johann, 37
Heger, Fritz, 105
Heimatblock: campaign of 1930, 113–
14, 116–17, 291 (n. 54), 292 (n. 65);
cabinet negotiations by and about,
119, 133, 154; in NR, 122–24, 128,
142–44, 150, 158–60, 162, 164–65,
170–72, 301 (nn. 39–40); an issue
within HW, 125–27; 1931 campaign
in U.A., 129; unwilling to campaign
in 1932, 156–76; dissolved, 201
Heimatschützer, 246, 257, 259, 318 (n.
17)
Heimatschutzverband Oesterreichs, 131
Heimatschutz-Zeitung, 43, 47, 56, 74–
75, 105, 132, 166, 290 (n. 48)
Heimwehr: general impact on Austria,
1–2, 7–8, 47–49, 70, 74, 162, 170,
182, 195, 206–9, 222–23, 231–33,
236–37, 243, 263
 as fascist, 1, 5–8, 97–98, 125, 200–
201, 204–5, 236–37, 259–60, 263, 279
(n. 18), 287 (n. 22)
 as paramilitary movement, 2–3, 17–
18, 27–30, 36–38, 44–46, 50, 59–61,
79, 105–6, 109–10, 118, 120, 128,
130–31, 183, 231–33, 243, 246, 257,
263
 goals of, 2–3, 6–7, 36, 48–49, 72,
85, 89–91, 98–100, 128, 150, 209,
231, 233, 246, 263; stated by Steidle,
30, 61; stated by Pabst, 36, 93; stated
by Starhemberg, 168, 197, 204–6,
230, 248
 general leadership, 5–7, 28–32, 36,
38–39, 48, 51, 58–60, 71, 110, 147,
155; disputes in and over, 27–28, 30,
59, 92–95, 97–100, 102–7, 118–20,
124–30, 134–35, 143, 146, 156, 166,
186–87, 207, 225, 236–37, 251, 260–
62, 289 (n. 43), 320 (n. 37)
 as popular movement, 5–6, 47, 49,
69–70, 90, 92–93, 120, 131, 150–51,
208–9, 263
 putsch, 6, 21–23, 25, 27, 41–42,
46–47, 56, 61, 70, 81, 88, 115–16,
131, 134–42, 145, 150–51, 163, 180–
81, 212–17, 272 (n. 15), 284 (n. 49);

rumors about, 25, 37, 49, 53, 71, 82, 84, 88, 117, 180–81, 228, 248, 313 (nn. 11, 14), 315 (n. 39)

propaganda and threats, 6, 32–33, 49–50, 56, 64, 79–81, 86–88, 90, 93, 155, 200; by Steidle, 40, 44; by press, 43–44, 47, 75, 118, 142, 259–60; by Pfrimer, 65, 74, 113, 131–34, 137; by Spann, 74; by Starhemberg, 113, 136, 150–51, 155, 178, 199, 206, 212, 255, 257; by Fey, 195, 201, 218–19, 224, 228, 251–52

membership, 7–8, 38–39, 50, 59–60, 70, 90, 120, 122, 126–27, 142, 236–37, 249, 263, 276 (n. 47), 314 (n. 28), 317 (n. 6), 319 (n. 29), 320 (n. 37), 322 (n. 66)

auxiliary executive forces, 18, 20, 30, 36, 45–46, 52, 60–61, 109–10, 120–21, 136, 156, 180, 184–86, 210–11, 213, 220–21, 226–29, 237, 242, 247, 250, 312 (n. 1), 314 (n. 28)

armaments, 19, 21, 25–26, 60, 62–63, 96–97, 110–11, 141, 163, 172–74, 248

and Austrian army, 20, 31, 33, 36, 60–61, 63, 103, 226–27, 239, 243, 245, 247, 249–50, 253, 259

and Austrian police, 31, 103, 115–16, 139, 166, 180, 187, 206, 209, 243, 252, 259

rallies and marches, 32, 53–54, 56, 67, 80–81, 86; in the Tyrol, 26, 104, 118, 126, 155; in Car., 33–34, 41, 56; in U.A., 44, 108; in L.A., 55–56, 63–67, 75, 77, 84, 96–99, 126, 131–32, 147, 218–19, 257, 261, 286 (n. 17), 294 (n. 21); in Styria, 56, 131–32, 142, 146–48, 186; in Vienna, 24, 69–70, 76, 147, 178, 187–89, 199, 201–2, 225, 252, 306 (n. 36)

military organization and maneuvers, 37–39, 59–61, 211, 248

labor unions, 57–58, 287 (n. 22)

finances and financial support, 60, 257, 260, 320 (n. 42); German, 21, 27, 140, 273 (n. 24), 284 (n. 50), 303 (n. 4); domestic, 27, 29, 32, 50–51, 53, 63, 88, 92, 106, 124, 128, 156, 166, 257, 274 (n. 27), 316 (n. 55); Hungarian, 27, 58, 62–63; Italian, 63, 77–78, 81–82, 86, 103, 106, 144, 187, 228–30, 232, 251, 259, 305 (n. 33), 308 (n. 66), 319 (n. 28), 322 (n. 58)

demands for const. reform, 61, 70, 76, 78, 80, 84–91, 93–94, 280 (n. 6), 285 (nn. 56–57)

dictatorial schemes, 85–86, 137

as political party, 92, 94–95, 105–7, 109, 113–14, 130–31. See also Heimatblock

auxiliaries for women and youth, 94, 110, 247, 290 (n. 48)

demands for economic reforms, 123, 131–33, 150–51, 209, 295 (nn. 32, 37)

and FF, 195–97, 201, 204, 209–10, 224, 229–31, 233, 238, 245, 249, 251

demands for "renewal" in provinces, 212–16, 219, 312 (nn. 11–12, 14), 314 (n. 33)

See also Austria, cabinet crises in; Heimwehr subheading under Anschluss, Burgenland, Carinthia, Christian Social party, Church, Lower Austria, Nationalrat, National Socialists, Salzburg, Seipel, Schober, Styria, Tyrol, Upper Austria, Vaugoin, Vienna, Voralberg; Technische Nothilfe

Heinrich, Prof. Walter, 73, 88, 93–94, 265–66, 289 (n. 37); and Korneuburg oath, 98–100, 287 (n. 21); on 1934 constitution, 317 (n. 4)

Helmer, Oskar, 219

Hicks, Maj. W. W., 59–61

Hilfspolizei, 184, 305 (n. 26)

Hiltl, Col. Hermann von, 24, 40–42

Hirtenberg Weapons Affair, the, 110–11, 163, 172–74, 185, 302 (n. 63)

Hitler, Adolf, 7, 28, 144, 172–73, 175–77, 233, 239, 247; and German-Austrian HS, 95, 162, 185, 301 (n. 33); and Starhemberg, 109, 113–14, 145–46, 156–58, 237, 289 (n. 41), 321 (n. 55); and Austria, 145, 175–77, 184, 190, 192–93, 203, 206, 245, 260; and Mussolini, 206, 256, 259; and Nazi putsch, 239, 242, 245

Hofmann, Dr. Josef, 135, 140, 296 (nn. 40, 42)

Hoyos, Count Rudolf, 246

Hueber, Dr. Franz, 266; min. of justice, 112; liaison with Nazis, 114, 147, 178, 186, 257, 267, 321 (n. 55); HB deputy in NR, 122, 154, 164, 300 (n. 16); HW leader in Sbg., 166, 306 (n. 43)

Hülgerth, Field Marshal Ludwig, 126, 128–29, 135–37, 143, 162, 266, 320 (n. 37); opposes putsch, 115, 136,

140; gov. of Car., 222; becomes vice-chan., 263

Hungary, 2, 32; bolshevism in, 18, 20; and HW, 21, 25, 27, 36, 47, 49, 51, 58, 62–63, 65–67, 77, 82, 114–15, 120, 138; and Bgld., 21–22, 27; and Austria, 83, 87, 96, 167, 179, 227; and Germany, 227; and OSS, 315 (n. 48). *See also* Bethlen, Gömbös, Hirtenberg Weapons Affair

Italy, 2, 6, 32, 41; and HW, 27, 49, 51, 53, 61, 63, 65–67, 77–78, 103, 114, 120; and South Tyrol, 62–63; and Austria, 62, 87, 96, 103, 167, 179, 193, 205, 227–28, 242, 254, 256, 305 (n. 33), 322 (n. 58); and Germany, 205, 256; and Ethiopia, 245, 251–52. *See also* Hirtenberg Weapons Affair, Mussolini

Jakoncig, Dr. Guido, 94, 104, 124, 127–28, 163, 178, 288 (n. 35), 300 (n. 16); as min. of trade, 160, 163–65, 170–71, 186–87, 300 (n. 27), 305, (n. 32)

Jánky, Gen. Béla, 62–63

Jansa, Gen. Alfred, 250

July 1927, 9, 16–17, 44–49, 56, 74

Kammerhofer, Konstantin, 78, 125, 136, 162–63, 166, 301 (n. 34); and German-Austrian HS, 178, 185–86

Kanzler, Rudolf, 21–28, 273 (n. 24), 309 (n. 73)

Karg-Bebenburg, Baron Artur, 58, 128, 140

Karwinsky, Carl, 201–2, 212, 238, 241, 253, 311 (n. 88)

Kerekes, Dr. Lajos, 2, 62, 65, 76, 140, 164

Kernmaier, Ferdinand, 222

Körner, Gen. Theodor, 50

Korneuburg oath, 97–103, 105, 107, 128, 159, 231, 287 (nn. 20–23)

Kubacsek (HW leader in Gloggnitz), 207

Kunata-Kottulinsky, Count, 135, 297 (n. 52)

Kunschak, Leopold, 52, 101–2, 119, 134, 217, 236, 247, 260, 287 (n. 22)

Lahr, Maj. Fritz, 152, 224, 252, 261, 309 (n. 69)

Lamberg, Count Karl Othmar, 131, 135–38, 140–41, 301 (n. 33)

Landbund, 12, 15, 157, 160; and CSP, 23, 43, 82, 112, 120, 154, 159, 197, 291 (n. 54); and const. reform, 80, 84–85; versus HW, 99–101, 196, 199–200, 204–5, 216–17, 222–23, 239; and Schober, 112, 114, 117. *See also* Austria, cabinet crises in; National Estates Front, Schumy, Winkler

Langoth, Franz, 46, 115, 167, 180, 195, 223, 306 (n. 41); liaison with Nazis, 204, 206, 309 (n. 69)

Lausanne Protocol, 164–68

League of Alpine Provinces, 32, 34, 36, 40, 51

League of Nations, the, 30, 96, 134, 155, 251–52, 312 (n. 14)

Legitimism, 22, 25, 27, 144–46, 249–50, 255, 260, 298 (n. 69)

Lengauer, Josef "Sepp," 57, 122–23, 125, 159, 162, 297 (n. 52), 301 (n. 39)

Lerchenfeld, Count Hugo, 42, 66, 82–83, 102, 104, 109, 119–21

Lichtenegger, Fritz, 57, 122–23, 171

Linz program, 40, 50, 108, 210

Little Entente, 41, 62, 64, 173, 175, 227–28, 250, 255–56

Lower Austria, 11, 13, 222; HW in, 24, 29, 35, 38, 46, 51, 58, 60, 62, 64, 121, 220, 319 (n. 29); Styrian influence in, 55, 57–58; leadership rivalry in, 96–98, 125, 147, 298 (n. 68); HW clash with SB in, 180. *See also* Bauernbund, Raab, Reither

Ludendorff, Gen. Erich, 28, 30

Ludwig, Eduard, 116, 225, 310 (n. 81)

Lustig-Prean, Gen. Heinrich, 59, 128, 280 (n. 35), 293 (n. 12)

Mandl, Fritz, 145, 172–73, 186, 252, 303 (n. 63), 305 (n. 33)

Matt, Maj., 126, 186

Mayer, Prof. Arno J., 5–6

Mayer, Maj. Friedrich, 46, 110, 290 (n. 50)

Mayrhofer, 222–23

Messersmith, G. S., 247, 250, 262

Meyszner, August, 135, 137–38, 145, 162, 297 (n. 52)

Miklas, Wilhelm, 111–12, 151, 155, 159–60, 224, 229, 239–40, 243, 251, 259

Military assistance corps, 197, 226–27,